# Cases on Survival and Sustainability Strategies of Social Entrepreneurs

Charles Oham
*University of Greenwich, UK*

A volume in the Advances in Business Strategy and Competitive Advantage (ABSCA) Book Series

Published in the United States of America by
IGI Global
Business Science Reference (an imprint of IGI Global)
701 E. Chocolate Avenue
Hershey PA, USA 17033
Tel: 717-533-8845
Fax: 717-533-8661
E-mail: cust@igi-global.com
Web site: http://www.igi-global.com



Library of Congress Cataloging-in-Publication Data

Names: Oham, Charles, editor.
Title: Cases on survival and sustainability strategies of social entrepreneurs / Charles Oham, editor.
Description: Hershey, PA : Business Science Reference, [2022] | Includes bibliographical references and index. | Summary: "This book outlines the reactive and proactive approaches social enterprises implement to establish themselves in the market taking into consideration the multiple bottom lines (social, financial and environmental) they aim to balance"-- Provided by publisher.
Identifiers: LCCN 2021023996 (print) | LCCN 2021023997 (ebook) | ISBN 9781799877240 (hardcover) | ISBN 9781799877257 (paperback) | ISBN 9781799877264 (ebook)
Subjects: LCSH: Social entrepreneurship--Case studies. | Social responsibility of business--Case studies. | Strategic planning--Case studies.
Classification: LCC HD60 .C3775 2022 (print) | LCC HD60 (ebook) | DDC 658.4/08--dc23
LC record available at https://lccn.loc.gov/2021023996
LC ebook record available at https://lccn.loc.gov/2021023997

This book is published in the IGI Global book series Advances in Business Strategy and Competitive Advantage (ABSCA) (ISSN: 2327-3429; eISSN: 2327-3437)

British Cataloguing in Publication Data
A Cataloguing in Publication record for this book is available from the British Library.

All work contributed to this book is new, previously-unpublished material.
The views expressed in this book are those of the authors, but not necessarily of the publisher.

For electronic access to this publication, please contact: eresources@igi-global.com.

# Advances in Business Strategy and Competitive Advantage (ABSCA) Book Series

ISSN:2327-3429
EISSN:2327-3437

Editor-in-Chief: Patricia Ordóñez de Pablos, Universidad de Oviedo, Spain

## MISSION

Business entities are constantly seeking new ways through which to gain advantage over their competitors and strengthen their position within the business environment. With competition at an all-time high due to technological advancements allowing for competition on a global scale, firms continue to seek new ways through which to improve and strengthen their business processes, procedures, and profitability.

The **Advances in Business Strategy and Competitive Advantage (ABSCA) Book Series** is a timely series responding to the high demand for state-of-the-art research on how business strategies are created, implemented and re-designed to meet the demands of globalized competitive markets. With a focus on local and global challenges, business opportunities and the needs of society, the **ABSCA** encourages scientific discourse on doing business and managing information technologies for the creation of sustainable competitive advantage.

## COVERAGE

- Tacit Knowledge
- Joint Ventures
- Small and Medium Enterprises
- Value Creation
- Cost Leadership Strategy
- International Business Strategy
- Competitive Strategy
- Differentiation Strategy
- Balanced Scorecard
- Entrepreneurship & Innovation

IGI Global is currently accepting manuscripts for publication within this series. To submit a proposal for a volume in this series, please contact our Acquisition Editors at Acquisitions@igi-global.com or visit: http://www.igi-global.com/publish/.

The Advances in Business Strategy and Competitive Advantage (ABSCA) Book Series (ISSN 2327-3429) is published by IGI Global, 701 E. Chocolate Avenue, Hershey, PA 17033-1240, USA, www.igi-global.com. This series is composed of titles available for purchase individually; each title is edited to be contextually exclusive from any other title within the series. For pricing and ordering information please visit http://www.igi-global.com/book-series/advances-business-strategy-competitive-advantage/73672. Postmaster: Send all address changes to above address. 

# Titles in this Series

***For a list of additional titles in this series, please visit:***
***http://www.igi-global.com/book-series/advances-business-strategy-competitive-advantage/73672***

***Critical Analysis and Architecture for Strategic Business Planning***
James McKee (Independent Researcher, Australia)
Business Science Reference • © 2022 • 289pp • H/C (ISBN: 9781799880738) • US $215.00

***Multidisciplinary Perspectives on Cross-Border Trade and Business***
Asmat-Nizam Abdul-Talib (University Utara Malaysia, Malaysia) Norhayati Zakaria (University of Wollongong in Dubai, UAE) and Samshul-Amry Abdul-Latif (Universiti Utara Malaysia, Malaysia)
Business Science Reference • © 2022 • 375pp • H/C (ISBN: 9781799890713) • US $225.00

***Cases on Digital Strategies and Management Issues in Modern Organizations***
José Duarte Santos (Instituto Superior Politecnico, Spain)
Business Science Reference • © 2022 • 365pp • H/C (ISBN: 9781799816300) • US $195.00

***Employee Share Ownership and Impacts on Organizational Value and Behavior***
Sara Elouadi (Hassan II University, Casablanca, Morocco)
Business Science Reference • © 2022 • 255pp • H/C (ISBN: 9781799885573) • US $215.00

***ICT as Innovator Between Tourism and Culture***
Célia M.Q. Ramos (University of Algarve, Portugal) Silvia Quinteiro (University of Algarve, Portugal) and Alexandra R. Gonçalves (University of Algarve, Portugal)
Business Science Reference • © 2022 • 319pp • H/C (ISBN: 9781799881650) • US $215.00

***Handbook of Research on Big Data, Green Growth, and Technology Disruption in Asian Companies and Societies***
Patricia Ordóñez de Pablos (The University of Oviedo, Spain) Xi Zhang (Tianjin University, China) Mohammad Nabil Almunawar (Universiti Brunei Darussalam, Brunei) and José Emilio Labra Gayo (University of Oviedo, Spain)
Business Science Reference • © 2022 • 415pp • H/C (ISBN: 9781799885245) • US $295.00

***For an entire list of titles in this series, please visit:***
***http://www.igi-global.com/book-series/advances-business-strategy-competitive-advantage/73672***

IGI Global
PUBLISHER of TIMELY KNOWLEDGE

701 East Chocolate Avenue, Hershey, PA 17033, USA
Tel: 717-533-8845 x100 • Fax: 717-533-8661
E-Mail: cust@igi-global.com • www.igi-global.com

*In memory of my father*
*Hyacinth Chukwunenye Oham 1930-2013*
*Teacher, Lecturer, Author and Principal*

# Table of Contents

# Detailed Table of Contents

absence of police protection, etc., these enterprises thrive. This chapter employs a case study method where 15 African immigrant entrepreneurs were targeted to determine how social capital is used to expand and sustain their businesses.



Provision of housing is vital to all the members of any country, and even a fundamental right of every person in a society to be housed properly. While the state has a primary role to play in reallocation of resources to meet the needs of the majority and ensure 'public good', the economic status of developing nations has made this a complex issue. The developing world has increasingly come to rely on voluntary action, especially the social enterprise movements. There are marked differences in the approaches to tackling the social housing issue in the developed and developing world, from the point of view of the role played by social enterprises in this area. This chapter takes a comparative look at the role played by social entrepreneurs and social enterprises in the area of social housing in the developing and developed world by looking at some specific examples and case studies and concludes that in the developing world the social enterprise movement has a stronger role to play.



The purpose of this paper is to present a social entrepreneur and his social enterprise from Istanbul, Turkey. It is aimed to provide a real-life example for social entrepreneurship readers which would show the entrepreneurial motives, the start-up problems, market struggles, and the hardships caused by the COVID-19 pandemic. Changing the world is hard work. Social entrepreneurs are the pioneers that accept the hard work and take action. As the examples are more visible, more people can be inspired to step in. This case study hopes to be a means of inspiring new social entrepreneurs.

# Preface

Social entrepreneurs do business in hostile environments as they compete for market share with the private sector and, at the same time, address business, societal and governmental failures through their mission. To effectively accomplish their objectives, social entrepreneurs must engage in strategy not only for their short-term objectives rather they should be concerned with the long-term direction of the business and its implementation while addressing current operational challenges, such as a lack of funding, expertise, skills, knowledge etc. Secondly, social entrepreneurs must work collaboratively for the collective progress of all actors in the social economy if systemic change is going to be achieved.

Through case studies, this book aims to bring to the fore effective strategies that social entrepreneurs adopt to secure the long-term future and remain socially, environmentally, and financially sustainable.

*Cases on Survival and Sustainability Strategies of Social Entrepreneurs* outlines the reactive and proactive approaches social entrepreneurs implement to establish themselves in the market taking into consideration the multiple bottom lines (social, financial, and environmental) they aim to balance.

Research conducted by Macke et al. (2018) found that strategy as a research line in social entrepreneurship was found to be conspicuously absent as social enterprise research percolated around three themes: social inclusion and social economy, social economy and economic development, and networks and social innovation. This significant gap in social enterprise research is being addressed by *Cases on Survival and Sustainability Strategies of Social Entrepreneurs*. We attempt to address all aspects of social enterprise strategy with this book to plug the gap in social enterprise capacity building and business development.

Several books have addressed social entrepreneurship; however, this book focuses on the practical steps social entrepreneurs take strategically to sustain the social enterprise venture. The book will enable social entrepreneurs to understand and apply strategic management models whilst reviewing practical cases and research in the field of social entrepreneurship in the chapters of this work.

The COVID-19 pandemic has hit the global economy hard, through which many social enterprises have been impacted by the loss of earned income and an inability due to restrictions to further their social, financial, and environmental objectives. It is envisaged that the post-pandemic recovery of social enterprises will continue for the foreseeable future. It is encouraging to note that social entrepreneurs are not known to shy away from challenges in their communities. They have a history of doing business in hostile or fiercely competitive markets when addressing inequality and market failure. Social enterprises also challenge the private and public sectors as they address societal failure through a blended value approach (Nicholls, 2006). The role of social enterprise is seen as an alternative or complementary provider for goods and services in many economies including the rural areas (Hazenberg & Hall, 2014; Munoz, 2011; Farmer et al., 2012, cited in Macaulay, et al., 2017).

Failure or success in most social enterprises is dependent on the crafting of a simple but effective strategy. Sometimes these plans are an intended strategy and, in other cases, they are reactionary to internal and external influences impinging on the organisation. In other cases, a new strategy emerges from an intended one and turns out to be effective (Mintzberg & Waters, 1985). We find all these scenarios at play in the chapters of this book.

This textbook highlights cases of survival and sustainability strategies deployed by social entrepreneurs in facilitating transformative change in their local communities.

I am pleased to note that chapters in this book are written by or about social entrepreneurs. Several research methodologies are used to understand the phenomenon of strategy and sustainability in social enterprises. Howbeit qualitative, they include case studies, autoethnographic reports, reflective practice, action research and literature reviews.

Another objective of this book is to explore cases that reflect the lived experiences of social entrepreneurs who conduct strategy at all levels (micro, small or large). The cases reveal how social entrepreneurs formulate and implement plans and take corrective action when entrepreneurial objectives fail.

This book has been written during the COVID-19 pandemic and lockdown; a time of great uncertainty that has seen many social enterprises struggle yet doing great work in their communities. We also explore how social enterprises are getting involved in and supplying innovation that contributes to the fight against the COVID-19 pandemic.

The text will provide students and researchers of social entrepreneurship and practitioners with the tools used to apply strategic management models whilst reviewing practical case studies in this book. *Cases on Survival and Sustainability Strategies of Social Entrepreneurs* is developed for students of entrepreneurship who are involved in researching social entrepreneurship at an undergraduate and postgraduate level. Each chapter has a research methodology that has been adopted by the authors to accommodate rigorous research into social enterprise strategy. It is pertinent to address the critical issues affecting social entrepreneurs in a post-pandemic era and provides students and practitioners with relevant concepts of strategy and entrepreneurship that will instigate sustainability.

*Cases on Survival and Sustainability Strategies of Social Entrepreneurs* are critical to the "new normal" social entrepreneurs find themselves, a post-pandemic world where uncertainties exist and the only constant thing is change itself. The importance of having an effective strategy for developing short- and long-term objectives for the social entrepreneur is an essential skill. Strategy, whether done for a small- or large-scale social enterprise, is indispensable and social entrepreneurs should use relevant frameworks such as the strategic analysis framework (Chapter 1) to formulate and implement a unique strategy for their ventures. It starts by making an attempt to do environmental scanning through research, considering a range of options and making a choice, analysing and reviewing the adopted strategy as an ongoing and iterative process.

## ORGANIZATION OF BOOK

### Chapter 1

This chapter explores the theory and practice of strategy that social entrepreneurs deploy to run their ventures in a sustainable way. A critical link between strategy and practice of social enterprise is discussed in detail in this chapter. The chapter focuses only on the strategic management framework and adapts it to include business analytical tools that social entrepreneurs use such as TOC, ABCD, Forms of Capital, SROI, etc. Social entrepreneurs run businesses to generate earned income and reinvest profits back into the business for a social purpose rather than for personal gain like an entrepreneur. Social enterprises include and mean different things to different people, they include a spectrum of trading organisations, such as cooperative societies, charities involved in a trading activity like charity shops, civic enterprises set up by local governments, credit unions and microcredit organisation run by social entrepreneurs. SE missions and characteristics enable them to be very attractive to the public and stakeholders.

### Chapter 2

COVID-19 is a relatively new disease and most victims are in low income, people-facing jobs. The most economically disadvantaged in society are less able to comply with certain non-pharmaceutical interventions (NPIs) partly due to their financial situation. Hope for the Helpless (H4H), set up as part of a micro social enterprise to cater for rough sleepers in London, UK, is at the heart of the COVID-19 response to the homeless there. A lack of financial resources or capital can constrain social entrepreneurs and restrict their ability to create social capital. However some social entrepreneurs have been able to innovatively leverage on previous relationships to augment their resource base because engagement with stakeholders is critical. The study explores one such relationship between H4H and a local health centre. It is hoped that this study will uncover survival strategies for social entrepreneurs to succeed and thrive in a post COVID-19 world.

## Chapter 3

The chapter is focused on social entrepreneurship and, after providing a comprehensive literature review on the topics, aims at providing evidence of the decision-making process of social entrepreneurs and of the strategies they implement by focusing on a single case study, namely “Parallelo”. Parallelo was founded in 2017 by four young Italian social entrepreneurs with the aim of promoting social inclusion of fragile categories and foreign people. Their “formula” is the “social lab” involving creative craftsmen that collaborate in the design and creation of sustainable products based on recyclable/discarded materials. By implementing a narrative approach, the case study is developed following step by step the social enterprise establishment and development. In doing so, the study aims at contributing to the social entrepreneurship field of research and at providing insights for practitioners about how decisions are made and strategies implemented within social entrepreneurial teams.

## Chapter 4

This chapter interrogates the notion of social capital and its potential impact in enhancing or undermining the socio-economic efforts by migrants in Durban, South Africa. Tshishonga argues that it is through entrepreneurship that entrepreneurs transform their innovative and creative ideas into business enterprises and job creation. This chapter is concerned about migrant social entrepreneurial endevours as a source of livelihoods within the informal economic sector. Informal businesses initiated by migrants have proven to be successful and sustainable compared to that of the locals. Despite the challenges faced by migrants entrepreneurs such as financial deficit, xenophobia, anti-foreign policies, victimization, violence and harassment absence of police protection, etc. these enterprises thrive. This chapter employees a case study method where 15 African immigrant entrepreneurs were targeted to determine how social capital is used to expand and sustain their businesses

## Chapter 5

Provision of housing is vital to all the members of any country, and even a fundamental right of every person in a society to be housed properly. While the state has a primary role to play in reallocation of resources to meet the needs of the majority and ensure 'public good', the economic status of developing nations has made this a complex issue. The developing world has increasingly come to rely on voluntary action, especially the social enterprise movements. There are marked differences in the approaches to tackling the social housing issue in the developed and developing world, from the point of view of the role played by social enterprises in this area. This chapter takes a comparative look at the role played by social entrepreneurs and social enterprises in the area of social housing in the developing and developed world by looking at some specific examples and case studies and concludes that in the developing world the social enterprise movement has a stronger role to play.

## Chapter 6

The purpose of this paper is to present a social entrepreneur and his social enterprise from İstanbul, Turkey. It is aimed to provide a real-life example for social entreprenurship readers which would show the entrepreneurial motives, the start-up problems, market struggles and the hardships caused by the Covid-19 pandemic. Changing the world is hard work. Social entrepreneurs are the pioneers that accept the hard work and take action. As the examples are more visible, more people can be inspired to step in. This case study hopes to be a means of inspiring new social entrepreneurs.

## Chapter 7

This study aligns with the objectives of this volume, presenting cases reflecting social entrepreneurs' lived experiences, seeking understanding and conveying learning from practitioners and their emergent approaches – embedded in contextual realities. Adopting an interpretative approach this chapter presents First Fruit Group (FFG) as an illustrative case derived from a broader study – highlighting various dimensions of entrepreneurial parenting identified as core elements in the nurturing process at FFG and manifested in the relationship between social entrepreneur and mentee. Evidently fundamental for FFG's growth, it extended strategic vision and raison d'être continuity in leadership succession – motivating new opportunity exploitation and sustaining the group's enterprising expansion.

## Chapter 8

This chapter addresses graduate unemployment through student entrepreneurship in the context of South African higher education. The graduate unemployment rate of South Africa is estimated at 33.5% for the youth (15-24) and 10.2% for those aged 25-34. Unemployed graduate phenomenon as depicted by the FeesMustFall campaign is exacerbated by untransformed curriculum which does not provide students with relevant skills matching the labour demands. In this regard, the chapter argues that student entrepreneurship remains one of the strategies university-based youth or students could not only a space to gain business skills and experience, but also a forum where they can put their creative ideas into income generating projects. The chapter first looks at student entrepreneurship and the challenges faced by tertiary students. Second, it explores the opportunities created through entrepreneurship, the challenges faced by student entrepreneurs and finally the support needed to run successful student entrepreneurship.

## Chapter 9

Social enterprises (SE) have long been recognised as a significant part of society and as a yardstick for the wider concern of community stakeholders to the general wellbeing and quality of life of the population. Furthermore, in countries that have embraced the free market with limited government particularly in post financial crisis enforced austerity fiscal budgets, the role of the SE is extremely important in contributing to community wellbeing. Now the COVID-19 pandemic of 2020 has dealt a crushing blow to many economic, social and entrepreneurial activities with its associated lockdowns and government mandated restrictions on economic activities. It is imperative given the devastating economic impact of the epidemic and subsequent lockdowns that efforts to encourage SE and social entrepreneurship be redoubled and receive government assisted training for these efforts. Creating robust and effective learning pathways informed by the need to support a building back better ethos is key to the future of social innovation and social enterprise based economic activities.

## Chapter 10

A key remit of any consultant is to assist the client or organization they work with to achieve their objectives by mapping out a strategy for developing and sustaining the work of the organization. The aim of this chapter is to use an autoethnographic method and semi structured questioning to reflect on our consultancy activity with social enterprises and not for profit organisations. As a part of their lived experience of engaging with clients, a group of diverse consultants reflect on their work of providing consultancy services to community groups, academics, and organisations.

## REFERENCES

Hazenberg, R., & Hall, K. (2014). Public Service Spin-Outs in the UK: Towards a Theoretical Understanding of the SpinOut Process. *Policy and Politics*. Advance online publication. doi:10.1332/147084414X13988685244243

Macaulay, B., Mazzei, M., Roy, M. J., Teasdale, S., & Donaldson, C. (2018). Differentiating the effect of social enterprise activities on health. *Social Science & Medicine*, *200*, 211–217. doi:10.1016/j.socscimed.2018.01.042 PMID:29421468

Macke, J., Sarate, J. A. R., Domeneghini, J., & Aparecida da Silva, K. (2018). Where do we go from now? Research framework for social entrepreneurship. *Journal of Cleaner Production*, *183*, 677–685. doi:10.1016/j.jclepro.2018.02.017

Mintzberg, H., & Waters, J. A. (1985). Of strategies deliberate and emergent. *Strategic Management Journal*, *6*(3), 257–272. doi:10.1002mj.4250060306

Munoz, S.-A., Steinerowski, A., Farmer, J., & Stephen, K. (2011). Community social enterprises as a response to the service needs of ageing rural populations. *Journal of Social Management*, *2*(September), 23–43.

# Acknowledgment

The editor would like to thank the following individuals from different parts of the world who kindly offered their time and expertise to review this book, they are: Professor Alessia Pisoni, Mr Andre Mostert, Mrs Carol Udoye, Dr Cyril Onwubiko, Don Mac Donald, Dr Titilayo Oshodi, Dr Ela Burcu Uçel, Professor Fidelis Emoh, Gloria Oham, Hannatu Sulley, Dr Jeff Gow, Dr John-Paul Okeke, Ms Julie Omage, Dr Kumar Kotecha, Rev. Fr. Dr. Louise Ezeilo, Maurice Ekwugha, Mercy Adegboye, Morenike Ajayi, Dr Nathaniel Massa, Dr Ndwakhulu Tshishonga, Princess Ositaoleribe, Tommy Hutchinson, Dr Richard Hull, Dr Yaz Osho, and Mr Boluwaitife Ajibola.

The social enterprise community are indebted to all of you.

Thank you!

# Introduction

Dave Mann, a local pastor at Bonny Downs Baptist Church, London, UK, in partnership with four churches, ran a free food service during the first COVID-19 lockdown. The service was oversubscribed by residents who had no recourse to public funds due to their immigration and refugee status and those waiting for their benefits to be processed. He describes the joy on the faces of children whilst he delivers the much-needed groceries. Most times children take the food items off his basket before he puts it down. A challenge engulfed the project, as the needs grew, there was a lack of funding to sustain the initiative. Dave and his team came up with an idea to solicit funds to sustain the project. They set up a crowdfunding page and solicited support from local churchgoers and residents who donated generously. Their Just Giving page has had over £12,000 in donations in a short space of time.

From Dave's initiative, a "service innovation" has emerged: Dave's group realised that some people self-isolating were unable to get their groceries. They recognised an opportunity to fill the gap by providing a free shopping delivery service. Once someone provides funds, Dave's group does the shopping and delivers at their door.

Sustainability challenges such as a lack of funds are not uncommon to social entrepreneurs all over the world. However, issues such as a lack of funding and resources can be mitigated if approaches to strategic planning are initiated at the concept phase of the project. Many social enterprises react to needs by initiating projects without much strategic planning which could reduce the risk and difficulties they run into at some stage. We discuss this in detail in Chapter 1 whilst in the other chapters of this book the need for strategy is evident in the cases discussed.

One thing about Dave is that he is a faith-based social entrepreneur who has been practising social enterprise for over 20 years. Spirituality can also lead to enterprise and innovation due to the tangible and intangible assets possessed in religion. This is known as spiritual capital or value when used to create social impact (see Chapter 7 on entrepreneurial parenting). We now know that needs are increasing in our communities and government agencies need the support of local community organisations. Whilst the incidence of domestic violence, hunger, poverty and mental health and wellbeing challenges are on a sharp increase, social entrepreneurs can rise to these challenges whether they are faith-based or secular. This book underscores this fact.

Several forms of capital were deployed for Dave's project including "spiritual capital". Capital is not only monetary, it also includes human capital in terms of volunteering, befriending the lonely and those presenting with mental health needs, the use of specialist skills and knowledge; soft skills. Environmental capital includes land, buildings and outdoor resources such as natural habitats etc. Tangible assets that can be used immediately are religious and community buildings that can be converted into hospitals, hostels, and logistical centres. Cultural assets such as festivals, markets, legends and symbols can be leveraged for social entrepreneurial objectives. Gifts and donations of groceries to Food Banks and other initiatives to distribute to those in need are all a form of capital. Intangible assets are our level of faith and hope amid the gloom, provision of friendship and emotional support to those who have been affected by this pandemic through online help services to those isolated or facing loneliness.

The predominant value system that focuses on the short-term gain over the long-term sustainability of the society, environment and economy has obliterated the productivity, self-reliance, and security of most countries. Such orientation left in its trail millions of unemployed and unskilled people due to a lack of social and capital investment by governments over the decades. For instance, at a time when many countries were grappling with their emergencies and the world went into lockdown, the UK was unable to rely on other countries as usual for essential supplies – medicines, personal protective equipment, and ventilators. It was a critical time for most developed countries that had outsourced their manufacturing capabilities to low-cost regions of the world. The COVID-19 pandemic revealed that a change to our business philosophy was needed. We need a different way of doing things that brings about the sustainability of our communities from a local to a global level. A social enterprise philosophy is one solution due to its multiple bottom lines that focus on the social, environmental, and financial goals all at the same time. Cases of Survival and Sustainability Strategies showcases a more sustainable approach that addresses the challenges faced in society such as poverty, unemployment, climate change, housing and healthcare by using social entrepreneurship models.

Dave did not have all the money to provide groceries for the people in need but, as he started, people began to support and donate. We now need more Dave's to act on social needs than ever before, be it climate change, deforestation, pollution of our waterways, air quality in our cities and action on corruption and bad governance, human rights abuses in Africa and the developing world with the complicity of the developed nations need to be addressed.

The United Nations Sustainable Development Goals (SDGs) cannot be achieved without social entrepreneurship and social innovation models included in the mix of actions needed. In this book, we showcase an engagement with those left out of the debate who need to be included in democratising involvement and participation. The good news is that, all over the world, we have human capital made up of skilful and compassionate people, as well as technology to create a sustainable future for all. As social entrepreneurs hone their strategies, there is scope for collaboration and social innovation that leads to survival and sustainable social enterprises.

In many cases as noted in this book, social entrepreneurs think of social entrepreneurship first before they practice or run a social enterprise. This is a profound statement that demonstrates that the mind with its cognitive prowess is the most important area that instigates social entrepreneurial action. In this book, we identify the cognitive process in terms of social entrepreneurial initiation either as a proactive, reactive or emergent strategy. However, it is not always structured and logical. Therefore, effective strategic planning tends to be the missing link with most social enterprises. Chapter 1 provides the theoretical basis for strategic planning in a social enterprise. We state the case for an intentional and skilful approach to using strategy that is not reactive or by trial and error. The more sustainable a social enterprise the higher their social impact. Other chapters in the book focus on the practical side that reveals relevant themes in social entrepreneurship.

The key to survival and sustainability is that social entrepreneurs need to "think sustainability" by having an operational to implement their plans. All over the world, social entrepreneurs are tackling climate change, decolonisation of the curriculum, poverty, gender-based violence, mental health, loneliness, and injustice. Other challenges that social entrepreneurs will address are food security, pollution, data protection, surveillance capitalism, conservation, political innovation in countries to promote good governance in the developing world, and much more.

In many cases, as noted in this book, social entrepreneurs carry out interventions without assistance from the government and sponsors. In other cases, institutional support comes in at a later stage, therefore having a well-crafted strategy that addresses pressures from the business environment will bring about survival and sustainability that will keep the good work going.

Every case in this book is divided into chapters. They are structured uniquely by the author to allow for the originality of each case study as there are different research methodologies for studying a phenomenon.

In Chapter 1, we explore the applied theories of strategic management i.e., how strategies are made by analysing the strategic management framework and providing relevant examples and links to other chapters to buttress the concepts of strategy, innovation, social enterprise, leadership and management used in sustaining social enterprises. The link between strategy and practice of social enterprise is analysed in detail. Some of the models and tools used in the strategic management framework are discussed in this chapter. Examples of strategy are also provided in this chapter to shed light on how strategy affects all functions of the business. A key feature of this chapter is the "how-to" of strategy that is outlined as a step-by-step approach to doing strategy. The chapter outlines the framework of strategy that is built upon in the later chapters demonstrating the link between theory and practice.

Chapter 2 is a case study on adaptive leadership relevant to micro-social enterprises addressing the impact of Covid-19 on people in low-income classifications and people-facing jobs. Hope for the Helpless (H4H), was set up as part of a micro-social enterprise to cater for rough sleepers in London, UK. The chapter explores the challenges of finance that can constrain social entrepreneurs and restrict their ability to create social impact. However, the social entrepreneurs, in this case, have been able to innovatively leverage previous relationships to augment their resource base. The study explores the relationship between H4H and a local health centre. Some survival strategies for social entrepreneurs to succeed and thrive in a post-COVID-19 world is uncovered in this chapter.

In Chapter 3, a case study of the decision-making process of social entrepreneurs and the strategies they implement to run the venture is presented. Focusing on a single case study, namely "Parallelo" designed as a "social lab" involving creative craftsmen that collaborate in the design and creation of sustainable products based on recyclable and discarded materials. By implementing a narrative approach, the case study follows the step-by-step process of establishing and developing the social enterprise. In doing so, the study contributes to the social entrepreneurship field of research by providing insights for practitioners on how decisions are made, and strategies implemented within social entrepreneurial teams to achieve survival and sustainability. The case demonstrates that leadership is a critical aspect of the strategic process.

Chapter 4 interrogates the notion of social capital and its potential impact in enhancing or undermining the socio-economic efforts of migrants in Durban, South Africa. This chapter addresses migrant social entrepreneurial endeavours as a source of livelihoods within the informal economic sector. Informal businesses initiated by migrants have proven to be successful and sustainable compared to that of the locals. This chapter employs a case study method where 15 African immigrant entrepreneurs were engaged to determine how social capital is used to expand and sustain their businesses. It demonstrates that various forms of capital apart from money could be used to support social entrepreneurs. This study highlights a critical need for enterprise support models that provide business development interventions to migrant and indigenous entrepreneurs.

In Chapter 5, a comparative look at social housing in the developed and developing countries is explored. The chapter reveals the potential for social enterprises to fill the gap in housing provisions for people in the developing world.

Chapter 6 is a case study of a social entrepreneur and his social enterprise supporting animal welfare from İstanbul, Turkey. It provides lived experience of entrepreneurial motives, start-up problems, market struggles and the hardships caused by the Covid-19 pandemic. The study underscores the challenges social entrepreneurs face and how they navigate various obstacles through determination and hard work to achieve social impact. This chapter underscores the importance of strategy to the social entrepreneur.

In Chapter 7, an interpretative approach to researching social entrepreneurship is demonstrated by presenting First Fruit Group (FFG) social enterprise as an illustrative case derived from a broader study – highlighting various dimensions of entrepreneurial parenting identified as core elements in the nurturing process at FFG and manifested in the relationship between social entrepreneur and mentee. The chapter explores the phenomenon of spiritual capital in social entrepreneurship and establishes its connection with entrepreneurial parenting critical to entrepreneurial success and sustainability. It exposes aspects of leadership and mentoring in the social enterprise which should be a key part of the strategy. A model of entrepreneurial parenting is developed that creates new resources for the social entrepreneur. The chapter highlights a strong connection between faith and entrepreneurship and how it leads to self-efficacy.

In Chapter 8, the case study examines the high graduate unemployment rate in South Africa. This is a social problem. Social entrepreneurial academics and practitioners demonstrate leadership and determination as they set out to mitigate this social problem. They strategically influence policy both at a political and institutional level. This is because the unemployed graduate phenomenon is exacerbated by an untransformed curriculum that does not provide students with relevant skills matching labour demands. Student entrepreneurship remains one of the strategies students can use to gain business skills and experience, but also a forum where they can put their creative ideas into income-generating ventures. The case study demonstrates that strategy is critical in developing policy and curriculum development to enhance graduate employment and enterprise that can transform a community.

In Chapter 9, the authors review social enterprise training provision across Europe given the disrupting effects of the COVID-19 pandemic. Supporting robust and effective learning pathways is one key to stimulating economic activities that would benefit a wide range of stakeholders including the vulnerable and marginalised.

Chapter 10 is a collective of social enterprise and non-profit consultants reflecting on their lived experiences (phenomenology) of doing consultancy with clients. The consultants interviewed share relevant tips for those considering consultancy interventions from routes into consultancy, terms of reference (TOR), mentoring, partnership, collaborations, pricing policy and managing the consultancy project.

A critical theme running through this book is that survival and sustainability should start from the planning phase.

The themes covered in this book include strategic planning, leadership, unemployment interventions, social housing, social enterprise start-up, graduate employment through enterprise, training and development, faith-based social enterprises, entrepreneurial parenting, and social enterprise consultancy. Financial and environmental sustainability and animal welfare are also covered in this book.

Although, the themes cover some of the issues social enterprises address, the principles can be applied to all sectors of social enterprise endeavours.

# Chapter 1
# Strategic Formulation and Implementation of Social Entrepreneurs

**Charles A.C. Oham**
*University of Greenwich, UK*

**Okeoma John-Paul Okeke**
*University of Wales Trinity St. David, UK*

## EXECUTIVE SUMMARY

*This chapter explores the theory and practice of strategy that social entrepreneurs deploy to run their ventures in a sustainable way. A critical link between strategy and practice of social enterprise is discussed in detail in this chapter. The chapter focuses on the strategic management framework and adapts it to include business analytical tools that social entrepreneurs use. Social entrepreneurs run businesses to generate earned income and reinvest profits back into the business for a social purpose rather than for personal gain like an entrepreneur. Social enterprises can mean different things to different people, they include a spectrum of trading organisations, such as cooperative societies; charities involved in a trading activity like charity shops; civic enterprises set up by local governments; credit unions and microcredit organisations run by social entrepreneurs. Social enterprise's mission and characteristics enable them to be very attractive to the public and stakeholders.*

DOI: 10.4018/978-1-7998-7724-0.ch001

After reading this chapter you should be able to:

1. Appreciate the importance of strategic planning to social entrepreneurs;
2. Describe and analyse some of the models and tools social entrepreneurs use to craft a strategy for their ventures;
3. Develop a strategy for a social enterprise initiative by applying the strategic management framework;
4. Be able to understand the underlying theories, constructs, concepts, and principles of the strategy used by social entrepreneurs in subsequent chapters by making connections with the key theories and models in this chapter;
5. Review practical cases and examples of strategic planning and how this can assist Social Entrepreneurs.

## INTRODUCTION

The crafting of strategy is an important skill that social entrepreneurs should have. This is because strategic planning leads to success by setting the scene for the acquisition of vital resources (human and material). 'Think and plan for victory' is a key strategic theme in the *Art of War* by Sun Tzu; a popular and classic Chinese military manual used by military and business leaders all over the world. The book encourages generals to 'outthink' the enemy rather than to 'outfight' as this will give victory with less cost. In social entrepreneurship, the 'enemy,' a metaphor, is a lack of resources and the persistent challenges facing humanity and the environment. Strategy is about thinking and planning the best course of action with minimal cost.

A social entrepreneur runs a business to generate earned income (profits) by selling goods and services to people, governments, and businesses. When profits are realised, they are reinvested into the social enterprise to further its mission, unlike private enterprises that disburses the profits to their owners and shareholders (Oham 2016). Please read Chapter 3 for a detailed definition and discussion on social entrepreneurship.

Social enterprises can assume different legal forms, they include a spectrum of trading organisations, such as cooperative societies, charities involved in a trading activity like charity shops, civic enterprises set up by local governments, credit unions and microcredit organisations run by social entrepreneurs, Company Limited by Guarantee and Community Interest Companies (CIC) (Galera and Borzaga, 2009). For example, the London Early Years Foundation (LEYF) is a social enterprise that provides childcare services in 37 nurseries around London. LEYF ploughs back all its profits to further its mission to increase social impact by training staff, employing local people, providing apprenticeship opportunities, and supporting mothers and fathers returning to work by looking after their children. LEYF also supports less affluent parents with free nursery places so their children can access early years education (SEUK, 2021). As demonstrated by the LEYF, social enterprises plough back their profits and resources into their business objectives to increase social impact.

Social enterprises are conceptualised as hybrid organisations, having in their DNA, the coexistence of two or more values (social, economic, and environmental) i.e., they have the 'best of both worlds' adopting best practices from both the private and not-for-profit sector. Fair-trade organisations (a form of social enterprise) act as hybrids having a strategy of generating revenue from trading activity and the social advancement of farmers as a social objective (Doherty et al., 2014). An example of a fair-trade organization is Kuapa Kokoo, producers of Devine Chocolate; they are a fair-trade cooperative started in 1993 and supply over 1,000 tons of cocoa to the European Union each year (Devine Chocolate, 2021).

A key feature of social entrepreneurship is social innovation which is the design of new ideas that work for the public good rather than sole commercial gain. Social entrepreneurship can stimulate social innovation during the process of strategising and managing the social enterprise (Edward-Schatcher and Wallace, 2017). An innovation strategy can enable social enterprises to adapt in situations of turbulence especially when board members and external stakeholders are actively engaged in planning and decision making to find solutions (Ramus et al., 2019). Increasing board diversity (gender, race, religion, and disability, etc.) is a form of governance innovation that instigates many solutions to societal challenges e.g. Work Integration Social Enterprises(WISE) create jobs and training opportunities for unemployed people.

Social businesses are one form of social enterprise demonstrating the richness and diversity of the social enterprise landscape that, sometimes, can be nuanced. Studies found social businesses sit at the interface of civil societies and markets; they bridge the gap between market-based action and the social needs of their constituents such as a cooperative society set up for members' benefits. Social business has a long history of the potential for social change which has been exemplified in the United States where community development corporations were established to catalyse economic growth by investing in job creation, business development, real estate, and affordable housing in target communities (Jager, 2010). Drawing on this, it is crucial that social businesses have a strategy to guide their intentions.

Taken together, this suggests that strategy is concerned with the direction and scope of an organisation over the long term with the aim of gaining advantages for the organisation through the combination of resources within a changing environment to fulfill market and stakeholder expectations (Johnson and Scholes, 1999). Strategy is about how organisations, in this case social enterprises, achieve their objectives (Grant and Jordan, 2013). The objectives of social enterprises hinge around multiple bottom lines which include **social objectives** – creating employment opportunities, providing education and health services, **environmental objectives** – running an environmentally sustainable business and **financial objectives** – to become profitable. As such, there are three critical questions and aspirational goals that a social entrepreneur must consider to be able to develop an effective strategy, for their social enterprise which are as follows:

1. **Where are we currently as a social enterprise?** This can be answered by using tools such as a SWOT analysis, conducting internal surveys, focus groups and consultations with staff and stakeholders or writing a business plan/proposal for social enterprises that have not started training.
2. **Where we want to be as a social enterprise:** This can be achieved by a clear vision of the difference the social enterprise would like to make in a few years' time by starting now.
3. **What should we do to get there as a social enterprise?** A practical strategy is formulated with business analytical tools seen in Figure 1.1 and decisions taken are implemented.

*Figure 1. Strategic analytical framework*

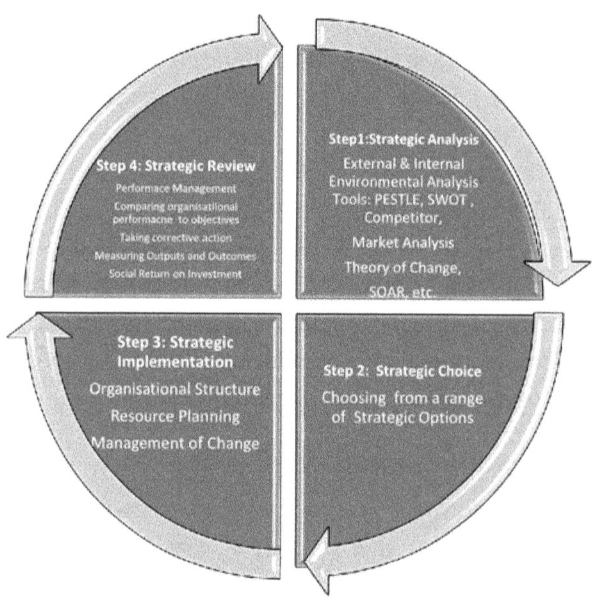


Strategic management involves having a vision of the future, formulating, setting, and selling a clear plan, setting objectives and measurement systems for the business

(Clegg et al., 2010). With a strategy, success can be attained, and risk mitigated by the social entrepreneur who develops an effective plan of action to grow the venture. In simplistic terms, strategy is planning wisely for organisational success. Johnson et al., (2009) list three levels of strategy; namely, corporate, business, and functional strategy. Corporate strategy deals with the wider industry and its attractiveness to the social enterprise e.g., how the environmental influences such as governments' decisions, interest rates, demography, and technology, etc. affect the social enterprise.

Business strategy, also known as competitive strategy, focuses on the competitive advantage that asks the question of how the social enterprise should compete against other businesses delivering the same products or services. This can be achieved when the social entrepreneur understands and focuses on their unique selling proposition i.e., what makes the business different and better than their competitors. The social entrepreneur should ensure that corporate and business-level strategies are conducted simultaneously to achieve sustainability and avoid the challenges of doing strategy in 'bits and pieces;' that could lead to a lack coordination of the whole business. For example, on 3rd June 2008, ECT Recycling CIC was acquired by May Gurney Limited from ECT Group CIC. ECT Group is one of the largest social enterprises in the United Kingdom providing a range of transport and recycling services in many parts of the country. In September of the same year, ECT Group divested itself of its rail business, which was acquired by the British American Railway Services, a company set up by Iowa Pacific Holdings (ECT Charity, 2021). Considering this case through a strategic lens, ECT Group had grown quickly and had become multifaceted since its founding in 1979, branching into several transport segments from disability transport, bus services, recycling, and train services. The decision to sell some of its subsidiaries could have been a business-level strategy to focus on a few segments by streamlining; to become more efficient and avoid over trading and taking on more than it could handle. Reviewing this case from a corporate strategy perspective, this period was the time of the global banking crises that led to recession in most developed countries. Banks had liquidity problems and had to be bailed out by many governments; they also withdrew a lot of lending facilities leading to cashflow problems for many businesses. So many companies went out of business during this period. It seems most likely that ECT's board wisely had to divest some of their business units to improve their cashflow situation and avoid the risk of exposing themselves to any form of turbulence in the business environment.

Larger social enterprises develop their strategy in three ways, by aligning their social objectives (e.g., addressing social needs such as providing health and employment interventions) with the business or financial objectives (increasing earned income through contracting, trading and retail), while the second element is leveraging organisational core competencies (e.g., expanding on what they do very well e.g. Hackney Community Transport (CT-Plus) based in London UK started out by providing disability transport for Hackney Borough Council. CT Plus has evolved into a major bus service provider for Transport for London (TFL)and the regions.

Functional strategy relates to everyday operations that keep the social enterprise functioning effectively and moving in the right direction. It involves day-to-day planning of activities such as purchasing raw materials, organising staff rotas, distributing products, etc.

To attain sustainability, social entrepreneurs strategically adopt some actions such as partnering with other organisations by pooling their resources together to achieve synergy (Austin et al., 2006). On the other hand, many not-for-profit organisations develop social enterprise subsidiaries as a fundraising strategy to generate sustainable income for the parent organisation (Alter, 2006). For example, charity shops belonging to major charitable organisations in the UK such as the Red Cross are a form of social enterprise because they are trading in goods and services. The profits realised are ploughed back into the parent humanitarian and relief organisation. Other Not-for-Profit organisations or social entrepreneurs, establish social enterprise subsidiaries as a strategy to address social needs as CT Plus has done and, at the same time, generate income and provide employment. This is an embedded form of social enterprise where the social objectives are also the business objectives (Alter, 2006).

Strategy as a research line in social entrepreneurship was found to be conspicuously absent as social enterprise research percolated around three themes: social inclusion and social economy, social economy and economic development, and networks and social innovation (Macke et al., 2018). This demonstrates a critical gap in social enterprise research and education given that strategy is critical to the survival of a social enterprise. Most social entrepreneurs practice strategy in a reactive or unplanned way. Their strategy formulation is unstructured and poorly articulated by the social entrepreneur. Strategy is crucial to a social enterprise and there is a need for it to be taught in a way that enables social entrepreneurs to easily craft it iteratively. Many social entrepreneurs started without a planned strategy but an idea to solve a problem. The challenge with this approach is that it does not prepare the social entrepreneurs for challenges or to facilitate a review of their performance and activities systematically and logically to enable sustained growth.

The solution is to use a strategic framework that will enable the social entrepreneur to be proactive and aware of the environmental factors (Political, Economic, Social, Technological, Legal and Environmental) affecting their social enterprise and to make and implement decisions from a range of options. By default, many social entrepreneurs who recognise a need or opportunity are involved in some aspects of strategy development to attract funding from funders or lenders and to satisfy other stakeholders. They do this by conducting feasibility studies, writing business proposals and plans which include market research, marketing strategies, budgets, cashflows, sales forecasts, monitoring and evaluation, and an exit strategy, etc. (Beugre, 2017). This is a good start however; these aspects of strategy need to be systematic and a part of a holistic strategic framework. One best practice is to ensure that marketing, funding and income generation strategy, are core elements of the strategic formulation process rather than a standalone activity. Time and resources must be spent in getting this right. A social enterprise's mission and objectives can be achieved when the strategy is used as a strategic management tool to determine the external factors affecting the venture and to implement the best options from a range of choices. Strategy can also be used as a change management tool to address any internal issues affecting the venture with the aim of transforming the business e.g., any weakness because of internal factors e.g., leadership, management style, decline in sales or service, human resource policy, or reputational damage, etc.

Strategy is a 'juggling act' with the social entrepreneurs 'eyes on the balls'. A study on 22 social enterprises in Hong Kong found that social enterprises that do not balance the objectives of their social mission and profit generation were less sustainable and competitive (Levy et al., 2019). The evidence from this study indicates that social enterprises with a Board providing oversight and regularly involved in strategy were more competitive. Therefore, a comprehensive strategy that addresses investment objectives, funding sources, operations, and governance is critical to survival and sustainability.

Sustainability of a social enterprise is crucial and relevant in a post-Covid 19 reality. It has been acknowledged that, although differences of opinion exist, there appears to be some agreement that sustainability can be viewed, for some, as long-term economic growth or financial viability of a firm, and for others, it could be about addressing the issues of climate change, or population growth or even resource imbalance (Hailey, 2014). With this book, we contextualise sustainability as an intention to fund the future of social enterprises predominantly by earned income and a mixture of other forms of funding such as grants, donations, merchandising, and unrelated business income, etc. Social entrepreneurs with a sustainability mindset, focus on addressing the ethical and moral concerns around the social and environmental issues affecting society whilst keeping their eyes on the finances of the business (Calic and Masakowski, 2016). Some of the social and environmental issues they address include poverty alleviation, climate change, health, education, and human rights whilst ensuring that income is generated, and finances are managed wisely. Sustainability in social entrepreneurship can be considered through theoretical perspectives, from simple conceptualisations, in which sustainability is referred to as ensuring the existence of the organization, whilst maintaining its objectives and deeper notions that sustainability is a way of life (Okorley and Ndenimah, 2012, Bagnoli and Megahi 2009). Social entrepreneurs practice sustainability not because it leads to long-term profit but because it is the right thing to do.

Recycle, Reuse, and Repair is a popular phrase that social entrepreneurs use to reduce costs, increase environmental sustainability, and extend their impact. Planning for sustainability is considered a viable strategy by stakeholders because it increases social impact and, in the long run, more outputs and outcomes are achieved. Furthermore, many people have become acquainted with the UN Sustainable Development Goals (SDGs) which, in a sense, is a strategic fit with social enterprise objectives that was being addressed long before.

Continuous entrepreneurial activity and the effective use of social and business models is a prerequisite for a sustainable social enterprise (Sabella and Niveen, 2016). Sustainability factors for community-based programmes include community participation, involvement of the staff as well as the community, stability of the organization, the type of leadership, and the effectiveness of the programme which reflects an understanding of the community and stakeholders (Ceptureanu et al., 2018).

The objective in social finance is to increase social impact through improving the social, environmental, and economic development of society, especially in deprived communities. It is worth stating that social finance focuses on satisfying the needs of society and the economy while considering social, cultural, ecological, and economic sustainability (Hayday, 2016).

A robust funding strategy for a social enterprise will target several sources of funds. They include grants from government and foundations, loans from commercial banks and investors, bonds, philanthropy, and crowdfunding by capitalising on social media and the internet.

## STEPS IN STRATEGY FORMULATION

Social entrepreneurs conduct strategy either knowingly or unknowingly in three ways. Firstly, they may have an intended strategy from the onset; secondly, they may have a reactive strategy by responding to external or internal turbulence e.g., an economic downturn, and thirdly, an emergent strategy that develops from the failure of an intended strategy (Mintzberg, 1987). Like any other entrepreneur, a social entrepreneur should practice strategy intentionally to survive and sustain their mission.

Outlined below are the steps taken when a strategic management framework is used to develop an organisation's capability.

**Step One:** Strategic Analysis Should Come First.

Strategic analysis has two major components: internal and external analysis, these are done within the context of a strategic management framework (see Figure

1 ). The external process involves corporate level strategy while the internal process involves business and operational levels of strategy. The strategic management framework underscores the importance that strategy should be formulated in a systematic way rather than an ad-hoc approach that picks one strategic tool e.g., a business plan while leaving others undone e.g., stakeholder analysis, monitoring and evaluation, reviews, consultations, surveys, etc. Strategy works best when it is done systematically following the relevant stages in the strategic management framework. For example, reviewing the strategy whether planned or unplanned is very important because it enables the social entrepreneur to evaluate what worked and what should be discontinued.

The most basic tool for strategic analysis is the SWOT framework that stands for Strengths, Weaknesses, Threats, and Opportunities. SWOT is a very uncomplicated way of looking at the organisations' capability. It enables the social entrepreneur to consider how to build on their strengths and mitigate any weaknesses and threats that are identified. Doing a SWOT analysis is just one piece of the puzzle and other tools of assessment should be incorporated in the strategic analysis phase. Business analytical tools that have been adapted to the mission and values of a social enterprise include SOAR- which stands for Strengths, Opportunities, Aspirations and Results, or Asset Based Community Development (ABCD) which is an effective method for identifying resources in the community that the social enterprise can access from the community and its networks. The Theory of Change can be used as a strategic analysis tool before a project is started and is valuable for strategic reviews. The deployment of more tools to the strategic analysis process provides the social entrepreneur with greater insights and options due to the inherent weakness in all tools. For example, SWOT is not a comprehensive tool for analysing the external issues affecting the social enterprise. Therefore, SWOT should at least be complemented with the PESTLE or its extended version PRESTCOM model which is effectively used for market research. PESTLE/PRESTCOM is an acronym for Political, Regulatory, Economic, Social, Technological, Legal, Competitive, Organisational, and Market factors that can affect the social enterprise. The social entrepreneur should interrogate these drivers with questions, such as, what are the regulatory factors affecting our childcare social enterprise? In other words, are there any licenses required to run a childcare service. Once all the factors are analysed, the social entrepreneur will be in a better position to formulate an effective strategy with a set of objectives. Strategic analysis is the first step in crafting a strategy for the social enterprise. This allows the social entrepreneur to scan the environment and analyse the drivers impacting the venture.

**Step Two:** Making a Strategic Choice from a Range of Options.

Once the analysis of potential opportunities and strengths of the social enterprise is conducted in step one, a range of options will likely emerge. Among the array of options, the social entrepreneur must make a choice on which option to pursue based on a robust strategic analysis that addresses the internal and external issues affecting the social enterprise. For example, should they start a nursery school or an after-school club? The strategic choice should be based on the capability and available resources that the social enterprise possesses to deliver the initiative successfully. It does not make business sense to go into projects that they do not have the resources to execute.

To maximise services to their target groups, social enterprises adopt a strategic choice to grow and increase the scale of their activities either by growing organically, as in the case of the First Fruit case study on entrepreneurial parenting (see Chapter 7) or by replicating mergers or acquisitions and social franchising models. Social entrepreneurs use their connectedness and community embeddedness to access financial and other resources to address prevailing social needs and this should be considered when making a strategic choice.

Earned income generation in social entrepreneurship sustains a social enterprise and its mission can be sustained from commercial revenue, internal reserves, grants, donations, and forms of loan finance, and these options should be considered at the analysis stage. The options should also include the legal structure to adopt to overcome income and capital constraints, for example, to avoid unnecessary payment of tax, some social enterprises in the UK create an umbrella charity where profits from their companies are transferred to the charity before it is deployed for social objectives e.g., most charity shops on UK high streets are of a different legal entity than their parent organisation e.g., Oxfam. This allows transfer of funds from the company to the charity to ringfence income from taxation thereby releasing funds for a social purpose.

**Step Three:** Strategic Implementation.

At this stage, the social entrepreneur implements their chosen objective. For example, if they have decided to start a nursery school, action should be taken to get it up and running. This is where the business plan comes in handy. The business plan addresses market research, the operations, marketing, and financial functions of the business. During the business planning phase, the business model to adopt should be considered i.e., how the social enterprise will generate income, for example, should the nursery school charge fees to parents or should they offer it free to parents or subsidise them and claim it back from the Government? The business model is a critical success factor; it includes revenue sources, cost structure, and investment size (Beugre, 2017). Normally, consultants or funders would ask 'what is your business model?' This means how will they generate earned income. One example is the social model of the Ecosia search engine which is to plant trees while their business model is to generate revenue from advertisements such as Google.

**Step four:** Strategic Review.

For existing social enterprises, social entrepreneurs must gather information for monitoring and measuring the social impact of their activities from the onset. This can be done using systems for monitoring and evaluation to capture data for regular reviews and evaluations. Having a system that captures information such as attendance forms simplifies the process of analysing and reviewing the data. Furthermore, competitive advantage can be attained by evaluating the social enterprise's activity, outputs (quantifiable deliverables), and outcomes (longer-term impact as a result of the intervention). Some of the tools used for monitoring and evaluation include registration documents – hard copy and electronic, website trackers, sales forecast, cashflows, actual budgets, bank statements, video recordings, beneficiary outputs, long-term outcomes, terms and conditions of contracts, reports, participant feedback and evaluation, etc. Outcomes are changes resulting from outputs over a longer period of time. These are normally qualitative in nature as opposed to outputs that are mostly quantitative. Social Return on Investment (SROI) is a method used for calculating the social impact and demonstrates the social value of an intervention, it is a move away from only measuring the economic value of an intervention but demonstrates a ratio of benefits to cost (Ashoka, 2021). SROI makes it possible to record value and success at different levels that could have gone unnoticed, this includes benefits for the participants, community, and society. Calculating SROI also assists with increasing knowledge development and learning that can be shared within the community and networks (Deloitte, 2021).

The illustration below shows how one-way social return on investment can be calculated.

## Example: Calculating Social Return on Investment for a Training Project

Participants- Trainees 200
Outcomes (Trainees in Jobs) 180, (Trainees starting a business) 20
Number of sessions 40
Hours of Volunteer Work 960 hours x £20per hour =£19,200
Number of volunteers 10
Bus Donated by a company for the project (valued at £20000)
Reduction in crime and antisocial behavior in the area (£30,000)

Food and drinks donated by local supermarket (£2000)
Discounted Hall Hire for training (valued at £8000)
Extra 100 participants trained (100 x 1000 per participant = £100000
Grand Total Match Funding = £179,200

*Table 1*

| Year | Match Funding | Grant | Total Project Cost |
|---|---|---|---|
| 1 | £179,200 | £100,000 | £279,200 |

*Table 2.*

| Cost Based on Target Agreed | | Cost Realised on Achieved Outcome | | Benefit Realised on Achieved Outcome | | Savings |
|---|---|---|---|---|---|---|
| No of Trainees | Cost per Trainee | Number of Trainees | Cost per Trainee | Total Number of Participants | Total | |
| 100 | 1000 | 200 | 500 | 200 | £279,200 | £179,200 |

*Cost based on target agreed reflects the number of trainees agreed and the cost of participants

**Cost realised on achieved outcomes reflects number of trainees realised and the change in cost based on funding

***Benefit achieved outcome reflects the true cost of the achieved outcome per trainee

**** Savings reflects the amount of the savings the project has saved by including the total match funding which is £179,200

Social Return on Investment (SROI) is calculated as follows (Investopedia, 2021):

$$\frac{\text{Social Impact Value (SIV) } 279200 - \text{Initial Investment Amount (IIA) } 100000}{\text{IIA } 100000 \times 100\%} = 2.79$$

SROI for this project is £2.79 for every £1 invested or spent. This demonstrates to stakeholders, including funders or the government, that the project produces a high return on any donations provided significant value for money spent.

## POLITICAL, POLICY AND REGULATORY DRIVERS AND THEIR IMPACT ON SOCIAL ENTREPRENEURSHIP

Some governments' strategy for the promotion of social enterprise has been through a Global Citizen Strategy functioning as a Social Entrepreneurship regulator and facilitator. Such close proactive positioning of government provides opportunities for global influence. Furthermore, some states operate on an international vs national strategy or globalism vs localism approach. Such an approach defines a government's nature of the partnership with either national, international, or local assistance social enterprise (SE) strategies (Forouharfar et al., 2019). For instance, the UK operates a Global Citizen Strategy through the British Council and Department of International Development that has global reach in many countries. Whilst most developing countries focus on the national and local development of social enterprises (see Chapter 8 on Graduate Entrepreneurship in South Africa).

Social enterprises are distinct and vary in their profile from rural to urban social enterprises; they also vary from one organisation to another. Rural policy and social enterprise domains need to be considered to respect the distinctiveness of social enterprises based in rural communities. This is because rural social enterprises operate differently and, by governments understanding of their particular needs and challenges, they will be able to formulate effective policies aimed at supporting SEs (Steiner and Teesdales, 2017). Steiner and Teesdale's study demonstrates that, in many situations', policy requirements need to be flexible to accommodate the needs of SEs. The study has important implications for the global SE movement in terms of governance and funding criteria, for example, one key area not discussed is how sole trading social entrepreneurs are enabled. This is because some social entrepreneurs do not follow a prescribed democratic or governance model and operate as it suits them. A governance framework can affect the objectives and intentions of a social entrepreneur if they are to access resources from that government. Currently, many funders, including governments, have come to accept that faith-based organisations may have in their constitution clauses that demonstrate their religious values (Dinham, 2007). This is encouraging more involvement of faith-based organisations in social entrepreneurship. Therefore, governance flexibility is needed to accommodate a diversity of social entrepreneurs to overcome resource limitations.

Social entrepreneurs must understand the policy context and how it influences their organisations positively or negatively if they are going to conduct an effective and efficient strategic analysis. Therefore, the tools for strategic analysis are vital and a social entrepreneur should be conversant with the use of business analytics tools to craft strategy effectively and advise governments on the support they need.

## DEVELOPING A STRATEGY TO BUILD CAPACITY

Due to lack of capacity or resources to measure social impact, getting hard output and outcome evidence has affected many social enterprises from demonstrating performance and social impact (Steiner and Teasdale, 2017). Furthermore, difficulties have been known to exist in measuring the impact of social enterprises due to definitional inconsistencies and other factors such as a lack of management skills (Peattie and Morley, 2008). However, the studies by Molecke and Pinkses (2017) showed that one-way social entrepreneurs were navigating this challenge by having a bricolage perspective in capturing and interpreting data on social impact. Social entrepreneurs employ alternative methodologies which, in a sense, demonstrate their resilience and innovativeness to make things work. They are seen to construct new methodologies of how to capture data that accounts for social impact and in so doing, delegitimise formal methodologies. Some of the tools used to measure social impact are SROI, social impact, and efficiency strategies. These tools demonstrate the social value of the intervention that may have gone unnoticed and are, therefore, undervalued.

Although measuring performance can be complex, social enterprises may not be operating efficiently in terms of generating earned income, managing staff and volunteers, and meeting their social objectives for various reasons such as the wrong motives by staff or a lack of competence (Royce, 2007). There is a constant need for social entrepreneurs and enterprises to acquire leadership, managerial, team building, and financial skills that build the capacity of the social enterprise to improve performance (Peattie and Morley, 2008). The capability approach is being applied to improve social enterprise capabilities, focusing primarily on human development (Wongtschowski, 2015). Staff development should be a key strategic objective of social entrepreneurs that will lead to sustainability. Human capital and, most specifically, leadership are major resource constraints in social entrepreneurship. Studies found that the success of programmes may be attributed in part to individual and group cultural learning and the appropriateness of the servant-leader approach (Martin and Noviceic, 2010). Leadership development can play a salient role in social entrepreneurship growth as the study suggests. A key attribute of leadership is having a clear vision of the difference the social enterprise wants to make and bringing people together to achieve the mission.

A key reason for social entrepreneurship is to sustain the social outcomes that an organisation provides for its beneficiaries. Whilst in most cases, investment, procurement, or funding decisions by donors are linked to performance, without an uninterrupted source of income, the good that places solutions to long-term societal and environmental concerns cease (Boschee, 2006). Increasingly, social impact measurement is becoming critical to managing social enterprises and attracting funding. To attest to this fact terms such as social finance, social bonds, and social impact are new lexicons that have entered social enterprise parlance (Malcolm, 2016).

Social entrepreneurs are developing new tools to access locked-up resources that address government, societal, and market failures. These tools are developed based on a construction of reality brought about by social interactions and their experiences built up over time. The Schwab Foundation for Social Entrepreneurship set up the Global Exchange for Social Investment (GEXSI) to render the global social capital market more efficient and transparent (Pamela Hartigan, 2006). The idea was to accumulate and combine social capital with other forms of capital platforms so that social entrepreneurs with replicable models can find the financial and the in-kind of support they need. The United Nations Task Force of the Social and Solidarity Economy (UNTFSSE) has focused on setting up a knowledge hub for Sustainable Development Goals (SDGs). The development of Solidarity and Social Economy (SSE) for SDG programmes, conducting an education gap analysis at the global level, and supporting of governments' efforts towards the UN resolution on SSEs (Social Economy News, 2021) are key objectives.

Regional differences exist in the income generation of social enterprises in the US compared to those in Europe. A study by Edward-Schatcher and Wallace (2017) found that European social enterprises were more dependent on grants, subsidies, and government assistance compared to those in the US who demonstrated scale and rigor by being self-financed through trading activity. This evaluation demonstrates that social entrepreneurs in the UK may require enterprise training. However, research by Anderson and Dees (2006) observed that social entrepreneurship has evolved from charity and not-for-profit models, therefore, there would be similarities between social enterprises in both countries in aspects of income generation.

Furthermore, some social enterprises are started because of an emergent strategy exacerbated by resource constraints (Boschee, 2007). To generate income, the charity develops a product or service and monetises it. Many US social enterprises have been early adopters of trading and earned income generation models. Aiming for self-sufficiency, social enterprises have their roots in charitable activities and not-for-profit models that were starved of funds either by government funding cuts, governance restrictions, and bars on trading by the Charity regulatory body due to the risk associated with trading (Boschee, 2007; Oham et al, 2009). In the UK, one of the oldest and most effective forms of social enterprise has been the trading arms of established charities such as Oxfam, Red Cross, Barnados, etc. (Hare et al., 2007).

Social entrepreneurship provides a significant degree of autonomy and scope for objectives to be scaled up, whilst not being subject to restricted funding conditions as they generate earned income rather than using grant income (Seanor and Meaton, 2007). Generating earned income is a key feature of social enterprises although this may come with the risk of business failure. Therefore, it is important that monitoring and evaluation of all functions of the business (operations, marketing, finance, human resource, and business development) becomes part of daily practice. This will make the strategic review process effective and efficient. Having discussed the development of a strategy to build the capacity of social enterprises, this chapter now moves on to highlight some of the key terms used in crafting strategy.

## THE 'MIND' OF THE SOCIAL ENTREPRENEUR: DEVELOPMENT AND EMANCIPATION STRATEGIES

Now we turn to the evidence drawn from a study carried out by Chandra (2018) that identified development narratives social entrepreneurs construct to represent and develop their work. Findings were that social enterprise development narratives were more pragmatic and solution-centric with less political ideology than development narratives. Their narrative contains development models reframed in new ways to address contemporary development challenges with a bottom-up approach that encourages local ownership and collaboration with stakeholders. The study also identified the increasing importance of social enterprises in the development sector (Chandra, 2018). This finding alludes to the increasing role social enterprises play within the social economy ecosystem. Furthermore, Chandra (2017) found social entrepreneurship to be emancipatory for those social entrepreneurs studied as many gave up a life of crime and focused on assisting people in need, and invariably emancipated themselves from a life of crime. These benefits outweigh any perceived and actual challenges a social entrepreneur may encounter when starting an initiative.

## REFLECTIONS ON CAPITAL LITERACY FOR SOCIAL ENTREPRENEURS

In 2013, a social enterprise academic was funded by the Higher Education Entrepreneurship Group to run a conference promoting social entrepreneurship in higher education. One of the outputs of the project was the development of an explainer video resource to encourage social entrepreneurs to understand the capital landscape given that access to finance is a major challenge they will face. The idea was that, through a deeper understanding of the nature of capital, social entrepreneurs could unlock other forms of capital to resource their ventures.

Capital Literacy for Social Entrepreneurs is based on the theory of the forms of capital postulated by Pierre Bourdieu who considered forms of capital other than money (Bourdieu, 1986). The project also builds on the Asset Based Community

Development model (ABCD) developed by Northwestern University that identifies hidden assets for community development.

Capital Literacy for Social Entrepreneurs identifies seven types of capital that can be interchangeably used to achieve entrepreneurial objectives. They are social, economic, environmental, cultural, symbolic, human, and spiritual.

To date, this project has developed several explainer videos that have had over 50,000 online views on YouTube. Other projects include website resources, book chapters, articles, workshops, and conferences (www.capitalliteracy.org). Some of the collaborating organisations include the British Council, several universities, and other non-profit organisations.

This project demonstrates that raising funds or financing is a critical need for social entrepreneurs and a strategy that enables social entrepreneurs to scan the external environment for alternative or supplementary capital is essential. This is because many social entrepreneurs focus on economic capital. However, with a robust strategy, they could identify other forms of capital available for use.

## CONCLUSION

This chapter has explored strategy formulation in social enterprises and highlighted the importance of strategic planning for social entrepreneurs. Strategy is a very critical part of the management process that social entrepreneurs should be actively involved in. The chapter discussed in-depth the need to apply a preferred strategic management framework that takes into consideration the purpose of the social enterprise. Having a strategy facilitates sustainability when the key vision, mission, and objectives are clear and relevant strategic management tools are used. Within this chapter, some of the underlying theories, constructs, concepts, and principles of strategy and sustainability in the context of social entrepreneurship have been discussed. The following chapters will clearly, and in some cases through the readers critical analysis, buttress the points covered in this chapter by highlighting practical cases in social entrepreneurial practice.

## REFERENCES

Anderson, A., Drakopoulou Dodd, S., & Jack, S. (2009). Aggressors; winners; victims and outsiders, european schools' social construction of the entrepreneur. *International Small Business Journal*, *27*(1), 126–136. doi:10.1177/0266242608098349

Anderson, A., & Starnawska, M. (2008). Research practices in entrepreneurship. *Entrepreneurship and Innovation*, *9*(4), 221–230. doi:10.5367/000000008786208731

Anderson, A., & Warren, L. (2011). The entrepreneur as a hero and jester: Enacting the entrepreneurial discourse. *International Small Business Journal*, *29*(6), 589–609. doi:10.1177/0266242611416417

Anderson, A. R., Drakopoulou Dodd, S., & Jack, S. L. (2012). Entrepreneurship as connecting: Some implications for theorising and practice. *Management Decision*, *50*(5), 958–971. doi:10.1108/00251741211227708

Baggot, R. (2013). *Partnership for Public Health and Well-being, policy, and practice*. Palgrave Macmillan.

Beugre, C. (2017). *Social Entrepreneurship Managing the Creation of Social Value*. Routledge.

Boschee, J. (2006) Social Entrepreneurship: The Promise and the Perils in A. Nicholls Social Entrepreneurship New Models of Sustainable Social Change, New York, Oxford University Press.

Bourdieu, P. (1986). The forms of capital. In J. Richardson (Ed.), *Handbook of Theory and Research for the Sociology of Education*. Greenwood.

British Council. (2015) *Social enterprise landscape in Ghana*. British. https://www.britishcouncil.org/sites/britishcouncil.uk2/files/social_enterprise_landscape_in_ghana_report_final.pdf

Burns, P. (2011). *Entrepreneurship and small business start-up, growth and maturity*. Palgrave Macmillan.

Ceptureanu, S., Ceptureanu, E., Luchian, C., & Luchian, I. (2018). Community based programs sustainability. A multidimensional analysis of sustainability factors. *Sustainability*, *870*(10), 1–15. doi:10.3390u10030870

Chan-Serafin, S., Brief, A., & George, J. (2013). How Does Religion Matter and Why? *Religion and Organisational Sciences*, *24*(5), 1585–1600. doi:10.1287/orsc.1120.0797

Chandra, Y. (2017). Social entrepreneurship as emancipatory work. *Journal of Business Venturing*, *32*(6), 657–673. doi:10.1016/j.jbusvent.2017.08.004

Chandra, Y. (2018). New narratives of development work? Making sense of social entrepreneurs' development narratives across time and economies. *World Development*, *107*, 306–326. doi:10.1016/j.worlddev.2018.02.033

Chanphirun, S., & Peter, V. (2014). Understanding the concept of the entrepreneurial university from the perspective of higher education models. *Higher Education, 68*(6), 891–908. doi:10.100710734-014-9750-0

Charity, E. C. T. (2021) *A brief history of Ealing community transport.* https://ectcharity.co.uk/files_uploads/A_Brief_History_of_ECT_Charity_(April_2016).pdf

Dees, J. (2007). *Taking social entrepreneurship seriously transaction social science and modern society.* 44(3): 24-31, 2007 Academic Press.

Defourny, J., & Nyssens, M. (2010). Social Enterprise. In K. Hart, J.-L. Laville, & D. Cattani (Eds.), *The Human Economy: A Citizen's Guide* (pp. 284–292). Polity Press.

Deloitte. (2021). *Is It Worth It.* https://www2.deloitte.com/content/dam/Deloitte/global/Documents/gx-is-it-worth-it.pdf

Department of Trade and Industry. (2002). *Social Enterprise: A Strategy for Success.* DTI.

Devine Chocolate. (2021). *The Beginnings and Structure of Kuapa Kokoo | Blog - Divine Chocolate.* http://www.Devinechocolate.com/devineworld

Dinham, A. (2007). *Faiths and frontiers on the starship: Boldly going as faith-based entrepreneurs?* Faith-Based Regeneration Network. http://www.fbrn.org.uk/files/STARSHIP.pdf

Doherty, B., Huagh, H., & Lyon, F. (2014). Social Enterprises as Hybrid Organisations: A Review and Research Agenda. *International Journal of Management Review, 16*, 417-436.

Edwards-Schachter, M., & Wallace, M. (2017). 'Shaken but not Stirred': Sixty years of defining social innovation. *Technological Forecasting and Social Change, 119*, 64–79. doi:10.1016/j.techfore.2017.03.012

Forouharfar, A., Rowshan, S. A., & Salarzehi, H. (2019). Social entrepreneurship strategic grid: Visualizing classification, orientation and dimensionality in the strategic paradigms of governmental-scale social entrepreneurship (A literature-based approach). *Cogent Business and Management, 6*(1), 1644714. doi:10.1080/23311975.2019.1644714

Good Finance. (2021). *Measuring Social Impact.* https://www.goodfinance.org.uk/measuring-social-impact

Grant, R., & Jordan, J. (2013). *Foundations of Strategy.* Willey.

Hailey, J. (2014). *The sustainable NGO: Why resourcing matters*. INTRAC Online. Accessible via https://www.intrac.org/sustainable-ngo-resourcing-matters/

Hare, P., Jones, D., & Blackledge, G. (2007). Understanding social enterprise: A case study of the childcare sector in Scotland. Social Enterprise Journal, 3(1).

Hayday, M. (2016). Managing Trends in Finance and Social Finance for Social Enterprise. In C. Oham & D. Macdonald (Eds.), Leading and Managing a Social. Academic Press.

Investopedia what factors go in calculating social Return on Investment. (n.d.). https://www.investopedia.com/ask/answers/070314/what-factors-go-calculating-social-return-investment-sroi.asp

Jager, U. (2010). *Managing Social Business: Mission Governance Strategy and Accountability*. Palgrave Macmillan. doi:10.1057/9780230292420

Johnson, G., & Scholes, K. (1999). *Exploring Corporate Strategy* (5th ed.). Prentice Hall Europe.

Johnson, G., Sholes, K., & Whittington, R. (2009). *Fundamentals of Strategy Pearson Education*. Academic Press.

Martin, J., & Novicevic, M. (2010). Social entrepreneurship among Kenyan farmers: A case example of acculturation challenges and program successes. *International Journal of Intercultural Relations*, *34*(5), 482–492. doi:10.1016/j.ijintrel.2010.05.007

Molecke, G., & Pinkse, J. (2017). Accountability for social impact: A bricolage perspective on impact measurement in social enterprises. *Journal of Business Venturing*, *32*(5), 550–568. doi:10.1016/j.jbusvent.2017.05.003

Oham, C., & Durkin, C. (2016). Social Innovation Management and Capital Literacy. In C. Oham & D. MacDonald (Eds.), Leading and Managing a Social Enterprise in Health and Social Care. Academic Press.

Oham, C., Stewart, J., & Cornish, Y. (2009). Social Capital Social Enterprise and Community Development. In J. Stewart & Y. Cornish (Eds.), *Professional Practice in Public Health* (pp. 191–206). Devon Reflect Press Devon.

Peattie, K., & Morley, A. (2008). *Diversity and Dynamics Contexts and Contributions*. Social Enterprise Coalition and Centre for Business Relationships, Accountability, Sustainability and Society Cardiff University. Available at http://orca.cf.ac.uk/30775/1/SE%20Monograph%20Published.pdf

Ramus, T., Cara, B.L., Vaccaro, A., & Brusoni, S. (2019). Social or Commercial? Innovation Strategies in Social Enterprise at Times of Turbulence. *Business Ethics Quarterly, 28*(4), 463-492.

Royce, M. (2007). Using human resource management tools to support social enterprise: Emerging themes from the sector. *Social Enterprise Journal, 3*(1), 10–19. doi:10.1108/17508610780000718

Royce, M. (2009). *Management for Social Enterprise*. Sage.

Sabella, A., & Niveen, L. (2016). A strategic perspective of social enterprise. *Journal of General Management, 41*(4), 71–89. doi:10.1177/030630701604100405

Social Enterprise UK. (2021). *The London Early Years Foundation*. Social Enterprise UK.

Steiner, A., & Teasdale, S. (2017). Unlocking the potential of rural social enterprise. *Journal of Rural Studies, 70*, 144–154. doi:10.1016/j.jrurstud.2017.12.021 PMID:31787801

Whittington, R. (1993). What is Strategy and does it matter? Thomson Business Press.

Wongtschowski, A. (2015) social enterprise capabilities and human development *DPU Working Paper* No.174, Special Issue on Capability Approach in Development Planning and Urban Design

# Chapter 2
# Adaptive Leadership in Micro Social Enterprise Teams:
## Exploring Innovative Healthcare Partnerships

**Maurice Ekwugha**
*University of Greenwich, UK*

## EXECUTIVE SUMMARY

*COVID-19 is a relatively new disease, and most victims are in low income, people-facing jobs. The most economically disadvantaged in society are less able to comply with certain non-pharmaceutical interventions (NPIs) partly due to their financial situation. Hope for the Helpless (H4H), set up as part of a micro social enterprise to cater for rough sleepers in London, UK, is at the heart of the COVID-19 response to the homeless there. A lack of financial resources or capital can constrain social entrepreneurs and restrict their ability to create social capital. However, some social entrepreneurs have been able to innovatively leverage on previous relationships to augment their resource base because engagement with stakeholders is critical. The study explores one such relationship between H4H and a local health centre. It is hoped that this study will uncover survival strategies for social entrepreneurs to succeed and thrive in a post-COVID-19 world.*

COVID 19 has hit the global economy hard; and its spread from the early 2020s has meant nations had to shut down their economies to deal with it. The devastating impact of this situation took its toll on health services in the UK and the government had to put measures in place to protect the NHS. Unfortunately, such measures

DOI: 10.4018/978-1-7998-7724-0.ch002

discouraged close contact with the most vulnerable groups and people were often reluctant to engage with them due to fear of infection, social distancing, lockdowns, and so on. The impact also spilled on to social enterprises which are often known to augment the efforts of health and social care.

The NHS is diverse but it has a common standard to work towards, namely: putting the enhancement of the patient experience first and delivering the highest standards of clinical care and services possible. According to Chakravorty et al. (2020) COVID-19 is a new disease with a disproportionately high death rate among the Black and Ethnic Minority (BAME) community compared to the rest of the UK, and most victims are in low income, people-facing jobs, and are therefore at a higher risk for infection and thus more desperate for a remedy. Atchison et al (2020) found that the most economically disadvantaged in society are less able to comply with certain non-pharmaceutical interventions (NPIs) like social distancing, 7-day isolation and 14-day quarantine measures, partly due to their financial situation. The high proportion of ethnic minorities in East London situates the Hope for the Helpless (H4H) based in Stratford East London, which is part of a micro social enterprise, at the heart of the COVID-19 response, particularly to the homeless there.

H4H was set up in 2018 as part of a micro social enterprise to cater for the rough sleepers around the Stratford city centre in East London, UK. What started out as a small and infrequent food stall soon ballooned into a full-blown organisation providing food, clothing and other basic amenities, as well as sundry assistance to about 100 rough sleepers on a weekly basis.

The H4H team is comprised of a team leader, four regular members and upwards of five other volunteers. The H4H team leader's role includes supervision and monitoring of the team members; investigating incidents and complaints; reporting any issues, writing reports; attending to enquiries from clients and other team members, and giving regular updates and feedback to the parent organisation. The team is proactive. The homeless arrive to be served warm food and provided with clothing in a well-lit welcoming environment; and the floors clean and conducive to their health and well-being. However, the service is also reactive. The team is alert to promptly deal with any routine occurrences. For example, dealing with rowdy individuals or when a sick person inadvertently vomits on the floor while waiting to be served. Sometimes, individuals may occasionally come in with more information s. For example, if a homeless person needs somewhere to spend the night, the team leader will personally contact a homeless shelter or call upon another team member to do so.

At the busiest of times on Saturday evenings, the H4H venue is a beehive of activity as various team members play their roles serving clients and performing their various duties. The tables are set at 8 p.m. and the homeless form an orderly queue of about 20 to 25 initial attendees waiting to be served a hot meal. On the whole, about 100 people are served on a Saturday night.

Some NHS trusts are social enterprises (e,g, Bromley Healthcare CIC) or run social enterprises as a part of their functions. However, some staff of NHS organisations that are not social enterprises, while not officially involved, have found a way to informally collaborate with social enterprises in innovative ways. Likewise, some social enterprises have been able to innovatively leverage on their previous relationships with NHS staff to augment their resource base in light of developments resulting from the pandemic. A lack of financial resources or capital can constrain social entrepreneurs and restrict the ability of social entrepreneurs to create social capital (Thompson et al., 2000).

H4H's East London base has enabled partnerships with nearby organisations and institutions, including a close bond with a particular NHS health centre in the area comprised of a GP surgery and other community health service providers. Oham and Mcdonald (2016) say engagement with stakeholders is critical to developing a social enterprise within healthcare. In the health centre, the GPs emphasise working in partnership with the local community to provide high-quality, safe and effective services. However, the current COVID-19 pandemic posed a new challenge.

On the GP side, the infection management team had a bigger role to play during the COVID-19 lockdown particularly in encouraging hand hygiene, cleaning of medical and office equipment, monitoring waste streams, changing clinical curtains, ensuring a thorough environmental clean between patients, managing different patients based on status, and especially translating and disseminating relevant government directives. The national guidance was taken as best practice which bestowed further responsibilities such as providing information on track and trace, and the summary and adaptation of national guidance for a primary care setting. This also involved interpreting an average of 20 national guidelines and policies each day, because it was felt the guidance was not specific to primary care and seemed more suited to secondary care.

GP staff shortages were handled by juggling staff in batches to take two- to three-week periods off while working from home. Before the pandemic, the GP practice had regular weekly in-house meetings every Thursday where all issues pertaining to their service were discussed. At the advent of the pandemic, the GP surgery started a 30-minute morning huddle at 9 a.m. to communicate changes, share information and ensure everyone was up to speed with new developments in policies and practice in a fast-paced environment. The meeting was informal with no set agenda and coordinated by the GP lead for the day. To ensure continuity, each lead GP hands over directly to the next lead GP.

The social entrepreneur and the (H4H team faced a similar challenge. They had to find solutions and also obtain clarification of government measures, as well as an understanding of how to implement them within their particular context. They also had to find ways to engage with the needy, now dispersed to various places, and often with no online presence. The social entrepreneur had to find ways to glean knowledge, information and support in the short and longer term.

One of the H4H team leader's roles involved regular interactions with the various service providers within the health centres, and their managers, to assist with the logistics of providing healthcare for the homeless where necessary. For example, the H4H team leader is armed with an exhaustive list of homeless shelters and other services that could help facilitate the rehabilitation of a recovering homeless patient. In practical terms, the team leader's role within the health centre, in catering to the needs of a rough sleeper, could take the form of soliciting transportation for a homeless patient discharged by the GP but who is having difficulty getting to the next rendezvous.

## LEADERSHIP, TEAM AND HEALTH CENTRE MICROSYSTEMS

The H4H team leader's role included serving as a point of contact, assisting and providing timely logistics to the GP surgery and community services. Figure 1 shows the various linkages and relationships between the team and the NHS management and staff within the health centre. Hartley and Benington (2010) defines one concept of leadership in terms of personal qualities, organisational positions, and as a social process. Leadership based on personal qualities emphasises the leader's personality traits, skills, capabilities, behaviours and standards. Successful leaders of this type are approachable, have a listening ear, and are ready to encourage and support team members. An example of poor leadership would be a leader who is aloof and seems to have a hidden self-centred agenda outside of the team's stated objectives.

Leadership based on the organisational position emphasises the leader's formal role. Hartley and Benington (2010) say 'a formal position within an organisation, such as chief executive or team leader brings with it the legitimacy to lead others,' and that, from a process perspective, leadership is about relationships and engaging the hearts and minds of stakeholders if they must achieve their goals. The aspiration to develop a leadership role could be based on a leadership model for the NHS hinged on the three Ps of purpose, partnership and performance i.e., providing and justifying a clear sense of purpose; motivating teams to work efficiently; and focusing on improving system performance (Storey and Holti, 2013).

When H4H commenced operations in 2018, none of the current team members were a part of the parent social enterprise besides the team leader. 'A' came in the first week, then 'B', and 'C' joined a few months later. When new team members arrive, it is the team leader's job to show them around, enumerate their responsibilities and

*Figure 1. Team microsystem*

team expectations; and instruct them on how to work in the particular environment of a social enterprise where maintaining excellent hygienic standards while working around rough sleepers, is a major underlying issue. For example, currently, 'B' has taken an extended leave and a volunteer worker is in their place. This has informed a directive leadership approach from the team leader because although enthusiastic, the new staff often leaves waste containers lying around and doesn't clear up after themselves. Also, they are not familiar with the prevailing organisational culture e.g., food service starts at 8 p.m. promptly, and therefore all areas must be tidy and everything set by 7.30 p.m. These preferences were flagged up by the senior management at subsequent team meetings. And thus, buttressing the argument that individual styles; team processes; and organisational cultures are interconnected.

Tuckman and Jensen (1977) sets out a team development model in the following stages: *forming, storming, norming, performing* and *adjourning* (see Figure 2). On their initial arrival, different team members acted differently. When 'A' joined she had not worked with the organisation before and was also new to the job role. She worked dutifully during the forming stage but the storming phase was a challenge. She needed coaching but would often ignore instructions and when corrected, would assume she was being unfairly treated. That was a sign that the team leader had to lead differently.

*Figure 2. Team development path (Tuckman and Jensen, 1977)*

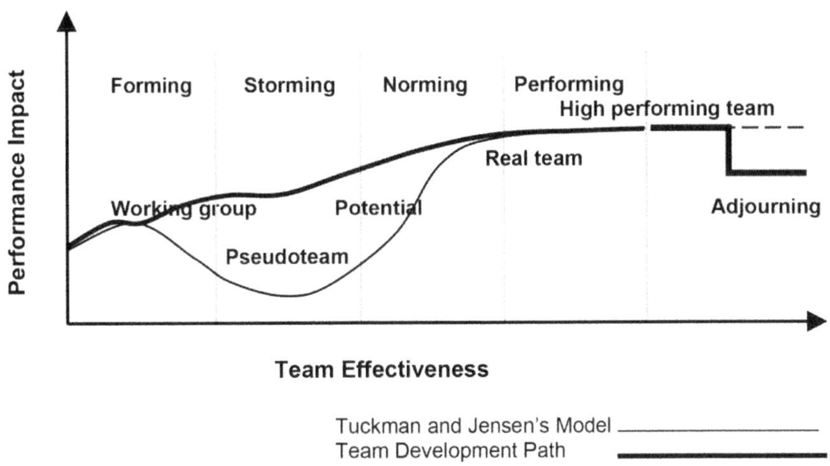


A team meeting was arranged, the proper procedure explained, and each member had to do a trial run. Then, it was explained that everyone had to get along for the work to move forward. This brought about a change in 'A' because the team leader had adapted his leadership style towards 'A' from a *coaching* to an affiliative one.

Teams are often dynamic. At the forming stage, 'teams' are not yet a team. Members may come and go at different stages and each new individual's performance necessitates a leadership style adjustment. Thus, it can be difficult to accurately determine the stage of overall team development because while some might be forming, others are in the storming, norming or performing phase within the same period. In fact, Tuckman and Jensen's model calls teams at the forming phase, 'working groups'. Katzenbach and Smith (1973) say 'teams differ fundamentally from groups because they require both individual and mutual accountability.'

Individual proficiencies and preferences on particular tasks may affect the performance of the team. The exclusive task needs of each microsystem within the centre have to be clarified to each new team member, whilst also emphasising team and individual needs (Adair, 1973). John Adair bases his 'action-centred leadership' on the recognition of individual, task and team needs (See Figure 3). Also, West

(2012) argues that 'teams are composed of a variety of emotional, social and other human needs that the team as a whole can either help to meet or frustrate.'

Before they joined our team, 'B' had worked in a different team within the organisation. Their previous background meant their forming stage was relatively short. 'C' wasn't happy to move to a different site when they arrived, however, partly perhaps, due to the warm welcome they received, and the team leader's experience with the two members already settled in, for example, providing them with keys to their personal locker the moment they arrived; they were cheerful and friendly. It seemed that they had a relatively brief forming stage and also seemed to skip the storming stage altogether because they got on well with everyone. Thus, the transition of the team from the *norming* to *performing* phase seemed almost natural. Evidence from the team reflexivity questionnaire showed that this was a highly task effective team. This could be because the team is quite small and the stages are cycled through quickly.

*Figure 3. Action centred leadership (Adair, 1973)*

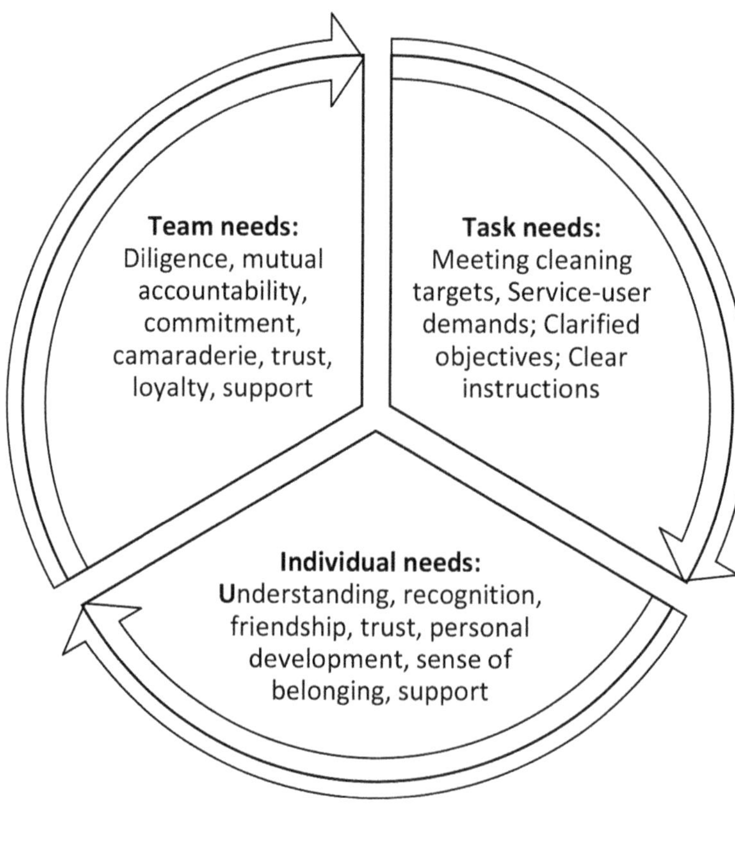

Recently, the team climate was affected by arrangements of the new senior manager to introduce monthly service-user meetings and action plans. The team was mandated to do a periodic deep clean of the service areas frequented by the service users. The task was challenging because the cleaning performance standards were raised from 90–95% and rectification forms highlighting any faults were also introduced, in addition to the weekly audits and arbitrary spot checks that already monitor team performance in the area. Management instructions were expected to be carried out without additional support or required training. Increased frequency of impromptu checks put added pressure on the team. This made team members more defensive with less time for team discussions which, in turn, affected team morale and cohesiveness e.g., 'A's performance, although still high, seemed to wane a little. 'B' has currently embarked on a prolonged sickness absence. 'C' seemed to have recovered the 'storming phase' they skipped, and became more vocal and questioning about the stringent regime the team now had to deal with. It seemed as though the team was in the adjourning stage.

## CONFLICT PREFERENCE

A minor conflict arose between two team members which was raised in the service users meeting. This highlighted issues around making sense of how positive elements of conflict may lead to improvement. This presented an opportunity to adapt learning from NHS staff ideas. The potential conflict situation arose between 'A', an old hand, and 'B' a voluntary staff who was hardworking, but not familiar with her surroundings and also uncertain about some of her responsibilities. Experienced team member 'A' was assigned to coach 'B' on the finer points of her role. Conflict resulted from this.

The team leader's informal leadership role meant he often adopted a relationship-oriented conflict preference (Whetten and Cameron, 2015). Thus, he tended to be more accommodating. Conflicting priorities meant that he had to judge between competing tasks. And depending on the situation, he was more likely to accommodate and then collaborate or compromise. However, if the situation was temporary, low priority or required time for tempers to cool, an avoiding posture could be employed. Thus, a compromising posture was likely to be adopted for minor disputes; a collaborating posture for major issues with far-reaching consequences; and an accommodating posture for other people's emergencies.

So 'A' and 'B' were called to a meeting to find out what their concerns were. 'A' said 'B's standards were poor, seemed irritated when corrected and had stopped talking to her. 'B' said 'A' was pressuring her. It was explained to 'B', that 'A' just wanted to help, and to 'A', that 'B' felt unduly pressured. The need to work together to improve the service was stressed to both parties. Firstly 'B' was instructed to apologise to 'A' for misinterpreting her motives. Then 'A' was asked to apologise to 'B' for raising her voice and putting extra pressure on her. They both apologised to each other and the team leader insisted on handshakes. Both did so. Then the mood was lightened when the team leader suggested they go the extra mile and hug each other. Everyone laughed and returned to their various stations. Later, it was observed that normal relations had resumed between the two. Thus, by insisting on the mutual goal of service improvement, the situation was moved from a people-focused to an issue-focused conflict.

## PUSHING FOR CHANGE

An area of service that required change in order to meet team challenges was the issue of NHS staff feedback. Whilst the social enterprise did receive some feedback from its service users, there was no direct feedback from the NHS staff themselves about H4H activities, how they felt, and where their efforts could be improved. It is felt that direct contact between the social entrepreneurs and the NHS staff in this way will drive improvement and put the team leader in a position to receive meaningful feedback and also influence management decisions in an adaptive way (Heifetz, 1994). For example, in a consultation about a major reorganisation, the team leader asked a series of questions which might have had an impact in management making certain changes. Developing a leadership role along those lines is worth considering.

Another area where improvements could be considered is in encouraging donations from individual health centre staff. This also encourages staff to have a more personal involvement in the success of the enterprise outside of the official organisational setting. Thus, the H4H team may need to do things differently and adapt their activities to staffs' own particular circumstances. This could mean new ways of soliciting for funds which would bring new challenges, for example, finding the right time to approach staff who are often very busy.

To push for change, the team leader may view his role as leading informally i.e., without authority. Heifetz (2006) says such people exercise leadership momentarily by impressing upon a group and sometimes by powerfully articulating an idea that strikes a resonant chord. For example, a staff assistant could speak up at a meeting even although they have no authority to do so. To do this, the team leader could make an effort to influence the line manager by including the initiative in the service-user meeting agenda.

To implement the team leader's funding plans, they would need to brainstorm with their team on possible approaches to the project. They would need to speak to their line manager and arrange for a meeting whenever possible about the modalities of designing an NHS staff feedback survey form, and communicating those views to the health centre manager and reception manager about displaying the feedback forms. They will need to contact the practice manager and other team leaders and service providers, to informthem of the initiatives.

## SCOUTING AND SCOPING

The study explores the team dynamic within the H4H team and how its leadership is able to learn from its partnership with the management and staff of a local health centre to ensure its sustainability. It examines the inner workings of the health centre during the COVID-19 pandemic and how the social enterprise was able to glean knowledge, information and support from the health centre to enhance its own practices and procedures. This was also with a view to leveraging the on-going relationship with health centre management and staff to augment the resource base of the enterprise in light of the effects of the current pandemic.

This study explores the lived experiences of a social enterprise team in partnership with staff in an East London health centre. The study adopts a qualitative approach that enables collation of first-hand information from real-life sources using ethnographic and phenomenological frameworks (Vivar et al., 2011). The approach captures the lived experience of the H4H team and NHS staff, ensuring that rich data, which would otherwise have been lost or overlooked, is captured. It ensures subjects are treated in greater detail and hitherto unheard responses are rehashed and documented fully.

A semi-structured questionnaire comprising 30 questions that explored the individual perceptions and experiences of health centre management and staff during the COVID lockdown period was used. The questions ranged from the physical impact of COVID; effectiveness of government policies; supporting vulnerable groups; to, the structures put in place by the health centre to tackle the COVID situation, and so on. One-to-one interviews were also conducted with GP and nursing management to further capture any adaptive practices and procedures they employed in the crisis.

A sample size of 23 health centre staff from the GP and community branches was used. The number of staff respondents comprised of nine GP staff, eleven community nursing staff, one auxiliary staff and two other staff who omitted to indicate their departments in the questionnaire and chose to remain anonymous. The GP surgery has a staff strength of 50 comprising 15 GPs, seven nurses and healthcare assistants, 23 non-clinical staff and five managers. The nursing team is made up of 19 nurses and six support workers.

Two of the respondents had recovered from OVID-19. Practically all of the respondents cited children and family as their greatest worry. All respondents recognised the lockdown as the most effective government measure against the pandemic. Many days of nerves, edginess, anxiety and anger were also a common theme among most respondents.

Four of the nursing staff indicated they were happy with the technological structures in place since the lockdown, particularly the provision of laptops which enabled them to work from home. Five GP staff also indicated the technological structures in place were effective. Four respondents each cited mental health structures as the next best structure provided. This was followed by leadership and communication, and then teaching and learning. None cited financial structures as effective. Rather, two of the nurses cited the homeless as the most vulnerable group and provision of shelter as an issue to be addressed. However, one GP staff felt that food distribution was fairly effective.

Before the study, the team leader viewed nurses as useful assistants who simply helped doctors with their valuable work. But results from the study, through the various inquiries and research, showed that the nurses' skills and experience are absolutely vital to the smooth running of the whole healthcare system, particularly during a pandemic such as COVID. results also showed that some of the health centre staff are concerned about the plight of the more vulnerable in society. Thus, the H4H team could make some gains if they could tap into the goodwill gestures arising from this.

The study involved PDSA cycles, as well as a three-phase Action Research method that included semi-structured interviews, observation notes and feedback surveys, (Senior and Fleming, 2006). The theoretical foundations of Action Research lie in Gestalt psychology i.e., change can only be successfully achieved by helping individuals reflect on, and gain new insights, into the totality of their situation (Burns, 2004). A constructivist approach to interviewing was adopted to encourage a meaning-making experience and the active collaboration of interviewer and interviewee (Hiller and DiLuzio, 2003). In order to move the scoping phase forward, evidence was gathered qualitatively and by undertaking a critical appraisal of potential resources using PROMPT criteria (The Open University) to ascertain the presentation, relevance, objectivity, method, provenance and timeliness of the evidence.

Multiple methods of inquiry were used, including emails, public databases and meeting notes obtained from attending service-user meetings, and in particular, using published materials; noticing artefacts; and observing other's actions and talk (Open University, 2010). Minutes of meetings are important because of what actions they suggest others will be taking over a period of time and the keeping of field notes is absolutely vital to doing a good productive inquiry.

To avoid the danger of stereotyping, artefacts were studied insofar as they were able to highlight and corroborate other information already received. The reason for this is because symbols are ambiguous, and one can only test one's insight into what something may mean if one has also experienced the culture at the deeper levels of values and assumptions. Also, it is especially dangerous to try to infer the deeper assumptions from artefacts alone, because one's interpretations will inevitably be projections of one's own feelings and reactions (Schein, 2004).

The team leader attended the service-user meetings as an informal adaptive leader. Heifetz (2006) says, 'over time a person who begins without authority may have to construct, strengthen, and sometimes broaden her base of informal authority in order to get more leverage.' The team leader gained the support of most high-impact stakeholders and continued to liaise with various other stakeholders and chase up the practice manager to whom the idea of sponsoring the introduction of collection boxes and an awareness poster was suggested. The practice manager wanted to know how much it would cost and what the surgery's contribution would be.

The project involved introducing collection boxes and an awareness poster for NHS staff using the Plan, Do, Study, Act (PDSA) cycle approach (Langley et al, 2009) as a pilot, and then Action Research to introduce change that could lead to better staff participation in generating funds. Previous consultations with colleagues presented options such as providing collection boxes with clear labelling; training; and staff awareness. The change was for the team to introduce collection boxes at strategic and easily accessible areas for centre staff. It was expected to contribute to the financial standing of the social enterprise division. Timing was a very important factor during the improving phase. The simple chart (see Figure 4) gives an idea of the timescale of events.

*Figure 4. Meeting schedule*

| Item No. | Action | Resp | Week 1 | Week 2 | Week 3 | Week 4 | Week 5 |
|---|---|---|---|---|---|---|---|
| | | | | | | | |
| | Speak to H4H Team | Me | | | | | |
| | Speak to Line Manager | Me | | | | | |
| | Speak to Health Centre Manager | Me | | | | | |
| | Speak to Nurse Team Leader Manager | Me | | | | | |
| | Speak to Receptionist Manager | Me | | | | | |
| | Speak to Practice Manager | Me | | | | | |
| | Speak to Frontline Staff | Me | | | | | |
| | Speak to Health Centre Manager | Me | | | | | |

## PLAN DO STUDY ACT (PDSA)

The advantage of using the PDSA cycle (Figure 5) is that improvements can be tested on a smaller scale before introducing improvements on a larger scale. Thus, changes can be refined over time in small cycles avoiding any costly errors.

- **Plan:** For the pilot, the first step would be to place a collection box at a strategic location for a specified time (one week) and inform the team to monitor this.
- **Do:** Observe and record how often contributions were made to the box.
- **Study:** The team removes the box to manage any issues arising e.g., size being too small.
- **Act:** Using the previous example, arrangements are made with management for a larger size box to be used in the next PDSA cycle.

Having made the requisite adjustments, results in this cycle will determine the decision to continue with the primary objective of rolling out the project throughout the centre, using Action Research or to test further PDSA cycles in the three areas of labelling, staff training, awareness, etc., before fully implementing the initiative.

Having addressed the issues from the first cycle, the box is returned to its place and the frontline staff, and other teams, are informed with the same deadline. Again, the process is observed and the findings recorded. Perhaps this time the issue might be the colour of the box, whereby comments are noted and further adjustments made. And then another cycle, but this time the box is placed at an easily accessible location to staff. It should be carefully observed by the team and the frontline staff whether staff use the box or not or do something else such as speak to the receptionist about it. In this way, staff response to the box is observed within a specified period as to how many are likely to use or ignore it. The team leader and members will also be on hand for any staff concerns such as the box causing an obstruction; still being too small to be noticed; or confusion on how to use it.

To successfully execute the project, regular cooperation of the team, line manager, practice manager, estates manager, lead practice nurse and the receptionist manager are essential. When approached, the practice manager wanted to know what the project was about; how it would affect their service; what part they are likely to play; issues of confidentiality and the communication channel to be used. A draft copy of the questionnaire was emailed to her. The practice manager seemed likely to have a negative opinion to any financial commitment. However, this was tempered by a healthy interest in the prospect of a positive image.

*Figure 5. PDSA Cycle*

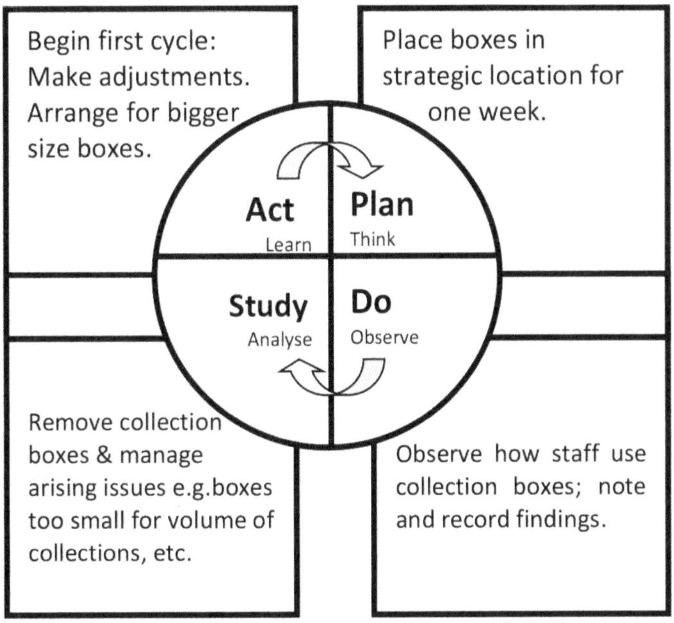


## ACTION RESEARCH

Action Research is a qualitative research approach that lends itself to studying research participants in their natural settings with the purpose of informing community change. As an iterative enquiry process, it balances problem-solving actions implemented in a collaborative context in order to understand the underlying cause to enable future predictions about organisational change (Reason and Bradbury, 2000 cited in Moore et al. 2011).

The term 'Action Research' was coined by Kurt Lewin (1946) based on his reasoning that, 'to be successful there has to be a 'felt-need' i.e. an inner realisation that change is necessary. This involves a three-pronged process that allows groups to address three questions:

- Change requires action, and is directed at achieving this;
- Recognising that successful action is based on analysing the situation correctly; and
- Identifying all possible solutions and choosing the most appropriate to the situation at hand (Bennet, 1983).

Action Research involves continuous cycles of taking action followed by observation and reflection on the consequences. Here, a three-phase cycle was used (See Figure 6).

*Figure 6. Action research cycle*

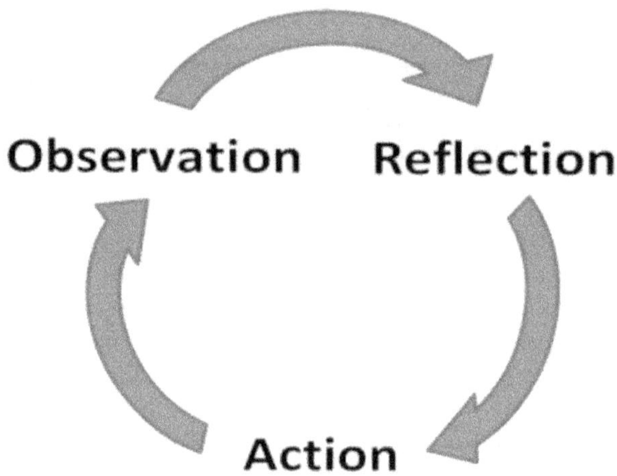


First phase of the Action Research cycle:

- **Situation:** Description of problem.
- **Objective:** Planned improvement i.e. what do you hope to achieve?
- **Action:** Implementation of initial course of action underpinned with relevant theories. and frameworks.

Second phase of the Action Research cycle: Utilising relevant methods of enquiry e.g., interviews, audits, questionnaires, meeting notes, records, etc.

Third phase of the Action Research cycle:

- Reflection: Encountering a particular situation and drawing conclusions from it;
- Critical Reflection: Going beyond simply thinking about the immediate how and why of what happened, to look at deeper factors involved in any situation;
- Developing theories about the situations we find ourselves in and our behaviours within them;
- Testing these theories by weighing them against the evidence.

Factors involved in a situation may include: assumptions, underlying beliefs, responsibilities, circumstances, policies, and so on.

## REFLEXIVE TOOLS

Structured debriefing (Gibbs, 1998): (See Figure 7).

- **Description:** Describe what happened without drawing any conclusions.
- **Feelings:** Describe feelings and reactions without drawing any conclusions.
- **Evaluation:** What was good about what happened? And what was bad about what happened?
- **Analysis:** Understand the situation or event. Understand the pressures, motivations and viewpoints of others. Draw on outside experience and ideas from expertise in evaluating theory; How does your experience differ from others, and, why does your experience differ from others?
- **General Conclusions:** General conclusions of your evaluation.
- **Specific Conclusions:** What you have learned about your personal situation, and your ways of behaving in that situation?
- **Personal action plans:** What would you do differently next time? What action points will you carry forward from this analysis?

The Groningen Reflective Ability Scale is a measure of one's ability to reflect (Aukes, et al., 2007). It has three sub-scales:

- **Self-reflection:** Exploring thoughts and appraising experiences;
- **Reflective communication:** Degree of openness and taking responsibility; and
- **Empathetic reflection:** Empathising with others and embracing different ways of thinking (See Figure 8).

*Figure 7. Three-phase action research*

| **Phases** | **Action** |
|---|---|
| Action | Situation:<br>Social enterprise revenue generation from pandemic fall out<br>Objective:<br>Planned improvement to introduce awareness poster to NHS staff<br>Action:<br>1)Use PDSA with team as springboard to launch action<br>2)Design poster; arrange placement of posters in acceptable location<br>3)Week-long implementation |
| Observation | Semi-structured interviews<br>Questionnaires<br>Observation, notes<br>Records, evaluation of options |
| Reflection | **Structured Debriefing (Gibbs, 1998)**<br>**Description**: Meetings with Stakeholders<br>**Feelings**: Happy with meeting attendance<br>**Evaluation**: Enablers –GPs, Line Mgr in full support , positive staff response; Blockers – HCM; NTL<br>**Analysing feedback:**Resistance to collection boxes due to possible pile up of used clothes in a clinical setting.<br>**Pressures**: Initial improvement followed by slump (Kotter, 1995); Choosing appropriate design, suitable location; resources; costing the project; allocating responsibilities; determining timescale, etc. Similarities - GPs in single location; Differences – various interdependent community services regularly interacting with wide variety of service users within and outside the centre.<br>**General Conclusion**: Improvement fairly successful; more to be done to change staff behaviour towards social enterprise.<br>**Specific conclusion**: Tend to avoid conflict and disengage from difficult stakeholders; discovered that 'less impactful' players can be more helpful than expected e.g. practice manager more accommodating than health centre manager and nursing team leader.<br>**Personal action plans**: Need to negotiate more; and monitor projects on weekly cycle |

*Figure 8. Team leader's reflective ability*

| | Strongly agree | Agree | Neutral | Disagree | Strongly disagree |
|---|---|---|---|---|---|
| I want to know why I do what I do | 5 | | | | |
| I am aware of the emotions that influence my behaviour | | 4 | | | |
| I do not like to have my clinical decisions discussed | | | 3 | | |
| I do not welcome remarks about my personal functioning | | | 3 | | |
| I take a closer look at my own habits of thinking | 5 | | | | |
| I am able to view my own behaviour from a distance | | 4 | | | |
| I test my own judgements against those of others | | 4 | | | |
| Sometimes others say that I do overestimate myself | | | 3 | | |
| I find it important to know what certain rules and guidelines are based on | | 4 | | | |
| I am able to understand people with a different cultural / religious background | | 4 | | | |
| I am accountable for what I say | 5 | | | | |
| I reject different ways of thinking | | | 3 | | |
| I can see an experience from different standpoints | | 4 | | | |
| I take responsibility for what I say | 5 | | | | |
| I am open to discussion about my opinions | | 4 | | | |
| I am aware of my own limitations | | | 3 | | |
| I sometimes find myself having difficulty in illustrating an ethical standpoint | | | 3 | | |
| I am aware of the cultural influences on my opinions | | 4 | | | |
| I want to understand myself | 5 | | | | |
| I am aware of the possible emotional impact of information on others | 5 | | | | |
| I sometimes find myself having difficulty in thinking of alternative solutions | | | | 4 | |
| I can empathize with someone else's situation | | | 3 | | |
| I am aware of the emotions that influence my thinking | | 4 | | | |

| | |
|---|---|
| **Overall** | **91** |
| **Self Reflection** | **86** |
| **Reflective Communication** | **77.09** |
| **Empathetic Reflection** | **70** |

## SOCIAL INNOVATION AND IMPROVEMENT

Social innovation occurs when challenges are addressed by creating social value (benefit to society rather than an individual) from new ideas or applications and new combinations of old things (Young, 2006). The widely held belief that the values and principles of privately owned enterprises are considered to be the unquestionable 'norm' and are seen by some to be more efficient in the delivery of public services (Kay et al., 2016), means social enterprises are often overlooked. In public health discourse, the role of social enterprise is often viewed as an alternative or complement to mainstream provision. Yet, not-for-profit organisations are improving the management of public health. Their added value lies in their ability to be independent, innovative, flexible, and responsive (NHS, 2008).

The contributions of social enterprises through change or strategic management initiatives by introducing social innovation and new management practices, help to mitigate many social ills ranging from poverty and food scarcity to health issues. Through social innovation and social enterprises, health practitioners are developing simple but effective tools to combat these challenges. It is critical that policy enactors factor in this group of stakeholders in their consultation, planning and interventions as this will build critical mass in terms of cost-savings, the use and leveraging of already existing resources, and other factors. However, there is still a significant gap in knowledge of how such activities can impact upon the social determinants of health (Macaulay, et al., 2017). Cottam (2010) says to look at both new and entrenched social issues, recognising what people have to offer and distiling the approach into participation and social contribution.

Innovation is also about maintaining improvement in a rapidly changing world to meet the distinctly challenging the demands and expectations of an increasingly savvy public. That involves adapting for a continuous change in how revenue generation is handled and how surrounding issues are perceived by service users, staff and stakeholders.

A novel innovation within the study would be introducing a returns form. This is a process innovation because it seeks to redesign the organisational process of collecting and returning collection envelopes from staff. The health centre manager considered this unnecessary. However, data has shown that less than half of all collection envelopes are labelled i.e., 48% and 51% before and after the campaign respectively, hence the collection returns form is an alternative means of tracking individual staff donations.

Because 'improvement is a continuous cycle rather than a one-off initiative' (Open University, 2014), some improvements can affect other services negatively. Thus, there is a need to have measures in place to dilute unforeseen consequences to the wider system e.g., implementing a collection returns system may put more strain on overstretched nurses' time for their patients. Therefore, assessing the time between collections becomes relevant. The solution of dedicating a particular staff in charge of H4H collections is also an option. However, all these changes may lead to further inquiries as to whether the fall in H4Hdeeper problem. According to Rodgers (2010), 'perhaps the toughest innovation is to find a way to persuade people that the status quo is not satisfactory.'

As innovations go, this project is rather localised and lacking in experiential stature compared to wider innovations such as the introduction of 'Sourced by Oxfam' ethnically sourced new products. But Figure 9 shows that the longer-term possibilities and wider implications of socially-led revenue drives in the health centre are limitless.

*Figure 9. Radical and incremental change*

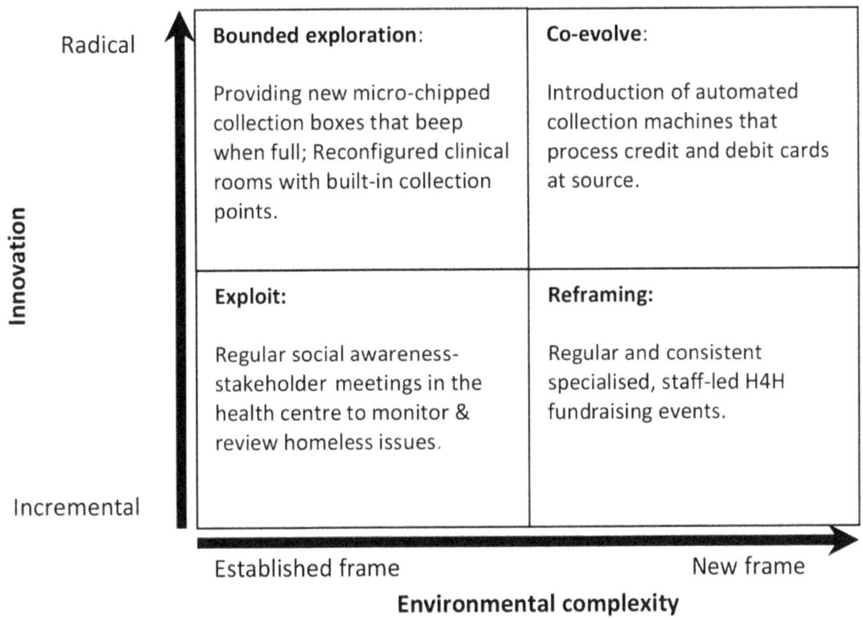


The temptation to declare an improvement without any learning would have distracted from the required learning or necessary adjustment to the team leader's methods or approach. However, there is room for improvement and further investigation into why staff reverted to type after the initial success in the week immediately following the awareness campaign launch. Kotter (1995) says, managers may be tempted to declare victory with the first clear performance improvement, but, until changes sink in deeply into a company's culture, new approaches are fragile and subject to regression. Also, it is advisable for the team leader to use the new-found credibility to tackle even bigger problems (Kotter, 1995) and avoid complacency after the initial success.

Realist evaluation is an important tool for its distinct viewpoint on how intervention brings about change, and is alive and alert to the importance of stakeholders as key sources for eliciting programme theory and providing data on how the programme works (Pawson and Tilley, 2004). In the event of sharing learning, diverse stakeholders may need different kinds of information. In realist evaluation, the end product is never a pass or fail verdict on an intervention but an understanding of how its inner workings produce diverse effects. (Pawson and Tilley, 2004). Figure 10 shows senior management support for the project from a realist evaluation context. Initially, it was thought that most opposition would be encountered from the Practice Manager and the GPs. But, it turned out blockers emerged from community service, in particular the Health Centre Manager and Nursing Team Leader.

*Figure 10. Realist evaluation*

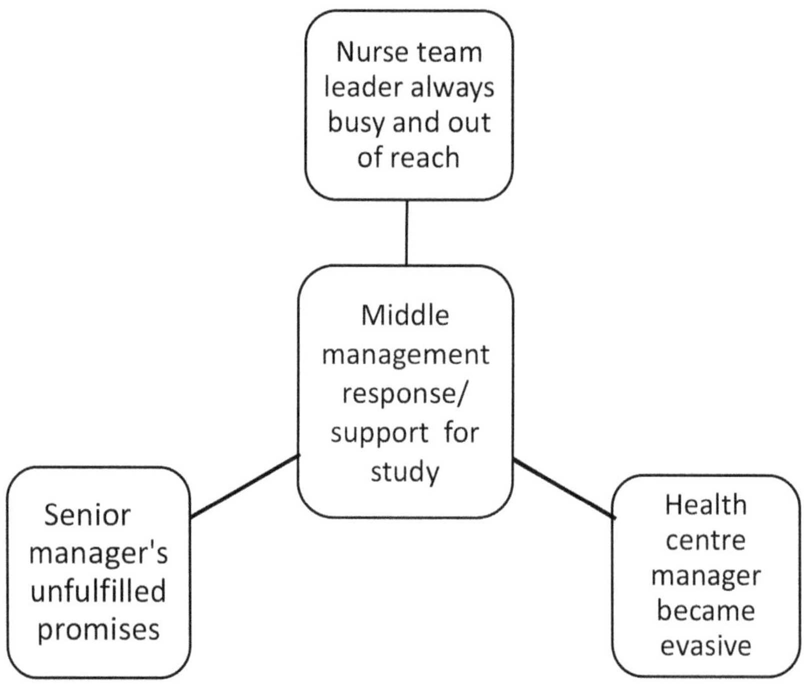


## CONCLUDING REFLECTIONS

This project was supposed to provide an avenue for NHS staff to contribute to the H4H social enterprise division through the introduction of collection boxes at a conspicuous location in the centre. In doing so, staff training and awareness were relegated to the fourth turn of the PDSA cycle whereas recent scoping endeavours revealed they ought to represent the major focus of the improving phase. Although it had always been the intention to use the PDSA and AR models to execute the project, other various scoping inquiries including meetings and discussions, made it clear the initiative would meet with some objections. For example, in the second user meeting, the practice manager asked the question; 'Should we encourage staff to bring used clothing into the clinic?' This prompted a more critical approach at what could reasonably be achieved. This also made the team leader look more closely at the power dynamics in the centre as it related to GPs, nurses, managers and their staff. Before the study, the team leader viewed nurses as an extremely useful appendage to the valuable work doctors are doing. But through various inquiries and informal chats leading from scoping the initiative, a clear appreciation that nurses were an intrinsic, highly skilled and irreplaceable link in the complex NHS care centre puzzle began to develop.

*Figure 11. Team leader's emotional intelligence*

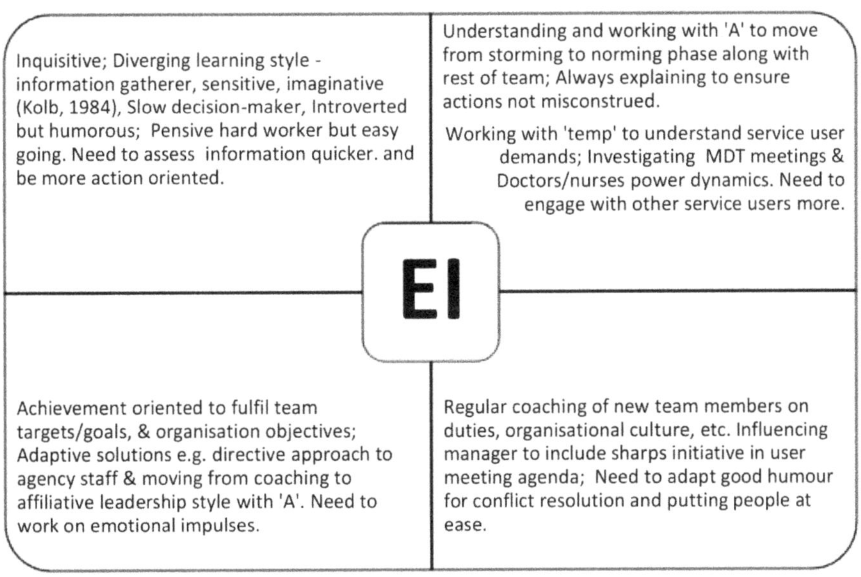


For example, one nurse was approached about the multi-disciplinary team (MDT) meetings with GPs and how they resolved issues. She said, 'GPs point out issues to us because we are in the frontline.' Another nurse further explained, 'the relationship between the GPs and nurses is cordial. GPs refer patients to nurses. Nurses see the patient and report on progress. But GPs are now more involved with resource allocation, and have greater control because they may escalate any lapses upwards.' However, another nursing manager didn't agree that the doctors had the upper hand in the relationship. And when asked if emotional aspects were ever discussed at the MDT meetings, she said, 'No, we don't discuss emotions. The major concern is for the health of the patient.' This supports Ballatt and Campling (2011) who suggest that, 'the rational approach has become somewhat dominant in the NHS such that issues of efficiency crowd out sufficient concern for the emotional life of the patient.'

*Figure 12. Adaptive leadership process*

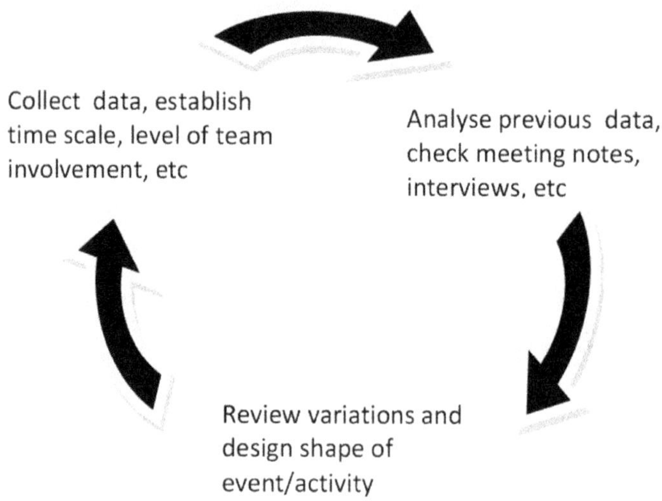


One area where social enterprises can profit from a partnership with the NHS is in adaptive leadership. Adaptive leadership has its advantages. But it is considered risky dangerous work because it challenges people to disengage from their comfort zone and accommodate needed adjustments. Heifetz (2006) supports this when he says, 'people fail to adapt because of the distress provoked by the problem and the change it demands.' Applying adaptive leadership can equip a leader with a better understanding of his competencies (Goleman et al, 2002) and why certain actions are taken. This also helps a leader play to his strengths while recognising disadvantaged areas with a view to making critical adjustments. This governed the decision of the H4H) team to embark on an awareness campaign rather than the introduction of collection boxes.

## REFERENCES


Adair, J. (1973). *Action-Centred Leadership*. McGraw Hill.

Atchison, C. J., Bowman, L., Vrinten, C., Redd, R., Pristera, P., Eaten, J., & Ward, H. (2020). Perceptions and behavioural responses of the general public during the COVID-19 pandemic: A cross-sectional survey of UK Adults. *BMJ (Clinical Research Ed.)*. Advance online publication. doi:10.1101/2020.04.01.20050039

Aukes, L., Geertsma, J., Cohen-Schotanus, J., & Zweirsta, R. (2007). The development of a scale to measure personal reflection in medical practice and education. *Medical Teacher*, *29*(2-3), 177–182. Advance online publication. doi:10.1080/01421590701299272 PMID:17701630

Ballatt, J., & Campling, P. (2011). *Intelligent Kindness: Reforming the Culture of healthcare*. RCPsych.

Brown, G. (2017). *My Life, Our Times*. Penguin Random House.

Burnes, B. (2004). Kurt Lewin and the planned approach to change: A re-appraisal. *Journal of Management Studies*, *41*(6), 977–1002. doi:10.1111/j.1467-6486.2004.00463.x

Chakravorty, I., Daga, S., Bhamrah, J.S., Menon, G., Dave. S., Chakravorty, S., Bhala, N. & Mehta, R. (2020). Self-reported occupational risk for COVID-19 in hospital doctors from Black Asian and Minority Ethnic Communities in UK. *The Physician, 6*(1). doi:10.38192/1.6.1.9

Coulter, A. (2004). When I'm 64: Health choices. *Health Expectations*, *7*(2), 95–97. doi:10.1111/j.1369-7625.2004.00269.x PMID:15117383

Francis, R. (2013). *Report of the Mid Staffordshire NHS Foundation Trust Public Inquiry: Executive Summary*. The Stationary Office.

Gibbs, G. (1988). *Learning by Doing: A Guide to Teaching and Learning Methods*. Further Education Trust.

Goleman, D. (1995). *Emotional intelligence*. Bantam Books.

Goleman, D. (2000). Leadership that gets results. *Harvard Business Review*, *78*(2), 78–90.

Hartley, J., & Benington, J. (2010). *Leadership for healthcare*. The Policy Press.

Hay Group. (2015). *Iceberg Model*. Mary Seacole Workshop 1 Slides.

Heifetz, R. (1994). *Leadership Without Easy Answers*. The Belknap Press of Havard University Press.

Heifetz, R. (2006). Mobilizing for adaptive work. In Making Policy Happen. Routledge.

Hiller, H., & DiLuzio, L. (2004). The interviewee and the research interview: Analysing a neglected dimension in research. *Canadian Review of Sociology and Anthroplogy*, *41*(1), 1–26. doi:10.1111/j.1755-618X.2004.tb02167.x

Katzenbach, J.R., & Smith, D. (1993). The discipline of teams. *Harvard Business Review, 83*(7-8), 162–71.

Kolb, D. A. (1984). *Experiential learning: Experience as the Source of Learning and Development*. Prentice-Hall Inc.

Langley, G. L., Nolan, K. M., Nolan, T. W., Norman, C. L., & Provost, L. P. (2009). *The Improvement Guide: a practical approach to enhancing organizational performance* (2nd ed.). Jossey-Bass Publishers.

Mary Seacole Programme. (2015). *Participant Learning Journal: Leadership Workshop One*. NHS Leadership Academy.

Meyer, J. (2000). Qualitative research in health care: Using qualitative methods in health related action research. *BMJ (Clinical Research Ed.)*, *320*(7228), 178–181. doi:10.1136/bmj.320.7228.178 PMID:10634744

Morgan, G., Gliner, J., & Harmon, R. (1999). Definition, purposes, and dimensions of research. *Journal of the American Academy of Child and Adolescent Psychiatry*, *38*(2), 217–219. Retrieved March 10, 2020, from https://www.jaacap.org/article/S0890-8567(09)62901-4/pdf

Naidoo, N. (2011). What is research? A conceptual understanding. *African Journal of Emergency Medicine*, *2011*(1), 47–48. Retrieved March 10, 2020, from https://www.researchgate.net/profile/Navindhra_Naidoo/publication/265704878_What_is_research_A_conceptual_understanding/links/54197fc60cf2218008bf83cf/What-is-research-A-conceptual-understanding.pdf?origin=publication_detail

Oham & McDonald. (2016). *Leading and Managing a Social Enterprise in Health and Social Care*. Community Training Partners.

Pawson, R., & Tilley, N. (2004). *Realist Evaluation*. University College London.

Ramsey, C. M. (2012). Developing Productive Inquiry, Section 4, (B839), Making a difference: the management initiative. The Open University.

Schein, E. H. (2004). The levels of culture. In Organizational Collaboration: Themes and Issues. Routledge.

Senior, B., & Fleming, J. (2006). The Leadership of Change. In *Organizational change* (3rd ed.). Prentice Hall.

Sparrow, S., & Robinson, J. (1994). Action Research: an appropriate design for research in nursing? *Educational Action Research, 2*(3). doi:10.1080/0965079940020304

Storey, J., & Holti, R. (2013). *Towards a New Model of Leadership for the NHS*. National Leaderrship Academy.

The Open University. (2014). *'Unit 6: Your initiative: developing options for action', B718: Mary Seacole Programme*. The Open University.

The Open University. (2015). *'Methods of inquiry: other sources of information', B718: Mary Seacole Programme*. The Open University.

The Open University. (n.d.). *Evaluating the quality of information: The PROMPT criteria*. Available at http://learn.open.ac.uk/mod/oucontent/view.php?id=451704

Thompson, J., Alvy, G., & Lees, A. (2000). Social Entrepreneurship: A New Look at the People and the Potential. *Management Decision, 38*(5).

Tuckman, B., & Jensen, M. (1977). Stages of small-group development revisited. *Group & Organization Studies*, *2*, 419–427.

Vivar, C. G., Canga Armayor, A., & Canga Armayor, N. (2011). *Qualitative Research Proposal: A Model to Help Novice Researchers*. Available at: https://www.researchgate.net/profile/Ana_Armayor/publication/282700875_Qualitative_research_proposal_A_model_to_help_novice_researchers/links/56447b0608ae451880a7d221/Qualitative-research-proposal-A-model-to-help-novice-researchers.pdf?

West, M. (2012). *Effective Teamwork: Practical Lessons from Organizational Research*. BPS Blackwell. (Original publication 1994)

Wheatley, M., & Frieze, D. (2011). *Walk Out Walk On: A Learning Journey Into Communities Daring to Live the Future Now*. Berrett-Koehler Publishers.

# Chapter 3
# Young Social Entrepreneurs and Social Challenges:
## The 'Parallelo' Case Study

**Alessia Pisoni**
*University of Insubria, Italy*

**Nicoletta Sciutti**
*University of Insubria, Italy*

## EXECUTIVE SUMMARY

*The chapter is focused on social entrepreneurship and, after providing a comprehensive literature review on the topics, aims at providing evidence of the decision-making process of social entrepreneurs and of the strategies they implement by focusing on a single case study, namely "Parallelo." Parallelo was founded in 2017 by four young Italian social entrepreneurs with the aim of promoting social inclusion of fragile categories and foreign people. Their 'formula' is the 'social lab' involving creative craftsmen that collaborate in the design and creation of sustainable products based on recyclable/discarded materials. By implementing a narrative approach, the case study is developed following step-by-step the social enterprise establishment and development. In doing so, the study aims at contributing to the social entrepreneurship field of research and at providing insights for practitioners about how decisions are made and strategies implemented within social entrepreneurial teams.*

DOI: 10.4018/978-1-7998-7724-0.ch003

## INTRODUCTION

Social entrepreneurship is increasingly attracting the interest of scholars and practitioners due to its positive impact on economies and its peculiar characteristics. When social organisations are financially autonomous, they are considered an efficient way to provide public services and improve the general welfare. In this respect, social entrepreneurship is intended as a process aimed at social change, involving local communities and improving their wealth. Social enterprises are often established in changing environments that oblige them to be adaptable and flexible in order to provide, in the fastest and most efficient way, the best service and product possible to clients. In this respect, 'change', 'adaptability' and 'flexibility' appear to be key terms to bear in mind while navigating this multifaced field of study.

The term 'social entrepreneurship' was initially perceived as strictly linked to public organisation and to the non-profit sector (Waddock and Post, 1991). It was intended as a solution to solve market voids and to sustain activities that could not generate revenues (Campbell, 1997). It has also been conceptualised as a 'multidimensional construct involving the expression of entrepreneurially virtuous behaviour to achieve the social mission, a coherent unity of purpose and action in the face of moral complexity, the ability to recognise social value creating opportunities and key decision-making characteristics of innovativeness, proactiveness and risk-taking' (Sullivan Mort, Weerawardena and Carnegie, 2003, p. 32). Only recently, its relevance for the private sector was underlined (Thompson, 2000). The key aspect remains the 'social mission'. However, social enterprises are diversified in terms of activity and form which make it even more difficult to determine the theoretical framework one needs to refer to (Bacq and Janssen, 2011).

Accordingly, scholars agree on the fact that social entrepreneurs require special leadership and innovative abilities (Abu-Saifan, 2012; Waddock and Post, 1991). In this respect, Abu-Saifan (2012) asserts that a social entrepreneur has a mission: to create social value for its customers. In doing this, they are socially alert, i.e., they recognise and pursue new opportunities to fulfil its mission. Entrepreneurial alertness come from 'skills, experiences, attitudes and special insights' (Murphy and Coombes, 2009, p. 333). According to Zahra et al. (2009), social entrepreneurs may be great visionaries, able to recognise worldwide social issues and then mobilise competent divisions in order to help reaching their vision. They are often defined as 'visionary individuals' (Bacq and Jannsen, 2011, p. 382) or as people with 'visionary insights' (Bacq and Janssen, 2011, p. 397). But also as people who mix visionary creativity with problem-solving rational creativity. Consequently, social entrepreneurs are totally concentrated on their vision and also focused on opportunity definition. Moreover, entrepreneurial vision is accompanied by a thoughtful strategic plan that helps in reaching long-term goals (Schwab foundation, 1998). To stay focused, a strong motivation is fundamental. In this regard, the main reasons that lead a social entrepreneur to start a social business activity are related to the desire for change and making a difference, meeting locals' necessities and solving social problems (Shaw and Carter, 2007). Accordingly, only a few social entrepreneurs want to become their own boss or be independent (Shaw and Carter, 2007). By contrast, social entrepreneurs are strongly motivated by the social aims they pursue. In other words, they want to feel that their job is useful (Sullivan Mort and Weerawardena, 2006).

The Chapter is structured as follows: Firstly, we present the relevant contributions published in the field of social entrepreneurship, with a particular focus on its characteristics, its broad definition and the importance of delineating clearer boundaries to this concept in order to avoid an overlapping between it and other social activities and initiatives. Moreover, also the delineation of the main peculiarities typical of social entrepreneurs by which it is possible to distinguish them from commercial entrepreneurs will be analysed. Secondly, we present a single case study we chose and discuss findings arising from the analysis. Lastly, concluding remarks and suggestions for future research directions complete the chapter.

## SOCIAL ENTREPRENEURSHIP AS A RESEARCH DOMAIN

As anticipated, social entrepreneurship as a research domain is increasingly attracting the attention of scholars. The term social entrepreneurship has gained different connotations over the years. In the past, it was mostly defined as an approach adopted by public organisations in order to cover the market's voids improving the resources' allocation (Waddock and Post, 1991). According to this description, it was intended to be a public instrument aimed at better distributing resources among communities in order to enable the setting up of activities that otherwise wouldn't create revenue (Campbell, 1997). Only starting from the last years of the 20th century, scholars have begun specifying the definition, underlining the social driven purpose of these kinds of enterprises (Prabhu, 1998). In particular, as stated by Mair and Martı´ (2004), social entrepreneurship is strictly linked to the concept of social innovation. This latter is an approach to innovation that implies the satisfaction of social problems as a main purpose, through the combination and recombination of the available resources. With this clarification, social entrepreneurship assumes a higher value that differentiates it from the general concept of entrepreneurship. As anticipated in its name, this approach to innovation enables not only the creation of profit and economic value, but more especially of benefits for the society. These advantages mainly consist in solutions to the so-called 'Grand Challenges' concerning the improvement of living conditions for humanity and especially for disadvantaged people in the world (Colquitt and George, 2011). In particular, 'Grand Challenges' consist of shared visions and objectives addressing the Global community's initiatives (Edler and Fagerberg, 2017).

More specifically, by improvement of living conditions it is intended: poverty reduction and elimination, making – as an example – healthcare and education accessible for everyone, promoting equality, inclusion, peace and, finally, protecting the environment. In relation to this, social entrepreneurship is an instrument in the alleviation of these challenges, also through the introduction of social innovation whose purpose is firstly the solution to these constraints and, only in a second phase, the generation of profit that can be beneficial for the community in difficulty. Moreover, despite the fact that, at the beginning social entrepreneurship was more referred to a public intervention, as stated by the Canadian Centre for Social Entrepreneurship (2001), this approach is also taken by both the private and the voluntary sector. In addition to this, social enterprises, that are the concretisations and the outputs of social entrepreneurship, operate in different industries such as healthcare, manufacturing and education (Pomerantz, 2003). Moreover, it has to be underlined that more definitions and descriptions exist and they change depending on the geographical context and the school of thought (Bacq and Janssen, 2011).

However, as reported in the *Stanford Social Innovation Review*, in an article entitled *Social Entrepreneurship: the case for definition* (Martin and Osberg, 2007), there are three main components where it can be possible to delineate social entrepreneurship while differentiating it from other social practices. Firstly, being an approach to entrepreneurship, it is fundamental to underline the fact that it consists in a process rather that something static. Consequently, the peculiar characteristics of this approach can be found analysing the steps involved in the innovation process itself. The innovation process consists of the phases occurring from the ideation of a new product or service to its launch (George, McGahan and Prabhu, 2012). As a consequence, entrepreneurship is defined as an approach characterised by the continuous research of opportunities to catch, with the consequent implementation of new ideas aimed at generating value (economic, social or both). This process can be represented by a cycle composed by the different steps an entrepreneur experiences in order to implement her or his new idea (Eisenmann, 2013). In particular, the first phase consists in the individualisation of an opportunity that can come from the necessity to cover a problem or to improve a determined situation in order to make a positive change. These changes can occur at a political, economic, social, technological, environmental or legal level. After this, a second phase is involved. At this level, the entrepreneur has to generate the idea and a strategy to implement it according to the resources at their disposal. When resources are mentioned, they consist not only of material resources but also human resources with their soft and technical skills and, finally, founding. After this, the entrepreneur can start with the activity contemporarily building an ecosystem, a strong network composed by other entities such as universities, public authorities, other enterprises from both for profit and not-for-profit sector, to create a sustainable business whose values, efforts and resources can be shared (Adner and Kapoor, 2010). Once the business has grown, further developments and improvements to it can be applied according to the change in the needs of the target they serve. Moreover, starting from the experience already lived, and the deep knowledge of the target market, together with the innate capacity to forecast new needs, an entrepreneur can also generate a completely new idea starting from zero, in order to create an added value compared to the previous offer, in this way, restarting the entrepreneurial process that can be defined a never-ending cycle (Teece, 2010).

Also, in the case of social entrepreneurship, there are some steps to be considered. First of all, there is the identification of a problem. In this particular case, the specific challenge to face consists in a '*stable but inherently unjust equilibrium that causes exclusion, marginalization or suffering of a segment of humanity that lacks financial means or political clout to achieve transformative benefits*' (Martin and Osberg, 2007). In this first step, the social entrepreneur identifies social problems that can be addressed. Examples of these can be found among the Sustainable Development Goals (SDGs)set up in the Agenda 2030 by the UN. The points contained in this document consist of social challenges concerning the improvement of more sustainable living conditions for the whole of humanity. This means finding long-term strategies to reduce poverty, allow health and education services for everyone, contribute to peace building around the world while also paying attention to the environment protection (United Nations). All these voids can be identified by entrepreneurs because of their target market knowledge. This knowledge is due to the fact that they are part of that community or because they have experienced a period of their life there, staying in contact with local people from whom they could have understood their characteristics and needs while perceiving the necessity to make a dramatic change to improve their lives (Gupta, 2013). In addition to personal skills, and the will to acquire new ones through the direct experience, there is also a deep interest in social matters whose solutions become real missions. The second step in the social innovation process regards the identification of an opportunity (Martin and Osberg, 2007). In fact, once the problem is defined, the entrepreneur has to understand how to practically solve it and, first and foremost, understand what the opportunity is under a void and the sufferance of people living in a particular disadvantaged status. What distinguishes social entrepreneurship from entrepreneurship for profit is its social purpose. As a consequence, the identification of a social opportunity is followed by the creation of a social value proposition to set as the purpose, meaning and reason to exist of that activity. The social value proposition consists of the idea and values by which the founder has been influenced and inspired (Payne, Frow and Eggert, 2017). Moreover, it also represents the opportunity itself on which the enterprise finds its roots. This aspect is crucially important for social enterprises, because that is their peculiar factor without which they could be categorised as a normal enterprise. In particular, these core values have to respect proper characteristics. They have to be inspiring, meaning that they have to be emotional and able to create a desire in people to be part of such a reality that pursues the creation of benefits for the humanity. In addition to this, they also have to respect creativity. The purpose and mission of the company has to be innovative even if it challenges a known and consolidated status quo (Emerson, 2003). It has to be a strong value that can be used as a 'call to action' to push people to join a common cause, also fighting a challenging status quo, based on inequality dictated either by a stagnating culture or dictatorial politicians or forced by the difficult economic conditions that don't allow people to live in a wealthy enough way. The final phase consists of the effective creation of a new equilibrium through the launch of the social entrepreneurial idea (Martin and Osberg, 2007). The impact on the target to serve has to be an alleviation of suffering and a remedy to the social problem. This peculiarity is essential in social entrepreneurship, where profit creation is not a priority (Hibbert et al., 2001). Moreover, in order to precisely address the needs of the target served, social enterprises usually have direct control on the entire supply chain process, in order to perfectly match the demand. Keeping production under control also enables better monitoring of costs occurring during the innovation process, to allow people to afford the products and services offered. An adding contemporary benefit is the setting up of an ecosystem where solid continuity of the social values of the enterprise can be sustained and shared. An ecosystem consists of interactions between individuals and an organisation, which cooperate to create new value to satisfy customers' needs (Moore, 1993). Collaboration is essential in entrepreneurship in general, but in social entrepreneurship is fundamental. As it is an innovative approach, based on the resolution of social and common shared social and living challenges, many efforts have to be dedicated in the maintenance of the new equilibrium impeding return to the previous status that caused suffering to the target audience. As sustained by the UN's SDGs, social change must be sustainable, meaning it must bring benefits now, whilst also taking into account future generations. Collaboration is also especially fundamental considering the importance of skills local communities can bring. As they represent the market they serve, they are also the main sources of market knowledge, fundamental to implement an innovative solution that perfectly addresses their needs and respecting their technical capabilities. At the same time, social enterprises usually also have the ability to create employment in the communities to serve, with the consequent creation of economic benefits to the people they help.

The importance of networking is also underlined by the explanation of the concept of 'Social Capital'. This latter consists in the value created by a social enterprise (Dubos, 2017). It can be divided into three dimensions: the structural, the relational and, finally, the cognitive capital. The structural capital is composed by all the relations on which the enterprise is based or that it creates. This concept underlines the fact that creating relationships is an asset for the company and also an achievement itself. The relational capital is more linked to an individual. In fact, it is the sum of all those relations and dealings that a person has with others always in relation to the company. In this respect, relationships among employees are also understood. Finally, cognitive capital is the creation of a shared meaning among a community. This meaning consists of awareness creation concerning the urgent need to solve a social problem, with the consequent acquisition of the same values on which the firm is based (Liao and Welsch, 2003).

The high number of definitions (see Table 1) and absence of a unique completed description of the approach often leads to confusion between social entrepreneurship and other social activities. Two main examples of activities that most of the time are confused with social entrepreneurship are social service provision and social activism (Martin and Osberg, 2007). The first consists of all those caring initiatives organised by one or more individuals with the aim of solving a particular social problem for a precise community or group of disadvantaged people. This kind of activity is very limited, not only from a geographical viewpoint, but also from a resources' perspective. In fact, whoever organises such initiatives has limited resources that are expected to finish (Orloff, 2020). Consequently, once there are no more assets, the projects cannot continue. Moreover, as they are focused on the needs of a determined community with its particular needs, these projects are independent and without a network whose components share the same value and purpose, with the consequent lack of possibility to receive help from these entities. The vulnerability of social service provision, together with the absence of a long-term vision, make it different from social entrepreneurship, whose purpose and outcomes must be sustainable and have stable services. On the other hand, social activism happens when an individual, once they have identified a social problem, starts working as a motivator of people to raise the importance of the issue and mobilize them to do something together to fight t and resolve it. In this respect, charisma and communication skills are essential. In fact, the entrepreneur must be able to find creative ways to inspire people whilst taking into account the possibility of criticisms. In this case, what differentiates this practice from social entrepreneurship is that, in this latter approach, the entrepreneur has a direct orientation to the solution of the problem being able to set up their own enterprise aimed at facing a certain challenge. In contrast, social activists have an indirect approach to the problem (Martin and Osberg, 2007). They want to solve it through other individuals and organisations such as NGOs, governments, workers and consumers. Another reason why it is important to distinguish between the two concepts, is the fact that activists are usually famous people whose role has an historical and shared meaning that can be linked to the achievement of important social goals that can be found in history books and have marked important steps of the society's development. For this reason, calling them entrepreneurs could create confusion among people (Martin and Osberg, 2007). Moreover, it is also possible to distinguish social activists from social entrepreneurs by considering the forms on which they usually base their speeches and their influencing activities on consolidated and well-known social problems. On the other hand, social entrepreneurs are defined as 'visionaries' (Bacq and Janssen, 2011, p. 397) who are able to predict new urgent social issues. Thanks to this ability, they can create completely new needs whilst also offering a contemporary solution to them. At the same time, the value proposition for which the offer is produced becomes an instrument to reach a higher goal different to profit. In fact, the main aim is the company's mission itself, which coincides with the resolution of a social challenge.

Despite these chances to delineate a clear and precise definition of social entrepreneurship several definitions already exist. However, growing interest demonstrated by scholars in relation to this field, is due to a number of different factors. Firstly, scholars are interested in general by what entrepreneurs do. They are increasingly fascinated by their inspiring stories reporting not only the positive side of the medal concerning the final success, but also the initial efforts and failures experienced to set up their enterprise (Verstraete, 2002). Moreover, scholars are focalizing their studies especially on the ideas social entrepreneurs develop and make real improving peoples' lives (Mort, Weerawardena and Carnegie, 2003). More specifically, with the increasing level of poverty and inequalities characterising the entire world comprehending both developing and developed countries, social entrepreneurship can be the right approach in order to prevent and then find solutions to these issues. Moreover, as it is a flexible approach to the market, meaning it is an entrepreneurial approach that adapts its offer according to the needs and the characteristics of the market, their flexibility is also under the attention of scholars and practitioners that aim to promote such an approach in a society that constantly change and need to be innovated very often (Prabhu and Jain, 2015). Another factor attracting the interest of researchers is their innate imperative in driving social change with long-term benefits. In doing so, scholars are also motivated by the need to preserve and give more value to social enterprises. This necessity is due to the fact that without a clear definition and description of these enterprises, it is also difficult to valorize them. This aspect can have bad consequences on the image of the company especially concerning its values and mission, with the probability to create misunderstanding among the target market and the potential investors too. In the first case, it is possible that people might confuse these kinds of firms for 'for profit' firms that aim to produce revenue. This can happen especially when people don't get the proper information about the activities, in particular about the story, the mission and value proposition. At the same time, this can also cause confusion

*Table 1. The definition of social entrepreneurship*

| Definitions of social entrepreneurship | Reference |
|---|---|
| Creating or elaborating a public organization so as to alter greatly the existing pattern of allocation of scarce public resources. | Waddock and Post (1991) |
| Social purpose ventures provide communities with needed products or services and generate profit to support activities that cannot generate revenue. | Campbell (1997) |
| Entrepreneurial organizations whose primary mission is social change and the development of their client group. | Prabhu (1998) |
| The process of adding something new and something different for the purpose of building social capital—focuses on actions taken by private sector actors. | Thompson et al. (2000) |
| Innovative dual bottom-line initiatives emerging from the private, public and voluntary sectors. The 'dual bottom line' refers to the emphasis placed on ensuring that investment generates both economic and social rates of return. | Canadian Centre for Social Entrepreneurship (2001) |
| The use of entrepreneurial behaviour for social ends rather than for profit objectives; or an enterprise that generates profits that benefit a specific disadvantaged group. | Hibbert et al. (2001) |
| Social entrepreneurship is a multidimensional construct involving the expression of entrepreneurially virtuous behaviour to achieve the social mission, a coherent unity of purpose and action in the face of moral complexity, the ability to recognize social value-creating opportunities and key decision-making characteristics of innovativeness, proactiveness and risk-taking. | Mort, Weerawardena and Carnegie (2003) |
| Social entrepreneurship creates innovative solutions to immediate social problems and mobilizes the ideas, capacities, resources, and social arrangements required for sustainable social transformations. | Alvord, Brown, and Letts (2004) |
| A process consisting in the innovative use and combination of resources to explore and exploit opportunities that aims at catalyzing social change by catering to basic human needs in a sustainable manner. | Mair and Martı´ (2004) |
| Social entrepreneurship may be defined as a professional, innovative, and sustainable approach to systemic change that resolves social market failures and grasps opportunities. | Saïd Business School (2005) |
| First, we view social entrepreneurship as a process of creating value by combining resources in new ways. Second, these resource combinations are intended primarily to explore and exploit opportunities to create social value by stimulating social change or meeting social needs. And third, when viewed as a process, social entrepreneurship involves the offering of services and products but can also refer to the creation of new organizations. | Mair and Martı´ (2006) |
| Any definition of the term 'social entrepreneurship' must start with the word 'entrepreneurship.' The word 'social' simply modifies entrepreneurship. If entrepreneurship doesn't have a clear meaning, then modifying it with social won't accomplish much, either. | Martin and Osberg, 2007 |
| The term social entrepreneur is ill-defined (Barendsen and Gardner, 2004; Weerawardena and Mort, 2006), it is fragmented, and it has no coherent theoretical framework (Weerawardena and Mort, 2006). | Abu-Saifan (2012) |

Source: Personal elaboration (combining different academic contributions)

with charities. In this case, people could under evaluate the work behind the firm. Despite the important role played by charities, together with their efforts to help people in need, they don't usually imply such an innovation process like an enterprise that has many costs to sustain. Moreover, charities help people in need without properly making their target independent from the solution of their problems. On the other hand, a social entrepreneurship's aim is the elimination of the problem from the roots, whilst also giving interested people skills and capabilities to reach their goal to escape from suffering (Van Iwaarden et al., 2009). At the same time, as social entrepreneurship starts from the concept of entrepreneurship, it is important to remember that each enterprise and entrepreneur, needs resources especially at the beginning. Funding encompasses economic, material and human resources. It is also important to differentiate these companies from other activities. Recognising the social mission and values on which the new enterprise is based, together with the underlining of the many efforts of the entrepreneur and people working for these realities, is crucially important. The more details given, the higher the possibility of greater funding. By demonstrating that they are a real enterprise and, with the addition of a positive social mission, it is possible to increase the credibility of the company. This step is crucially important especially for social enterprises whose founders usually use capital coming from donors while for-profit companies are usually initially founded by the family members of the entrepreneurs (Bacq and Janssen, 2011).

In conclusion, social entrepreneurship does not present a unique clear definition, but scholars are working to delineate its boundaries with the aim of better understanding the innate capabilities of social entrepreneurs who have the will to increase awareness about the important role played by social enterprise contemporarily avoiding confusion with other kinds of social activities. Social enterprises possess a socially driven mission that creates social capital and a deep sustainable social change that solves crucial humanitarian problems.

## SOCIAL ENTREPRENEURS' UNIQUE CHARACTERISTICS

As previously pointed out, our aim is to devote a deeper assessment in understanding the specific characteristics of the social entrepreneur. Accordingly, a wide literature review has been performed. According to Waddock and Post (1991) social entrepreneurs are leaders who work to implement 'catalytic changes; in the perception of social-related issues with the consequent capability to influence the Governments' agenda making social problems a priority to solve. Social problems are characterised by complexity also due to the fact that they are fixed in a certain society or community where people are used to live in suffering without seeing the possibility to change.

In addition, according to Abu-Saifan (2012, p. 25), the social entrepreneur is 'a mission-driven individual who uses a set of entrepreneurial behaviours to deliver a social value to the less privileged, all through an entrepreneurially oriented entity that is financially independent, self-sufficient, or sustainable'. Consequently, the social entrepreneur is someone who has the capability to see opportunities of change and to address unmet needs, where others live in a passive way despite their suffering (Thompson, Alvy and Lees, 2001).

In order to better analyse the profile of social entrepreneurs, it is worth noting that social entrepreneurs are the first of all entrepreneurs. All entrepreneurs share peculiar traits identified by a considerable amount of contributions published over the years with the aim of understanding the driving factors that push an individual to pursue such a career. First of all, an entrepreneur is an innovator. By innovation, we refer to the propensity to engage in new idea generation, experimentation, and research and development activities. In implementing innovation, entrepreneurs allow a constant change that perfectly matches the fast changes of the society and their needs creating adding value (both economic and social). For this reason, they are also called 'change agents' (Gartner, 1989). Another peculiar characteristic of entrepreneurs is proactivity, which to be considered as the ability of someone who always anticipates new trends before others (Seibert, Crant and Kraimer, 1999). A proactive behaviour allows entrepreneurs not only to identify new solutions to launch on the marketto solve an existing problem, but also to predict and create new needs. The third entrepreneurial characteristic is creativity, according to which, an entrepreneur can combine and recombine resources to produce tailor-made solutions to serve the target (Radjou and Prabhu, 2016). At the same time, entrepreneurs are also people who dedicate their life to their ideas, missions and creations. Their enterprises become their scope and their mission in a way that does not allow them to stop thinking about it. Due to all these efforts, they can be described as highly committed. Moreover, especially during the first phase of their business, when everything is new, resources are scarce and there is higher risk of failure, they demonstrate persistence and determination in reaching their goals despite all the obstacles they will face (Tang, 2008). This behaviour is also due to the high ambition. Ambition is not only related to the will to make money, but in contrast is also related to the achievement of a mission with the consequent creation of added value. It means to have a great vision and the perspective to create something that will create benefits from different perspectives (Verheul and Van Mil, 2011). All these characteristics sometimes allow entrepreneurs to succeed and also to accept failures as chances to learn avoiding making the same mistakes more than once. Moreover, an entrepreneur is also the person who has to represent theirown company. As a consequence, to make it possible to create a business that fits with their mission and vision, it is crucially important to share their own values, creating a shared company culture among employees, to express the value proposition of the company to all stakeholders. In doing this, the entrepreneur also needs to be a leader, i.e. they must be able to influence others to understand and agree about what needs to be done and how to do it (Yukl, 2013). In this respect, charisma or idealised influence is the part of leadership that plays with emotions (Antonakis, 2012). Northouse (2018) assumes that followers see the leader as a model to deeply respect and trust. Charismatic leaders usually share their own vision with subordinates to set a common mission to be pursued and to create a sense of ownership among them. In doing so, good communication skills are essential. Both direct and indirect communication allows the entrepreneur to express themselves clearly, creating a channel with the stakeholders with which to influence them. Finally, an entrepreneur must be able to develop the managerial skills necessary to implement the required business processes (Malach-Pines et al., 2002).

As stated by Thompson, Alvy and Lees (2001), social entrepreneurs can be compared to normal entrepreneurs for all the above-listed characteristics. Despite this, there are factors discriminating the two profiles. According to Abu-Saifan (2012) four factors distinguish social entrepreneurs from common entrepreneurs. Social entrepreneurs: 1) are mission-driven; 2) act entrepreneurially by being: mission leader, emotionally charged, change agent, opinion leader, social value creator, socially alert, manager, visionary and, last but not least, highly accountable; 3) act within entrepreneurially oriented organisations characterised by innovation and openness; 4) act within financially independent organisations that execute earned-income strategy ('deliver social value while remaining financially self-sufficient'). More specifically, social entrepreneurs are visionaries. Their ideas are defined as visions, something that predicts the opportunity to improve a social condition trapping a certain community that for this reason cannot live in a wealthy way. In other words, attention to social concerns is at the base of their activities. Their social visions are also due to their social alertness that makes them more inclined to help others instead of making money (Thompson, 2002). Their mission is not the creation of a solution with an economic value, but it is the benefits that this solution can directly or indirectly bring to a particular community living in difficulties (Mort, Weerawardena and Carnegie, 2003). Quite often, social entrepreneurs have also to be brave in fighting against a consolidated state of mind or cultural, economic or political barriers, in order to set up a concrete change in something that does not work in the society. As a consequence, it is sometimes difficult for them to involve people, especially locals, to understand their values and vision. This is why social entrepreneurs also act as activists in order to share their thoughts and their mission. Accordingly, social entrepreneurs are also defined as people *'who create sea-change movements, either quickly over time, and have a major impact'* (Martin and Osberg, 2007). In this way, they aim to become real motivators of people, and in doing so, they have to demonstrate their innate communication (House and Baetz, 1979), transformational leadership (Odumeru and Ifeanyi, 2013) and creativity skills (Okhomina, 2010).

Abu-Saifan (2012) distinguishes among Non-Profit and For-Profit social entrepreneurs. Very often, social entrepreneurs are thought to be exclusively non-profit oriented. Also, when they are for-profit social entrepreneurs, their main purpose is not the creation of social value or social capital. By contrast, they aim to maximize sales in order to create economic benefits for the society around it. In addition, social entrepreneurs aim to reach their objectives without creating any competition with people. Moreover, they are accomplishment driven, meaning that they are motivated by the achievement of a main challenge.

In conclusion, as stated by Gartner (1988), there are characteristics that both social and non-social entrepreneurs share whilst others are peculiar traits by which a distinction between both profiles can be made. As entrepreneurs, social entrepreneurs

*Table 2. Characteristics of the social entrepreneur: A summary*

| Peculiar characteristics of social entrepreneurs | References |
|---|---|
| -Innovative in using and combining resources<br>-Emotionally charged<br>-Socially alert and social value creator<br>-Leader (both mission leader and opinion leader)<br>-Change agent ('catalytic changes' in the perception of social-related issues)<br>Could be for-profit or not-for-profit oriented (but social wealth creation remains the priority) | Gartner (1988); Waddock and Post (1991); Campbell (1997); Prabhu (1998); Thompson et al. (2000); Hibbert et al. (2001); Mort, Weerawardena and Carnegie (2003); Mair and Martı´ (2004, 2006); Alvord, Brown and Letts (2004); Abu-Saifan (2012) |
| **Unique abilities of social entrepreneurs** | |
| - To identify a stable, but unjust equilibrium causing exclusion and suffering of disadvantage community to achieve benefits<br>- To identify opportunities where others see problems<br>To create a social value proposition inspiring others, and to call them into action in the social change<br>To realise a new equilibrium alleviating suffering<br>To influence a Governments' agenda | Waddock and Post (1991); Thompson, Alvy and Lees (2001); Martin and Osberg (2007) |
| **Common entrepreneurs vs. social entrepreneurs** | |
| The social entrepreneurial process involves:<br>- Innovation, creativity<br>- Social vision and shared values<br>- Social alertness and motivation based on a social aim<br>- Activism<br>**But** also considers other typical characteristics of entrepreneurs:<br>- Creativity and innovation<br>- Determination, ambition and commitment<br>- Leadership, charisma, and communication skills<br>- Managerial competences | Gartner (1988) |

Source: Personal elaboration

can be defined innovators, change agents, creative and proactive for their ability to create a change (social, economic, political, technological) predicting a future need. They are also persistent, committed, determined and ambitious because of their will to use all their efforts in reaching their goals and, in the continuous determination they have, even if they risk failure. Moreover, entrepreneurs are leaders, charismatic, good communicators and able to inspire others, motivating them to pursue the same shared values of the company and of the entrepreneurs and company's culture. Finally, they also have managerial skills in order to understand the management and organisation process of the business. In addition to these common characteristics, there are specific unique traits that delineate the profile of social entrepreneurs. Firstly, they are defined as leaders who work to implement 'catalytic changes' in the perception of social-related issues with the consequent capability to influence the Governments' agenda, making social problems a priority to solve (Mair and Martı´, 2004). Consequently, they are social visionaries (Zahra et al., 2009), social value activists motivated by a social aim and are socially alert. All these characteristics delineate the profile of a social 'super hero' who, through an innovative approach, aim to make deep changes in the society, to alleviate suffering. They may also aim to make profits but this is not their priority. By contrast, commercially-, and for profit driven entrepreneurs are characterised by a need for achievement, a locus of control and they are also driven by accomplishment, are Machiavellian, strategic thinkers and risk bearers (Gartner, 1988).

## THE PARALLELO CASE STUDY

A single case study, namely Parallelo[1], has been chosen for this chapter. It is the first project of Officina Casona, a social enterprise founded in 2017 by four young Italian social entrepreneurs with the aim of promoting social inclusion of fragile categories and non-indigenous people. Following a qualitative case study methodology (Einsehardt, 1989), to collect data, we conducted a series of interviews – and informal chats – with the founders, carried out field visits, and triangulated data, we collect documentary information from the company, the website and available local news. By implementing a narrative approach, the case study was developed following the social enterprise's establishment and development step-by-step. We started with an event history (Langley, 1999) to trace the chronology of the main events that happened in the company's history (see Figure 1). In doing so, we aimed at providing evidence of the decision-making process of social entrepreneurs and the strategies they implemented to carry on their business.

As mentioned, the initial team was formed by four young (under 30 years old) Italian friends strongly motivated at working in the social field. The Founders' background was a good mix of knowledge. Considering education, they cover fields such as economy and management, foreign languages and mediation, design and architecture, and communication. Also,, in terms of work experience they are pretty varied, ranging from the startup world to fields of marketing and communication. Almost all founders have previous experience in the social field; either as employee or volunteers.

Before officially establishing the social enterprise – which happened in 2017 – the four founders encountered the typical challenges that characterize a 'start-up' phase of each project, i.e., to evaluate the willingness and commitment of each team member in joining the entrepreneurial adventure, finalise the initial idea (evaluate the feasibility of the project) and test the business model. In this phase, a strong motivation is essential to pursue the initial challenges: learn how to become entrepreneurs and how to scratch from the ground up (either considering knowledge needed or resources). Sentences such as '*we were enthusiastic about the idea of concretely contributing in something useful for the society*', '[our strong motivation] *allow us to keep problems and challenges in the background*' were often recalled during the interviews. The founders' goal/mission – that initially motivated them to start the company – acted as the main driver that pushed them to the next level. In those years, Italy was experiencing a massive migration of desperate people crossing the Mediterranean Sea with rickety boats hoping to reach Europe and start a new life. If they were lucky enough to reach the Italian coasts, migrants and refugees were given first-aid assistance, then access to a first- and a second-line reception phase. Without entering into too much detail in explaining what the Italian law ruled, the second-line reception system was conceived for asylum seekers and beneficiaries of international protection and includes some education/training activities aimed at promoting their social inclusion. Within this framework/context, the founders identified the social opportunity and gained inspiration to finalise the social value proposition characterising their project.

The name they picked for the first project was Parallelo (parallel in English), because Officina Casona was their first idea and Parallelo was their first 'parallel' project. Moreover, parallel is a word that remains more or less the same when translated in different languages and is, therefore, easy to understand. Based on this, they defined the Parallelo's mission as: '*A place for runaways from each parallel from the world*'.

In 2016, the founders launched the association with the aim of creating engagement around the project before legally incorporating the social enterprise and starting activity. The association involved 60 associates along with 200 active volunteers. In 2017, they officially established the Social Enterprise and launched the Parallelo project, thus allowing them to participate in a call launched to assign confisca4ed properties (related to criminal confiscation) to social projects. Then, the founders

*Figure 1. Timeline of main events in the company history*
*Source: Personal elaboration*

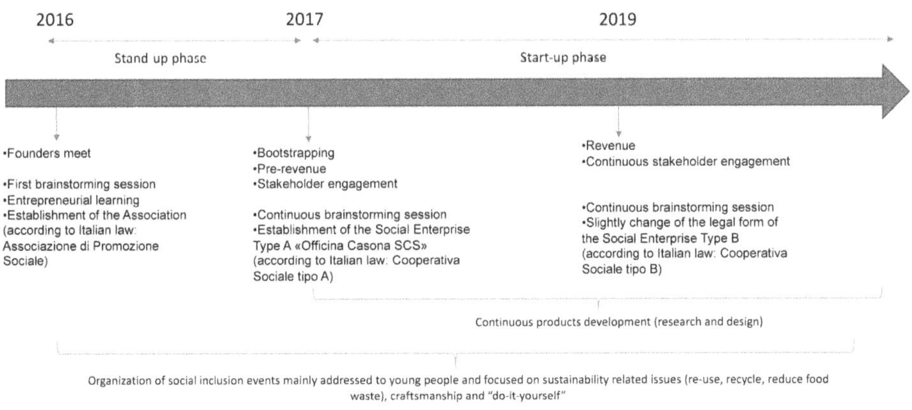


opted for an initial bootstrapping which was essential to cover the initial expensed and launch the company given their financial constraints

The four founders decided to meet weekly to make those decisions needed to carry out activities. Before being implemented, every action was discussed and evaluated in depth among the assembly.

The Parallelo's 'formula' was conceived as a 'social lab' involving creative craftsmen that collaborate in the design and creation of sustainable products based on recyclable/discarded materials. The social lab aims to promote social inclusion of fragile categories and foreign people by actively involving them in the creation and production process. More specifically, labs regard:

- Carpentry
- Pottery
- Cyclomechanics
- Bookbindery
- Tailoring
- Communication.

As anticipated, products are based on recyclable/discarded materials. The product's creation involves considerable design activity to make them cool and attractive. Quoting from their social annual report: '*by providing new life to used or discarded materials we implement the circular economy principles, thus reducing our environmental impact. By implementing a sustainable and responsible consumption behavior we boost the social impact of our project*'. More specifically:

- Paper comes from local companies;
- Ceramic products are produced with water and clay;
- Bikes are donated from individuals, associations or public institutions;
- Discarded wood and pallet;
- Leather and fabrics from local companies;
- Jeans from individuals and textile companies.

Products are then sold to the public either through the shop they have created where the labs are carried out or online. Each product represents a way to communicate the social project and its social mission. Besides being useful, sustainable and cool, each product tells a story, the story of who has realised it. In this respect, the package includes the stylised face, hands and a brief story of the person who has produced it. In doing so, they make a unique product, as unique as the individuals and their story. Moreover, with training activities being the most important one of their business model, the brief story of who made the product also represents an effective way of communicating the social mission.

In 2017, their primary activities were focused on ‘training’. Initially, their programme was organised around the above-mentioned labs and involved 12 non-Indigenous people (either asylum seekers or beneficiaries of international protection) who changed every 6 months. More specifically, whilst learning ‘how to do a job’ – each one specifically related to the above-mentioned labs – these indigenous people also learn technical terms needed to work in that field. This was the ‘Parallelo’ initial formula. However, after some changes introduced in Italian law and related to the support granted to asylum seekers or beneficiaries of international protection, the founders were somehow ‘forced’ to ‘pivot’ their initial idea and change their legal status from Social Enterprise type A to type B. In Italy, a Social Enterprise type A should generate revenues mainly from training activities. Once the Governmental support for training activities devoted to asylum seekers or beneficiaries of international protection were substantially reduced, the founders needed to find a solution to integrate the business model with new revenue streams. That is why they needed to change their legal status to type B, which also allows revenue from sources other than training. Reporting from the interviews ‘*it was not an easy decision to make. We need to change skin, and we feel forced by the external environment to do that’*.

By entering the ‘start-up phase’, the sustainability of the project is based on its ability to self-sustain by generating revenue. Therefore, along with the production and other activities related to fixing and restauration, tailor-made/personalised products, the founders are also involved in the organisation of events, communication services and marketing of social projects, craftsman workshops and training activities for fragile categories and indigenous people. More specifically, training is performed in partnership with local reception centres and labour market insertion services, and is based on practical activities characterised by an increasing level of difficulties. These represent alternative revenue streams other than that related to selling products they create to the public.

Their products and activities have been increasingly appreciated by the public over the years, thus also allowing them to hire people belonging to fragile categories as defined by the Italian law (L. 381/91). Nowadays, they employ ten people, five Italians, three fragile persons (two out of which are also refugees), and four are refugees and asylum seekers.

As young social entrepreneurs, literally scratching from the ground, the founders are used to facing continuous challenges. However, the latest challenge, related to the COVID-19 pandemic, has been particularly tough to address. Due to social-distancing measures and mobility restrictions, the training activities offered to the public have been suspended for a long period of time. Also, production activities suffered a substantial slowdown, which had an immediate impact on the lower number of products available for sale. '*We were worried not to be able to cover all the costs we bear to carry on the productions*'. However, their good reputation and the positive impact their activities had shown so far, ensured them a donation that helped them get through the revenue decrease due to the pandemic.

## DISCUSSION AND CONCLUSION

Social entrepreneurship is a process involving an innovative approach in the use of resources with the aim to satisfy the needs of disadvantaged communities while alleviating their suffering (Mair and Martı´, 2004). These social issues can be grouped in the UN's SDGls included in Agenda 2030, such as poverty reduction, equal access to educational end healthcare services, peace building, environment protection, and the general creation of inclusiveness and equal opportunities for everyone (United Nations). The social driven purpose of social entrepreneurship is the discriminative factor by which it is possible to distinguish it from the general more profit-driven idea of entrepreneurship. As stated by Martin and Osberg (2007), all these features influence and are also reflected in the innovation process. In fact, the first step is characterised by the identification of a social problem or a status of sufferance to solve. Starting from this, the social entrepreneurial process enables in the identification of a problem providing a real opportunity that will be transformed into an enterprise that can be conceptualised as the concretisation of social entrepreneurship. During the entire process, the creation of a local network among which to share resources and skills will be fundamental. In fact, social entrepreneurship is community and collaboration based. Finally, the benefits will be visible through the benefits occurring in the community served. This change will have to be sustainable and also visible in the future.

Moreover, the case study presented in this chapter provides an interesting story. The four young friends aiming to pursue a social mission thus promoting the inclusion of non-indigenous and fragile people by performing a wide range of activities. As stated, the framework within which the initial idea came from was the one characterised by the massive migration from Africa that Italy was experiencing (and still is) in the considered timeframe. They not only demonstrated how passion and motivation can help in pursuing a social mission, but also showed how it is possible to perform these activities in a 'modern' way, the one they conceived with the labs. Thus, promoting social inclusion – and sensitising the society – also through effective communication of their social mission.

To conclude, some limitations of this study must be noted. The findings deriving from a single case-based study, are limited to the case study analysed and are therefore difficult to be generalised. Nevertheless, the case study provides useful insights – about the challenges encountered and how these have been faced – by young social entrepreneurs aiming at initiating a social project.

## ACKNOWLEDGMENT

Authors would like to thank Parallelo's founders for their invaluable support and availability in providing information about their activities.

## REFERENCES

Abu-Saifan, S. (2012). Social entrepreneurship: Definition and boundaries. *Technology Innovation Management Review*, *2*(2), 22–27. doi:10.22215/timreview/523

Adner, R., & Kapoor, R. (2010). Value creation in innovation ecosystems: How the structure of technological interdependence affects firm performance in new technology generations. *Strategic Management Journal*, *31*(3), 306–333. doi:10.1002mj.821

Antonakis, J. (2012). Transformational and charismatic leadership. *The Nature of Leadership*, *2*, 256-288.

Austin, J., Stevenson, H., & Wei-Skillern, J. (2006). Social and commercial entrepreneurship: Same, different, or both? *Entrepreneurship Theory and Practice*, *30*(1), 1–22. doi:10.1111/j.1540-6520.2006.00107.x

Bacq, S., & Janssen, F. (2011). The multiple faces of social entrepreneurship: A review of definitional issues based on geographical and thematic criteria. *Entrepreneurship and Regional Development, 23*(5-6), 373–403. doi:10.1080/08985626.2011.577242

Brockhaus, R. H. (1982). The psychology of the entrepreneur. Encyclopedia of Entrepreneurship, 39 - 57.

Campbell, S. (1997). Social entrepreneurship: How to develop new social-purpose business ventures. *Health Care Strategic Management, 16*(5), 17–18. PMID:10179045

Colquitt, J. A., & George, G. (2011). Publishing in AMJ—Part 1: Topic choice. *Academy of Management Journal, 54*(3), 432–435. doi:10.5465/amj.2011.61965960

Costa, P. T. Jr, McCrae, R. R., & Kay, G. G. (1995). Persons, places, and personality: Career assessment using the revised NEO Personality Inventory. *Journal of Career Assessment, 3*(2), 123–139. doi:10.1177/106907279500300202

Di Domenico, M., Haugh, H., & Tracey, P. (2010). Social bricolage: Theorizing social value creation in social enterprises. *Entrepreneurship Theory and Practice, 34*(4), 681–703. doi:10.1111/j.1540-6520.2010.00370.x

Dubos, R. (2017). *Social capital: Theory and research.* Routledge.

Edler, J., & Fagerber, J. (2017). Innovation policy: What, why, and how? *Oxford Review of Economic Policy, 33*(1), 2–23. doi:10.1093/oxrep/grx001

Eisenmann, T. R. (2013). Entrepreneurship: A working definition. *Harvard Business Review, 10*, 1–4.

Emerson, J. (2003). The blended value proposition: Integrating social and financial returns. *California Review Management, 45*(4), 35–51. doi:10.2307/41166187

George, G., Mcgahan, A. M., & Prabhu, J. (2012). Innovation for inclusive growth: Towards a theoretical framework and research agenda. *Journal of Management Studies, 49*(4), 661–683. doi:10.1111/j.1467-6486.2012.01048.x

Germak, A. J., & Robinson, J. A. (2014). Exploring the motivation of nascent social entrepreneurs. *Journal of Social Entrepreneurship, 5*(1), 5–21. doi:10.1080/19420676.2013.820781

Gupta, A. K. (2013). Tapping the entrepreneurial pPotential of grassroots innovation. *Stanford Social Innovation Review, 11*(3), 18–20.

Harding, R. (2007). Understanding social entrepreneurship. *Industry and Higher Education, 21*(1), 73–84. doi:10.5367/000000007780222723

Liao, J., & Welsch, H. (2003). Social capital and entrepreneurial growth aspiration: A comparison of technology- and non-technology-based nascent entrepreneurs. *The Journal of High Technology Management Research, 14*(1), 149–170. doi:10.1016/S1047-8310(03)00009-9

Malach-Pines, A., Sadeh, A., Dvir, D., & Yofe-Yanai, O. (2002). Entrepreneurs and managers: Similar yet different. *The International Journal of Organizational Analysis, 10*(2), 172–190. doi:10.1108/eb028949

Markides, C. (2006). Disruptive innovation: In need of better theory. *Journal of Product Innovation Management, 23*(1), 19–25. doi:10.1111/j.1540-5885.2005.00177.x

Martin, R. L. & Osberg, S. (2007). Social Entrepreneurship: The Case for Definition. *Stanford Innovation Review*, 28-39.

Moore, J. F. (1993). Predators and prey: A new ecology of competition. *Harvard Business Review, 71*, 75–86. PMID:10126156

Murphy, P. J., & Coombes, S. M. (2009). A model of social entrepreneurial discovery. *Journal of Business Ethics, 87*(3), 325–336. doi:10.100710551-008-9921-y

Nicole, B. (2003). *The Base of the Pyramid (BOP): Reperceiving Business from the Bottom Up.* Global Business Network (GBN) Working Paper.

Northouse, P. G. (2018). Leadership: Theory and practice. *Sage (Atlanta, Ga.).*

Odumeru, J. A., & Ifeanyi, G. O. (2013). Transformational vs. transactional leadership theories: Evidence in literature. *International Review of Management and Business Research*, 2(2), 355–361.

Okhomina, D. A. (2010). Entrepreneurial postures and psychological traits: The sociological influences of education and environment. *Research in Higher Education*, 2–20.

Orloff, A. (2020). *Remaking modernity: Politics, history, and sociology.* Duke University Press.

Payne, A., Frow, P., & Eggert, A. (2017). The customer value proposition: Evolution, development and application in marketing. *Journal of the Academy of Marketing Science, 45*(4), 467–489. doi:10.100711747-017-0523-z

Prabhu, J., & Jain, S. (2015). Innovation and entrepreneurship in India: Understanding jugaad. *Asia Pacific Journal of Qualitative. Management, 32*(4), 843–868.

Radjou, N., & Prabhu, J. (2016). Frugal innovation. How to do better with less. *The Economist.*

Schafer, D. S. (1990). Level of entrepreneurship and scanning source usage in very small businesses. *Entrepreneurship Theory and Practice*, *15*(2), 19–21. doi:10.1177/104225879101500204

Seibert, S. E., Crant, J. M., & Kraimer, M. L. (1999). Proactive personality and career success. *The Journal of Applied Psychology*, *84*(3), 416–427. doi:10.1037/0021-9010.84.3.416 PMID:10380421

Shaw, E., & Carter, S. (2007). Social entrepreneurship: Theoretical antecedents and empirical analysis of entrepreneurial processes and outcomes. *Journal of Small Business and Enterprise Development*, *14*(3), 418–434. doi:10.1108/14626000710773529

Sullivan, M. (2003). Social entrepreneurship: Towards conceptualisation. *International Journal of Nonprofit and Voluntary Sector Marketing*, *8*(1), 76–88. doi:10.1002/nvsm.202

Tang, J. (2008). Environmental munificence for entrepreneurs: Entrepreneurial alertness and commitment. *International Journal of Entrepreneurial Behaviour & Research*, *14*(3), 128–151. doi:10.1108/13552550810874664

Teece, D. J. (2010). Business models, business strategy and innovation. *Long Range Planning*, *43*(2-3), 172–194. doi:10.1016/j.lrp.2009.07.003

Thompson, J. L. G., Alvy, G., & Lees, A. (2000). Social entrepreneurship: A new look at the people and the potential. *Management Decision*, *38*(5), 328–338. doi:10.1108/00251740010340517

United Nations. (n.d.). *The 17 Goals. Department of Economic and Social Affairs.* Retrieved from: https://sdgs.un.org/goals

Van Iwaarden, J., Van Der Wiele, T., Williams, R., & Moxham, C. (2009). Charities: How important is performance to donors? *International Journal of Quality & Reliability Management*, *10*(2), 2–22. doi:10.1108/02656710910924143

Verheul, I., & Van Mil, L. (2011). What determines the growth ambition of Dutch early-stage entrepreneurs? *International Journal of Entrepreneurial Venturing*, *3*(2), 183–207. doi:10.1504/IJEV.2011.039340

Verstraete, T. (2002). Essay on the singularity of entrepreneurship as a research domain. *Éditions de l'ADREG.*

Waddock, S. A., & Post, J. E. (1991). Social entrepreneurs and catalytic change. *Public Administration Review*, *51*(5), 393–401. doi:10.2307/976408

Weerawardena, J., & Mort, S. G. (2006). Investigating social entrepreneurship: A multidimensional model. *Journal of World Business*, *41*(1), 21–35. doi:10.1016/j.jwb.2005.09.001

Yukl, G. (2013). *Leadership in Organizations* (Global edition). Pearson.

Zahra, S. A., Rawhouser, H. N., Bhawe, N., Neubaum, D. O., & Hayton, J. C. (2008). Globalization of social entrepreneurship opportunities. *Strategic Entrepreneurship Journal*, *2*(2), 117–131. doi:10.1002ej.43

## ENDNOTE

1 See https://parallelolab.com/

# Chapter 4
# Towards Enhancing Migrant Social Entrepreneurship Through Social Capital in Durban, South Africa

**Ndwakhulu Stephen Tshishonga**
*University of KwaZulu-Natal, South Africa*

## EXECUTIVE SUMMARY

*This chapter interrogates the notion of social capital and its potential impact on enhancing or undermining the socio-economic efforts by migrants in Durban, South Africa. Tshishonga argues that it is through entrepreneurship that entrepreneurs transform their innovative and creative ideas into business enterprises and job creation. This chapter is concerned about migrant social entrepreneurial endeavours as a source of livelihoods within the informal economic sector. Informal businesses initiated by migrants have proven to be successful and sustainable compared to that of the locals. Despite the challenges faced by migrant entrepreneurs such as financial deficit, xenophobia, anti-foreign policies, victimisation, violence, and harassment, absence of police protection, etc., these enterprises thrive. This chapter employs a case study method where 15 African immigrant entrepreneurs were targeted to determine how social capital is used to expand and sustain their businesses.*

## INTRODUCTION

In the African continent, South Africa was the last country to gain independence in 1994 through democratic elections (Jeeves and Cuthbertson, 2008). After being

DOI: 10.4018/978-1-7998-7724-0.ch004

subjected to decades of colonial and apartheid regimes, South Africa adopted a political economy that reinforced social and economic discrimination, exclusion and marginalization, especially for people of colour. Since the arrival of Europeans on South African shores, the country went through various political and economic administrations from the Dutch, Germans and later the English but subsequently the white Afrikaners became the settler colonisers (Mashel and Qobo, 2017). The political and economic processes under apartheid culminated in a sad reality which brutally contributed not only to the dispossession of the indigenous landowners but also visibly stripping people of their livelihoods. Natural resources like diamonds, gold and others were monopolised by European settlers, for their benefit locally and for the enjoyment of their folks back in Europe. For Mashele and Qobo (2017: 2), colonialism and apartheid in South Africa was part of this European accumulation process. Mashele and Qobo (2017: 2) posit that the marginalisation of natives in South Africa could not be secured without their total economic disempowerment. This implies that the deprivation of means of livelihoods occurred through moving the African people from their fertile land or subjecting them to exploitable labour. Admittedly, South Africa, like any African country suffers from the legacy of slavery, colonialism and apartheid as well as economic, socio-economic injustices and systems (Amtaika, 2017, Maathai, 2009 and Ng'ambi, 2018). These systems left Africans with mass poverty, infectious diseases and poor health, scarcity of human capital and underdevelopment, thus rendering the continent to be uncompetitive internationally (Ng'ambi, 2018). A myriad of economic crises, the adoption of neo-liberal economic policies and its failure to uplift the poor in the developing nations (Lawrence, 2018), has failed to bring the 'political kingdom' as promised by Nkrumah as this has not resulted in economic dividends and economic emancipation (Mills and Herbst, 2012).

The attainment of political liberation in 1994 existed alongside staggering economic growth with the poor and previously disadvantaged blacks bearing the brunt of Apartheid legacies and the adoption of neo-liberal policies (Eloff, 2017). In order to revive and democratise the economy, attempts were made by the ANC-led government to redress the situation (The Presidency, 2019). Such commitment saw the enactment of macro-economic policies and programmes such as the Reconstruction Development Programme (RDP) in 1994, GEAR in 1996, Accelerated and Shared Growth Initiative for South Africa (ASGISA) in 2006, the National Growth Path in 2010 and the National Development Plan (NDP) in 2012 to redress socio-economic injustices of the apartheid regime (Du Preez, 2013, p. 94). The rationale behind these policies was to grow the economy and further advance socio-economic development. However, with the colonial-apartheid economy being intake, South Africa is failing to realise its dream of being a developmental state, based on state intervention, especially in the planning of macro-economic policies (Rautenbach, 2017). Thus, without an effective state, a powerful and competent bureaucracy and state capacity as well as active citizenry, the implementation of socio-economic policies will be impossible (NDP, 2012). South Africa would join other Africa nations who have dismally failed to achieve economic development post-independence.

Since independence, South Africa witnessed the influx of migrants from other parts of the world, especially migrants from the African continent. The convergence of pull and push factors at hand with such immigration has led to mistrust of these migrants. An estimated 2.9 million migrants settled in South Africa at mid-year 2020, the most industrialized economy in the region and a particularly attractive destination for those in search of education and better opportunities (World Migration Report 2020). Other African countries bearing the burden of hosting international migrants are the Democratic Republic of the Congo (952,871) and Angola (656,434) who were estimated to be the three countries hosting the highest number of international migrants in the sub-region at mid-year 2020 (UN DESA, 2020).

The opportunities available for semi-skilled labour in sectors such as construction, mining and services are major migration drivers throughout the region. The United Republic of Tanzania and South Africa attract high-skilled labour in financial services. Upskilling trends are on the rise among semi-skilled migrants to South Africa, while commercial agriculture absorbs the large majority of low-skilled migrant labour to the country (AU, 2017; UNCTAD, 2018: 81-85). In the context of South Africa, OECD/ILO (2018, p. 24) highlighted that:

*Immigrants are well-integrated into the labour market in terms of employment and unemployment rates, and in general do not seem to displace native-born workers. The contribution of immigrant workers to GDP is estimated to be close to 9% in 2011, and just below their share in employment. Nevertheless, immigration is raising income per capita in South Africa, while immigrants also make a positive net fiscal contribution.*

This year, South Africa celebrated 27 years of democracy; the question is, how has democracy helped to improve the lives of the poor for the better while there is a prevalence of poverty, unemployment and inequality (The Presidency, 2019)? It is hard to talk about a healthy and thriving democracy in South Africa while there is a socio-economic situation camouflaged by poverty, unemployment and inequality (Terebracnch, 2012). The end of apartheid in South Africa and conflicts in many parts of Africa, accelerated the movement of people across the continent (Segatti and Landau, 2011). There are diverse reasons for people's movements, chief among them, conflicts and political instability resulting in forced migration in search of peace and economic opportunities. For immigrants, these new forms of mobility offer the promise of moving out of poverty whilst, at the same time, posing new governance challenges.

Migration has to do with the movement of people while immigration underlies such movement from one's own country to another country (Giddens & Sutton, 2013). Thus, migration is underpinned by international and domestic mobility (Landau & Segatti, 2013). The rise of international migration and the emergence of globalization has rendered the world an 'immigrant society' (Heywood, 2013, p 166). Attached to migrations are the push and pull factors (Giddens & Sutton, 2013). Push factors entail adverse political circumstances and conditions that made people leave their counties of origin whilst pull factors such as the economic opportunities often attract the movement of people. Push factors, according to Giddens and Sutton (2013, p. 706), refer to dynamics within a country of origin, which force people to emigrate. Pull factors are those features that attract immigrants such as prosperous labour markets, better overall living conditions and lower population density (Giddens and Sutton (2013, p. 706). Positively, Landau & Segatti (2013, p. 355) argue that migration could address inequality and open opportunities. In South Africa, and the rest of the African continent, migration and migrant entrepreneurial activities contribute to more inclusive economic growth of the host nations (NDP, 2012). This is despite the perceptions of the political elite and officials regarding the migrants or foreigners being a threat to the country's development, national stability and social services (Tella, 2016). In the African continent, challenges such as political instability, diseases, unemployment opportunities, human rights abuse, corruption and poverty have contributed to fellow Africans fleeing their country of origin to South Africa (Mlambo, 2019 and Tella, 2016). The reality is that, since 1994, there has been an flux of people from other African countries and many of them have resorted to entrepreneurship for their economic survival (Mahlobo, 2016). Thus, the presence of immigrants has sparked the entrepreneurial culture and further challenged locals to be creative in developing entrepreneurial businesses owned and managed by them rather than depending on the state for employment (Mahlobo, 2016). However, the question remains what lessons can be drawn from some of the vibrant and successful migrant entrepreneurs without throwing Afro-xenophobic tendencies towards immigrants?

It is against this background that this chapter interrogates the notion of social capital and its potential impact in enhancing or undermining the socio-economic efforts by migrants in Durban, South Africa. Tshishonga (2020) argues that it is through entrepreneurship that entrepreneurs transform their innovative and creative ideas into business enterprises and job creation. An empirical study was conducted through the use of individual interviews with 15 immigrant entrepreneurs operating in the Durban Central Business District. This chapter was guided by three core questions: 1) How does social capital enhance immigrant entrepreneurship? 2) What opportunities are available for immigrant entrepreneurs through social capital? 3) What are the social and economic benefits of using social capital in immigrant entrepreneurship? 4) What are the challenges faced by immigrant entrepreneurs? The findings in this chapter re-affirm the key role played by social capital, not only in facilitating the start-up and sustenance of immigrant entrepreneurial businesses, but also forge the pathways towards accessing information and networks for socio-economic survival. While economic opportunities and challenges might be similar for both natives and immigrants, the study revealed that immigrant entrepreneurs are confronted by perpetual challenges, chief among them, lack of financial support, xenophobia and constant harassment by the law enforcement agencies and natives.

This chapter, therefore, argues that social entrepreneurship is a means of creating employment and financial independence. The chapter employs qualitative research methods. Empirical data was solicited from selected participants. These were recruited under a purposive and random sampling. The participants were migrant entrepreneurs who had grown their enterprises through the assistance of countrymen or fellow migrants. Participants introduced each other to participate in the study and it snowballed from there until the required number was achieved.

# BACKGROUND

## Entrepreneurs, Entrepreneurship, and Social Entrepreneurship

Worldwide there is an intrinsic link between migrants, migration and migrant (social) entrepreneurship. Despite their qualifications, skills and jobs, migrants like any other person have to socially and economically survive and one of the ways has been to embark on entrepreneurial small business in the host country. Therefore, social enterprises have become the source of securing livelihoods by migrants. Thus, social entrepreneurship has the potential to provide training and employment for clients while generating income for social service programmes (Anderson, 2014; Roy et al., 2014). In the midst of pressing socio-economic challenges, entrepreneurship has been claimed to be a self-determined pathway out of poverty and structural inequalities (Doering-White, Sanchez & Creasey, 2021). For communities and immigrants who, for long, have suffered from colonial and neo-colonial extractive economies, ranging from land dispossession to predatory lending, Lewis (2019) opines that small business ownership could be instrumental in promoting economic stability and autonomy.

The word entrepreneur is attached to the innovative and creative ideas for socio-economic businesses and enterprises. Entrepreneurs are, therefore, distinguishable from other business people through their critical thinking for innovation, ability to take risks and handle complex situations and capability to transform meagre resources into productive asserts (Pieterse, 2021). It is evident that entrepreneurs create micro-enterprises as the source of socio-economic survival and unemployment turns out to be the driving force for the development of entrepreneurial activities (Pieterse, 2021). An entrepreneur is a person who is action oriented, highly motivated, and who takes risks to achieve goals, therefore, entrepreneurship becomes a practice used by an entrepreneur to advance their innovative ideas (Mohammed, 2018). Entrepreneurial activities carried out by entrepreneurs aim to make profit and provide social services and goods for people. Economically, migrants and migrant entrepreneurs are mostly affected by the host nation's economy and its economic policies. Their peripheral status not only renders them vulnerable to anti-immigrant policies and the labour market, but also leaves them open to be massively abused and economically marginalised (Sahin et al., 2006). Sahin, Nijkamp and Baycan-Levent (2006) argue that entrepreneurship is one of the pathways towards escaping unemployment in a host country and, as such, migrants are obliged to opt for self-employment. Entrepreneurship affects the economy both directly and indirectly and, at various levels, through innovation, competition and restructuring (Wennekers et al., 1999). Empirical research has shown that both a higher rate of new business start-ups and rate of turbulence (the sum of start-ups and closures) enhance, after a certain time lag, economic growth and job creation (Carree et al., 2003).

*Figure 1. Entrepreneurial activity in the commercial and wider environment*
*Source: Adopted from Ahmad & Seymour, (2008 cited in Afewerki, 2015, p. 9)*

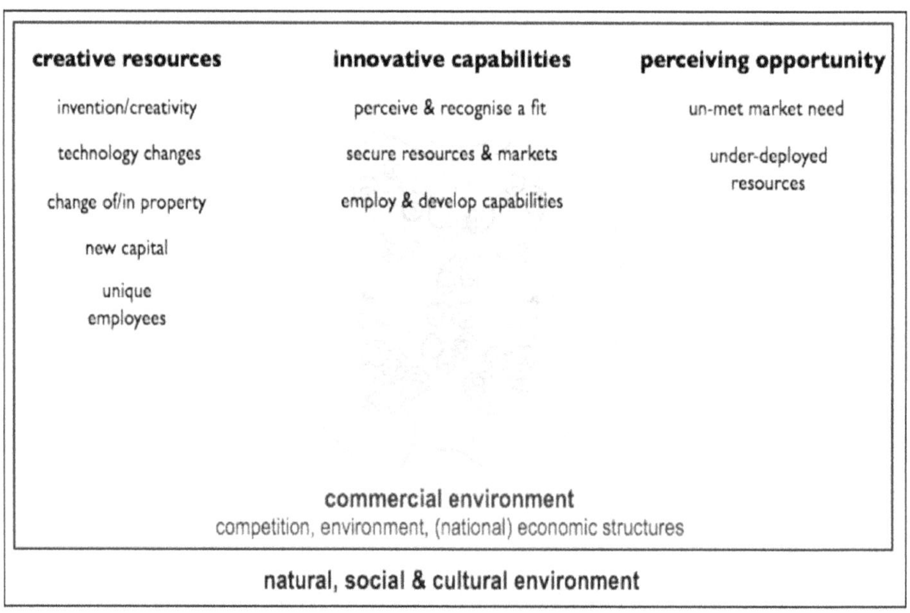

For Gallardo-Vázquez, Costa and Valdez-Juárez (2020), entrepreneurship is not only a necessary strategy that entails the emergence of a business idea and the creation of a company, but also constitutes true entrepreneurial capital. The prevalence of poverty and unemployment internationally has led people to delve into social entrepreneurship as an alternative pathway towards addressing these socio-economic challenges. Central to successful and sustainable entrepreneurial enterprises has been the interface of innovation, creativity and intellectual capital as drivers for organisational performance (Popescu, 2020). For entrepreneurial businesses' success, there is an interface of creative resources, innovative capabilities and perceiving opportunities as well as the commercial environment (Ahmad & Seymour, 2008).

According to Ahmad & Seymour (2008), this can be done by entrepreneurs assuming:

*The risk-taking role of an entrepreneur; entrepreneurs' role of innovation or the creation of new products, services, processes, identifying new markets or creation of new firms; the arbitrage role of an entrepreneur as well as the process of change, appearance and/or creation.*

Social entrepreneurship is inclusive of non-profit organisations that apply business expertise to become efficient in providing and delivering social services (Hoogendoorn, Pennings and Thurik, 2012). Included in this category are socially responsible businesses established to offer innovative solutions to socio-economic and ecological challenges using market-based models (Dorado, 2006). Social entrepreneurship is underpinned by four schools of thought: 1) the Innovation School of thought, 2) the Social Enterprise School of thought, 3) the EMES approach and finally 4) the UK approach (Hoogendoorn, Pennings and Thurik, 2012, pp. 118–119). The Innovation School is more concerned about individual entrepreneurs who thrive on tackling social problems and meet social needs through innovative means. At the centre of the Social Enterprise School, are entrepreneurs who create non-profit organisations geared towards generating income whilst, at the same time, are able to drive their social missions. To sustain their activities, non-profit organisations adopt business models and further venture into activities that generate income independent from donor or government subsidies. Although the EMES School is still centred on enterprises, its main focus is community and how the founding members of the associations or cooperatives are able to exercise their autonomy and participatory decision-making powers (Hoogendoorn, Pennings and Thurik, 2012). The last School is the one based in the UK, which is based on partnership, and its business ventures have social dimension that ensures any surplus is reinvested back into the business or the community for mutual benefit (Hoogendoorn, Pennings and Thurik, 2012, p. 119). For example, Courtney Lewis (2019) claims that ownership of small businesses advances economic stability and autonomy within communities that suffered from colonial and neo-colonial extractive economies, ranging from land dispossession to predatory lending. However, entrepreneurship has been criticised by authors such as Prahalad (2006) and Servon (2011) (also see Doering-White, Sanchez and Creasy, 2021) who indicated that there is more emphasis on individual responsibility by entrepreneurship which makes it overlook the structural inequalities and broader patterns of discrimination.

## Migrants and Migrant Entrepreneurship

Migrant entrepreneurship is a sub-set of mainly businesses initiated and run by migrants with a specific socio-cultural and ethnic background or migrant origin. Immigrant entrepreneurship is more of a group phenomenon and context and the environment matters for the success of migrant entrepreneurs (Gordon, 2010). Vinogradov (2008) argues that immigrant entrepreneurship is often a product of interactions that take place between immigrants themselves and within a group and between a group and the environment in which they operate. Such convergence and interactions provide immigrant entrepreneurs with greater insight on how they can set up their businesses based on financially sound, profitable, growth oriented, and sustainable ventures principles and values (Afewerki, 2015). In the context of migrant entrepreneurship, several scholars have highlighted the impact of different migrant group cultures on entrepreneurship. Choenni, (1997, cited in Sahin, Nijkamp and Baycan-Levent, 2006, p. 5) was able to distinguish between what they call 'normal entrepreneurship' and migrant entrepreneurship. Orientation on migrant products, on migrant market customers or on indigenous migrant business strategies were cited as some of the features which set migrant entrepreneurs apart from the other entrepreneurs. Thus, migrants and their movement is part of human intervention and unrestricted movement of labour across the SADC region and the entire African continent is said to be of economic value and help in the regional integration (NDP, 2012).

Viewed from a socio-economic perspective, migrant entrepreneurship and entrepreneurs themselves play an important role in the economy of the host country. Behind the migrant entrepreneurs are push factors prompting them to start their own self-employment. For migrant entrepreneurs, self-employment, in this case, is not only a means of earning a living; it is also a way of recognition and social acceptance (Veciana, 1999). Motivation, support, access to information and willingness to take risks are often cited as fundamental attributes for migrant entrepreneurs to initiate and run their own businesses (Masurel et al., 2005) Whilst others are pushed to start entrepreneurial business because of the acquired knowledge and available business opportunities to be exploited in the host country (Sahin, Nijkamp and

Baycan-Levent, 2006). Above these factors, assimilation and acculturation lay the foundation for immigrants to navigate their informal businesses. Thus, through acculturation, immigrants adopt and assimilate into the local cultures and languages whilst, by assimilation, foreigners are able to gain social membership and better integrate further into the host country (Bartram, Poros and Monforte, 2012). In this case, making money becomes the result of time, knowledge and innovation's investment into the business, not an ultimate goal for the great entrepreneurs like Raymond Ackerman. Raymond Ackerman argues that:

*Money should not be the main motivating factor in starting a business. People should go into business to work on something they enjoy and the money will follow. (cited in Mahlobo, 2016, p. 172)*

It is clear that passion, innovative ideas and culture of co-ownership are fundamental building blocks for successful entrepreneurial ventures. In the modern era, immigrant entrepreneurial ventures are no longer embarked on only for survival due to obstacles encountered in the host country (Waldinger et al., 1990), but are also triggered by immigrants' willingness to exploit business opportunity and make money (Chrysostome, 2010).

Socially and economically, migrant entrepreneurship plays a decisive role in growing the economy of the host country. Attesting to this, Afewerki (2015, p.4):

*Immigrant entrepreneurship can play a significant role in value creation and thereby have a positive impact on the host economy's social welfare. Entrepreneurship can be an important instrument in the integration process of immigrants. It can also be an important source of employment to a lot of immigrants and this in turn can relieve huge burden from the welfare state and generate income to the regions where these immigrants settle in. Furthermore, it can provide further entrepreneurship and employment to other immigrants through networking along the supply chain, thereby contributing to innovation, which in turn can have a positive impact on the overall economy.*

Immigrant entrepreneurship is linked to a process of moving into a new country from the country of origin to create or run a business venture (Ngota, Sisulu, Rajkaran and Mang'unyi, (2019). Essentially, an immigrant entrepreneur uses their information, skills and knowledge to initiate a business activity as part of a self-employment drive (Aaltonen and Akola, 2014). Evidence from studies done on immigration entrepreneurship, is that entrepreneurial enterprises undertaken by immigrants contribute to job and wealth creation of the host country (Dalhammar, 2004, Doering-Whitea, Sanchez, and Creasey, 2021).

Cantillon and Marx emphasised that profit may motivate people towards business entry and self-employment. The desire to take risk and a spirit of adventure may be another motive (Knight, 1921). Some have greater access to information or knowledge and wish to exploit that advantage (Kirzner, 1973). The entrepreneur may be driven, not only by economic motives but also by psychological motives such as the desire to innovate and create new products (Schumpeter, 1934).

The tendency or ability to become self-employed also differs between natives of a country and migrants; immigration involves taking risks and this is also the case for entrepreneurship. Migrants are therefore considered to have an appropriate attitude or mindset to start a business (Verheul et al, 2001).

## Contextualising Social Capital Within Migrant Entrepreneurship

Social capital in this chapter is employed as an analytical framework towards gauging its role and importance in growing and sustaining the migrant entrepreneurial businesses. Social capital is associated with informal rules, norms and long-term relationships that facilitate coordinated action and enable people to undertake cooperative ventures for mutual advantage (World Bank, 1997). Social capital manifests itself through networks, norms and social trust inherent in associations whose members work together in concerted collaborative action. It is also the store of goodwill (Putnam, 1993). More importantly, Putman, et al, (1993, p. 35) associates social capital with features of social organisations such as networks, norms and trust that facilitate action and cooperation for mutual benefits. Social capital, according to Łukaszewska-Bezulska (2014), is concerned with relations between individuals and groups, in this, the individual migrants and their associations. Within the immigrant community, the importance of social capital has been captured by Massey (1999) who describes it as the grease and fuel of migration, while Faist (1997), associates social capital and networks as part of the social space in which migration takes place. In essence, social capital is an invaluable resource for immigrants (Wahlbeck and Fortelius, 2019). However, Łukaszewska-Bezulska (2020) argues that the quality of social capital depends on two factors: the strength and type of bonds tying an individual to others and the individual's particular migration experience.

Social capital theory depicts social interactions and their valuable and beneficial advantage to the community (Bayat, 2005 and Grewe, 2003). The existence and strengths of social capital in a community are reflected in the coordinated or collected actions of individuals, organisations, and community institutions as they work together towards a common goal in the community (Yunus, 2017). Social capital theory emphasises the importance of social networks, communication, social structures, and social relationships (Yunus, 2017). According to Putnam (1994), the critical component of social capital are the networks of civic engagement as the links that connect people. Tristan (2004) said that social capital theory encompasses the notion that social relationships are productive, which is social capital. This theory gives various dimensions of the complex social world that enable social capital. Both participation and social capital have something familiar (Yunus, 2017).

Social Capital Theory concentrates on the actions people take to acquire or maintain social relationships that turn into resources used for an individual or community benefit (Heydayat, 2014). Social Capital is about building and using social relationships to generate intangible and tangible benefits in the short- or long-term for the community (Grewe, 2003). Social Capital Theory is applied in a variety of disciplines, including community development, political science, and sociology (Bayat, 2005). Social capital refers to relationship structures that rely on the obligations, expectations, and trustworthiness of those involved (Teles, 2012). The author further argues that social capital is dependent on the social structures that exist between people, which make it possible for those involved to take specific actions and be able to get things done that they would not have been able to do on their own. Putnam (2000) defines social capital as voluntary civic associations, and decentralised institutions will close the vacuum left by the states, further becoming a prime site of policy and practice for locality governance and development.

Social capital is expected to facilitate bottom-up development that may help to reduce the problems of social exclusion and inequalities (Grewe, 2003). In particular, the communities that live in poverty are faced with interrelated barriers that manifest not only in economic exclusion but also from the cumulative process of isolation and disadvantage in the community (Teles, 2012). However, social capital rebuilds community-based activism and helps marginalised members of the community overcome their weakened ability to participate fully in matters that affect them (Yunus, 2017). For example, in South Africa, there are immigrant groupings and associations created to offer social and business support especially since the emergence of xenophobic attacks directed against foreigners (Crush and Ramachandran, 2015). Crush and Ramachandran (2015, p. 31) further note that levels of xenophobia are highest among self-employed immigrants. On the other hand, Teles (2012) believes that social capital is an asset that improves people's capacity to mobilize collective action. Jacob in Soithong (2011) describes social capital as an idea that explains the significant role of public institutions and community engagement at the local level.

Putman, et al, (1993) differentiated three types of social capital as bonding, bridging social capital and linking social capital. Bonding social capital theory is more focused on the connections between people with similar characteristics and interests and tends to reinforce homogeneity and exclusivity (McGonigal et al. 2005). Bonding social capital refers to within-group relations where the members of the group are fair, such as race, gender, socioeconomic status (Yunus, 2017). Thus, bonding social capital is expressed through the close-knit relations of friends and families who can be depended on for basic survival in times of stress. Bridging social capital theory is concentrated on connections between people from diverse contexts and is seen as inclusive (McGongal et al. 2005). Bridging social capital is more concerned with between-group relations, and the individuals involved are more dissimilar to each other (Grewe, 2003). It enables people to 'get by'; bridging social capital enables people to get ahead. Linking social capital theory focuses on relationships among people with different powers and allows access to resources, ideas, information, and knowledge within a community (McGonigal et al. 2005).

## FINDINGS AND ANALYSIS

### Profile of Participants

Ten immigrants running entrepreneurial businesses were interviewed in Durban Central Business District (CBD). The migrants are represented by an equal number of gender, five females and five males. The profile in Table 1 reflects that participants originated from various African countries such as Malawi, Zimbabwe,

*Table 1. List of participants*

| Participant # | Qualifications | Gender (M/F) | Age | Country of Origin | Years in SA | Type of Business |
|---|---|---|---|---|---|---|
| 1 | High School | F | 35 | Congo | 8 | Hairdresser |
| 2 | High School | F | 28 | Lesotho | 7 | Hawker |
| 3 | Primary School | F | 34 | Somali | 11 | Take-away kitchen |
| 4 | University | M | 38 | Burundi | 7 | Car Mechanic |
| 5 | University | F | 37 | Congo | | Plumber |
| 6 | High School | M | 40 | Nigeria | 9 | Tuck-shop |
| 7 | High School | M | 32 | Zimbabwe | 7 | Computer Mobile technician |
| 8 | Primary School | M | | Somali | 12 | Tuck-Shop |
| 9 | University | M | | Ethiopia | 5 | Car Guard |
| 10 | Primary School | F | 33 | Somali | 6 | Take-away kitchen |
| P#11 | High School | M | 29 | Tanzania | 8 | Salon |
| 12 | High School | M | | Malawi | 4 | Construction |
| 13 | Primary School | F | 26 | Congo | 11 | Nail Technician |
| 14 | Primary | M | 35 | Congo | 6 | Selling vegetables |
| 15 | University | M | 26 | Burundi | 15 | Language Centre |

Source: Author's analysis

Nigeria, Somalia, Lesotho, Ethiopia, and Congo DRC. In terms of the ages of the participants, the youngest migrant entrepreneur was 35 while the oldest was 53 years old. The criteria to select participants for this chapter was based on their experience, insight and exposure of running entrepreneurial business as immigrants in Durban Business District.

Concerning trade or businesses undertaken by immigrants, most of the participants were in the informal sector with females in the fast-food business being a common enterprise for most Somali women with the exception of two who ran crèches for Somalis only. Male participants were more involved in running tuck shops and uber driving.

## Need for Entrepreneurship Among Migrant Community

All the participants interviewed for this chapter were involved in informal economic activities. Emanating from their profiles, entrepreneurship is the only career path for most of the migrants residing in Durban. Whilst some expressed dismay over the lack of migrant friendly policies in South Africa, others took the available business opportunities in the informal sector. Those who managed to obtain residential status, managed to register their companies in order to operate legally.

One participant commented that:

*The entrepreneurial culture is not foreign to Africans. In Somalia, it is a generational preoccupation for many to run successful and more advanced entrepreneurial adventures. My family in particular has been doing cross-border trading in Yemen, Saudi Arabia and Kenya selling khat and other goods. So entrepreneurship is the only survival livelihood I grew up knowing.*

Learning a trade either through formal schooling or through experienced family members or relatives is a novel way of acquiring skills and expertise. In some contexts, the entrepreneurial spirit and culture has been prompted through the scarcity of resources, hence van Ransburg (2012, p. 65) argues that:

*The more enterprising Africans become, the more they will grow in self-confidence and belief in their ability to survive and prosper even in the violent seas of society.*

Most of the migrants enter the informal economic sector not by choice, but through circumstances, which require them to survive socially and economically. One participant bemoaned that he could not stay in Zimbabwe because he could not survive economically. He further indicated that he specialises in fixing fridges and since there were no jobs for foreigners, he had to do other piece jobs.

*I have to diversify my skills by learning new trade. For me to acquire such skills and knowledge like plumbing and electric work, I have to volunteer to work with my friend who has a registered company in plumbing, painting and electrification and I am also a driver for uber.*

It became evident that bonding capital, together with bridging networks, were instrumental in affording Takunda a chance to learn a new trade without necessarily going to university or a technical college. Accordingly, entrepreneurship continues to serve as a pathway to economic inclusion especially for marginalised people and immigrants (Lutomia, Bravo and Seck, 2019). A Nigerian entrepreneur commented that:

*I run a clothing shop, where I sell male and female clothes and shoes. My shop was open through the help of my Nigerian brother who sold the store to me as he was leaving for Johannesburg. Before I opened my clothing shop, I was working as a security guard at one of hotels in Durban.*

A Malawian immigrant entrepreneur indicated that he runs a construction company building houses and putting up ceilings boards. He got involved in construction as he had building skills the learned in Malawi. He started building houses in Malawi and, upon arriving in South Africa, he naturally went into an industry he was familiar with. He demonstrated that he now enjoys better living standards than he did in Malawi because the South African currency is stronger. He managed to buy a van to make his work easier if he has to go and build in far-flung parts of Durban.

## Social Capital in the Context of Migrant Entrepreneurship

Among causes, a distinction runs between strong and weak social ties. Further distinctions run between *bonding* social capital (strong ties among close relations), *bridging* social capital (weak ties among people from diverse backgrounds but of similar socioeconomic status) and *linking* social capital (or 'friends in high places'). Considerations of cultural difference or 'ethnicity' apply across these different dimensions of social capital and take on cultural hues, that is, each applies within and across cultural settings. The question of cultural difference and social capital arises in three different contexts: immigration and migration, transnational enterprise, and ethnically diverse societies.

In the context of this chapter, social capital can be analysed from three perspectives as highlighted by Łukaszewska-Bezulska (2020). Such perspectives entail local environment/ neighbourhood capital, ethnic diaspora capital, and the individual capital of the subject (migrant). Among the migrants and migrant communities, social capital and migration networks, socially, economically or religious become the only source of survival, especially on arrival. Viewed from the cumulative causation theory, migration networks are understood as sets of interpersonal ties that link migrants, former migrants, and non-migrants in origin and destination areas through the bonds of kinship, friendship, and shared community origin (Massey et al. 1993). Such bonds are used to forge social and economic opportunities for migrants, especially in the informal sector.

The local environment plays a decisive role in the success or failure of immigrant businesses. One male from Somalia said:

*The local environment is a determining factor for my business. If the environment is hostile like the one we operate under, my business suffers greatly. Right things are tense in the Durban CBD most of our colleagues from all over Africa who ran clothes and beauty stalls in the open market were kicked out yet they were paying rent to the Municipality. You know why they were removed it is because they are foreign. We are scared. The environment is not conducive for conducting business at the moment. However some of us have fictitious kinships and can survive while some of have no kinships.*

The ownership or lack of social capital by an individual immigrant or community has an impact on the entrepreneurial ventures pursued by migrants. Unlike other immigrants, Somalis have strong social ties which help them to run their enterprises successfully.

## Opportunities Through Social Capital and Migrant Entrepreneurship

Migrants depend on their ethnic groupings and associations already in existence in South Africa, be it Somalis, Zimbabwean, Nigerian, etc. For the establishment of businesses, immigrants heavily rely on their ethnic diaspora capital to establish their entrepreneurial businesses. Depending on the push factors in their countries of origin, most immigrants arrived in South Africa without financial back-up, hence entrepreneurship becomes the only pathway for economic survival. Participants were asked to share the opportunities available to them as migrant entrepreneurs in Durban. Table 2 highlights the opportunities available to migrant entrepreneurs in Durban.

Most of the socio-economic opportunities for immigrants are created through strong ties and networks forged in South Africa or back in their country of origin (Adida, 2014). These groups are reproduced in the migrant communities overseas where ethnic associations have usually been formed. From evidence provided by participants, it was clear that ethnic associations in the case of Durban were

*Table 2. Opportunities for migrant entrepreneurs*

| Opportunities for Migrant Entrepreneurs | |
|---|---|
| Car guarding and customer care is a very tiring job, but through the service we are providing one is able to get that little money for transport and feed the family (Participant 9) | For me it was a dream come true to be able to open my own tuck-shop and at the moment I have created employment for three local ladies (Participant 3) |
| Working in the informal sector is all about hustling, but since I registered my company, I am able to get small contracts for plumbing, carpentry and electrification of premises and homes (Participant 5) | Despite offering a service to our clients, the Salon has become the focal point for connecting with people from home and generating some little money to pay for rent and sending the surplus back home. (Participant 11) |
| Being a technician especially operating computers and telephones is in demand. That is apart from the stiff competition, I managed to generate my rental money, school fees for my son and am buying food (Participant 7) | For me self-employment gives me the urge to work hard and to be innovative in assessing what people back home in Lesotho want so that the clothes I sell already have a market even before I cross the border (Participant 2) |
| The economic hardships in my country made me to make something out of nothing. When I established my takeaway, people could not believe that it will be a success (Participant 10) | I saw a gap in teaching migrants languages such as English, French for their integration into the local culture. I registered the Centre specialising in providing translation and teaching non-English speakers English (Participant 15) |
| Both local and immigrants need vegetables and through the money I obtained from my family I was able to buy a van to stock and sell vegetables in the city and other suburbs adjacent to Durban CBD (Participant 14) | I learnt entrepreneurial skills and car mechanics from my family, especially my brother. These skills came in handy hence I was able to establish an internet cafe to repair customers computers (Participant 4) |

Source: Participants' responses

fundamental in providing social and moral support at times such as bereavement and fatal sickness. Pieterse (2003, p, 10) reiterates that social capital among immigrants transcends any tangible economic and social value for the establishment of business, hence in times of tragedy, memberships are able to rely on existing associations. Ethnic associations exist alongside other networks such as national associations and have been helpful in terms of providing seed money for establishing small businesses. For example, Somalis in Durban use old boys' networks, professional associations, class-based networks, women's clubs and other networks to keep afloat in their business endeavours.

*When I arrived from Somalia I had nowhere to sleep, no money. I went to a Somali brother who ran a tuck-shop and I told him I had just arrived and had nowhere to go. He did not hesitate to take me in. He introduced me to people from my own town. All these good people helped me now you see this car I use to drive for uber I got the money from my community. They helped me buy a car because I am an experienced driver.*

A Congolese entrepreneur added that:

*I run a hair salon and do artificial nails for ladies and also do haircuts for both men and women. I had to learn this skill to start my business because I do not have qualifications to get a decent job. I rent one room for the business.*

The immigrants interviewed highlighted that social capital is their mainstay. Many arrive in the country with only the clothes on their backs, without knowing anyone, no education and no money but, because they are migrants, their countrymen take them under their wing. In the Somali communities, resources are often pulled from other Somalis to assist newcomers in starting their own enterprises. Money owed is repaid slowly after the newcomers have established themselves. The circle of social capital continues like that in immigrant communities. It is clear that social capital has provided an access to social networks and economic opportunities for most of the migrant entrepreneurs to success in running their businesses.

*Table 3. Social capital among entrepreneurs*

| | Nationality | Social Capital among Entrepreneurs | | |
|---|---|---|---|---|
| | | Bonding | Bridging | Linking |
| 1 | Congolese | Medium | Strong | Strong |
| 2 | Ethiopian | Strong | Strong | Strong |
| 3 | Burundi's | Strong | Medium | Strong |
| 4 | Mosotho | Weak | Medium | Strong |
| 5 | Tanzanian | Medium | Strong | Strong |
| 6 | Zimbabwean | Medium | Medium | Strong |
| 7 | Somalis | Strong | Strong | Strong |
| 8 | Malawi | Medium | Medium | Strong |
| 9 | Congo | Medium | Medium | Strong |
| 10 | Lesotho | Medium | Medium | Weak |

Source: Author's analysis

Table 3 shows that participants had strong linking capital. Bonding and bridging was rated as medium. From the individual and collective networks, migrant entrepreneurs managed to support each other, share and learn the skills of shared-ownership, management and economic empowerment (Dooms and Pillay, 2020).

## Challenges Faced by Migrant Entrepreneurs in Durban City

Immigrant entrepreneurs in broader South Africa and Durban in particular, are confronted by numerous challenges. Some of these challenges range from ambiguous policy frameworks, lack of protection of foreign businesses, demanded protection fees by local law enforcement, operating without financial subsidy, xenophobic attacks, police harassment and confiscation of their goods. These factors render immigrants running businesses in Durban vulnerable to attacks. These challenges limit them from operating effectively and efficiently. A slow-growing economy affects both native South Africans and immigrants although at different scales. For example, the World Bank Group (2018, p. 21), affirms that due to a weak economy and skills constraints, South African entrepreneurs find it difficult to either start or expand their businesses.

*Table 4. Challenges faced by migrant entrepreneurs*

| **Challenges faced by Migrant Entrepreneurs** | |
|---|---|
| I am unable to get any loan or any assistance from the refugee social services or small business at EThekwini municipality because I don't have South African citizenship | The challenge that he first had was that people first did not support him in buying clothes from his shop because they were saying he is a foreigner; he then employed an African lady to work for him as a saleslady and then people started to buy because they believe the lady is the owner of the shop |
| As a migrant entrepreneur, the challenge I often face is theft at night. Thugs have on several occasions smashed my cars now I have built a fence to protect the cars. South Africans accuse us of taking their jobs yet we create our own jobs as we cannot get into the mainstream job market | My container was broken into at night. We get harassed daily and some immigrants have been killed. I now have security bars to protect the container |
| Robbery and looting motivated by xenophobia where stock and cash were taken at gun point | I operate in my two-roomed accommodation and due to the demand, the rooms have become too small for the business. People want to buy at night even if the shop is closed. There is a lot of bullying from South Africans and they tend to use intimidation and loot our goods |
| It is hard for her to get loans and financial assistance from EThekwini Municipal because she is illegally living in the country hence, she cannot be considered without legal documents to be in South Africa | As a migrant I am not supported by the municipality. I cannot access opportunities like tenders because I don't have a work permit to apply for one. |
| Bullying and constant harassment by South Africans is a huge challenge. We are threatened daily and told to go back to our home countries | |

Source: Authors Analysis

Immigrants surviving in the informal economy experience daily harassments and their businesses are targeted for looting by locals. Somalis, in particular, have been under attack in townships where they run tuck shops. Locals accuse them of undercutting local businesses by selling cheap, and sometimes expired goods. Thus, competition of scarce resources and limited economic opportunities led to Afro-xenophobic hatred and attacks against African nationals (Mlambo, 2019). Politicians and officials who pronounce anti-immigrants sentiments further fuel tensions between the natives and fellow African immigrants (Mosselson, 2010). Such utterances have implications for the health, security and economic prospects of immigrants living in South Africa. Due to such discrimination particularly from those high in government, they (foreign individuals), according to Mlambo (2019, p. 60) find it difficult to access basic needs such as healthcare services, banking services, and employment opportunities, thus, experience social exclusion and systemic discrimination.

Immigration, whether voluntary or forced migration create other challenges which are beyond economics. Due to housing shortages, most of the immigrants running their businesses in Durban are either renting, squatting with friends or family members whilst others stay in the Townships. This, on its own, has implications for urban infrastructure services, health and education (Çelik, 2019). These challenges are an add-on to the already existing 'hostile environment' exacerbated by South African immigration policy (Hill, 2018) and xenophobia. Unhealthy competition and anti-immigrant businesses by both locals and government in Durban render immigrant entrepreneurs 'economic detour' a concept used by Doering-White, Sanchez & Creasey (2021, p. 48) to imply the tendency of minority entrepreneurs to open businesses that offer social capital at the expense of profit.

## FUTURE RESEARCH DIRECTIONS

This chapter explored the potential and role of social capital in enhancing immigrant social entrepreneurship in Durban. Social capital is a sustaining element within businesses which are formed and run by migrants in South Africa and Durban in particular. This chapter only focused on immigrants in the Durban business centre, therefore, it is recommended that a comparative study should be conducted to cover all migrants in the big cities in South Africa. Such a study could benefit both the locals and immigrants to work together. Focus should be on how policies could be formulated drawing lessons from immigrant businesses. The findings of such a study could not only benefit the National Department of Small Business and its sub-units in various spheres of government but will also help in curbing the scourge of xenophobia in South Africa. Key to the study will be its emphasis on the impact of immigrant entrepreneurship on direct and indirect job creation, skills transfer and economic development in the host country.

## CONCLUSION

Social capital plays a central role in immigrant entrepreneurship and is key in sustaining migrants' social and economic lives in South Africa. Durban is one of the South African cities with a vibrant culture of entrepreneurship, where either natives or migrants irk a living from the entrepreneurial activities. Although the informal economic sector is populated by the locals, for immigrants, it is the only sector where they can secure their livelihoods. Thus, lack of social security due to high unemployment makes locals and immigrants to compete in the informal sector (Cebekhulu, 2018).

Business-wise immigrants have proven that they can survive at all odds. Despite all the challenges faced by immigrant entrepreneurs, social capital; inclusive of individual connections (binding) and socialisation through migrant communities, associations and structures developed in the host country and in diaspora (bridging) and such, these are used to link social capital especially with national and international bodies responsible for looking after the welfare of the immigrants, asylum seekers and refugees.

## REFERENCES

Aaltonen, S., & Akola, E. (2014). *Lack of trust - The main obstacle for immigrant entrepreneurship?* University of Turku. Retrieved from: http://www.pyk2.aalto.fi/ncsb2012/aaltonen.pdf/

Adida, C. L. (2015). *Immigrant Exclusion and Insecurity in Africa*. Cambridge University Press.

Amtaika, A. (2017). Is Democratisation of Africa a Process or an Experiment" The Dissection of the Democratic Theory. In A. Amtaika (Ed.), *The Democratisation of Africa: Dynamics and Trends* (pp. 3–30). Pan African University Press.

Anderson, S. G. (2014). *New strategies for social innovation: Market-based approaches for assisting the poor*. Columbia University Press. doi:10.7312/ande15922

Bartram, D., Poros, M. V., & Monforte, P. (2012). *Key Concepts in Migration*. SAGE Publications.

Cebekhulu, A. (2018). *Umhlaba Uyahlaba! The World is Thorny! Wandsbeck*. Reach Publishers.

Celik, S. (2019). Evaluation of the Migration Phenomenon as an Economics Dimension. In Immigration and Refugee Policy: Breakthroughs in Research and Practice (pp. 1-7). IGI Global.

Chisala, C. (2020). Immigrant Entrepreneurship in Africa: A Zambian Perspective. In Impact of Immigration and Xenophobia on Development in Africa (pp. 224- 245). IGI Global.

Crush, J., Cikanda, A., & Skinner, C. (2015). Migrant Entrepreneurship and Informality in South African Cities. In Mean Streets: Migration, Xenophobia and Informality in South Africa (pp. 25-59). Southern African Migration Programme, the African Centre for Cities and the International Development Research Centre.

Crush, J., & Ramachandran, S. (2015). Doing business with Xenophobia. In Mean Streets: Migration, Xenophobia and Informality in South Africa (pp. 25-59). Southern African Migration Programme, the African Centre for Cities and the International Development Research Centre. doi:10.2307/j.ctvh8r45r.6

Dalhammar, T. (2004). *Voices of entrepreneurship and small business- Immigrant enterprises in Kista* [Unpublished PhD Thesis]. Royal Institute of Technology.

Doering-Whitea, J., Sanchez, J., & Creasey, H. (2021). Entrepreneurship as a community practice strategy: Lessons from Detroit. *Journal of Community Practice*, *29*(1), 46–61. doi:10.1080/10705422.2021.1881935

Dooms, T., & Pillay, P. (2020). Black entrepreneurship journeys. In A. Cawe & K. Mabasa (Eds.), *Beyond Tenderpreneurship: Rethinking Black Business and Economic Empowerment* (pp. 336–358). Mapungubew Institute for Strategic Reflection.

Dorado, S. (2006). Social entrepreneurial ventures: Different values so different process of creation, no? *Journal of Developmental Entrepreneurship*, *11*(4), 319–343. doi:10.1142/S1084946706000453

Eloff, T. (2017). *Turning Point: South Africa at the Crossroads*. Tafelberg.

Giddens, A., & Sutton, P. W. (2013). *Sociology* (7th ed.). Polity Press.

Gileya. (2017). *The typology of a personality in social philosophical dimension. Peculiarities of a marginal personality in the modern world*. Academic Press.

Gordon, S. L. (2010). Migrants in a 'state of exception' xenophobia and the role of the post-apartheid state. In Contemporary Social Issues in Africa: Cases in Gaborone, Kampala and Durban (pp. 45-64). Africa Institute of Africa (AISA).

Heywood, A. (2013). *Politics* (4th ed.). Palgrave MacMillan. doi:10.1007/978-1-137-27244-7

Hoogendoorn, B., Pennings, E., & Thurik, R. (2012). Conceptual Overview of What We Know about Social Entrepreneurship. In J. Defilippis & S. Saegert (Eds.), *The Community Development Reader* (pp. 117–124). Routledge.

Jokela, M. (2008). Personality predicts migration within and between U.S. states. *Journal of Research in Personality*.

Justyna Łukaszewska-Bezulska, J. (2020). The role of social capital in labour-related migrations: The Polish example. *Journal of International Migration and Integration, 3*, 1–8. Retrieved May 9, 2021, from. doi:10.100712134-020-00776-z

Kandler, C., & Bleidorn, W. (2015). The Genetic and Environmental Contributions to Personality Differences and Development. The International Encyclopedia of Social and Behavioral Sciences (2nd ed., pp. 884-890). doi:10.1016/B978-0-08-097086-8.25011-3

Landua, L. B., & Segatti, A. (2013). Urbanisation and migration: The governance of mobility and spatial inequalities. In U. Pillay, G. Hagg, & F. Nyamnjoh (Eds.), *State of the Nation South Africa 2012-2013*. HSRC Press.

Lawrence, P. (2018). Challenging the Hegemony of Neoliberal Economics: Is Another Way Possible? In Building Blocks Towards an African Century: Essays in Honour of Thabo Mbeki, Former President of the Republic of South, Africa (pp. 136-165). Johannesburg: Real African Publishers.

Lewis, C. (2019). *Sovereign entrepreneurs: Cherokee small-business owners and the making of economic sovereignty*. University of North Carolina Press. doi:10.5149/northcarolina/9781469648590.001.0001

Łukaszewska-Bezulska, J. (2014). Social capital and migrations: an analysis of interactions in light of particular theoretical concepts - Problemy Polityki Społecznej - Numer nr 4 (2014) - BazEkon - Yadda, Problemy Polityki Społecznej. *Studia i Dyskusje, 27*(4), 23–40. Available at: http://www. problemypolitykispolecznej.pl/images/czasopisma/27/PPS-27-23-40.pdf

Lutomia, A. N., Bravo, J. B., & Seck, F. (2019). Becoming an African Hair Salon Entrepreneur in the United States of America. In Immigration and Refugee Policy: Breakthroughs in Research and Practice (pp. 31-51) IGI Global.

Maathai, W. (2009). *The Challenge for Africa: A New Vision*. William Heinemann.

Mahlobo, T. (2016). *The New Economy: Ancient Hope for Modern Economies*. Johannesburg: LCBN Ltd. and LEAD2020.

Mills, G., & Herbst, J. (2012). *Africa's Third Liberation*. Penguin Books.

Mlambo, D. N. (2019). A South African perspective on immigrants and Xenophobia in post-1994 South Africa. *African Renaissance*, *16*(4), 53–67. doi:10.31920/2516-5305/2019/16n4a3

Mohammed, A. A. (2018). *Entrepreneurship Lecture Notes*. https://www.researchgate.net/publication/326190494_Entrepreneurship_lecture_note

Mosselson, A. (2010). There is no difference between citizen and non-citizen anymore: Violent xenophobia, citizenship and the politics of belonging in post-apartheid South Africa. *Journal of Southern African Studies*, *36*(3), 641–655. doi:10.1080/03057070.2010.507570

Ng'ambi, H. C. (2018). Advancing the Developmental Goals of Africa through Rare and Total Leadership: The case of Thabo Mbeki. In Building Blocks Towards an African Century: Essays in Honour of Thabo Mbeki, Former President of the Republic of South, Africa (pp. 70-100). Johannesburg: Real African Publishers.

OECD/ILO. (2018). *How Immigrants Contribute to South Africa's Economy*. OECD Publishing. doi:10.1787/9789264085398-en

Pietersen, E. (2021). Entrepreneurship leadership. In E. van Zyl (Ed.), *Leadership in the African Context* (2nd ed.). Juta and Company Ltd.

Prahalad, C. K. (2006). *The fortune at the bottom of the pyramid*. Pearson Prentice Hall.

Roy, M. J., Donaldson, C., Baker, R., & Kerr, S. (2014). The potential of social enterprise to enhance health and well-being: A model and systematic review. *Social Science & Medicine*, *123*, 182–193. doi:10.1016/j.socscimed.2014.07.031 PMID:25037852

Rudigi, R. J. (2010). 'The journey from death to life: I was told that life is out there' - a case study of Congolese immigrants in Durban, South Africa. In Contemporary Social Issues in Africa: Cases in Gaborone, Kampala and Durban (pp. 65-78). Africa Institute of Africa (AISA).

Sahin, M, Nijkamp, P., & Baycan-Levent, T. (2006). *Migrant Entrepreneurship from the Perspective of Cultural Diversity*. file:///C:/Users/TSHISH~1/AppData/Local/Temp/Migrant_Entrepreneurship_from_the_Perspective_of_C.pdf

Servon, L. J. (2011). *Bootstrap capital: Microenterprises and the American poor*. Brookings Institution Press.

Terreblanche, S. (2012). *Lost in Transformation: South Africa's search for a New Future Since 1986*. KMM Review Publishing Company.

Tshishonga, N. (2021). Economic Survival: Towards balancing the Financial and Intellectual Act? In Higher Education, Community Engagement and Entrepreneurship in Southern Africa (pp. 68-95). Cambridge Scholars Publishing.

World Bank Group. (2018). *An Incomplete Transition: Overcoming the Legacy of Exclusion in South Africa*. UCT Press.

## KEY TERMS AND DEFINITIONS

**African Immigrants:** People from Africa who have voluntarily come to live in the US or other countries.

**Entrepreneur:** A person who undertakes the process of creating wealth by identifying opportunities, taking risks, seizing the opportunities in order to supply good and services needed in the market.

**Entrepreneurship:** A process undertaken by an entrepreneur to create wealth in a society or a firm.

**Host Country:** A recipient country of immigrants. In this case South Africa and its cities.

**Immigrant:** A person who moves from one country to settle in another country of which s/he is not a citizen.

**Immigrant Entrepreneurship:** A process of creating wealth or entrepreneurial enterprises in a host country undertaken by an immigrant.

**Immigration:** An act by an immigrant to settle in a foreign country. Therefore, immigration is the permanent movement of people to one country from another.

**Informal Enterprise:** A firm employing workers between 1 to 10 people with a capital injection of less than USD 10,000.

**Native:** An indigenous person born and a citizen of the host country.

**Social Capital:** Is a term used to reflect the norms, values, and networks as well as formal or informal relationship.

**Social Entrepreneurship:** Is an entrepreneurial practice where entrepreneurs start organisations or businesses with both social and economic purposes.

**Social Network:** Entails the connection between people from the same community who rely on communicating with each other for purposes of an outcome such as jobs, business, and relationships.

**Xenophobia:** That is the concept described to denote the dislike, resentment, and stereotype against immigrants for various reasons.

# Chapter 5
# A Comparative Look at Social Housing in Developed and Developing Countries:
## The Role for Social Enterprises

**Fidelis Ifeanyi Emoh**
*University of Botswana, Botswana*

**Don Macdonald**
*University of Greenwich, UK*

**Charles Oham**
*University of Greenwich, UK*

**Gladius Kulothungan**
*University of Wales Trinity St. David, UK*

## EXECUTIVE SUMMARY

*Provision of housing is vital to all the members of any country, and even a fundamental right of every person in a society to be housed properly. Whilst the state has a primary role to play in reallocation of resources to meet the needs of the majority and ensure 'public good', the economic status of developing nations has made this a complex issue. The developing world has increasingly come to rely on voluntary action, especially the social enterprise (SE) movements. There are marked differences in the approaches to tackling the social housing issue in the developed and developing world, from the point of view of the role played by sSEs in this area. This chapter takes a comparative look at the role played by SEs and SEs in the area of social housing in the developing and developed world by looking at some specific examples and case studies and concludes that in the developing world the SE movement has a stronger role to play.*

DOI: 10.4018/978-1-7998-7724-0.ch005

# INTRODUCTION

There is no single definition of social housing across the nations. However, definitional issucs cxist particularly around the position of cooperatives; time-limited subsidies, and the role of private suppliers. Definitions may relate to ownership – notably non-profit organisations and local authorities (e.g,. the Netherlands and Sweden); who construct the dwellings (e.g., Austria and France); whether or not rents are below market levels (e.g., Ireland and England); the relevant funding and/or subsidy stream (e.g., France and Germany); and most importantly, in almost all of the countries, the purpose for which the housing is provided. In some countries, social housing is formally available to all households (e.g., Austria and Sweden) but, in most cases, it is directed at those who cannot serve their own housing needs (e.g., the Netherlands and England).

In the developed world, the principle of social housing is that where the private sector is unable to provide the required level of affordable accommodation for all those who need it, the state must intervene to ensure that those on low incomes are provided for. The provision of social housing is seen as a key remedy to housing inequality, as rent increases are limited so they remain affordable to those most in need. In the UK, Social housing is the term given to accommodation, which is provided at affordable rates, on a secure basis to people on low incomes or with particular needs. Social housing properties are usually owned by the state, in the form of councils, or by non-profit organisations such as housing associations. As of 2015, 17% of all households in England were social housing (Mullins, Czischke, & van Bortel, 2012).

## Social Landlords

The varying definitions of social housing mean that it is impossible to provide strictly comparable figures on the supply of social housing – rather we must use each country's definition which reflects their views of the nature and importance of social housing. A SE, on the other hand, is defined as a business or other hybrid organisation characterised by the delivery of social value as the principal aim as opposed to maximising profit for the owners/shareholders; and the ongoing production of goods or the provision of services to generate an income that covers costs and potentially allows for a surplus (ILO, 2016). A SE's primary objective is to address social needs through a financially sustainable business model where surpluses (if any) are mainly reinvested for that purpose. It is a business venture that exists to fix a social or environmental problem and uses its profits for this purpose (Coetzee, 2016). Social landlords are SE based on their objectives and characteristics. Beugre

(2017) notes that the meaning, practice and governance of SE could vary from country to country. They can be identified as a SE based on the following characteristics:

- Have a clear social and/or environmental mission set out in their governing documents;
- Generate the majority of their income through trade;
- Reinvest their profits to further their mission and objectives;
- Risk-taking propensity; be autonomous of state or private control;
- Be majority controlled in the interests of the social mission;
- Passion and alertness; and
- Be accountable and transparent.

## The Scene From the Developed World

In the UK, the central government's Department of Trade and Industry (DTI) defines SE as 'businesses with primarily social objectives whose surpluses are principally reinvested for that purpose in the business or the community, rather than being driven by the need to maximize profit for shareholders and owners' (DTI, 2004). The West Midlands Social Economy Partnership (WMSEP) defines SE as 'a collective term for an organisation that is driven by particular social and community values, whilst aiming to operate effectively and sustainably within a competitive business framework i.e., helping the community as well as maintaining a viable business (WMSEP, 2004). According to Alter (2007), the UK Social Enterprise Coalition also supports the UK Government definition which many of its members were actively involved in helping to develop: A SE is a business with primarily social objectives whose surpluses are principally reinvested for that purpose in the business or in the community, rather than being driven by the need to maximise profit for shareholders and owners.

In Belgium, as in several European countries, SE has a dual meaning. The first meaning generally speaks to service organisations that are developing commercial activities. The second refers to those cooperatives or associations with initiatives specifically aimed at the occupational integration of people excluded from the labour market (Defourny & Nyssens, 2001). This second definition stems from the specific social service need around SEs that have developed in Europe causing them to be associated with employment creating initiatives e.g., Work Integration Social Enterprises (WISE). This common definition is most closely aligned with the American academic concept of a social purpose organisation whose programming for participants includes activities that simultaneously generate revenue. In Europe, SEs come in a variety of forms including employee development trusts, social firms, intermediate labour market organisations, community businesses, or charities' trading arms (OECD, 2003).

These country specifics demonstrate that social entrepreneurship is a continuum consisting of a variety of not-for-profit organisations with a trading dimension. They include charitable trading organisations such as charity shops, social firms that employ people with disability, cooperative groups, and voluntary and community trading organisations. This demonstrates that some SEs have evolved over the years from one form of not-for-profit organisation to another whilst others start as SEs from the onset (Oham, 2016).

### The Decreasing Investment From the State

The decreased investment in social housing is part of a larger shift, often associated with neoliberalism, from government-provided housing to a greater focus on partnerships between government, not-for-profit and private sectors for housing provision in the developed world (Beer, Kearins, & Pieters, 2007; Kleit & Page, 2015). In line with trends in other welfare systems such as healthcare, childcare and social care, housing provision has experienced reduced state investment, privatisation and commissioning of public services from third-sector organisations in the developed world (Mullins, Czischke, & van Bortel, 2012). The changes have involved a shifting role for government as the state seeks to 'steer' rather than 'row' or 'direct' rather than 'directly implement' (Beer et al., 2007, p. 13). We have to keep these developments in view as we look at the social housing scene in the developed world.

## SOCIAL HOUSING AND ENTERPISE IN NEW ZEALAND

Conceptualisations of SE in New Zealand are influenced by a variety of ideologies which, in turn, contributes to diversity in SE activity. Trading not-for-profits and community economic development organisations tend to be located more towards the social end of the socio-economic continuum, whereas business-oriented social innovation organisations are more likely to be found at the economic end of the spectrum. Unique to New Zealand are a range of Maori organisations. Often *iwi* (tribal) based, these organisations typically draw on cultural traditions to guide and inform their practice. Dey and Grant (2014) demonstrate how the activities of many of these Maori organisations may be considered as a SE.

Community housing providers currently operating in New Zealand could be seen to fall under the SE umbrella and are more likely to identify with the not-for-profit and/or community development positioning than social innovation. In some areas, such as Auckland, partnerships between local and state government, property developers and sometimes community organisations, has seen the creation of special housing areas. These areas are created with the intention of fast-tracking the availability of social and affordable housing in designated areas. There are also many Maori *iwi*-based housing options around the country, such as the kaumatua (elder) housing offered by many Maori Consistent with the general SE context in New Zealand, a lack of resourcing and supportive infrastructure are key challenges facing all of these social housing providers.

## State Subsidised Housing

Within the New Zealand context, social housing is recognised as a subset of affordable housing, i.e., where a household spends no more than 30% of its gross income on housing costs, whether for rent or mortgage. Statistics from 2009 indicated social housing at that time accounted for one in five dwellings in New Zealand, i.e., residents in these dwellings received some form of housing assistance, either as a tenant of a state-owned house or a recipient of a government-provided accommodation supplement (Housing Shareholders Advisory Group, 2010). In New Zealand, the government is the major supplier of social housing through Housing New Zealand Corporation; the next is the local government (Community Housing Aotearoa, 2015). A small number of NGOs and community groups provide some dwellings, albeit on a small scale. The dominant role of the state as a provider of such housing means, in reality, social housing more realistically equates to 'state-subsidised housing'.

Comparatively, New Zealand social housing is strong in terms of international benchmarks. For example, waiting lists are shorter and declining when compared to other countries, but the pressure is still evident and growing (Housing Shareholders Advisory Group, 2010). However, issues across the New Zealand social and affordable housing market vary significantly across the country due to local and regional conditions (Community Housing Aotearoa, 2015).

Community Housing Aotearoa (CHA) is an umbrella organisation established in 2005, representing 74 members, including local councils and not-for-profit organisations that deliver community housing solutions. Collectively, the member organisations provide at least 4,021 homes with a minimum of 9,700 beds. CHA estimates that over 15,000 people go home each night to a home operated by a not-for-profit community housing organisation. There are four member organisations in the Hamilton area. Two provide housing and residential support to people in or nearing retirement, one supports mental health patients with housing and associated social service support and the fourth supports people with disabilities (Community Housing Aotearoa, 2015).

Housing New Zealand Corporation (HNZC), the government-owned provider of state housing, owns around 65,000 houses and leases 3,000 more. In total, 4.5% of all residential properties across New Zealand are HNZC properties (New Zealand Government, 2015).

In 2014, the Cabinet agreed to a programme of reform that aims to improve the performance of the New Zealand government's investment in social housing including state housing. These reforms also sought to increase the number and diversity of social housing providers to increase choice and contestability. Ultimately, the government expects these reforms will grow the total quantum of social housing available to meet increasing demand (English & Bennett, 2015). The Housing Stakeholders Advisory Group summarises the objectives of the government's social housing reforms thus: that New Zealanders have access to housing that meets their needs and is affordable; that assistance is available to those most in need for the duration of their need, and be delivered cost-effectively; that a suitable business environment is created for investment in affordable housing by providers, including non-governmental organisations (NGOs) (HSAG 2010, p11).

Two new government bodies have been established as part of the reform process. The Social Housing Unit (SHU), Te Wāhanga Kāinga Pāpori, is a government agency established in 2011 as a semi-autonomous body within the Building and Housing Group of the Ministry of Business, Innovation and Employment. SHU's principle aim and priority is to facilitate an increase in the supply of social and affordable housing for New Zealanders by working with organisations, including not-for-profit, *iwi*, and private sector providers. The Unit allocates funding and facilitates partnerships, including land transfers and sale or lease of surplus state housing stock (SHU Website). Since its establishment, NZ$139 million has been provided in capital grants to community housing providers for development of 890 housing units (Ministry of Social Development, 2015). The Community Housing Regulatory Authority (CHRA) is another newly created entity rising from the reforms. Separate from the Social Housing Unit, but sharing some of their facilities, CHRA is also based within the Ministry for Business, Innovation and Employment. CHRA has been established to accredit and monitor community housing providers, with the power to intervene if necessary. CHRA's focus is to assist the emergence of a diverse range of CHPs, and create a more level playing field between the Housing New Zealand Corporation and CHPs. HNZC and community housing providers are both required to report to CHRA at the same level. The government strategy envisages an expanded role in the social housing market for Community Housing Providers, as these organisations are recognised by the government as better able to respond to the needs of specific tenants.

The government anticipates the availability of social housing to increase through a number of reform outcomes. Through its ongoing programme of sales, reinvestment and redevelopment, HNZC as part of its business as usual asset management, expects to see ownership of some of their properties transferred to Community Housing Providers. For example, in April 2015, HNZC announced the transfer of 2800 houses to the Tamaki Redevelopment Company, a joint venture housing provider established by Auckland Council (59%) and the New Zealand Government (41%) (English & Bennett, 2015). The New Zealand case demonstrates the role national and local government can play in stimulating civil societies' involvement in social housing.

## THE SOCIAL HOUSING SECTOR IN THE UNITED KINGDOM

### History and Background

The United Kingdom (UK) housing sector consists of a plethora of organisations that include profit and not-for-profit entities. These configurations of organisations have added value to the housing sector as various segmentations of residents have seen their needs and demands met by a diversity of housing associations. Housing providers include voluntary organisations such as housing associations that provide social housing, private landlords and the mortgage provision sector by financial institutions. Housing Associations were set up because of a range of social needs of people affected by homelessness, low incomes, foreign students' housing needs, immigration, and a lack of social cohesion. These needs were not adequately catered for by the public or private sector.

A major driver for social housing over the years has been government policy and funding, strategically noticing the value that the voluntary sector could provide to society. This has led to an array of large and small housing associations thriving within the social landlord ecosystem. Other drivers have been civil society and faith-based (see FFG in Chapter 7) organisations such as churches and faith based organisations that provide social action interventions (Oham and Macdonald, 2016). In the UK, around 1,700 registered housing associations provide 2.5 million homes for 5 million people in England with private finance playing a significant role in funding with £40bn of public sector grants levering in £60bn of private finance and creating a £15bn surplus. This is then reinvested to regenerate neighbourhoods, provide supported accommodation for those with special needs, create employment and provide services for families and young people.

Listed below are several types of organisations within the not-for-profit sector that have been involved in social housing.

Voluntary housing associations have a long history in the UK from the 1860s and even before. Almshouses were the first social housing, providing housing for the local elderly from the 10th century in England; the oldest still in existence dating from about 1132. They continue to provide this service to around 3,000 elders. From 1723, the Poor Law required local government in England to provide workhouses for the poor and needy, the first set up in 1631; this was the type of institution Charles Dickens described in Oliver Twist. Workhouses were phased out by 1948. Some Black and Ethnic Minority Housing Associations were set up in the 1970s and 1980s to address the unmet needs of ethnic minorities, examples include SHIAN Housing and ODU DUA Housing Association.

Mainstream housing associations were set up in the late 19th century as charitable ventures in London, along with other charities. This was propelled by Octavia Hill, the campaigner, providing some houses, as did other associations including the Guinness Trust and Peabody Trust. The sector expanded rapidly from the early 1970s after campaigners against slum landlords started taking practical action; examples, are the Notting Hill Housing Trust and Paddington Churches Housing Association (now Genesis). Some funding was charitable but housing development was mostly funded by the government until 1988; in this year, the grants were cut back and they were asked to use private-sector loans to make up the difference. Over time, the rate of a grant from the government has fallen from over 90% and sometimes higher before 1988 to usually well below 25% now.

## Hostels and Staff Housing

In 1912, the YMCA (England) started its first hostel and now provides 10,000 bed spaces for young people through a federation of local housing associations. The YWCA, which had provided 4000-bed spaces in the 1990s, decided to sell all its hostels because it could not afford to renew the fire escapes and other safety features (A more radical approach would have been to take out a social investment loan to fund the work, paying it back from revenue but these were not freely available then. This has been done by a social enterprise, Bristol Together).

The private sector has also been involved, with housing provided for employees; in fact, some companies built whole villages such as Bourneville built by Cadburys (now part of Kraft and no longer so community-minded) and Port Sunlight in 1888 by the Lever Brothers (now part of Unilever). In London, which has always been a high-cost area for housing, staff hostels were provided by employers such as John Lewis, the Metropolitan Police, and the Civil Service up until the 1990s.

## Governance of Housing Associations in the UK

Housing associations are regulated by, and receive significant funding from, central Government; both revenue and capital. Despite being funded and regulated by the Government, housing associations are independent of Government control. An example of their independence is that they have resisted the wholesale implementation of the 2015 UK Government's plan, previously thought to be a *fait accompli*, (which) would see housing association tenants offered the chance to buy their homes at high discounts.

Other housing associations are cooperatives, meaning that they are owned and controlled by people or groups with a shared interest and common purpose (e.g., staff) that brings about equity in terms of rewards and democratic control of governance. Faith-based organisations such as churches and their subsidiaries have also been at the forefront of social housing provision. Most have been renamed which this has masked their faith-based origins. Examples include Anchor House in Newham, London, owned and managed by the local Catholic Church who provide housing for homeless men. These voluntary organisations have strong community links as a result of their charitable and religious work in the community, allowing them to tap into various types of social and spiritual capital. Voluntary housing associations must follow strict governance rules; they are inspected by government-backed agencies and given ratings for a range of standards, including financial soundness, which is published annually. They are officially called Registered Social Landlords. They have built up a sphere of political influence, along with a bank of professional expertise, with specialist support and training available. This arrangement enables them to provide an additional array of specialist services in addition to housing. Social outcomes linked to housing association provision include drug and alcohol, mental health, disability and supported living as well as employment interventions to name but a few.

Further examples of housing associations providing additional services to general housing include employment and training projects (Genesis), community facilities (Peabody); although this has been reducing as austerity affects the UK. They also provide over 420,000 supported housing places for elderly, disabled tenants (Abinteg) and specialist client groups such as the mentally ill, in partnership with specialist organisations (St Landlords). Housing associations can be innovative by designing new services for their service users and utilising innovative designs, such as constructing flat-pack housing and sports fitness facilities and enterprises (YMCA).

## Expansion

Large housing associations have continued to expand and have also taken over smaller housing associations and this has caused some problems concerning communication with tenants. At the same time, funding for housing development was cut right back from 2010. New Housing projects often involve no direct government subsidy at all but are funded from reserves of the Housing Association and 'private borrowing' through the use of new forms of debt financing, which includes shared ownership, which is based on a tenant part renting/part buying a property.

Private finance plays a very significant role, although there are limitations; a financial adviser complained about the banks' willingness to refinance loans, although another expert stated that the strict regulatory regime protected the access to private finance from all size housing associations.

Since a big expansion from the 1970s, housing associations are now the main providers of social housing for rent in the UK, providing 243,000 units. In 2015, they built over 40,000 new homes in England, but are under pressure in a variety of ways. They invest six times as much funds as the amount that they generate from the private sector through loans and bonds, along with charitable fundraising, to match any government grants. This demonstrates the significant contribution housing associations bring to the UK housing sector and the economy in general, and it draws in stakeholders of housing associations who are impacted by its activities. It is therefore vital that housing associations are robust enough to fulfil their obligations to stakeholders.

However, as UK Government austerity bites, with a considerable reduction of investment by the Government in new homes by 60% between 2010 and 2015, rents are being increased radically, particularly in high-cost areas such as London. Under Government pressure, large housing associations have become more involved in building houses for sale, nevertheless, they are being criticised by many professionals in the sector and also a respected newspaper city editor for becoming too commercial. Home-ownership is very popular in the UK, more so than in other European countries and housing associations were also asked to take over various government housing estates through stock transfer arrangements. Many housing associations also provide much more than just general housing, including employment and training projects for tenants and others (Catalyst HA). A recent study identified that people in social housing find their housing associations provided more help than Government run job centres at putting them on the first step of the career ladder. Others provide a range of community facilities, such as community centres and youth and children's provision (Peabody) although it has to be said much of this additional provision has reduced as austerity bites while government funding has reduced since 2008.

UK Housing associations are a good example of a well-founded social enterprise sector as their income and profits generated by renting out homes is ploughed back to further their objective of housing provision. Their experience shows the pressures they must overcome, but also the opportunities. The situation in the developing world is very different. However, there are lessons from the UK experience which could be utilised in the developing world; these include political will by the government, states and local governments in enacting relevant policies that will stimulate the development of the social housing sector. In the UK, the local government is the biggest player in housing provision. Furthermore, there is a need for imaginative design by community champions and change agents that will trigger the required change in housing, involvement with stakeholders such as local chiefs and customary councils that robustly link with the community and investment by the private sector.

In the UK, approximately 70,000 social enterprises are contributing more than £18 billion (approx. R320 billion) to the UK economy and employing approximately one million people. (Social Enterprise UK Small Business Survey, 2013). Some UK government regeneration and social programmes with many housing associations at the forefront include Neighborhood Renewal, Local Strategic Partnerships, Compact, Sure Start, Big Society and Active Communities where these initiatives enhance social capital among marginalised people and deprived communities. In areas of negative social capital, housing associations in the UK have had to deal with anti-social behaviour, crime, low social cohesion and a lack of investment. These are critical issues that have had a huge impact on local communities especially those that have seen a decline in manufacturing and coal mining in the last 30 years. Many housing associations depending on their size have community development departments and officers who work as a catalyst to promote community cohesion thereby building up social capital of the area. Spiritual capital can be considered as a subset of social capital. It is defined as 'the fund of beliefs, examples and commitments that are generational legacies acquired through a religious tradition that attaches people to a transcendental source of human happiness and demands stewardship' (Malloch, 2008). Simply put, spiritual capital is the advantage stakeholders acquire as a result of their faith. This resource is described as the missing leg of the stool of economic development and has attracted immense attention (Malloch, 2005; Capaldi, 2005). A significant percentage of the housing associations in the UK were set up by Christians and church clergy. This demonstrates the critical role that faith can play in addressing critical housing needs in any country. For example, Paddington Churches Housing Association (PCHA), now Genesis Housing, was set up in 1966 by a group of church leaders who had insurmountable challenges getting people into decent homes at affordable rent. The organisation has grown to become a major player in the housing sector with a turnover above £261 million in 2014 (Genesis, 2014). In 1993, one of the authors of this chapter travelled on a business trip to Kaduna city in Northern Nigeria, he was referred to the Young Men's Christian Association (YMCA) hostel established in 1964 by German Missionaries to provide training and accommodation for students attending its vocational training. Each room had two bunk beds to accommodate four people. It provided temporary and affordable accommodation to many men on low income and those shuttling on business trips between Kaduna and other cities in Nigeria. The author had started a printing business and was in town to complete a printing contract. Although the hostel provided accommodation for its students at the vocational training centre situated within the compound, it also had surplus rooms to offer to the public.

## SOCIAL HOUSING AND ENTERPRISE IN SUB-SUHARAN AFRICA

Globally, the housing need is most acute in Africa, where the population will more than double by 2050. The opportunity and need for better housing are critical in Africa, with its rapidly shifting economic and demographic profile. The continent's population is the fastest growing in the world and is predicted to increase from 1.2 billion in 2015 to 2.5 billion by 2050, which will necessitate hundreds of millions of new homes (Tusting et al., 2019). Sub-Saharan Africa is particularly faced with the problem of housing and more especially social housing in terms of quality and quantity.

Sub-Saharan Africa is geographically made up of the area of the continent of Africa that lies south of the Sahara comprising the following countries; Angola, Benin, Botswana, Burkina Faso, Burundi, Cabo Verde, Cameroon, Central African Republic, Chad, Comoros, Democratic Republic of Congo, Republic of Congo, Cote d'Ivoire, Equatorial Guinea, Eritrea, Eswatini (formerly known as Swaziland), Ethiopia, Gabon, The Gambia, Ghana, Guinea-Bissau, Kenya, Lesotho, Liberia, Madagascar, Malawi, Mali, Mauritania, Mauritius, Mozambique, Namibia, Niger, Nigeria, Rwanda, Sao Tome and Principe, Senegal, Seychelles, Sierra Leone, Somalia, South Africa, South Sudan, Sudan, Tanzania, Togo, Uganda and Zambia.

Improved housing (defined as housing with improved water and sanitation, sufficient living area and durable construction) doubled during 2000–2015 with 134 (118–147) million Africans in the analysed countries gaining access to improved housing (Tusting et al., 2019). The study ranked the countries in Sub-Saharan Africa for improved housing from highest to lowest: Botswana, Gabon, Zimbabwe, Senegal, Gambia, Namibia, Congo, Swaziland, Cote d'Ivoire, Ghana, Cameroon, Nigeria, Guinea, Zambia, Burkina Faso, Kenya, Guinea-Bissau, Benin, Togo, Rwanda, Sierra Leone, Equatorial Guinea, Mali, Burundi, Tanzania, Angola, Liberia, Uganda, Sudan, Somalia, Mozambique, CAR, Malawi, DRC, Madagascar, Eritrea, Ethiopia and

South Sudan. However, unacceptable inequalities persist, with 53 (50–57) million urban inhabitants (47% [44–50%] of the total urban population of sub-Saharan Africa analysed) and 595 (585–607) million rural inhabitants (82% [80–83%] of the rural population) living in unimproved housing in 2015. The study revealed that nearly half of Africa's urban population still lives in unimproved conditions, which is partly explained by widespread unimproved sanitation.

Further studies by Tusting, et al., (2020) observed that poor housing, which includes inadequate drinking water and sanitation facility, is associated with health outcomes known to increase child mortality in Sub-Saharan Africa. Improvements to housing may be protective against many important childhood infectious diseases as well as poor growth outcomes, with major potential to improve children's health and survival across Sub-Saharan Africa. The study found that adequate housing is essential to human well-being but is neglected in public health and that children living in housing with improved drinking water and sanitation, sufficient living area, and durable construction had a reduced likelihood of four major causes of death: malaria (12–18% reduction), diarrhoea (8% reduction), growth failure (stunting: 17% reduction, wasting: 10% reduction, underweight: 15% reduction), and anaemia (11–13% reduction) after accounting for differences in levels of urbanisation, poverty, vaccinations, and other public health interventions. Improvements to housing may help reduce the burden of disease among children in Sub-Saharan Africa alongside wider poverty reduction.

According to Biehler, Choplin and Morelle (2019), the question of housing for working-class populations remains a recurrent issue in Sub-Saharan African cities, the 'social-housing' policies implemented by states following independence, and under the influence of lenders, have almost always benefited the most well-off. They questioned whether the 'participatory' alternatives now promoted by some Non-Governmental Organisations (NGOs) are enough to create a new model for social housing in Africa.

Their comparative history of social housing in three African capitals namely Ouagadougou in Burkina Faso, Yaoundé in Cameroon, and Nouakchott in Mauritania, three state capitals marked by a French presence (former colonisation and current cooperation) and the majority of whose residents are poor, highlighted several types of actions when it comes to housing, marked by three successive stages: the first phase of public intervention, followed by the withdrawal of the state and the enactment of a policy governing self-building, and finally a policy based on public-private partnerships coupled with more local initiatives funded by NGOs. Their analysis shows that the 'social' dimension of the housing produced is not always obvious. It also reveals a recurring pattern in these three cities, characterized by similar timetables: the first phase of state intervention, leading to the construction of housing complexes, followed by the withdrawal of public players in the name of 'structural adjustments', and finally a recent return to urban operations, with significant involvement on the part of private investors, where the rise of social housing now seems to be based on participatory experiments on a small scale. The study concluded that successive measures, supposedly aimed at building social housing, have declined decade after decade, essentially addressing a relatively affluent population, and remaining inaccessible to less well-off households.

## Nigeria

Social housing and social entrepreneurship are potential solutions to growing housing investment, but neither has gained a foothold and their impact is yet to be felt in Nigeria. Social entrepreneurship in Nigeria faces a dearth of empirical knowledge and findings, as the area is only just eliciting academic interest and debate (Iyortsuun, 2013). The National Housing Policy (2012) recommended social housing for three categories of Nigerians, namely: no-income group, that is, income less than or equal to 25 per cent of national minimum wage; low-income group, income above 25 per cent and up to 100 percent minimum wage and lower medium-income group, income above national minimum wage. The Nigerian housing policies were well-conceived with the fundamental elements of feasibility, affordability and limited time frame required for the completion of the programmes. To some extent, the various policies and programmes of housing in Nigeria have been able to make significant improvements in housing production and delivery. The housing policies provided guidelines for housing construction, maintenance and delivery.

Nevertheless, the policies and programmes are besieged by shortcomings like poverty, ever-increasing costs of construction and building materials, homelessness, weak institutional frameworks for housing delivery, administrative bottlenecks in plan approval collection of certificate of occupancy and, programme monitoring as well as review (Ibimilua & Ibitoye, 2015). However, none of the housing policies has been able to address the specific issues of social housing. It is only recently that the Federal Government of Nigeria disclosed a plan to raise a fund worth one trillion naira, in conjunction with private investors, to finance mortgages for low-income earners, under the social housing programme of the present Buhari Administration which The Vice President, Yemi Osinbajo disclosed at the 22nd Nigerian Economic Summit in Abuja. He said that the fund is a financial intervention fund to be named 'Family Homes Fund' and will be generated by aggregating funds from the private sector, local, and international investors. The Vice President explained that the fund would help the government intervene in mortgage financing for developers to build social houses according to government specification for low-income earners and that any Nigerian who can afford to contribute 30,000 naira a month would be able to own a house under the Federal Government social housing scheme (Vanguard,

October 17, 2016). Social housing policies, however, persist. The funding provision for social housing has been reduced from one trillion naira in 2016 to 200 billion naira in 2021. Nliam (2021) reported that the Nigerian Presidency had announced that the N200 billion facilities set aside for the Federal Government Social Housing Scheme are ready for disbursement to start the project.

This follows the finalization of the agreement with the Central Bank of Nigeria (CBN) with a guarantee from the Federal Ministry of Finance for the scheme, which is expected to be disbursed at 5% per annum. Under the Social Housing Programme, the Federal Government plans to support 1.5 million Nigerians to acquire low-cost houses either through mortgage options or a Rent-to-Own option.

## South Africa

South Africa is far ahead of all other countries in Sub-Saharan Africa in the issue of social housing and social enterprise. The country has, through an enabling law, the Republic of South Africa Social Housing Act No. 16, 2008 created the right atmosphere for social housing to thrive. The Act aimed to do the following:

Establish and promote a sustainable social housing environment; to define the functions of national, provincial and local governments in respect of social housing; to provide for the establishment of the Social Housing Regulatory Authority to regulate all social housing institutions obtaining or having obtained public funds; to allow for the undertaking of approved projects by other delivery agents with the benefit of public money; to give statutory recognition to social housing institutions, and to provide for matters connected therewith.

Social housing under the Act means a rental or cooperative housing option for low- to medium-income households at a level of scale and built formwhich requires institutionalised management provided by social housing institutions or other delivery agents in approved projects in designated restructuring zones with the benefit of public funding; while 'Social housing institution' means an institution accredited or provisionally accredited under this Act which carries or intends to carry on the business of providing rental or cooperative housing options for low- to medium-income households, on an affordable basis, ensuring quality and maximum benefits for residents, and managing its housing stock over the long term.

The Act provided some general principles applicable to social housing in South Africa that will act as a guide to Nigeria viz: in giving priority to the needs of low- and medium-income households in respect of social housing development, the national, provincial and local spheres of government and social housing institutions must ensure their respective housing programmes are responsive to local housing demands, and special priority must be given to the needs of women, children, child-headed households, persons with disabilities and the elderly; support the economic development of low- to medium-income communities by providing housing close to jobs, markets and transport and by stimulating job opportunities to emerging entrepreneurs in the housing services and construction industries; afford residents the necessary dignity and privacy by providing the residents with a clean, healthy and safe environment; ensure the sustainable and viable growth of affordable social housing as an objective of housing policy; facilitate the involvement of residents and key stakeholders through consultation, information sharing, education, training and skills transfer, thereby empowering residents; ensure secure tenure for residents in social housing institutions, on the basis of the general provisions governing the relationship between tenants and landlords, and between primary housing cooperatives and its members; the suitable location of social housing stock in respect of employment opportunities; the conversion or upgrading of suitable residential and non-residential buildings for social housing use; incentives to social housing institutions and other delivery agents to enter the social housing market; an understanding and awareness of social housing processes; transparency, accountability and efficiency in the administration and management of social housing stock; the creation of sustainable, viable and independent housing institutions responsible for providing, developing, holding or managing social housing stock; and the use of public funds in a manner that stimulates or facilitates private sector investment and participation in the social housing sector.

The Act provides for a Social Housing Regulatory Authority with the following functions among others: promote the development and awareness of social housing; promote an enabling environment for the growth and development of the social housing sector; provide best practice information and research on the status of the social housing sector.

The functions of social housing institutions under the Act include among others: acquire, develop, manage, or both develop and manage, approved projects primarily for low-income residents with the joint support of local authorities; promote the creation of quality living environments for low-income residents; re-invest operational surpluses generated as a result of funding provided in terms of the social housing programme, in further approved projects; consult with municipalities to develop social housing stock; seek permission from the Regulatory Authority for the sale of any properties in their ownership on the basis that such sales will not endanger the security of tenure of existing residents meeting the conditions of their tenancy and that the grant component of the proceeds receipts from such sale will be used to provide social housing.

The International Labour Organisation (2016) private and public procurement and the social enterprise project, the best-case studies from South Africa show the important role of the private and public sectors in supporting the growth and sustainability of social economy enterprises, through contractual agreements for goods or services, as well as through mentoring and enterprise development initiatives. By procuring goods or services from these social economy enterprises, the private and public sector have enabled them to create jobs and opportunities for income generation within their local communities, thereby increasing the involvement of beneficiaries in their local economy. Furthermore, through the work conducted by these enterprises, beneficiaries become more actively involved in the development of their communities, promoting greater social cohesion and social inclusion.

ILO (2016) show cased the Masisizane Women's Housing Co-operative as a success story of a social enterprise in South Africa involved in social housing that began by making bricks and grew to building houses. This women-owned a brick-making cooperative which provided decent, safe and secure housing for the community of Ivory Park while assisting the Gauteng Department of Housing in its service delivery objectives.

Masisizane was established in 1998 to address the lack of decent housing in Ivory Park. The informal cooperative started as seven women from the then informal settlement of Ivory Park, each contributing R25 a week to a savings club to buy bricks, doors and windows to build houses for themselves. At the time, the people of Ivory Park were living in informal shacks, and seasonal heavy rains often resulted in the flooding and destruction of homes, and sometimes even in death. The savings club eventually grew in number to include 24 women. This is when it decided that instead of buying bricks; members would learn to make their own bricks (it saw this as a viable business opportunity). The enterprise learnt how to make bricks from a group of builders in a neighbouring location, and would make about 10,000 bricks that it would sell to people in the area.

Whilst busy with their brick sales, a woman's home was destroyed by heavy rains. This woman also lost two of her young children in the destruction. Being women themselves, this tore at their heartstrings, and the cooperative decided to build her a brick house (with the help of a few men from the community). Masisizane used the bricks it made, and bought additional materials such as cement, windows, and doors to build a four-bedroom house, which was completed within one week. Masisizane then invited the Gauteng Provincial Department of Housing to the official unveiling, and the provincial Department donated money towards catering for the event, which was also televised.

Masisizane was approached by a company called Apex, who had seen them on television and offered a series of training initiatives to the members. Members were trained in welding, painting and also improving their brick-making skills. An outcome of the training was that members decided to build another four-bedroom house for an old woman and, once again, the enterprise invited the Gauteng Provincial Department of Housing to the official unveiling. At this stage, the Department realised the potential in Masisizane to build houses for the Ivory Park community.

The Masisizane Women's Housing Co-operatives provided decent housing to the members of the Ivory Park Community. With a focus on vulnerable women (mostly those affected by HIV/AIDS), Masisizane has played a pivotal role in supporting the most vulnerable members of their community.

Although the enterprise refers to itself as a cooperative, Masisizane Women's Housing Cooperative is registered as a not-for-profit organisation. Masisizane is registered on the Gauteng Department of Housing supplier database and received a contract from the department to build 250 units (houses). Masisizane became the Support Organisation for the People's Housing Process in January 2003 and after more contract renewals, it had completed a total of 1200 units (houses) for the community of Ivory Park through the Department of Housing. The reason for supporting social enterprises is simple – job creation, according to information supplied in an interview with a Gauteng Department of Housing representative. The Ivory Park RDP housing project was part of the People's Housing Process, a people-driven process in which community contribution and partnerships are encouraged. It made sense to appoint Masisizane as the contractor for the Ivory Park project as it was already assisting the community with housing development.

Through the contract with the Department of Housing, Masisizane was able to provide decent housing for the community. With the profits, it was also able to build a community crèche, also named Masisizane, and plant a vegetable garden to help feed the children that attend the crèche as well as needy families in the community.

## Lessons

- Small social enterprises and local community groups can deliver on large contracts and assist the government to achieve its service delivery mandates, as well as significant cost savings due to social capital and access to local labour and resources.
- Taking the initiative to show case completed projects can open up opportunities for a social enterprise to obtain more opportunities. Access to clients is an important aspect of growth and sustainability; marketing can increase such access.
- Challenges related to procurement processes, especially compliance issues and capacity building, can be overcome with the assistance of stakeholders. The Department of Housing – once it had identified Masisizane as a potential supplier – made a concerted effort to assist the organisation to develop its business plan as well as in its application process.
- Sustainability is ensured when an enterprise expands its product/service scope as well as its client base. Too much reliance on one single product/

service or one single client negatively affects the ability of a social enterprise to grow, increase profitability and remain sustainable (ILO, 2016).

## CONCLUSION AND RECOMMENDATIONS

The history and nature of social entrepreneurship and its influence on social housing as exhibited in our case studies from some countries in the Western world demonstrates that there is the potential to adopt and adapt certain policies and practices that would support the development and growth of social housing and social enterprise in Sub-Saharan Africa. In Sub-Saharan Africa, investment in the housing sector has been market-driven with some level of Government involvement; however, there is a non-existent voluntary housing sector due to a lack of capacity building of community organisations and civic societies. The good news is that the potential exists as there is munificence of faith-based and community development organisations that require capacity building to take on the challenge of providing affordable housing to the public. One potential is the grassroots network of faith-based organisations. Their assets, both human and physical, can be vital to the development of the social housing sector. Social housing can come in handy in major cities in Sub-Saharan Africa where people have been known to live in squalor. Various national and state governments could act as a catalyst for the development of an ecosystem of voluntary housing associations. There is much more that government can do to create an enabling environment for groups to be aware of and have the skills to set up building societies and housing associations that will drive through a range of innovations in the African housing sector.

For social entrepreneurship to succeed in the developing world, the fundamental issues of funding and official corruption must be addressed. Evidence has proven that official corruption is a barrier to economic growth and development, official corruption diverts funds and talents away from real investments into political rent-seeking (political lobbying, influencing judges, and currying favour with bureaucrats). This will have a negative impact on the development of a social housing market in any country (Krueger 1974; Murphy et al. 1991). Secondly, the actors working for sustainable change need to adopt strategies creatively to tackle the problem of funding. Housing Finance in Sub-Saharan Africa remains critically inaccessible for most people. Inaccessibility is defined by high-interest rates and short-loan tenures that make it untenable for mortgage seekers.

Key conclusions that emerged from the ILO (2016) study include:

- The social economy has the potential to create jobs, improve service delivery and foster greater social cohesion and social inclusion.
- Procurement policies and legislation are alienating and difficult.
- There is not enough conversation encouraging engagement with, and development of, the social economy.
- Support services, both financial and non-financial, are essential for the establishment and sustainability of social economy enterprises.

Social enterprises require administrative and business services and support to successfully navigate the procurement process, especially with writing proposals and business plans; obtaining/achieving certification and other compliance requirements; and registering on supplier databases. Mentoring can go a long way in building the capacity of emerging enterprises, helping them to become independent, self-sustainable business enterprises. Furthermore, social enterprises often require start-up or seed funding to establish their business (i.e., enterprise development funding). A lack of funding opportunities is a critical issue that can be addressed by political will, policy development and implementation by tapping into existing social capital. Given Sub-Saharan Africa's extensive resource base of social capital and long history and tradition of catalysing community self-help projects by clubs, town unions and abroad groups, a foundation exists for social innovation in housing provision in the region.

## REFERENCES

Alter, K. (2007). *Social Enterprise Typology*. Virtue Ventures LLC.

Beugre, C. (2017). *Social Entrepreneurship, Managing the Creation of Social Value*. Routhledge.

Capaldi, N. (2005). Introduction. In N. Capaldi (Ed.), *Business and Religion: A Clash of Civilizations?* M&M Scrivener Press.

Chimphondah, A. (2019). The Past, present & future of affordable housing in Africa. *Affordable Housing Investment Summit Africa.*

Coetzee, M. (2016). *Introduction to Social Enterprises in South Africa*. Presented at the Graduate School of Business, University of Cape Town.

Community Housing Aotearoa. (2015). *Details Matter: Taking Stock of the Community Housing Sector in Aotearoa*. Community Housing Aotearoa.

Defourny, J., & Nyssens, M. (2001). Belgium: Social Enterprises in Community Services. Academic Press.

Department of Trade and Industry (DTI). (2004). www.dti.gov.uk/socialenterprise/

Dey, K., & Grant, S. (2014). Maori Communities as Social Enterprise. In H. Douglas & S. Grant (Eds.), *Social Entrepreneurship and Enterprise. Concepts in Context* (pp. 194–216). Tilde University Press.

Emoh, F. I., Ajator, U. O., & Ugonabo, C. U. (2016). Urban infrastructure financing and management in Nigeria. *Global Journal of Advanced Research, 3*(6), 492–504.

English, B., & Bennett, P. (2015). *Social Housing Reform Programme: Overview (Paper one)*. New Zealand Government.

English, B., & Coleman, J. (2015). *Budget 2015: Social Bond to Focus on Mental Health*. New Zealand Government.

Genesis Housing Association. (2014). *Annual accounts*. https://www.genesisha.org.uk/PDF/Finance_Statements_2014.pdf

Grant, S. (2015). *Social Housing in New Zealand: Does Social Enterprise Fit into this Mix?* University of Waikato.

Ibimilua, A. F., & Ibitoye, O. A. (2015). Housing policy in Nigeria: An overview. *American International Journal of Contemporary Research, 5*(2).

International Labour Organisation. (2016). *Private and public procurement and the social economy project: best practice case studies from South Africa*. ILO.

Iyortsuun, A. S. (2015). A conceptual overview of social entrepreneurship and its relevance to the Nigeria's third sector. *International Journal of Small Business and Entrepreneurship Research, 3*(4), 32-51. www.eajournals.org

Kerlin, J. A. (2006). *Social Enterprise in the United States and Europe: Understanding and Learning from the Differences*. International Society for Third-Sector Research and The Johns Hopkins University.

Kerlin, J. A. (2010a). A comparative analysis of the global emergence of social enterprise. *Voluntas, 21*(2), 162–179.

Kerlin, J. A. (2010b). *Historical institutionalism and social enterprise development: Towards a conceptual framework for comparative social enterprise*. Working Paper. www.istr.org/resource/resmgr/Istanbul_abstracts/ISTR2010_0580.pdf

Krueger, A. (1974). The political economy of the rent seeking society. *The American Economic Review*, *64*, 291–303.

Malloch, T. R. (2005). Spirituality and Entrepreneurship. In N. Capaldi (Ed.), *Business and Religion A Clash of Civilizations?* M&M Scrivener Press.

Malloch, T. R. (2008). *Doing Virtuous Business: The Remarkable Success of Spiritual Enterprise*. Thomas Nelson.

Murphy, K. M., Shleifer, A., & Vishny, R. W. (1991). The allocation of talent: Implication for Growth. *The Quarterly Journal of Economics*, (May), 503–530.

Nliam, A. (2021). *N200bn social housing facility ready for disbursement*. https://von.gov.ng/amp/2021/05/31/n200bn-social-housing-facility-ready-for-disbursement

OECD. (2003). *The Non-Profit Sector in a Changing Economy*. OECD.

Oham, C., & Macdonald, D. (2016). *Leading and Managing a Social Enterprise in Health and Social Care*. Community Training Partners.

Oham, C., Stewart, J., & Cornish, Y. (2009). Social Capital, Social Enterprise and Community Development. In J. Stewart & Y. Cornish (Eds.), *Professional Practice in Public Health*. Reflect Press.

Social Enterprise Alliance. (2004). www.se-alliance.org

South Africa Social Housing Act No.16 of 2008.

Swann, S. L., & Morgan, M. (Eds.). (2002). Social capital: Insights from qualitative research. Academic Press.

The Nigerian National Housing Policy (2012).

Tusting, L. S., Bisanzio, D., Alabaster, G., Cameron, E., Cibulskis, R., Davies, M., Flaxman, S., Gibson, H. S., Jakob Knudsen, J., Mbogo, C., Okumu, F. O., von Seidlein, L., Weiss, D. J., Lindsay, S. W., Gething, P. W., & Bhatt, S. (2019). Mapping changes in housing in sub-Saharan Africa from 2000 to 2015. *Nature Research Letter*. doi:10.1038/s41586-019-1050-5

Tusting, L. S., Gething, P. W., Gibson, H. S., Greenwood, B., Knudsen, J., Lindsay, S. W., & Bhatt, S. (2020). Housing and child health in Sub-Saharan Africa: A cross-sectional analysis. *PLoS Medicine*, *17*(3). https://doi.org/10.1371/journal.pmed.1003055

Vanguard. (2016). *FG plans #1trn social housing scheme*. www.vanguard.com/2016/10/fgplans-n1trn-social housing-scheme/

Whitehead, C., & Scanlon, K. J. (Eds.). (2007). *Social Housing in Europe*. London School of Economics and Political Science.

# Chapter 6
# Hugging Like Koalas Do: The Story of KitapKoala, a Social Enterprise From Istanbul, Turkey

**Ela Burcu Uçel**
https://orcid.org/0000-0001-7210-9476
*İzmir University of Economics, Turkey*

## EXECUTIVE SUMMARY

*The purpose of this paper is to present a social entrepreneur and his social enterprise from Istanbul, Turkey. It is aimed to provide a real-life example for social entrepreneurship readers which would show the entrepreneurial motives, the start-up problems, market struggles, and the hardships caused by the COVID-19 pandemic. Changing the world is hard work. Social entrepreneurs are the pioneers that accept the hard work and take action. As the examples are more visible, more people can be inspired to step in. This case study hopes to be a means of inspiring new social entrepreneurs.*

## INTRODUCTION

*...the truth is, there are no superheroes. There is just us, and too often we are the ones that we keep waiting for. (Shiza Sahid, the co-founder of The Malala Fund (Pacor, 2015))*

We live in a world where the prominent mindset glorifies wealth, defines success in financial terms and uses up resources recklessly. The same mindset creates the perception that, if we want change, we need saviours to do that: there is not much

DOI: 10.4018/978-1-7998-7724-0.ch006

we can do as individuals. Movies and books keep telling us stories of superheroes that make a change and we know that we are not one. That very fact – *we are not superheroes* – might bring us to the understanding that if it's only us, then it is us, who should change the world.

Social entrepreneurs are the ones who stop waiting for someone as a saviour. They are clearly aware of the social problems and needs. They take responsibility and action to change what they are able to change. They accept the entrepreneurial risks and establish social enterprises. As businesses are widely seen as the fundamental causes of social, economic and environmental problems (Porter and Kramer, 2011), social enterprises are like superheroes that make a difference and contribute to a better image for 'the businesses' and, social entrepreneurs are 'panacea to failure in market and state mechanisms' (Parkinson and Howorth, 2008, pp.292) Businesses are 'increasingly judged on the basis of their relationships with their workers, their customers, and their communities, as well as their impact on society at large' (Social Enterprise Alliance, 2018, pp. 2). As a result of the social pressure towards businesses regarding the harm they cause, there has been an increasing corporate tendency on improving stakeholder welfare, in addition to maximising shareholder value (Awaysheh and Bonfiglio, 2017). Businesses engage in corporate philanthropy and emphasise acting in a socially responsible manner. This is how we distinguish social enterprises from commercial ones: their *value propositions*. While commercial enterprises primarily create financial value and personal wealth through satisfying needs and wants; social enterprises exist to create social value through solving social problems (Austin et.al., 2006). Commercial enterprises have financial and market-related goals whereas social enterprises have social goals (Certo and Miller, 2008; Van de Ven. Et.al, 2007).

Dees (1998) describes social entrepreneurs as change agents who have the mission of creating a sustainable social value whilst continuously innovating and pursuing new opportunities to serve that mission. Ashoka's (2012) definition is also similar 'Social entrepreneurs are individuals with innovative solutions to society's most pressing social problems.' They create new ways and models to solve social problems and add social value.

As mentioned earlier, businesses increasingly emphasise improving stakeholder value and developing responsible leadership practices. Similarly, social enterprises are now the focus of attention. Thus, experiential learning materials may well serve business and social entrepreneurship students and readers in their efforts to better understand this hot topic (Awaysheh and Bonfiglio, 2017; Short et. al, 2009). In such an attempt, this paper will present the short case of a social entrepreneur from Istanbul, Turkey and the social enterprise he created and will share their story.

## ESTABLISHING KITAPKOALA

Dr. Umut Kısa remembers the tiny little kitten he accidentally hurt in an attempt to protect it, when he was four. From then, he felt indebted to animals. After becoming an accomplished business person in publishing and at a certain economic welfare, he decided it was time to pay back in 2018. He wanted to take action to help animals in need. Inspired by a National Geographic documentary, he first thought of buying an ambulance and hiring the required staff which would respond to animals' emergencies. In a second thought, the plan did not sound like working in the long run. There were other options, like donating and volunteering to an NGO, or establishing an NGO, but these did not seem sustainable to him. s NGOs were experiencing a decline of support from philanthropists and governments (Alter, 2007). He wanted this effort to help, to be independent of him (or other donators) and his (or others') financial resources, so that it could last longer. The model he needed was one which would be self-sufficient in the long term and would continue even if he didn't have the resources needed for support: *a social enterprise.*

Like many other countries, Turkey was experiencing an increase in the social entrepreneurship efforts back then, in 2018. According to 2019 data, there are almost 9,000 social enterprises in the country, which generally operate in education, manufacturing, and creative industries. Most of them were established after 2015 and located in big cities like Istanbul, İzmir and the capital, Ankara. Their legal status varied: sole traders, associations, limited companies, cooperatives, corporations and foundations. Almost half (%55) is owned and operated by women. The leaders/ founders are mostly young (47%) and the vast majority is highly educated (%83) (British Council, Turkey, 2019).

Eighty-six percent of the social enterprises have reportedly developed a new model, product or service in the last year, which indicates being highly innovative. There are intermediary organisations in the country, which support the social enterprise ecosystem: co-working spaces, accelerators, and incubators. Additionally, research institutes, universities, local administrators, funding bodies and government agencies try to encourage and promote them.

Although the context seems promising, social entrepreneurs and enterprises operate in a quite unfavourable setting, as Turkey was listed last, among the 44 countries in providing necessary support and atmosphere (British Council Report on Social Enterprises in Turkey, 2019).

As a fan of the movie 'Star Wars' Dr. Kısa groups people in two: Jedis and those who stand on the dark side. The dark siders are people who solely focus on personal interest, whereas Jedis are the ones who think of themselves and others. Jedis are people who not only avoid hurting a fly but also help a fly when it is hurt. In deciding to start a social enterprise Dr. Kısa was motivated by this: He didn't want to ask for donations from the Jedis, because they were already doing what they could contribute to several causes. Given the fact that all resources are retained by the capitalist system, he needed a model which operated in the system, earned even than the dark siders and used the outcomes to serve a social goal. He says 'Even Marx (1867) wouldn't object if we used the surplus value for the animals'.

KitapKoala's philosophy, which is shared on company's web site, nicely communicates this mindset:

*Humans are intrinsically good. They do not want others to suffer, but they are not aware they should help, unless they see those in need. The NGOs – although they create a great amount of good – are far from getting support of the majority that fail to see those in need. That's why they have trouble in getting donations. Even if they get donations, as a result of bureaucratic costs, they lose their flexibility and mostly are able to continue with the short-term dedicated efforts of a few. The non-profit organisations are usually far from being result oriented. The organisations that have access to greatest resources are not the NGOs, they are the for-profits.*

*Thus, for-profits should fund the good cause. When for-profits are embedded with a social goal and they are managed by people who have entrepreneurial skills, great and strong resources can be retained.*

*KitapKoala is a for-profit organization with the social cause of funding the medical treatments of stray animals. In commercial enterprises, the profit is added to the shareholders' wealth, in KitapKoala the profit belongs to stray animals. That's why stray animals are the partners of KitapKoala's board of directors.*

*One of the main goals of our system is to set an inspiring example for other businesses to adopt similar business models.*

Dr. Kisa took a step and established a national online bookstore called KitapKoala with an initial capital of 100,000 TL. Then and now, the online bookstore industry is dominated by a number of giants in Turkey. They provide a huge variety of books, with fast delivery and low prices. Their huge sales volumes enable economies of scale and they can operate with satisfactory profit margins even at lowest prices. They usually have successful customer relationship marketing practices and they follow the motto: '*customer is always right*'. On the other side, there are small online bookstores, most of which are newly established and struggle to attract customers by decreasing the prices even further. They aim to grab a market share and wish to have enough sales volumes so that they can be profitable. Most of them cannot survive in the long-term but, in the meantime, they lower the prices to unsustainable levels.

## BUSINESS MODEL OF KITAPKOALA

That was how the market looked like when KitapKoala started business. The enterprise was named after the Koala bears for a reason:

Trying to keep up with the product variety, fast delivery and low prices of the giants and also competing with the even lower prices of other small online businesses...The only way to survive among them, was to differentiate (Porter, 2005). KitapKoala identified its target market as candid, real and sensible people who love books and created its one-of-a-kind way of communication with them. There is a special KitapKoala way of approaching the customers: *hugging them like Koalas do*. The way they address the customers via emails and on the phone; the way they designed the web site. Customers can find many books, with fast delivery and low prices in other bookstores, but KitapKoala offers them an extra Koala way of hugging. The cold corporate language that one experiences when buying from the giants, versus the Koalan language which warmly hugs you. Their motto is also different from the rivals: '*customer is right, only when he is right.*' So, KitapKoala wants to have customers who accept when they are wrong. They do not hesitate to avoid serving customers who do not empathise or try to understand the other party.

### The Mission

Dr. Kisa says he has seen many philanthropists and NGOs that lose focus because they want to answer every call for help and try to help everyone. Every time, the result was a failure. He believes keeping the initial mission and the goal in mind is the key to sustainable operations. Thus, KitapKoala identified its mission: *to help animals that suffer* and focused only on helping them. No other calls for support were answered.

### The System

Stray animals are a distressing social problem in Turkey. There is an estimated number of 130,000 stray dogs and 125,000 stray cats only in Istanbul, based on 2017 data (Istanbul Municipality Report, 2017). They face many threats in the streets: hunger, human violence, health problems, extreme weather conditions and other human-related risks, like traffic. They need human help for feeding and health problems. KitapKoala's mission starts here. They use the profits for stray animals' medical treatments. The previous year's profit constitutes the budget dedicated for the cause. The animal-lovers can apply to KitapKoala for funds granted to stray animals via the web site. The applications are evaluated and the budget is divided in order to help the maximum number of animals in need. KitapKoala has a partnering NGO,

HipDer. This NGO also aims to help stray animals. They identify animals in need of medical treatment, provide the treatment via a veterinarian and pass the bill to KitapKoala.

The partnering organisation was selected by KitapKoala's customers: an announcement was made on the web site, asking for an organisation to cooperate. HipDer was offered by the majority of customers.

KitapKoala solely relies on profits coming from the operations in reaching its social goal; no donations are accepted. Because they think that relying on external support will decrease their innovative capabilities and the organisational skills would become dull. Thus, they have two balanced priorities: ***economic value creation*** to fund ***social value creation*** (Peredo and McLean, 2006). They have a funding mechanism which is the bookstore and a program mechanism through which funds are provided for animals in need. These mechanisms are interdependent (Alter, 2007). In KitapKoala's case, the wealth generated is simply the means to the social end targeted (Dees, 1998). Thus, the company fits into the definition of an *integrated social enterprise*, offered by Fowler (2000); the income generating activity (bookstore) is directly aimed at creating social value (helping animals).

As Dees (1998) suggested, social enterprises can be placed along a spectrum: moving from purely commercial ones to purely philanthropic ones; KitapKoala falls somewhere near the latter end of that spectrum. It provides benefits for the social cause and invests in the business so that it is sustainable in the long-term (Dees, 1998).

Profits go to animals, but what happens when KitapKoala is not making profits? They set the system in such a way that funds are still provided even there are no profits. The medical treatments of animals are named as an expense of the company.

The cause KitapKoala serves does not provide any privileges in business operations. None of the suppliers provide any additional discounts or favours just because they have a cause. Some occasionally support KitapKoala in other ways. Besides this, 98% of customers prefer the brand because of its Koalan language, fast delivery and reasonable prices. Only 2% stick to KitapKoala for the cause and say that they would buy books from them even if they were the most expensive in the market.

## The Human Element

When the business was first established, KitapKoala didn't have any employees of its own. The employees of Dr. Kısa's other company worked for KitapKoala for some time. Now, after three years, the company has 15 employees. Dr. Kısa says, the employees are so devoted and committed to the cause and inspired by it that, KitapKoala is able to continue operations with only 15 people whereas their competitors have around 50 employees. The way they own the business and the way they feel about the cause is so powerful that, they triple the effort of competitors' employees. The organisational climate is warm; it is like a university campus. The employees are highly educated and qualified. This is another reason why the business can run operations with such a small number of employees. They create value, they innovate and come up with new ideas that contribute to the business and the cause. KitapKoala enjoys a very high human productivity.

Dr. Kisa passed the management onto the employees to focus on his other business. Now, there is a non-hierarchical organisation which is managed by a seven-member leaderless team. There are no titles. The team formulates and executes the strategy, continues operations and controls the processes. They use a 360-degree performance evaluation method in which all employees self-evaluate and are evaluated by their colleagues. 'Who to hire or fire' is also decided by the team. Although there is no officially assigned leader, – by all means – a lot of leadership takes place during decision making, conflict resolution and motivation processes (Choi and Schnurr, 2014).

Managing a social enterprise requires improving efficiencies and effectiveness in both the funding and programme mechanisms. It necessitates being able to apply different approaches in two sides. Thus, the team members should have blended skills and experience- business and social (Alter, 2007). KitapKoala ensured the system to work sound, via the fully empowered, young, qualified and dedicated employees.

## KITAPKOALA AND THE COVID-19 PANDEMIC

In February 2019, KitapKoala opened its first brick and mortar bookstore with a huge investment. It was one of the biggest bookstores in the country and was of huge excitement for the KitapKoala family. But things didn't go as expected and the Covid-19 pandemic started. It was an unknown illness and thus, required strict measures of isolation and protection. The following warnings and lockdowns caused a sharp decline in the number of shop visitors and sales. KitapKoala did not lay off any employees despite the severe economic situation. Dr. Kısa says 'We established the business to care for animals, is it possible to harm our own, in a hardship?' The shop was incurring a loss of 100,000 TL every month. The landlord gave a 50% discount for the first two months. But later, the loss was back.

After some time, the internet sales increased enormously. But this boom in sales was not favourable for KitapKoala. The system was able to handle 150 shipments a day; suddenly there were 350 daily shipments. They couldn't cope with the sudden growth. They were obliged to stop operations and close the web site for five days. In time, the sales were balanced and the system was able to overcome higher numbers of shipments than the normal. Additionally, online sales figures were able to compensate some percentage of the brick-and-mortar sales losses. But things went bad in the summer. Both online and shop sales dropped significantly. KitapKoala was incurring losses every month, it needed urgent financial support. This is a common problem for most social enterprises in Turkey, as 65% are looking for external financing to continue operations (British Council Report on Social Enterprises in Turkey, 2019). That's the point where Dr. Kısa stepped in. His commercial enterprise had receivables from a publishing house which was a supplier of KitapKoala at the same time. That receivable was transferred to KitapKoala and the financial trouble was dealt with. KitapKoala was in debt now to Dr. Kısa's company and problem was solved.

## KITAPKOALA - NOW

In its third year, KitapKoala has an asset size of 3 billion TL and 30,000 annual book sales despite the Covid-19 pandemic and the resulting economic crisis. It is able to compete with the giants in fast delivery and low prices. It has a 600 $m^2$ store on one of the most popular and crowded streets of Istanbul and despite having no profits, it funded the treatment of almost 100 stray animals.

The future looks promising. Dr. Kisa and the KitapKoala team has very positive expectations for the post-Covid business life. These tough times proved their strength: if KitapKoala is able to survive even in this extraordinarily hard circumstance, then it will do much better when things change for better.

## CONCLUSION

There are plenty of ways to define a social enterprise. If we choose to look at all the common characteristics that they have (Thompson and Doherty, 2006):

- SEs have a social purpose;
- SEs use their assets and the wealth they create for community benefit;
- SE profits are used for the cause;
- SEs try to serve community benefit (sometimes partly) by operating in a certain market;
- SE employees or members have some degree of control or role in governance;
- SEs try to have both healthy financial structures and successful social outcomes.

We see that KitapKoala sets a good example to examine and think over. Its story, the hardships and the solutions told, may light the way of and inspire future social entrepreneurs.

As the world becomes overwhelmed by social, environmental and financial problems, and people become more and more pessimistic, the value provided by social entrepreneurs becomes more visible. They are the agents who try to maximise social benefit. When it is a time of despair, it is a time of action. We know that we (agents) do not create the structures. However, it is impossible to create, maintain or change the structures without us (Sarason et.al, 2008, 2010). We also know that all humans are given all that it takes to change the world (Bornstein, 2005).

## REFERENCES

Alter, K. (2007). *Social Enterprise Typology.* http://www.virtueventures.com/setypology

Ashoka. (2012). Social entrepreneurship: Definition and boundaries. *Technology Innovation Management Review*, (February), 24.

Austin, J., Stevenson, H., & Wei-Skillern, J. (2006). Social and commercial entrepreneurship: Same, different, or both? *Entrepreneurship Theory and Practice*, *30*(1), 1–22. doi:10.1111/j.1540-6520.2006.00107.x

Awaysheh, A., & Bonfiglio, D. (2017). Leveraging experiential learning to incorporate social entrepreneurship in MBA programs: A case study. *International Journal of Management Education*, *15*(2), 332–349. doi:10.1016/j.ijme.2017.04.001

Bornstein, D. (2005). *How to change the world: social entrepreneurs and the power of new ideas*. Penguin Books.

British Council. (2019). *Report on Social Enterprises in Turkey*. https://www.britishcouncil.org.tr/programmes/education/social-enterprise-research

British Council, Turkey. (2019). *The State of Social Enterprise in Turkey*. Available at: https://www.britishcouncil.org.tr/en/programmes/education/social-enterprise-research

Certo, S. T., & Miller, T. (2008). Social entrepreneurship: Key issues and concepts. *Business Horizons*, *51*(4), 267–271. doi:10.1016/j.bushor.2008.02.009

Choi, S., & Schnurr, S. (2014). Exploring distributed leadership: Solving disagreements and negotiating consensus in a "leaderless" team. *Discourse Studies*, *16*(1), 3–24. doi:10.1177/1461445613508891

Dees, J. G. (1998). Enterprising non-profits. *Harvard Business Review*, *76*, 54–67. PMID:10176919

Fowler, A. (2000). NGDOs as a moment in history: Beyond aid to social entrepreneurship or civic innovation? *Third World Quarterly*, *21*(4), 637–654. doi:10.1080/713701063

Marx, K. (1959). *Das Kapital, a critique of political economy*. H. Regnery.

Municipality, İ. (2017). *Report on stray animals*. https://www.trthaber.com/haber/yasam/istanbuldaki-sahipsiz-kedi-kopek-sayisi-aciklandi-311559.html

Pacor, I. (2015). Shiza Shahid's 3 Lessons for Being a Change-Maker (Capes and Masks Not Included). *Educational Tours*. Retrieved from https://blog.eftours.com/ef/events/shiza-shahids-3-lessons-for-being-a-change-maker

Parkinson, C., & Howorth, C. (2008). The language of social entrepreneurs. *Entrepreneurship and Regional Development*, *20*(3), 285–309. doi:10.1080/08985620701800507

Peredo, A. M., & McLean, M. (2006). Social entrepreneurship: A critical review of the concept. *Journal of World Business*, *41*(1), 56–65. doi:10.1016/j.jwb.2005.10.007

Porter, M. E. (1985). *Competitive Advantage*. The Free Press.

Porter, M. E., & Kramer, M. R. (2011). Creating shared value. *Harvard Business Review*, *89*(1/2), 62–77.

Sarason, Y., Dean, T., & Dillard, J. (2006). Entrepreneurship as the nexus of individual and opportunity: A structuration view. *Journal of Business Venturing*, *21*(3), 285–305. doi:10.1016/j.jbusvent.2005.02.007

Sarason, Y., Dean, T., & Dillard, J. (2010). How can we know the dancer from the dance? *Journal of Business Venturing*, *25*(2), 238–243. doi:10.1016/j.jbusvent.2008.06.003

Short, J. C., Todd, W. M., & Lumpkin, G. T. (2009). Research in social entrepreneurship: Past contributions and future opportunities. *Strategic Entrepreneurship Journal*, *3*(2), 161–194. doi:10.1002ej.69

Social Enterprise Alliance. (2018). *Trends in giving report*. https://socialenterprise.us/article/trends-in-giving-report-2018/

Thompson, J. L., & Doherty, B. (2006). The diverse world of social enterprise. *International Journal of Social Economics*, *33*(5/6), 361–375. doi:10.1108/03068290610660643

Van De Van, A. H., Sapienza, H. J., & Villanueva, J. (2007). Entrepreneurial pursuits of self and collective interests. *Strategic Entrepreneurship Journal, 1*(3-4), 353–370. doi:10.1002ej.34

# Chapter 7
# Entrepreneurial Parenting Through Spiritual Capital:
## A Case Study on First Fruit Group Social Enterprise

**Charles A. Oham**
*University of Greenwich, UK*

**Nathaniel Massa**
*University of Malta, Malta*

## EXECUTIVE SUMMARY

*This study aligns with the objectives of this volume, presenting cases reflecting social entrepreneurs' lived experiences, seeking understanding, and conveying learning from practitioners and their emergent approaches embedded in contextual realities. Adopting an interpretative approach, this chapter presents First Fruit Group (FFG) as an illustrative case derived from a broader study – highlighting various dimensions of entrepreneurial parenting identified as core elements in the nurturing process at FFG and manifested in the relationship between social entrepreneur and mentee. Evidently fundamental for FFG's growth, it extended strategic vision and raison d'être continuity in leadership succession, motivating new opportunity exploitation and sustaining the group's enterprising expansion.*

## INTRODUCTION

This study aligns with the objectives of this volume, presenting cases reflecting social entrepreneurs' lived experiences, seeking understanding and conveying learning

DOI: 10.4018/978-1-7998-7724-0.ch007

from practitioners and their emergent approaches – embedded in contextual realities.

Adopting an interpretative approach, this chapter presents First Fruit Group (FFG) as an illustrative case study. It highlights a number of dimensions of entrepreneurial parenting identified as core elements in the nurturing process at FFG and manifested in the relationship between social entrepreneur and mentee. Evidently, fundamental for FFG's growth, it extended strategic vision and raison d'être continuity in leadership succession, motivating new opportunity exploitation. This contributed directly to sustaining the group's enterprising expansion.

Founded in a London borough by Rev Peter and Mrs Hannah Watherston in 1997, First Fruit grew into a group of social businesses and projects providing supported accommodation, employment and work-related training for homeless people and the long-term unemployed. Founded on Christian principles, FFG works with people of all faiths and none (First Fruit Group, 2021).

We extend Lindquist, et al.'s (2015) work on 'parental entrepreneurship' and role modelling, to include spiritual capital emanating from religion as a channel and leveraged source of entrepreneurial parenting in this context. This leads to dimensions of entrepreneurial parenting taking on a broader view of the concept which, in this case, are observed to sustain and enhance continuity in strategic vision and growth; aligned with the enterprise's social remit.

Emanating from exploratory research, in-depth semi-structured interviews are conducted with the current FFG Managing Director (MD). The concept of spiritual capital, a major area of growing research interest, is investigated. Drawing on established metaphorical perspectives, we explore how the entrepreneur's inductive mentoring and protracted nurturing, coupled with transcended strong spiritual faith was inculcated in her entrepreneurial endeavours and resilience in the face of challenges – inspiring decision-making manifested in subsequent exploited opportunities – extending and multiplying social value.

In this regard, our research converges ensuing findings from the perspective of three interrelated and mutually reinforcing entrepreneurial parenting dimensions we observed. We posit a *supernatural* dimension of entrepreneurial parenting drawing from strong spiritual capital, permeating a sense of higher purpose and deep-seated social mission. The *natural* dimension relates to the upcoming future-entrepreneur's conventional nurturing and mentoring by biological or 'adoptive' entrepreneurial parents. Eventually, both complementary dimensions are ultimately sustained by the recipient emergent *entrepreneur* who perpetuates this cycle; in turn evangelising social responsibility in their own organisation's culture, while fostering a strong enterprising attitude in their employees and future leaders – through conscientious nurturing and committed leadership.

Providing useful contextual insights on these dynamics, our study observes spiritual capital as a critical formative influence on the Managing Directors (MD's) development as a social entrepreneur. It also presents opportunities for further research informing trainers and policymakers through exploring potential adoption of various relevant aspects.

This offers potential to enhance mentoring, succession, and leadership aspects; as well as reinforcing organisational culture elements, towards building and sustaining visionary direction and entrepreneurial training. Such a perspective presents complementary awareness ensuring no stage in the nurturing and/or parenting process is left out in striving to enhance organisations' long-term sustainability in strategically providing enduring social value.

## BACKGROUND

Social enterprise and third-sector dynamics converge increasingly urgent attention on sustainability and value creation in social and environmental contexts. Current times arouse public awareness, clamouring for corporate social responsibility (CSR) and mounting regulatory pressure. Social demands and environmental concerns, spurned by incessant corporate scandals question shareholder primacy in employed capitalist ideals, sounding a clarion call (Geldres-Weiss et al., 2021). Held to account, this pressing call is today increasingly heeded by politicians and policymakers; sometimes also acknowledged by corporate industry titans themselves[1].

Yet even before today's in-vogue environmental, social and governance (ESG) expectations and mandated compliance, scholars perceived a long-apparent trend in progressive erosion of ethical and moral values in business, enterprise interaction and society. Combined with momentum-gathering disenchantment post-global financial crisis, this has seen a broad sentiment towards 'de-secularisation' and a call for the 'remoralising' of public life (e.g., Baker et al., 2011). For example, the recent work of economist and Nobel laureate Stieglitz and others, outlines the role of religion and ethics in economics and business in relation to sustainability, equity and mutually reinforcing social value. This has, in turn, seen the emergent notion of 'spiritual capital' – beyond the established domain of social capital (Fukuyama, 2005; Putnam, 2000).

Often attributed different terms, such as *religious-* or *faith-*, 'spiritual capital' is considered an enduring reserve that also accrues value in organisational and business interactions at various levels – whether manifested in resilience and an enduring belief in opportunities identified at the level of the entrepreneur; or in performance-enhancing cohesion and shared vision at the level of the organisation interfacing with its clients; or even at broader community level (Mas-Machuca & Marimon, 2019).

Particularly relevant in the context of faith-based social entrepreneurship, we consider spiritual capital as an effective basis enhancing entrepreneurial parenting and mentoring. In this case, given the extent of sustained nurturing for the purposes of coaching and succession, grooming next generation leadership; and the strongly shared religious belief and value systems – we extend the notion of parenting beyond the biological, to also include the intimate non-family mentoring and spiritual dimensions manifested in this context. This offers potential for useful insights and extending understanding on the dynamics at play. For example, Lundmark et al. (2017, p. 139) emphasise the importance of metaphors in theory development, underlining that the influence of such figuratively applied parent and familial leadership images extended on entrepreneurship theorising remains unexplored. Articulating value from such approaches, they note:

*Metaphors function through a comparison of concepts, where one is understood as the other (Morgan, 2006), but meaning is not just transferred from the source to the target domains; rather, meaning emerges through a blend of relationships between the source and the target (Cornelissen, 2006a, 2006b). [...] Thus, the use of metaphor is a creative act that offers a different way of understanding a phenomenon and challenges taken-for-granted ways of thinking (Morgan, 2006, 2016); that is, metaphors not only efficiently transfer complex ideas between two domains (Morgan, 1980, 2006), but they also help us discover new aspects of the domains and their related phenomena. (Berti, 2017; Black, 1962; Cornelissen, 2006b; Fauconnier & Turner, 1998)*

Thus, using FFG as a case, we explore the lived metaphorical manifestation of entrepreneurial parenting and spiritual capital dynamics in the context of social entrepreneurship and succession. We provide preliminary qualitative insights into their role in influencing continuity in an entrepreneurial direction, maintaining sustained social value creation, and enhancing enterprise growth through strategic vision and opportunity exploitation. This, while successfully preserving the organisation's raison d'être and social remit: 'harvesting skills for enterprise and mission' and 'more choice for those in need' (First Fruit Group, 2021).

The next section proceeds by consolidating broad theoretical perspectives and supporting literature converging at this nexus. Following that, the methodological approach is articulated. An overview case profile of FFG's MD is presented, and the discussion proceeds with findings emanating from the study. Finally, in concluding, salient observations are drawn, presenting practical relevance while outlining limitations and highlighting areas for further research.

# THEORY AND SUPPORTING LITERATURE

## Entrepreneurship, Parenting, and Metaphoric Manifestations

Entrepreneurs begin a journey of entrepreneurship through the exploitation of recognised opportunities, figuratively 'birthing' new ventures or start-ups. This results from various factors such as entrepreneurial learning vicariously achieved through role modelling, apprenticeships and mentoring; and a combination of push and pull factors (Jack & Anderson 1999; Bloemen-Bekx et al. 2019; Kuanunai, 2008). Such activity prospects sustainability, continuity and succession – not only at the level of the entrepreneur or enterprise (e.g., in the case of a family business succeeding to the next generation) – but also more broadly, in potential for perpetuating wellbeing and growth in socio-economic terms.

Together with personality traits, scholars researching pathways to successful entrepreneurship have long highlighted parenting influencing entrepreneurship (e.g., Bloemen-Bekx et al., 2019; Staniewski & Awruk, 2021) – upcoming generations' decision to become self-employed (Chlosta et al., 2010), as well as entrepreneurial competence (EC) and entrepreneurial interests (EI). Schmitt-Rodermund (2004) linked 'authoritative parenting' to adolescent EC among both students and small business founders. Similarly, Wijaya et al. (2018) empirically observed such parenting influencing risk propensity and EI – transmission taking place from parents to children, with even grandparents playing a role (Laspita et al., 2012). In their conceptual paper, Jiang et al. (2017, p. 13) posit that aspects of parenting, both inside and outside the family business context, 'contribute to the expression of entrepreneurial intentions and behaviours in adulthood', amplifying linkages between intentions and behaviors.

Lindquist et al., (2015) explore the origins of intergenerational association in entrepreneurship and find that parental entrepreneurship increases the probability of childrens' entrepreneurship by 60%. Yet aligned with our objectives, they further study such linkages among biological as well as adoptive parents. They contribute to the body of literature by decomposing intergenerational transmission of entrepreneurship into pre- and post-birth allowing them to measure the relative importance of nature and nurture in the reproduction of entrepreneurship from one generation to the other. Interestingly, their findings crucially reveal that, 'both biological and adoptive parents make significant contributions. However, the impact of post-birth factors (i.e., the influence of adoptive parents) is approximately twice as great as the impact of pre-birth factors (i.e., the influence of biological parents)" (p. 270).

In line with this predominant nurture element, and the contextual relevance of our study, we extend the notion of parenting beyond the biological – to include 'adoptive' entrepreneurial leaders who act in such a capacity. At FFG the founder,

Rev Watherston, developed a close sustained relationship with his staff as a result of spiritual capital – a subset of social capital which includes levels of reciprocity among people of a similar association or grouping, which can be a family, group or community (Oham, 2009). Aligned with our study's underpinning rationale, we extend the powerful case-relevant metaphors of family, parenting and propagation to beyond biological family association, transcending organisational and spiritual domains in this context.

It is not uncommon for committed founders leading close-knit dedicated teams to paternalistically or maternalistically refer to non-family employees as their 'children'; or even the organisation itself as their 'baby' or 'one family'. Indeed, in such cases 'family' has symbolic meaning and ideological significance – suggesting normative unity and commitment; shared values and understandings (Ainsworth & Cox, 2003; Haugh & McKee, 2003). A metaphorical family (Vincent Ponroy et al., 2019) is actually 'just like a family', based on 'the shared values of a sense of belonging, honesty, loyalty, trust and respect' (Haugh & McKee 2003, p. 141). Similarly, organisational leaders acting as role models or moral stewards are figuratively seen as and referred to as a 'parent' by their subordinates (Johnson, 2017, p. 843).

Complementarily, from a spiritual perspective, for example, 'God the Father' is attributed powerful divine paternal imagery in Christian theology (e.g., *Pater Noster*, The Lord's Prayer, also known as the Our Father; The Holy Bible, Literal Standard Version (2020), Matthew 6:9–13, and Luke 11:2–4). In this light, one observes biblical parallels aligned with biological, as well as human interactional and parental aspects in propagation, nurturing, growing, and enduring sustainability; also to be fruitful in perpetuating value and good, aligned with core aspects of (especially social) entrepreneurialism.

Whilst not intending to investigate any religious associations in their research on family firm identity maintenance by non-family members, Vincent Ponroy et al. (2019, p. 872) coincidentally observed the consolidation of earthly and spiritual parental metaphors. Non-family respondents in their study, referred to their 'religiously admired' founder as a 'incarnated god who knew everything'. Notwithstanding the founder's passing away, employees reported a persisting cult-like admiration, maintaining 'family' continuity in the absence of family involvement. Non-family members reverently likened this enduring aura of nurturing leadership and metaphorical family belonging as follows: 'It's like Christ and his apostles. It's affective. We knew the founder and we live his values, in a personal capacity, every day'. This ensured vision continuity beyond succession and maintaining a strong family firm identity through non-biological metaphorical 'family' members.

In our case study, this was clearly also evinced in FFG's founder, Rev Watherston's personality, his interaction with employees, and nurturing of future leaders; and reciprocated through their reverence towards him and dedication to his social enterprise's mission. Here, the vision and social sentiments he inculturates, combined with strong faith and shared religious belief, acted as a surrogate proxy for a 'biological' family.

## Entrepreneurship, Religion and Social Value

Entrepreneurship theories broadly postulate entrepreneurial intentions as a talent or trait, something that one may have acquired and accrued through nature and/or nurture (Tortella et al., 2009). Entrepreneurs can be found in almost all sectors of the economy, including the public sector where it is designated as civic entrepreneurship (Burns, 2011). Social entrepreneurship falls within the entrepreneurial spectrum; it is distinct from other forms of entrepreneurship (Lumpkin et al., 2013), and having an explicit social mission (Dees, 1998, 2007) may be based on having multiple bottom lines, where success and performance is gauged in terms of financial, social and environmental impact (Dixon & Clifford, 2007; Savitz & Weber, 2006). Trading for a social purpose generally sees profits ploughed back to further the organisations' social objectives (Oham, 2016). Schumpeter describes entrepreneurs as a lynchpin of socio-economic development, moving into areas of low productivity investing their resources with the aim of furthering their business objectives (Down, 2010). In this regard, economic or social value is generated aligned with the motives of the agent. Regardless of intention, entrepreneurs develop their host communities by creating employment opportunities and social development in the long run. Through this process, other entrepreneurs could be developed through role modelling, apprenticeships and mentoring (Jack & Anderson, 1999).

One often overlooked category actively engaged in economic activity is entrepreneurial religious groups (from various religious denominations, such as e.g., Christianity, Islam, Judaism, Hinduism etc. ...), such as, in this case, churches, priests, nuns, and lay communities. They creatively bring innovation and enterprise to their congregations and communities and are driven by an enduring mission and clear objectives effectively addressing social and economic needs in a sustained manner at various levels, sometimes even beyond their proximate localities (Dinham, 2007; Foster, 2006; Pearce et al., 2010). For example, in 1956, a 26-year-old Catholic priest seeking to address post-civil war decline and poverty in Spain established Mondragon. Father Arizmendiarrietta's cooperative has grown to employ more than 8000 employees today, generating annual revenues exceeding 12 billion Euros (Mondragon Corporation, 2020). Notwithstanding its social mission, Mondragon ranks 11th globally, alongside other renowned big corporate firms in Forbes' list of enterprises that are changing the world (Forbes, 2021). This outstanding, yet typical, case has attracted much attention in this context (Oham, 2016).

Scholars have also long drawn parallels and direct associations from religion informing CSR, and impacting human behaviour in this regard (c.f., Blum & Dudley, 2001). For example, in-depth studies on business executives established 'much inductive evidence of a relationship among their conception of God, norms and values, and business conduct' (Graafland et al., 2007, p. 331). Recently, conducting the first systematic review of literature on religion and CSR, van Aaken and Buchner (2020) consolidated and highlighted empirical evidence where 'intrinsic religiosity positively affects ethical CSR attitudes [and] extrinsic religiosity stimulates philanthropic CSR attitudes' (p. 925. See also Mazereeuw-van Der Duijn Schouten et al., 2014). Drawing on corporate decision makers' conceptions of God, norms and values to examine associations with socially responsible business conduct orientation, Graafland, et al. (2007) found that executives practicing monotheistic religions, were more strongly aligned with socially responsible decisions.

Indeed, studies on religion and entrepreneurship have been an area of interest for more than 100 years, starting with Weber's (1905) seminal work, 'The Protestant Ethic and the Spirit of Capitalism' (Carswell & Rolland, 2007; Cavanagh, 1999; Davidsun & Wiklund, 1996; Gibbs & Ilkan, 2008; Gotsis & Kortezi, 2009; Ibrahim & Angelidis, 2005; Kauanui et al., 2008; Lee et al., 2003; Malloch, 2005; Millman et al., 1999; Moris & Schindehutte, 2005; Morrison, 2000; Neal et al., 1999; Pearce et al., 2010; Weber, 1965). Due to societal shift in recent times, inquiry into what is known as 'spiritual capital' is starting to emerge. This nascent field of study considers the advantages of faith on entrepreneurial efficacy and economic development (Malloch, 2005, 2008; Oham, 2013; Rima, 2013). Social enterprises are part of the entrepreneurial spectrum and have seen growing research interest over the past 20 years (Nicholls, 2006). Faith-based social enterprises are ventures set up by social entrepreneurs as a result of their spiritual mission to do good in society by addressing social needs (Dinham, 2007; Oham, 2013). The role of religion and faith in entrepreneurship is, in certain contexts, recognised as critical. For example in Ghana, many interviewed social entrepreneurs point out that their faith and support from faith-based groups such as churches and mosques were invaluable in seeing them through when starting-up their social enterprise initiatives (British Council, 2015). Linkages between faith and social entrepreneurship are intertwined with the scope to increase social impact in many neighbourhoods. Furthermore, the influence of faith in society has also been noticed by policymakers in the UK and the USA (Baker et al., 2011; Dinham, 2007). Research on faith and entrepreneurship at this juncture is growing due to many factors including, for example, the complexities and increasing challenges in many economies and societies, and the search for alternative and complementary approaches to entrepreneurship.

## Consolidating Entrepreneurial Parenting and Spiritual Capital in Context

As already indicated, metaphors provide insights into aspects of phenomena needing in-depth study, extending boundaries and advancing the field of entrepreneurship (Lundmark, et al., 2019). Drawing from convergent literature, FFGs founding entrepreneur nurturing the apprentice is designated the 'Entrepreneurial Parent – Natural mentor' (EPN); while the relationship the entrepreneur has with the metaphysical source (God) is ascribed as the 'Entrepreneurial Parent – Spiritual' (EPS). The apprentice, eventually transitioning to MD shepherding the organisation forwards, in turn duly becomes an 'Entrepreneurial Parent' by reproducing the experiences and qualities found in their 'entrepreneurial parents', mentoring other upcoming social entrepreneurs e.g., staff – thereby completing the cycle of propagation and continuity – perpetuating entrepreneurial parenting. This thus leads to the continuous nurturing and creation of entrepreneurs as a default sustainability business process in FFG – multiplying value in society and localities. The 'Entrepreneurial Parent' functions as a protégée replicating their entrepreneurial parents' qualities, and parenting generations of other entrepreneurs through role modelling and mentoring.

In the FFG context, the MD entrepreneur's lived experience and development is studied, as engaged with their faith, they put it into action with the desired outcomes. These dynamics are explored through this faith-based social enterprise case study. The concept of spiritual capital is used to explain accrued advantages in this process resulting from peoples' shared faith and direction. The tangible and intangible resources an individual (entrepreneur) has due to their collective engagement and commitment to a religion is often seen as a subset of social capital and the missing leg in the stool of economic development (Malloch, 2005, 2008). In this case, we consider spiritual capital acting as a three-dimensional resource that the entrepreneur benefits from, enabling the eventually incumbent MD to attain their objectives; and in the process extend value and provide beneficial outcomes to stakeholders.

### Defining Spiritual Capital

Spiritual capital is defined as a set of values, ethical standpoints and visions for change held by individuals, groups and institutions; and a source of motivation for the percolation of other capitals (Baker et al., 2011). Spiritual capital's advantages arise because of engagement with religion in its broader sense (individual, institution, networks and stakeholders). It is also considered as the fund of beliefs linked to a transcendental source of human happiness and fulfilment (Malloch, 2005, 2010). Spiritual capital can be defined more widely as it differs from religious capital that explains patterns of religious beliefs and behaviour over lifecycles and generations

(Neuman, 1986). In some circles, spiritual capital may be seen as a derivative from the broader construct of social capital (Holt et al., 2012). It is a conceptual framework demonstrating the relationship underlying how spiritual capital instigates resilience and moderates turbulence in the life of entrepreneurs (Kolade & Egbetokun, 2019). From another perspective, spiritual capital may then contribute to the development of relationships that can, for example, help scale a business (Neubert et al., 2017). Vaconcelos (2020) thematically articulates six salient features of spiritual capital, namely: wealth, faith and belief, values, virtues, vision and benefits.

## CASE STUDY PROFILE AND METHODOLOGICAL APPROACH

### The FFG Managing Director

The current MD leads this faith-based social enterprise providing employment opportunities and social housing services to vulnerable people. Arriving from India aiming to read a PhD at Oxford University, a sudden change of events led young Christina Baby to start her career as a Business Development Officer at FFG. Twenty-five years later she is CEO and MD of FFG and Just Homes. Using thematic analysis, the concept of entrepreneurial parenting and mentoring emerges, demonstrating how the social entrepreneur developed her capacity to lead and function as an entrepreneur through the influence of significant others that played a key 'parenting' role in her development. Besides her enterprising biological parents who doubled as spiritual and entrepreneurial mentors; equally significant 'adoptive parents', were the FFG founders, an entrepreneurial priest and his wife – Rev Peter and Mrs Hannah Watherston.

Christina Baby shares her early experiences of observing her father and mother, George and his wife, Soosy Isaac, social entrepreneurs in India – followed by her solo move to the UK at a young age, where she unexpectedly got involved in social entrepreneurship with Rev Peter Watherston and his wife, who were serial social entrepreneurs in the London Borough of Newham (Oham, 2013). Before retiring in 2014, Peter and Hannah had long provided pastoral care. Peter actively and conscientiously trained and nurtured his staff and volunteers through role modelling, mentoring and apprenticeship – instilling core guiding principles. Most of his mentees have since risen to senior positions at FFG and in other organisations.

Rev Peter and Hannah started FFG in 1997, which they grew from a small employment support project into a multifaceted trading enterprise, with several subsidiaries including cafés, a furniture warehouse, a plastic recycling plant, a sewing facility, property maintenance, storage facilities, hostels for vulnerable women and social housing for single people. The global financial crisis of 2008 adversely affected

FFG when its major supplier and partner soon went out of business. This led to closure of three of their biggest subsidiaries: warehousing, storage and recycling. FFG has since restructured its operations and focuses on its social housing arm (Just Homes), cafés and a clothing recycling project. FFG's current turnover is just over one million pounds.

## Methodological Approach

A constructive interpretive approach is adopted exploring the phenomena under study – seeking understanding on how the entrepreneur constructs reality in entrepreneurial learning within such circumstances. The research is based on a purposively selected in-depth case study providing rich context, enabling the capture and observation of a number of insights on relational aspects and lived realities. The methodological approach promotes flexibility for rich interpretation through further investigation based on emerging insights. Within the context of this research, case-based methodologies are advocated. They are ideal for examining best practice as well as seeking insights and deep understanding of complex phenomena (Aastrup & Halldorson, 2008). With case studies, empirical events consolidating multiple data and methods are described and critically investigated towards establishing context-relevant insights and useful inferences (O'Leary, 2014). Case studies give bearing to an epistemological base and support for theory and framework development (Denzin & Lincoln, 2003; Schwandt, 1993; Yin 2003). Towards this end, the FFG MD was extensively interviewed. The interviews explored in-depth the experienced extent of entrepreneurial parenting, her understanding of spiritual capital, and their combined manifestation in her entrepreneurial stance and behaviour; and its implications on vision and mission continuity and concomitant outcomes on individuals. In consolidation, the approach adopted explores whether entrepreneurial parenting through spiritual capital, at an individual level, can be used to explain the nurturing of new entrepreneurs over time, in the context presented at FFG.

Building on earlier initial interviews with the original founder, Rev Watherston, and employees, qualitative data and insights for this exploratory research were primarily derived from narratives and in-depth interviews with the current FFG MD – who had been nurtured and mentored over a protracted period of time by her founding predecessor. Interviews took place over one month, on site at the premises with on average one hour's duration. Recorded interviews were transcribed and iteratively coded in relation to key emergent themes, also partially informed by the literature aligning with the study.

Additionally, important nuanced insights from ongoing periodic direct observation were also derived from association since one of the authors has been a member on FFG's board since 2012, which enabled an 'outside-insider' perspective, aiding with interpretation and providing institutional access for further probing and clarification when required, as well as availing of internal documentation, extensive notes and reflective journals were kept, consolidating additional rich insights.

## FINDINGS AND DISCUSSION

Outcomes from our preliminary research observe a prevalent critical form of spiritual capital in this case study. Entrepreneurial parenting and key emerging insights present three component dimensions, namely: Entrepreneurial Parenting-Spiritual (EPS); Entrepreneurial Parenting-Natural mentor (EPN); and the Entrepreneurial Parent-Entrepreneur (EPE), the individual who eventually becomes an entrepreneur him- or herself.

In this context, it was found that entrepreneurial parenting is facilitated by spiritual capital emanating from the mentors. Entrepreneurial parenting is seen as a critically important theme frequently emerging from the data following in-depth analysis.

Entrepreneurial Parenting within the FFG' context is enumerated in detail as follows:

One aspect deriving from the research question considers how spiritual capital may significantly influence (Christian) entrepreneurial activity. Analysis showed emergent coding for the 'Parenthood' theme to be significantly pronounced. It represented a key role that spiritual capital plays through the MD at FFG. The function of spiritual capital is deemed to provide a form of 'parenting' to entrepreneurs and staff – in the sense that the entrepreneur (MD) is nurtured and, in turn, nurtures others, also exhibiting a key aspect of parenting. Parenting as a literary term signifies a form of care, mentoring and protection, the 'upbringing' of a child. In this case, here it demonstrated the care and support provided by the mentor, the transcending of social vision evangelisation beyond succession; and its sustained value continuity perpetuated throughout the organisation.

Observations from qualitative data analysis revealed no less than 35 codes highlighting 'Parenting' characteristics. The respondent also made several references to the role of her father or father figures in her life. Here, one notes that fatherhood may not necessarily connote a male figure; rather it could also be a metaphor extending to the role of a mother or others imparting nurturing support. The following highlights the nature of entrepreneurial parenting experienced in this context:

*Code 13: ... when I was growing up; my Father used to tell me that the Christian life is to do justly, love mostly and walk completely with the Lord, he gave me my Christian values.*

*I found myself completely uprooted and my family meant a lot to me and I completely lost confidence and lost myself, but one passage that my father quotes and I have quoted and taken to heart is this "the Spirit of God will not take you where the grace of God will not protect you". I only realised the links when I came here [father's training and values]. When I have difficulty, I quote the scriptures and I have a breakthrough.*

Based on case evidence, here one observes our aforementioned three-dimensional nature of parenthood, revealing manifestations of this concept from the metaphysical (spiritual) to the physical (mentor to mentee), and then on an individual level as the new entrepreneur supports and mentors others in their team. Parenting can be described as a form of procreative influence on an entrepreneur's values. It represents the way an entrepreneur is developed and mentored in the practice of entrepreneurship; from the nascent stages, to apprenticeship, and mastery, with additional potential to develop and empower other entrepreneurs.

Parenting also infers a long-term perspective that counters and absorbs any pressure or temptation for short-term gains rather than long-term sustainability of the social enterprise and welfare of the entrepreneur. It is a unique patient approach to entrepreneurial action. Parenting in a way puts in check unsustainable or unethical entrepreneurial motives and introduces longer-term aspirations, plans and relationships, as revealed in our study. It was also evinced here that spirituality may present concepts contrary to typical business practice; such as questioning, openness and letting go, as opposed to conquest and control (Keller & Helfenburn, 2008). Evidently, the respondent was in a mentoring or nurturing relationship for several years up to the point where she gained the skills and confidence required to take on the MD role. In human resource terms, this is known as 'game keeping' rather than 'poaching' to fill vacancies (Torrington & Hall, 1998). Linking to Bourdieu's' forms of capital, this case study demonstrates the respondent applying her cultural capital to gain relevant skills to take on this position in combination with the human and social capital endowment she had (Bourdieu, 1986). However, the unique feature about these elements is that they evolve and flourish within the sound basis of a religious environment, thereby manifesting a spiritual form of capital. Ensuing data demonstrated the nobility of the Entrepreneurial Parenting concept – moral, ethical, and sustainable values, embodied and transferred to the protégé by the cultural capital of the respondent's parents and those she eventually worked with within FFG. Consequently, 'Parenthood' can be seen as an elevated aspect of service and values such as servant leadership, underpinned by humility, hope, altruism, and forgiveness that puts self-interest as the last priority, for example, as seen in Greek Orthodoxy and other religions (Gotsis and Kortezi, 2009).

Furthermore, other key traits of parenting observed in this case study were the ability to envision a desirable future and recognising and developing talent. This ability for opportunity and talent recognition is a key trait of entrepreneurs. It is an ability to see human beings as a unique creation with the right to humanise the world (Gotsis & Kortezi, 2009). However, in this case, the concept of opportunity recognition in entrepreneurship is now inward focused and interpersonal within the organisation. These traits are identified in Bink and Vale's entrepreneurial profiles demonstrating how entrepreneurs exploit opportunities that present themselves (Binks & Vale, 1990). A key component of spiritual capital is belief in a being that knows and wants the best for its agent. Christian scriptures point to God as a human developer who nurtures individuals, also encouraging them to maximise their talents (e.g., The Holy Bible, Literal Standard Version (2020), 1 Corinthians 12:4-11; Matthew 5:14-16, 6:1-4, 25:1-30; 1 Peter 4:10; Romans 12:3-8). A parallel Christian understanding of this could mean that the creator recognises potential in the midst of business challenges. This is reflected in the MD's statements:

*Code 13 .... I liked where he [FFG Reverend and founding CEO] was going with the project; I don't think that if I had not personally met him; I would have personally thought of [doing] what I am doing.*

Data revealed the code for potential identification. The mentor, in this case, adoptive 'parent' and founder, in some way kindled self-belief and exposed the potential of the novice, an eventual entrepreneur. For example, the respondent noted that her father, God and finally, her 'adoptive' mentor had played a positive role in her career. Regarding the latter, in time, the CEO had encouraged her to take on the role of MD when she did not feel confident in doing so. In all aspects of Entrepreneurial Parenting, a form of mentoring and skills acquisition is taking place in three dimensions: influencing the entrepreneur, the values of the enterprise and social impact on stakeholders. This observed influence is strong, enabling change to take place as evidenced:

*Code 9 ... My parents had a great influence on me, and my first introduction to social entrepreneurship was by my father who studied in the United Kingdom and went back [to India] to set up a social enterprise to give women a job. My parents made a stand at the time in the community to give women a job. They paid for every child of their entire workforce about 250 [to go to school].*

Another trait of parenting picked up from the data is that of a 'Servant King', a relationship described by the respondent who reflected on the humility of Jesus as He put aside His divinity to become human and go through suffering to serve humanity

(The Holy Bible, Literal Standard Version, 2020, Philippians 2:5). It emerged that from her early days, the respondent patterned her life in this way, and that all her mentors were people actively following this lowly principle.

*Code 20 ... Servant King is Jesus' words; Jesus said the first shall be the last ...*

Similarly, and often selflessly, effective parenting involves leadership, the ability to positively influence and give direction. The paradigm and ethos of leadership brings about the ability to challenge the mentee to extend their boundaries by coming out of their comfort zones and becoming highly productive – aspiring and realizing potential. This can be achieved by extending their influence or exceeding their objectives, such as entering new markets and developing new products or services. Fatherhood could also designate a challenge on the entrepreneurs' values to ensure that they are moral and ethical. There is a responsibility on the 'father' to ensure their protégée actualises their objectives. This is critical as parenting symbolises a compulsion to support or possibly go the 'extra mile'. The responsibility is coupled with patience, especially as the newly initiated may be 'finding their feet', negotiating existing protocols and may, as a result of inexperience, make costly mistakes. In a sense, in this case the mentee also operated as a leader, a sort of 'de facto' leader while understudying the mentor. This occurs as the entrepreneur engaged in projects or ventures requiring entrepreneurial leadership with their teams and customers. The respondent noted that:

*Code 20: ... it is my job to ensure that it is happening; if it is not happening, it sinks the boat; you have to lead, set the pace, encourage, review and criticise.*

This extract demonstrates the respondent had now come to understand a critical aspect of parenting is that of strong leadership.

Furthermore, parenting also epitomises self-reliance; in the natural sense of the word, one would not be a parent if the feature of procreation is non-existent. The respondent explained that while spiritual capital reveals some aspects of non-dependence on the external factors, the intention is to develop self-sustaining systems. The respondent gives evidence of parental figures – parents and mentors – being self-reliant. She noted that her founding predecessor's policy at FFG was not to apply for recurrent funding, rather to apply for capital funding grants whilst internally generating earned income through its business models. This can-do attitude went a long way in giving the organisation resilience in difficult times. It may have been a value that kept them going amidst the threat of completely winding up.

Another dimension of parenting revealed in the data extract was 'trust of God' – where the symbolic image of a child looking up to the father for all their needs come into play. The respondent revealed that for her, God seemed to always be there and that, time and time again, she and her team witnessed 'miracles' and the hand of 'God' in the affairs of the organisation. It led to strong faith as they saw a repetition of some form of 'Divine intervention' in their business dealings:

*Code 13i: ... I have confidence, if God wants me to go out and do something, I do it.*

Entrepreneurial parenting can be seen as a metaphor for sustainability not only for the organisation's objectives, but also for the employees. The parent has a natural inclination to perpetuate himself through acculturation and the reproduction of cultural capital (Bourdieu, 1986). The pantheistic nature of God in some religions underscores this fact (Cavanagh, 1999). Having a successor-in-waiting (succession planning) is a key factor for organisational sustainability and links closely to Bourdieu's work on cultural capital reproduction. Perpetuation in this case, seems to be a form of destructive innovation, where one culture is 're-cultured' into a more advanced or efficient one. This case demonstrates the value of spiritual capital in FFG, where there was a tendency to not be driven by short-term gain – an approach that directly led to the 2008 global financial crisis and a pitfall for so many entrepreneurs. Spiritual capital values empowered the founder and leaders at FFG to consequently establish a fundamental additional factor underpinning their leadership which essentially provided sustainable good value for their stakeholders.

Parenting breeds confidence as it nurtures novice entrepreneurs – as a new up-and-coming candidate is nurtured into an empowering relationship by the father figure through training and development, guidance and apprenticeship.

*Code 31: ... the founders have made a huge influence on me; they made me see things inside of me.*

Spirituality, in most cases, projects God as a Father and the source of true fatherhood. The Jewish name for God is Jehovah which means Father or Abba. We observe scriptures and faith literature as main sources of spiritual capital that furnish disciples with a rich history for understanding the nature of Fatherhood in God. For example, names and attributes of God linked to His miraculous work, as noted by the respondent:

*Code 16: ... you have to have a special experience with God to have spiritual capital, for people to come to you and ask to help. Once you have that kind of experience it is hard to deny God.*

Another aspect of effective parenting is the attraction of parent and child towards each other. This also plays out in the spiritual context, as those who have a relationship with this spiritual parent seem to have been attracted to His attributes in a mutual way; brought about as a result of a strong pull towards each other as a result of a common origination, as articulated in the following data excerpt:

*Code 12: ... When I came to the UK, I missed my dad terribly. The CEO [Rev, founder] was like my dad working with the less fortunate. I liked where he was going with the project. I don't think that if I had not met him, I would have personally thought of doing what I am doing [social enterprise]. I would have personally gone into teaching. He made me look at this; the rules and the background [parents and family history of social enterprise] clicked, and it started meaning something to me. I went for an interview for another job and the former CEO and Chairman was one of the interviewers. I was unsuccessful. However, he asked if he could interview me for another job and the Board agreed. If I had not met him and his wife, I would not have done what I was doing. He made me look at social enterprise, the rules and the background then clicked, and I could identify with it and it started making meaning to me.*

This kind of attraction normally initiated by a parent when potential is recognised, could be a shared interest and purpose, yet also perhaps vocational. However, it is reciprocated by the beneficiary. Similarly, parenting connotes protection by a stronger one; most entrepreneurs have attributed the challenges of business failure and the fear of losing as a barrier to entrepreneurial efficacy. The protection is seen on different levels of parenting. Firstly, from a transcendental level, for reassurance and support; and secondly, from a physical and individual level. The respondent claimed that she noticed the hand of God in her affairs attributing her success to an omniscient and omnipotent God.

*Code 13: ... the CEO asked me to be the Director, and I had declined because I did not have confidence, that's when they recruited a Managing Director, that's when "A" came in as the Director. Later, the founders came back to me and asked me to be a joint director. I said [to God] if you are giving me this mantle you should give me the strength to carry it.*

In another incident, the interviewee talks about God's protection on her and her biological father:

*Code 13 xi-xiv: ... One needs a personal experience with God to understand this. Until this happens, spiritual capital does not mean anything; it happened to me when*

*I was 18 years old. I hated languages at school, so I avoided the language exam in school and went to a mock debate, [I] did this debate, and I somehow passed this exam. A series of things happened, so my father decided to take me to the north of India. He took me to the home of where Gandhi was born. This was a long way from home as we came from Southern India, and we arrived late at night and found out that the Hotel we had booked had gone bankrupt and was out of business. Nowhere to go as the hotel we booked had been closed.*

*I said to my dad, what do we do now? My dad was confident in his God and had recited Psalm 24 "I will look up to the hill from whence comes my help". We prayed, and two people came up and said you look like strangers - this was 2:00 am, in the morning. They took us to a place where our accommodation and feeding was sorted out for six to seven days that we were there.*

*God did great things and [during] the entire period I felt God being there, so it was experiential. Spiritual capital has to be experienced i.e., people asked to help. Once you had this kind of experience, it is hard for you to deny God. That was when I felt God being there and sorting us out, because it was dangerous. My father [respondent evidently laden with emotion] ... this is when I understood my father's faith, I felt that I don't need to be someone else, I can have this relationship myself. If that is what has happened, you can experience it. You have to have a special experience with God to have spiritual capital, for people to come to you and ask to help you – once you had that kind of experience it is hard to deny God.*

*Spiritual capital has to be experienced; it didn't mean anything to me then [before the experience], and I knew some things about God [prior].*

It is vital that the translational nature and implication of the parenting theme applied here is understood within a multidimensional context. The instructions from the parent are vital to an entrepreneur, in some cases, they are a needed lifeline for success. A family experience was translated into constructive learning as the beneficiary, in this case, the ensuing entrepreneur, used her skills and experience as a resource in navigating the challenges that she encountered within an entrepreneurial setting.

These characteristics of parenting in our case point to various traits that make spiritual capital a critical part of entrepreneurial parenting and entrepreneurship. It also indicates the way the entrepreneur was influenced through parenting.

## Dimensions of Parenthood Exhibited

In consolidation, the theme 'Parenting' exhibited three dimensions emerging from our exploratory study – also substantiated by drawing from the literature on spiritual capital. The dimensions evinced include:

1. **Entrepreneurial Parenting:** The Supernatural (EPS), where God is recognised as a parent who cares.
2. **Entrepreneurial Parenting:** The Natural entrepreneurial 'parent' (EPN), the mentor supporting an entrepreneur.
3. **Entrepreneurial Parenting:** The Entrepreneur (EPE), where the parented individual and eventual entrepreneur in turn also exhibit entrepreneurial parenting qualities in their leadership.

Table1 presents the key parenting characteristics observed in relation to the three dimensions observed.

*Table 1. Emergent entrepreneurial parenting dimensions observed through the case study*

| 1. Entrepreneurial Parenting Dimensions | 2. Characteristics | 3. Unique differences between Entrepreneurial Parenting Dimensions |
|---|---|---|
| Supernatural (EPS) | - Patience of God<br>- Care of God<br>- Innovation - ideas from God<br>- Motivation - from God<br>- Protection - from God<br>- Guidance - from God<br>- Direction/Leadership - from God | - Transcendental in nature<br>- Intangible in nature<br>- Miracles - unexpected solutions to problems |
| Natural Mentor (EPN) | - Sacrifice of the Mentor<br>- Fallibility of Mentor<br>- Dependence on Mentor<br>- Support from Mentor<br>- Mentoring the Mentee<br>- Training of the Mentee<br>- Development of the Mentee | - Human limitations of the mentor e.g., mistakes being made<br>- Hand holding of Mentee |
| Entrepreneur (EPE) | - Self-Efficacy of the Entrepreneur<br>- Individuality of the Entrepreneur<br>- Mentoring by the Entrepreneur<br>- Coaching by the Entrepreneur | - Hands-on engagement on objectives<br>- Change agent in the community |

Source: Consolidated by the Authors from ensuing empirical observation

In the table presented, Column 1 indicates the different dimensions of Entrepreneurial Parenting established from our analysis of the data. In Column 2, the key characteristics observed for each dimension of Entrepreneurial Parenting established are presented. These characteristics distinguish each parenting dimension from the others in this context. In Column 3, are unique differences that highlight the nature of Entrepreneurial Spiritual Capital not seen in other dimensions due to its origination: e.g., the source, in the case of the Entrepreneurial Parent – *Supernatural*, *Natural Mentor* and *Entrepreneur/Individual*. These characteristics are drawn from our contextual case analysis. While ensuing supporting evidence is found in the preceding section contending with the findings and data analysis; their implications are consolidated next.

## Entrepreneurial Parenting: The Supernatural (EPS)

This is the relationship an entrepreneur develops with a transcendental source, in this case Christianity, that the MD is associated with. It is a relationship with God. It is a spiritual experience that is developed from an encounter between the entrepreneur and God. As already referred to, the social entrepreneur claimed that:

*Code 13: ... You have to have a special experience with God to have spiritual capital for people to come to you and ask to help you – once you had that kind of experience it is hard to deny God. Spiritual capital has to be experienced; it didn't mean anything to me then (before the experience), and I knew some things about God (prior)*

Entrepreneurial Parenting the Supernatural can be positioned as the source of all attributes that emanate from the concept. It is the progenitor of the other two dimensions that are observed in this case study.

## Entrepreneurial Parenting: The Natural Mentor (EPN)

This is the relationship that the entrepreneur had with her entrepreneurial father, a mentor; or a parental figure that has shaped the young upstart's worldview of entrepreneurship. It does not focus narrowly on the aspect of learning and applying business principles – it also encompasses all that spiritual capital stands for, such as morality, corporate social responsibility and the total care for humanity and nature (Malloch, 2005). From the interviews, the respondent claimed her 'father' (as well as her later 'adoptive' Reverend 'parent', FFG's founder) were her greatest influencers, giving her the tools, she needed to thrive and survive in her role as a social entrepreneur:

*Code 15: ... My Father told me about asking the sun to stand still when time is short, I ask God to stretch my time, this (task) has to be done today- I have two kids and a marriage and to manage, to look at the applications, I see that I have taken far to accomplish what I need to do.*

*Code 31: ... [Rev] Peter and Hannah have made a huge influence on me they made me see things inside of me.*

For Christina Baby, her relationship to the 'parent' also involves engaging in spiritual rituals such as prayer, communion, and bible study – unique to the organisational group. Rituals were regularly engaged in within the affinity group over the period, reinforcing the basis for this enterprising organisational culture:

*Code 15: ... Under the CEO, we had monthly staff meetings, shared communion together [sacramental Holy Communion]; we stopped when we moved to the warehouse. We try and pray once a week. Any day we are all here together, we pray. My managers are elders and pastors in their own churches. There are four staff meetings in a year when we have lunch together. So we do have some activity but is not regular.*

*God is good; we give thanks, prayer is important when faced with different situations. We had an issue with a supplier we dealt with the situation by prayer and when the issue was resolved we gave thanks together.*

*There are some regular and sometimes sporadic prayers when we are faced with difficult situations.*

*We now have a project in which all of us are praying for favour..."*

## Entrepreneurial Parenting: The Entrepreneur (EPE)

The practice of entrepreneurship by the MD exhibits a form of entrepreneurial parenting, as she conceives, nurtures and manages the venture – extending its social mission, creating value in the community. Sustaining this across succession requires effective leadership skills from the entrepreneur that are aligned to this context.

In this regard, all the experience the entrepreneur gained through mentoring, training and development herself, evidently became manifest in her own coordination of all organisational resources – including her leadership, as well as the coaching and nurturing of her employees and teams.

The respondent identified several remits giving credence to her leadership of FFG. As indicated this, for example, involved supervision, monitoring, evaluating, and developing employees. As already observed, the respondent elaborated on her leadership role as follows:

*Code 20 c: ... it is my job to ensure that it is happening, if it is not happening it sinks the boat, you have to lead, set the pace, encourage, review and criticise.*

This captures the role of leadership from an entrepreneurs' perspective. The whole process of leadership from the originator of parenting to the mentor and finally to the entrepreneur, demonstrated the intricate and complex nature of spiritual capital as it influenced and, in turn, reinforced the respective entrepreneurs.

Figure 1 presents the directional flow of parenting influence the entrepreneur is exposed to in FFG, this being cascaded directionally and emblematic of parenting.

*Figure 1. The dimensions of entrepreneurial parenting and directional influence in First Fruit Group*
*Source: Conceptualised by the Authors*

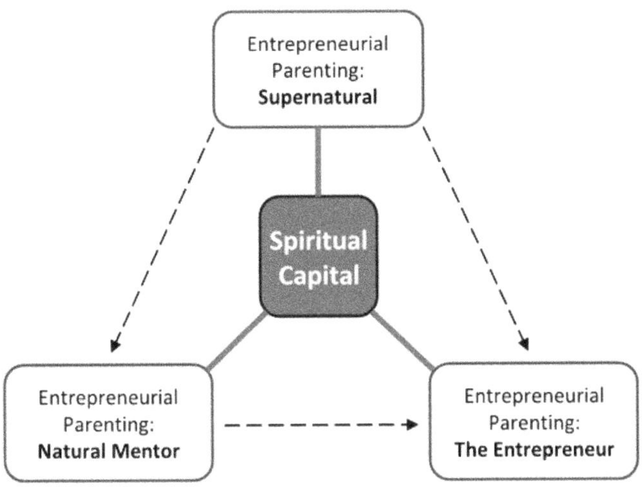


## CONSOLIDATING IMPLICATIONS AND CONCLUSION

In consolidation, our preliminary study explored the role of spiritual capital emanating from religion as a channel and source reinforcing entrepreneurial parenting at FFG. Multiple dimensions of entrepreneurial parenting influenced the respondent and have had a direct impact on the perpetuation of organisational values, as well as the nature, business objectives and enduring enterprising success of the organisation.

This study provides early insights seeking to demonstrate how entrepreneurial parenting is actualised through utilisation of spiritual capital in such contexts. In this case, entrepreneurial parenting played a critical role in the life of the current MD, Christina Baby, as she was exposed to several parental influences – whether from her own biological parents, or other significant 'adoptive' enterprising people she looked up to as guiding parental figures.

Over the years, FFG has been endowed with an embedded spiritual culture and a default subconscious visionary objective propagated by empowered subsequent leaders – that of training and developing entrepreneurs. This, likely an emergent strategy, since the training and developing of entrepreneurs *per se* was not originally, and is not explicitly, recognised as the core mission of the organisation. In this regard, it would be pertinent for future research to, for example, investigate what the impact would be if developing social entrepreneurs effectively became a stated core strategy at FFG. Essentially, FFG has been functioning as an 'entrepreneurial parenting organisation', noting that the current MD has herself developed and been reared in an environment of entrepreneurial parenting which, over time, involved biological, metaphysical, and mentoring dimensions of entrepreneurial nurturing.

We note that metaphors in this context represent close links and relationships existing in biology and theology, enhancing continuity and sustainability – as in the creation or sustaining of life. It would be valuable for further research and interdisciplinary studies to address this nexus in greater depth, to explore the possibility that there may be more that science and theology have in common – complementarity, rather than elements that divide these two domains. Applied perspectives here could bring considerable benefits both to society and the economy.

We further pose a question for future exploration in relation to training and development: What type of training and mentoring should specialist social entrepreneurs operating in certain areas (such as e.g., faith or environmental sectors) be offered? – given that in nature and biology, nurturing is context specific in terms of the environment and the needs of the species. This could have important ramifications in providing new perspectives for indicating complementary models of entrepreneurial learning and training that our business schools should also recognise or engage in as complementary or alternative approaches (Lucey, 2019). We note that, in this case, the social entrepreneur faced nuanced situations of dealing with spiritual capital that in some instances brought conflict upon herself and embraced cultural values, which in some ways may have been in dissonance or at odds with typically prevalent business practice and cultural norms.

In conclusion, the findings from this preliminary and exploratory case study provide useful insights in illustrating that entrepreneurial parenting can manifest in three dimensions: the supernatural, the natural mentor, and the individual nascent entrepreneur. At FFG, these were collectively supported, enhanced and reinforced by spiritual capital in this context. Our case study provides insights into these complex complementary processes of entrepreneurial parenting and suggests areas for further research and application.

## ACKNOWLEDGMENT

We would like to thank the First Fruit Group Managing Director, the Board and staff for the opportunity afforded us to conduct this study.

## REFERENCES

Aastrup, J., & Halldorsson, A. (2008). Epistemological role of case studies in logistics: A critical realist perspective. *International Journal of Physical Distribution & Logistics Management, 38*(10), 746–763. doi:10.1108/09600030810926475

Ainsworth, S., & Cox, J. W. (2003). Families divided: Culture and control in small family business. *Organization Studies, 24*(9), 1463–1485. doi:10.1177/0170840603249004

Baker, C., Stokes, P., Lichy, J., Atherton, J., & Moss, D. (2011). *Values, beliefs and attitudes in the era of late-capitalism: A consideration of the re-emergence and re-positioning of faith and spirituality as spiritual capital in the workplace.* https://www.chester.ac.uk/sites/files/chester/Values,%20Beliefs%20and%20Attitudes%20in%20the%20Era%20of%20Late%20Capitalism.pdf

Berti, M. (2017). *Elgar introduction to organizational discourse analysis.* Edward Elgar Publishing. doi:10.4337/9781784717056

Binks, M., & Vale, P. (1990). *Entrepreneurship and Economic Change.* McGraw-Hill.

Black, M. (1962). *Models and metaphors.* Cornell University Press. doi:10.7591/9781501741326

Bloemen-Bekx, M., Voordeckers, W., Remery, C., & Schippers, J. (2019). Following in parental footsteps? The influence of gender and learning experiences on entrepreneurial intentions. *International Small Business Journal, 37*(6), 642–663. doi:10.1177/0266242619838936

Blum, U., & Dudley, L. (2001). Religion and economic growth: Was Weber right? *Journal of Evolutionary Economics, 11*(2), 207–230. doi:10.1007/PL00003862

Bourdieu, P. (1986). The forms of capital. In J. Richardson (Ed.), *Handbook of Theory and Research for the Sociology of Education* (pp. 241–258). Greenwood.

British Council. (2015) *Social Enterprise Landscape in Ghana.* British Council. https://www.britishcouncil.org/sites/default/files/social_enterprise_landscape_in_ghana_report_final.pdf

Burns, P. (2011). *Entrepreneurship and small business, start up, growth and maturity.* Palgrave Macmillan. doi:10.1007/978-0-230-20848-3

Carswell, P., & Rolland, D. (2007). Religion and Entrepreneurship in New Zealand. *Journal of Enterprising Communities Peoples and Places in the Global Economy, 1*(2), 162-174.

Cavanagh, G. F. (1999). Spirituality for managers: Context and critique. *Journal of Organizational Change Management, 12*(3), 186–199. doi:10.1108/09534819910273793

Chlosta, S., Patzelt, H., Klein, S. B., & Christian, D. (2012). Parental role models and the decision to become self-employed: The moderating effect of personality. *Small Business Economics, 38*(1), 121–138. doi:10.100711187-010-9270-y

Cornelissen, J. P. (2006a). Making sense of theory construction: Metaphor and disciplined imagination. *Organization Studies, 27*(11), 1579–1597. doi:10.1177/0170840606068333

Cornelissen, J. P. (2006b). Metaphor and the dynamics of knowledge in organization theory: A case study of the organizational identity metaphor. *Journal of Management Studies, 43*(4), 683–709. doi:10.1111/j.1467-6486.2006.00607.x

Davidson, P., & Wiklund, J. (1996). Values, belief and regional variations in new firm formation rates. *Journal of Economic Psychology, 18*(2-3), 179–199. doi:10.1016/S0167-4870(97)00004-4

Dees, J. G. (1998, January/February). Enterprising nonprofits: What do you do when traditional sources of funding fall short? *Harvard Business Review*, 55–67.

Dees, J. G. (2007). Taking social entrepreneurship seriously. *Transaction Social Science and Modern Society, 44*(3), 24–31.

Denzin, N., & Lincoln, Y. (2003). *Collecting and interpreting qualitative materials.* Sage publications.

Dinham, A. (2007). *Faiths and Frontiers on the Starship: boldly going as faith-based entrepreneurs?* Faith Based Regeneration Network UK.

Dixon, S. E. A., & Clifford, A. (2007). Ecopreneurship—A new approach to managing the triple bottom line. *Journal of Organizational Change Management*, *20*(3), 326–345. doi:10.1108/09534810710740164

Down, S. (2010). *Enterprise Entrepreneurship and Small Business*. Sage.

Fauconnier, G., & Turner, M. (1998). Conceptual integration networks. *Cognitive Science*, *22*(2), 133–187. doi:10.120715516709cog2202_1

First Fruit Group. (2021). *About us*. https://www.firstfruit.org.uk/aboutus.htm

Forbes. (2021). *Change the World Rankings*. https://fortune.com/change-the-world/2020/search/

Foster, D. (2006). Exploring Cultural Mode Amidst Others in the Church of England. In A. Nicholls (Ed.), *Social Entrepreneurship New Models of Social Change*. Oxford University Press.

Fukuyama, F. (2004). *Social Capital and the Global Economy Foreign Affairs*. http://public.gettysburg.edu/~dborock/courses/Spring/p344/ps344read/fukuyama-social%20capital%20and%20globalization.pdf

Fukuyama, F. (2005). Building democracy after conflict: "Stateness" first. *Journal of Democracy*, *16*(1), 84–88. doi:10.1353/jod.2005.0006

Geldres-Weiss, V. V., Gambetta, N., Massa, N. P., & Geldres-Weiss, S. L. (2021). Materiality matrix use in aligning and determining a firm's sustainable business model archetype and triple bottom line impact on stakeholders. *Sustainability*, *13*(3), 1065. doi:10.3390u13031065

Gibbs, P., & Ilkan, M. (2008). The ethics of marketing in Islamic and Christian communities insights for global marketing. *Cross Cultural Management*, *15*(2), 162–175. doi:10.1108/13527600810870606

Gotsis, G., & Kortezi, Z. (2009). The impact of Greek orthodoxy on entrepreneurship: A theoretical framework. *Journal of Enterprising Communities People and Places in the Global Economy*, *3*(2), 152–175. doi:10.1108/17506200910960851

Graafland, J., Kaptein, M., & Mazereeuw-van Der Duijn Schouten, C. (2007). Conceptions of God, normative convictions, and socially responsible business conduct. *Business & Society*, *46*(3), 331–368. doi:10.1177/0007650306296085

Haugh, H. M., & Mckee, L. (2003). 'It's just like a family' – shared values in the family firm. *Community Work & Family*, *6*(2), 141–158. doi:10.1080/13668800302541

Holt, C. L., Schulz, E., Williams, B., Clark, E. M., Wang, M. Q., & Southward, P. L. (2012). Assessment of religious and spiritual capital in African American communities. *Journal of Religion and Health*, *51*(4), 1061–1074. doi:10.100710943-012-9635-4 PMID:22810197

Ibrahim, N. A., & Angelidis, J. P. (2005). The long term performance of small businesses: Are there differences between "Christian based companies and their secular counterparts"? *Journal of Business Ethics*, *58*(1-3), 187–193. doi:10.100710551-005-1413-8

Jack, S. L., & Anderson, A. R. (1999). Entrepreneurship education within the enterprise culture: Producing reflective practitioners. *International Journal of Entrepreneurial Behaviour & Research*, *5*(3), 110–125. doi:10.1108/13552559910284074

Jiang, D., Hayward, S. D., & Morris, M. L. (2017). Raising entrepreneurs: Can parenting style amplify entrepreneurial intentions and behaviours? *International Journal of Management and Enterprise Development*, *16*(1/2), 13–33. doi:10.1504/IJMED.2017.082544

Johnson, L. (2017). The lives and identities of UK Black and South Asian head teachers. *Educational Management Administration & Leadership*, *45*(5), 842–862. doi:10.1177/1741143217717279

Kauanui, S. K., Thomas, K. D., Sherman, C. L., Waters, G. R., & Gilea, M. (2008). Exploring entrepreneurship through the lens of spirituality. *Journal of Management, Spirituality & Religion*, *5*(2), 160–189. doi:10.1080/14766080809518698

Keller, J. G., & Helfenbein, R. (2008). Spirituality, economics, and education: A dialogic critique of "spiritual capital." *Spirituality. Economics and Education*, *5*(4), 109–128.

Kolade, O., Egbetokun, A., Rae, D., & Hussain, J. (2020). Entrepreneurial resilience in turbulent environments: the role of spiritual capital. In P. Sinha, J. Gibb, M. Akorie, & J. M. Scott (Eds.), *Research Handbook in Business and Management series*. Elgar Online. doi:10.4337/9781788973717.00028

Laspita, S., Breugst, N., Heblich, S., & Patzelt, H. (2012). Intergenerational transmission of entrepreneurial intentions. *Journal of Business Venturing*, *27*(4), 414–435. doi:10.1016/j.jbusvent.2011.11.006

Lee, K., McCann, P., & Ching, M. (2003). Christ and business culture: A study of Christian executive in Hong Kong. *Journal of Business Ethics*, *43*(1/2), 103–110. doi:10.1023/A:1022967300183

Lindquist, M., Sol, J., & Praag, M. (2015). Why do entrepreneurial parents have entrepreneurial children? *Journal of Labor Economics*, *33*(2), 269–296. doi:10.1086/678493

Lucey, T. A. (2019). Examining a measure of spiritual capital: Perceptions of business and education majors. *Citizenship, Social and Economics Education*, *18*(1), 3-15.

Lumpkin, G., Moss, T., Gras, D., Kato, S., & Amezcua, A. (2013). Entrepreneurial processes in social contexts: How are they different, if at all? *Small Business Economics*, *40*(3), 1–23. doi:10.100711187-011-9399-3

Lundmark, E., Krzeminska, A., & Shepherd, D. A. (2019). Images of entrepreneurship: Exploring root metaphors and expanding upon them. *Entrepreneurship Theory and Practice*, *43*(1), 138–170. doi:10.1177/1042258717734369

Malloch, T. R. (2005). Spirituality and Entrepreneurship. In N. Capaldi (Ed.), *Business and Religion A Clash of Civilizations?* M&M Scrivener Press.

Malloch, T. R. (2008). *Doing Virtuous Business: The Remarkable Success of Spiritual Enterprise*. Thomas Nelson.

Mas-Machuca, M., & Marimon, F. (2019). Holistic spiritual capital: Definition and its measurement. *International Journal of Organization Theory and Behavior*, *22*(1), 96–110. doi:10.1108/IJOTB-05-2018-0057

Mazereeuw-van der Duijn Schouten, C., Graafland, J., & Kaptein, M. (2014). Religiosity, CSR attitudes, and CSR behavior: An empirical study of executives' religiosity and CSR. *Journal of Business Ethics*, *123*(3), 437–459. doi:10.100710551-013-1847-3

Millman, J., Ferguson, J., Tricket, D., & Condemi, B. (1999). Spirit and community at South West Airlines: An investigation of a spiritual values-based model. *Journal of Organizational Change*, *12*(3), 221–223. doi:10.1108/09534819910273928

Mondragon Corporation. (2020). *Annual Report 2019*. https://www.mondragon-corporation.com/2019urtekotxostena/assets/downloads/eng/annual-report-2019.pdf

Morgan, G. (1980). Paradigms, metaphors, and puzzle solving in organization theory. *Administrative Science Quarterly*, *25*(4), 605–622. doi:10.2307/2392283

Morgan, G. (2006). Images of organization (updated ed.). Sage.

Morgan, G. (2016). Commentary: Beyond Morgan's eight metaphors. *Human Relations*, *69*(4), 1029–1042. doi:10.1177/0018726715624497

Morris, M., & Schindehutte, M. (2005). Entrepreneurial values and the ethnic enterprise: An examination of six sub Cultures. *Journal of Small Business Management, 43*(4), 453–479. doi:10.1111/j.1540-627X.2005.00147.x

Morrison, A. (2000). Entrepreneurship: What triggers it? *International Journal of Entrepreneurial Behaviour & Research, 6*(2), 59–71. doi:10.1108/13552550010335976

Neal, J. A., Benyamin, M., Lichtenstein, B., & Banner, D. (1999). Spiritual perspectives on individual, organisational and societal transformation. *Journal of Organizational Change Management, 12*(3), 175–186. doi:10.1108/09534819910273757

Neubert, M. J., Bradley, S. W., Ardianti, R., & Simiyu, E. M. (2017). The role of spiritual capital in innovation and performance: Evidence from developing economies. *Entrepreneurship Theory and Practice, 41*(4), 621–640. doi:10.1111/etp.12172

Neuman, S. (1986). Religious observance within a human capital framework: Theory and application. *Applied Economics, 18*(11), 1193–1202. doi:10.1080/00036848600000072

Nicholls, A., & Cho, A. (2007). Social Entrepreneurship: The Structuration Field. In A. Nichols (Ed.), *Social Entrepreneurship New Models of Sustainable Social Change*. Oxford University Press.

Nicholls, A., & Young, P. (2006). Preface to Paperback Edition. In A. Nicholls (Ed.), *Social Entrepreneurship New Models for Sustainable Social Change*. Oxford University Press.

O'Leary, Z. (2014). *The Essential Guide to Doing Your Research Project*. Sage.

Oham, C. (2013). Could there be treasures in our faith? The recognition and utilisation of spiritual capital values. In D. Singleton (Ed.), *Faith With Its Sleeves Rolled Up*. Faith Action.

Oham, C. (2016). Why Social Enterprise? In C. Oham & D. Macdonald (Eds.), *Leading and Managing a Social Enterprise in Health and Social Care*. Community Training Partners.

Oham, C., Stewart, J., & Cornish, Y. (2009). Social Capital Social Enterprise and Community Development. In J. Stewart & Y. Cornish (Eds.), *Professional Practice in Public Health* (pp. 191–206). Devon Reflect Press.

Pearce, J. A. II, Fritz, D. A., & Davis, P. S. (2010). Entrepreneurial orientation and the performance of religious congregations as predicted by rational choice theory. *Entrepreneurship Theory and Practice, 34*(1), 219–248. doi:10.1111/j.1540-6520.2009.00315.x

Putnam, R. (2000). *Bowling Alone: The Collapse and Revival of American Community*. Simon and Schuster.

Rima, S. D., & Lessens, R. (2005). *Spiritual Capital Research Project, Letter of Intent*. Metanexus Institute.

Savitz, A., & Weber, K. (2006). *The triple bottom line: How today's best-run companies are achieving economic, social, and environmental success - and how you can too*. Jossey-Bass.

Schwandt, T. A. (1993). Theory for the moral sciences: Crises of identity and purpose. In G. Mills & D. J. Flinders (Eds.), *Theory and concepts in qualitative research* (pp. 5–13). Teachers College Press.

Staniewski, M. W., & Awruk, K. (2021). Parental attitudes and entrepreneurial success. *Journal of Business Research, 123*, 538–546. doi:10.1016/j.jbusres.2020.10.039

The Holy Bible, Literal Standard Version (LSV). (2020). *Covenant Press, Covenant Christian Coalition*. Retrieved from http://self.gutenberg.org/

Torrington, D., & Hall, L. (1998). *Human Resource Management*. Prentice Hall Europe.

Tortella, G., Quiroga, G., & Moral-Arce, I. (2011). *Nature or Nurture? Factors of Entrepreneurship: A Comparative Approach*. Institute of Latin American Studies Columbia University.

van Aaken, D., & Buchner, F. (2020). Religion and CSR: A systematic literature review. *Journal of Business Economics, 90*(5-6), 917–945. doi:10.100711573-020-00977-z

Vasconcelos, A. F. (2020). Individual spiritual capital: Meaning, a conceptual framework. *Journal of Work-Applied Management, 13*(1), 117–141. doi:10.1108/JWAM-08-2020-0038

Vincent Ponroy, J., Lê, P., & Pradies, C. (2019). In a family way? A model of family firm identity maintenance by non-family members. *Organization Studies, 40*(6), 859–886. doi:10.1177/0170840619836707

Weber, M. (1905). The Protestant Ethic and the Spirit of Capitalism. In *Die protestantische Ethik und der Geist des Kapitalismus*. Academic Press.

Weber, M. (1965). *The Sociology of Religion*. Methuen.

Weber, M. (2011). The Protestant Ethic and Spirit of Capitalism. In S. Kalberg (Ed.), *The Protestant Ethic and The Spirit of Capitalism*. Oxford University Press.

Wijaya, N. H. S., & Rinaldi, E. (2018). Parenting Style, Risk Propensity, and Entrepreneurial Interest. *Proceedings of the 7th International Conference on Entrepreneurship and Business Management, 1*, 296-301. 10.5220/0008492102960301

Yin, R. (2003). Applied Social Research Methods Series: Vol. 34. *Applications of case study research* (2nd ed.). Sage.

## KEY TERMS AND DEFINITIONS

**Capitalism:** A prevalent economic and social system of privately controlled trade and industry where the primary objective is to maximise shareholders wealth and profit. Excessive focus on the sole objective of profits increasingly comes at the expense of other stakeholders' rights – where regulation to control for this is often trailing and playing 'catch-up'. The failures of capitalism in modern society are often claimed to be portrayed by the worldwide meltdown resulting from the recent 2008 global financial crisis, and widening disparity and wealth gaps in modern society.

**Corporate Social Responsibility (CSR):** A self-regulating business model that seeks to guide a business or organisation to be socially accountable – not only to itself and its shareholders (the owners), but also importantly to society and various publics – broadly, all stakeholders and the environment. Increasingly organisations, either engage proactively on such initiatives, or are conversely pressurised to do so, given a trend towards mounting pressure from both societal and political domains, resulting in increased oversight, regulation and compliance requirements.

**Entrepreneurial Parenting:** Refers to the nurturing and formative parenting role of parents who are enterprising or entrepreneurs – thus shaping the development of their children, who will likely be predisposed to engage in entrepreneurial activity themselves as a result of their upbringing and nurturing, inclusive of vicarious learning, shared beliefs and familial bonds.

**Environmental, Social, and Governance (ESG):** Sharing conceptual elements with CSR, ESG comprises three central factors used to evaluate companies and countries with respect to sustainability measures. Also, it is associated with sound governance, arguably safeguarding against unlawful, and, in some instances, unethical action and behaviour on all three aspects. It is increasingly built into compliance requirements and standards in many sectors, including financial investments.

**Metaphor:** A metaphor is a symbolic association or parallel operationalisation. Whilst not being exactly the same, there exists a direct similarity in praxis or function.

**Social Entrepreneurship:** Value creating activity and enterprise associated with social entrepreneurs – who pursue novel applications that have potential to solve community-based problems. Undertaking risk and effort to create positive changes in society, where beyond financial profits, sustainable enduring value is created for society and the environment. This is sometimes referred to as a 'triple bottom line'.

**Spiritual Capital:** Capital is generally considered to be a store of wealth or an asset that can be capitalised or drawn upon. Sometimes considered a subset of social capital, spiritual capital draws from fundamentals in philosophy, theology, sociology and economics. Broadly, spiritual capital refers to the accumulated value and potential accrued in an enduring collection spiritual and ethically informed beliefs, knowledge, values and dispositions that drive societal, organisational and interpersonal behaviour.

## ENDNOTE

1 See for example the 'Business Roundtable', an association of high-profile corporate CEOs responding to mounting disenchantment and CSR obligations, seeking to promote value in society, and enhance broader opportunities beyond maximising shareholders' wealth through commitments to employees and society.

# Chapter 8
# Addressing the Unemployed Graduate Challenge Through Student Entrepreneurship and Innovation in South Africa's Higher Education

**Ndwakhulu Stephen Tshishonga**
*University of KwaZulu-Natal, South Africa*

## EXECUTIVE SUMMARY

*This chapter addresses graduate unemployment through student entrepreneurship in the context of South African higher education. The graduate unemployment rate of South Africa is estimated at 33.5% for the youth (15–24) and 10.2% for those aged 25–34. Unemployed graduate phenomenon as depicted by the FeesMustFall campaign is exacerbated by untransformed curriculum which does not provide students with the relevant skills to match the labour demands. In this regard, this chapter argues that student entrepreneurship remains one of the strategies university-based youth or students could not only a space to gain business skills and experience, but also a forum where they can put their creative ideas into income generating projects. The chapter first looks at student entrepreneurship and the challenges faced by tertiary students. Second, it explores the opportunities created through entrepreneurship, the challenges faced by student entrepreneurs, and finally, the support needed to run successful student entrepreneurship.*

DOI: 10.4018/978-1-7998-7724-0.ch008

## INTRODUCTION

Across developed and developing nations, the problem of youth unemployment is perplexing and has reached a vantage point (Sankobe, 2019). Various reasons are attached to bulging youth unemployment and subsequent graduate unemployment. In the context of South Africa, jobless growth, lack of requisite skills, poor education and a mismatch of acquired qualifications in the labour market are among the key contributory factors towards rising youth unemployment and emerging graduate unemployment. It is, therefore, not surprising that unemployment among young people is the highest in the country with 38.2% (Stats SA, 2018). Internationally, youth unemployment is the highest. while in Africa, the labour force is unable to create new and sustainable jobs for young people including those with college or university qualifications (James, 2019). Youth unemployment remains one of the major challenges estimated to be sitting at 53%, making it the highest in the world (McCauley, 2019, p. 4). The scourge of youth unemployment made President Ramaphosa to declare it a national crisis in May 2019 (James, 2019). Youth constitute 55.2% of the 6.2 million South Africans who are actively seeking jobs. This is worsened by the slow economic growth and lack of investment in youth programmes. The graduate unemployment rate in South Africa is estimated at 33.5% for the youth (15–24) and 10.2% for those aged 25–34 (StatsSA. 2020). The unemployed graduate phenomenon as depicted by the FeesMustFall campaign is exacerbated by the untransformed curriculum that does not provide students with the relevant skills to match labour demands.

In this regard, this chapter argues that student entrepreneurship is one of the strategies university-based youth or students could use to escape socio-economic challenges. Through student entrepreneurship, university youth (students) not only gain business skills and experience, but also gain a forum through which they are able to put their creative ideas into income-generating projects (Tshishonga, 2020). Student entrepreneurship in a developing country like South Africa could be helpful in closing employment gaps created by the prevalence of poverty, unemployment, and income inequality. Student economic exclusion has been one of the major challenges faced by South Africa as it has a high youth unemployment rate of 55.2% which indicates some of the major economic participation issues faced by the youth (Stats SA, 2019). Since 2019, youth unemployment has increased at around 55.9% (StasSA, 2020). Students have watched their livelihoods being dictated by the high unemployment rates in the country and less effective government interventions to the solutions, which exclude them from their country's economy.

It is against the growing rate of university youth unemployment and underemployment that this chapter interrogates student entrepreneurship as the pathway towards addressing the scourge of graduate unemployment in higher education. This chapter is qualitative in nature and uses document analysis in the form of accredited articles, books and book chapters, as well as official government documentations to navigate entrepreneurship as a panacea to address the unemployed graduate challenge in the higher education sector.

## SCOURGE OF UNEMPLOYED GRADUATE

Globally, unemployment continues to be high with an estimated 18.3% of young unemployed graduates, meaning more than 73 million educated young people aged between 15–24 years are unemployed (Lam, 2014:2). The latter depicts that graduated youth unemployment rate is nearly three times higher when compared to the unemployment rate for adults. According to the World Bank (2013), the number is higher because there are about 300 million young graduates who do no productive work for living, while about 621 million youth are neither working nor educated. The problem of unemployment is exacerbated by the problem of youth graduating annually and hope to enter the labour market for the first-time yet there are few job opportunities.

*Figure 1. Graduates unemployment rates in selected countries and other country groupings (2013)*
*Source: OECD database (2014)*

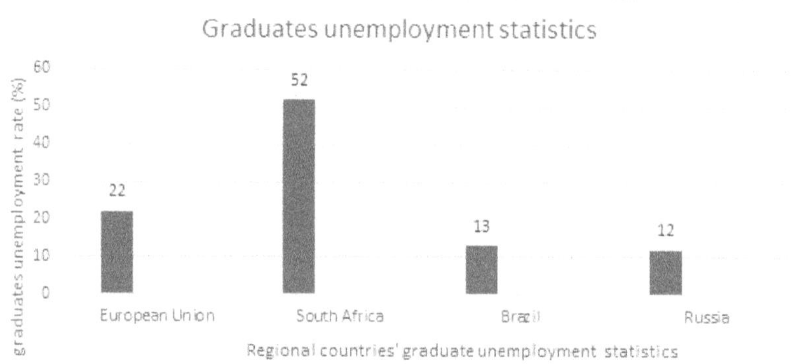


Figure 1 shows that the graduate unemployment rates remain high across many countries with South Africa's unemployment rate beyond 50 percent. On the other side, the European Union is just above 20 percent, meaning many of its countries have low unemployment rates for graduates (ILO, 2014; & IMF, 2014).

*Figure 2. Graduate unemployment in African regions*
*Source: World Bank (2011-2015)*

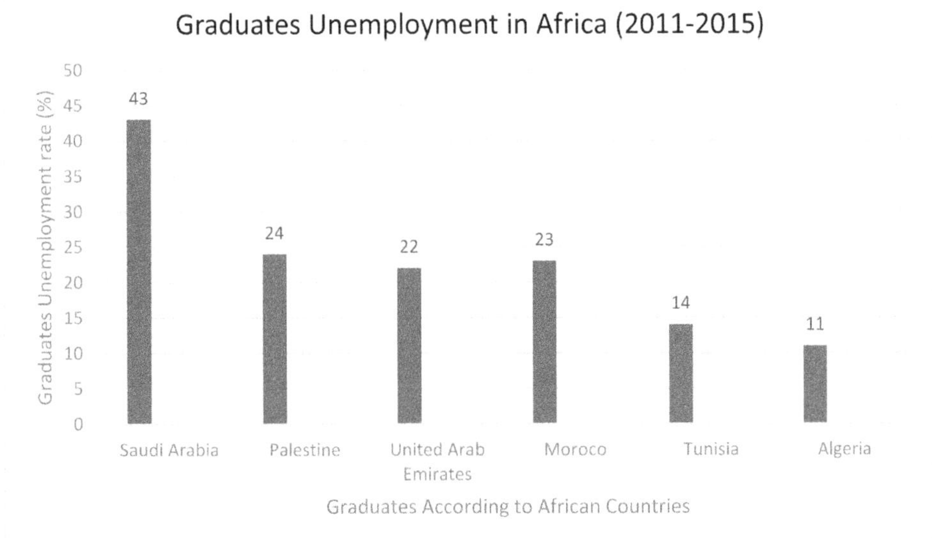


Figure 2 shows that the graduate unemployment rate is highest in Saudi Arabia followed by the Palestinian Territory, with Algeria at the bottom. The conclusions about African graduates' unemployment is made based on the selected African countries. In the majority of African countries unemployment rates are very high, meaning students still find it challenging to be hired after completing their tertiary studies(WEF, 2013).Drawing from the middle east and north African countries, the unemployment rate is high, although there is educational accomplishment. Actually, in some Middle East and North African (MENA) countries, educational accomplishment increases the chances of not finding employment because students graduate but securing a job becomes more difficult than finishing the tertiary training (ILO, 2015). Skill mismatches are a serious problem and, in most cases, relate to poor basic education, as a result, it becomes hard to find well equipped students, as a study done in [Nigeria, Tunisia, Saudi Arabia and Turkey], found (JA Worldwide, 2011:13). This reflects the challenge that university qualifications are no longer a passport for secure employment with continued university graduates' unemployment and underemployment in Africa (Honwana, 2013).

Unemployed graduates include all people who are 15 years and older, not working, but available for work, job searching, and have the necessary skills and knowledge for work (Barker, 2007:174). Therefore, the unemployed could be defined as people who take active steps to obtain the desired skills for work, are qualified and, capable and willing to start a job should they find one. Graduate unemployment is becoming a disturbing phenomenon among students and university youth. StatsSA (2020), reports that the age group between 15 and 24 are not only vulnerable due to their unemployability and underemployability but also account for 43.2% of the unemployed. Thus, the failure of the economy to create jobs, together with skill mismatches are among many reasons for the structural unemployment and emerging phenomenon of graduate unemployment in post-apartheid South Africa (The Presidency, 2019).

Without equality of opportunities, coupled with access to education, jobs and other economic opportunities, the scourge of graduate unemployment confronting university youth remains. South Africa is experiencing a sprouting challenge of graduate unemployment (The Presidency, 2019: 24). However, compared to those with less education, graduates have better prospects for employability and job opportunities. Figure 3 shows the importance of education. Those with (35.4%) and without (54.8%) matric qualifications count for a larger percentage of the unemployed youth while the graduates only 2.3% in total (StasSA, 2020).

*Figure 3. Proportion of the unemployed by education level, Q1: 2020*
*Source: StatsSA, 2020: 7*

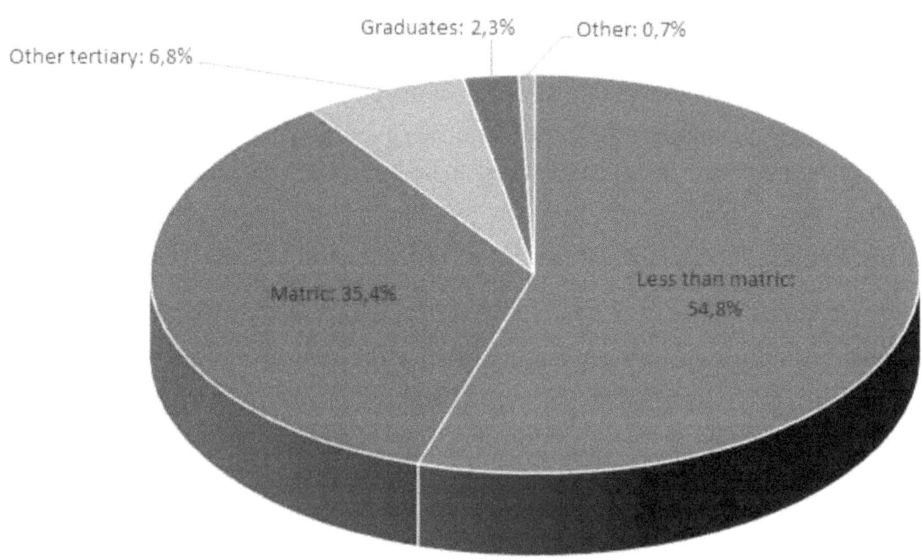


Education remains an important instrument for social mobility and attaining jobs. This situation is further aggravated by the reality that the majority of employable active university youth are unable to secure jobs post graduation (Tshishonga, 2020). Traditionally, formal education is often perceived universally as a legitimised vehicle for self and societal advancement (Omadjohwoefe, 2011). For Omadjohwoefe (2011), university graduates are despondent and hopelessly in search of jobs everywhere. The problem of graduate unemployment is attributable to corruption in governance, the population explosion, expansion of university enrolment and lack of entrepreneurship education in the university curricula (Omadjohwoefe, 2011).

*Figure 4. South African provincial unemployment rate for graduates (2018)*

In South Africa, unemployment is so high, and that could be caused by its geographical dynamics that include race and previous apartheid separate development, hence, there are often unequal employment opportunities among South African provinces (Sekatane, 2004:20). The unemployment of graduates could also be a result of vast rural areas (provinces) with more people receiving insufficient education that does not qualify them to sophisticated courses than in urban areas. This is evidenced by the fact that in all provinces, rural provinces like Mpumalanga have the highest percentage (74.4 percent) of unemployed graduates followed by KwaZulu Natal and the Eastern Cape at 74 percent and 73 percent, respectively. The province with the lowest youth unemployment rate is Gauteng at 59.5 percent, as shown in Figure 4.

South Africa is one of many countries both within Africa and internationally that are challenged by severe unemployment, especially the graduates (De Witte, Rothmann, & Jackson, 2012). High unemployment rates of graduates in South Africa are among the most pressurising social and economic challenges that face the democratic government and the Continent at large. In South Africa, graduates remain the most vulnerable group in the labour market because of the shift in economic demands and expectation of highly skilled labour (Graham & Mlatsheni, 2015; Statistic South Africa, 2017).

*Figure 5. Unemployment rate by education status: 2008 to 2017*
*Source: (From Statistics South Africa, 2017)*

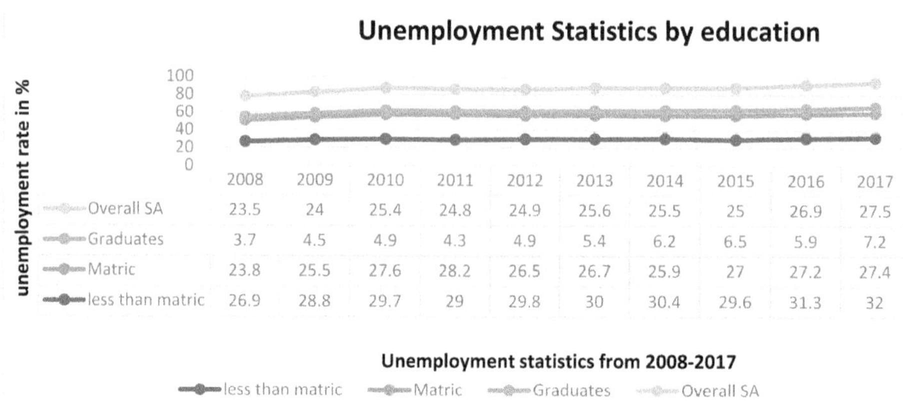


| | 2008 | 2009 | 2010 | 2011 | 2012 | 2013 | 2014 | 2015 | 2016 | 2017 |
|---|---|---|---|---|---|---|---|---|---|---|
| Overall SA | 23.5 | 24 | 25.4 | 24.8 | 24.9 | 25.6 | 25.5 | 25 | 26.9 | 27.5 |
| Graduates | 3.7 | 4.5 | 4.9 | 4.3 | 4.9 | 5.4 | 6.2 | 6.5 | 5.9 | 7.2 |
| Matric | 23.8 | 25.5 | 27.6 | 28.2 | 26.5 | 26.7 | 25.9 | 27 | 27.2 | 27.4 |
| less than matric | 26.9 | 28.8 | 29.7 | 29 | 29.8 | 30 | 30.4 | 29.6 | 31.3 | 32 |

Figure 5 shows the shifts in employment rates for graduates in matric and tertiary as well as the overall South African stats. Given the shift in labour demand, there is a slight increase in the employment rate, but the graduates are still likely to struggle in securing employment after graduation. This, however, is not a true reflection of the expected case. According to the Quarterly Labour Force Survey (QLFS) (Statistics South Africa, 2017), the graduate unemployment rate has slightly lowered by 0.8% in 2017 compared to the 2016 rate. Over 433,000 people, including graduates, who joined the labour force and were unemployed at the end of 2016 and beginning of 2017, approximately 58% were the youth (Statistics South Africa, 2017). The graduate unemployment rate remained at 7.3 percent from the last quarter of the year 2016 according to Statistics South Africa (2017). From 2008 to 2015, a closer inspection of the graduate unemployment rate depicts that there was 8.3 to 10.5 percent growth for South African graduates and the youth (Statistics South Africa, 2015). The above statistics depict that over the years, the labour market has been characterised by a shrinking job-security which requires constant up-skilling, experience for employability and ongoing training and development. The overall stats depict that South African people with no matric; with matric; and who graduated are experiencing a slow increase in terms of employment rate which symbolises that there are more graduates and job seekers than available opportunities.

## NOTION OF STUDENT ENTREPRENEURSHIP

Graduate unemployment has prompted students in different fields and faculties to resort to entrepreneurship as the pathway to address their socio-economic challenges. Opportunities created by universities saw students establishing and running small businesses within and outside campuses. Structural support by institutions of higher education push student entrepreneurs into pursuing entrepreneurship based on their studies (Singh, 2019: 20). Thus, student entrepreneurship as a strategy for closing the employment gaps created by the prevalence of poverty, unemployment and income inequality (Bailettai, 2011 & Jansen, de Zande, Brinkkemper & Stam, 2015). The concept of student entrepreneurship is defined as an economic development tool where knowledge obtained by students is utilised to translate such knowledge into income generating businesses (Bailettai, 2011). Marchand & Hermens (2014) defined student entrepreneurship as an individual attending academic classes at university while conducting innovative and entrepreneurial activities for revenue generation. Therefore, student entrepreneurship is a college or university student who may be attending entrepreneurial classes or not, while simultaneously conducting a business on/near campus where he/she is attending formal courses. The whole concept of student entrepreneurship is a form of entrepreneurship focused on student entrepreneurs in higher educational institutions or the youth in general.

The Global Entrepreneurship Monitor (GEM) (2013) has data from 69 countries which monitors the trends of economic growth which may be due to different entrepreneurial activities between nations. According to the GEM Report (2017), Africa is ranked the lowest with 17% of entrepreneurs expected to create jobs and North America being the highest with 29.5%. The high statistics in North America are due to high youth and student entrepreneurship successes in the US. This has seen students' businesses employ more than 350,000 people with a total number of 1.3 billion users using businesses invented in university dorms such as Facebook and windows software (Marchand, 2015: 267). With such differences between these two regions there is a gap in lack of student entrepreneurship research (Politis et al., 2011). From students' entrepreneurship a new concept was coined known as "Studentrepreneur". This concept was further explained as student entrepreneurs who attend university classes and simultaneously have on and off campus businesses generating income for themselves (Marchand, 2015: 269).

## FINDINGS AND ANALYSIS

### Reasons for Graduate Non-Employability

Various reasons are attributed to the scourge of students' unemployment worldwide and South Africa in particular. Some of the reasons are associated with the broader socio-economic trends beyond the students themselves and institutions of higher learning. While other factors relate to the issues of re-curriculum, exposure to integrated work placements and, most importantly, creative and innovative thinking among graduates themselves.

Higher education is meant to play a crucial role in training future leaders based on social demands and global market demands. Unemployment among the graduate university youth is further exacerbated by the lower skills and market skills mismatch. Admittedly, global competitiveness and the technological advancement have enormous demands on universities to produce graduates with cognitive skills and knowledge required by the labour market. Thus, Pauw, Oosthuizen and Van Der Westhuizen (2008: 45) argue that:

*Learners are inadequately prepared for both tertiary studies and entry into the labour market. Lack of, or inadequate career guidance means that they do not choose fields of study and types of qualifications with good employment prospects. In addition, lack of soft skills and workplace experience mean that employers are reluctant to employ graduates, preferring more experienced people instead.*

After finishing college education or any form of higher education, graduates expect a valued job compared to those of high-school graduates. However, the results prove differently since graduate unemployment is high (Winkelmann, 2009). The main objective of tertiary education has been focused on university and college access for students and about gaining more admission for students so that they can be equipped with the necessary information for work. However, while graduates want to have good jobs and decent incomes based on acquired knowledge, graduate students sometimes face unemployment after graduation (Hwang, 2017). Unemployment is challenging to the individual, especially the recently graduated because it leads to a financial crisis if the students are not employed after university, and this is often due the fact that they lack the skills and experience required. Arkes (2010) argues that if graduates do not have the intrinsic experience or skills to meet the needs of employers, then the unemployment rate will increase, and the certificate received would be unnecessary. The latter depicts that if the graduates lack career management, effective training, and discipline-specific skills, the unemployment rate is likely to escalate.

According to Hwang (2017: 5), the 'gap between students' developed skills and ability on campus and practical job requirements can be another reason for unemployment', it is often caused by mismatch of university choices against work requirements. Therefore, the unemployment of graduates is somehow dependent not only on the academic performances, but also on personal background that might have influenced course choice which eventually determines the route of job hunting. Another factor that determines whether one is likely to be employed include race, gender, and socio-economic factors, skills and experiences gained through college curricula which are sometimes not sufficient for a work entry-level position and that adversely cause unemployment to rise (Morley, 2001; & Pauw *et al.*, 2008). In addition, the education received in universities and training colleges is insufficient and limited to a general level, which does not produce the exact skills needed to be hired. Sparber & Fan (2012) explain that the traditional curricula provided from schools to colleges and to the workplace does not match the practical needs, and those differences contribute greatly to unemployment. Failure of the curriculum to develop the skills needed by the labour market led to graduates leaving universities without transferable skills and practical knowledge for employability or self-employment (Honwana, 2013).

Furthermore, Hwang (2017) provides contrasting reasons for high unemployment rates among graduates, noting that some graduates tend to be over-educated for entry-position in the labour market. From a work perspective, being over-educated means that the graduates exceed the social optimal level of education, making it difficult to be considered for junior position jobs. So, if there are available job positions that require basic bachelor-level skills and there are graduate who exceeds the level, it is highly possible that the over-educated will not be considered even for job interview. From an economic perspective, which focuses on structural unemployment, the graduate unemployment comes from mismatching between available jobs and wanting to do courses that already have limited spaces (Herz & Van Rens, 2011). It is therefore clear that, the surplus of graduates who have advanced degrees like honours or a master's degree can rarely be considered in labour that demands people with junior degrees, and this leads to the overeducated searching for a job based on their education level.

## Effects of Graduate Unemployment

Onoyase (2019) stipulates that graduates from higher institutions face the difficulty of not getting jobs immediately after graduating. According to researchers Sara (2008), and Tandama (2009), some years back, graduates used to be easily employed after graduating, however, in the current centuries the situation severely became difficult as the number of graduates continues to increase, yet there is a shortage of vacancies. The issue of graduate unemployment has forced graduates to go in search of self-employment and to go as far as wanting to volunteer in some companies. In Africa, graduates' unemployment is a very discouraging challenge because in ten graduates, only one student is likely to get work immediately. This is also affirmed by Balogun (2016: 63) who stresses that almost half of the 10 million African graduates turned-out of over 668 universities yearly do not get jobs, and that has a serious effect and concern among them, and some of the effects are due to the poor curricula. Onoyase (2019) mentioned that one of the reasons why graduates find it difficult to secure jobs after graduation is the inadequate curricula which yields no competency and that is a bad outcome. In South Africa, the inability of many graduates to secure employment indicates that education alone is not a solution for unemployment (Maseku, 2019). Sadly, having a higher education qualification does not guarantee or secure a job. With the current bleak economic situation, graduates enter into the job market with uncertainty about gaining employment (Pauw et al., 2008). Despite various interventions to address youth unemployment and employability, graduates included, joblessness remains high and is reaching a crisis point (Honwana, 2013 and Kruss, 2004). Graduate unemployment is a challenge not only for South Africa, but the entire African continent (Honwana, 2013). Consequently, due to graduate unemployment, graduates often suffer from depression. For Oluwajodu et al., (2015), the problem associated with unemployed graduates is also linked to their participation in criminal activities that undermines youth development in general, hence threatening the economy.

According to Adesina (2013), graduate unemployment as it is, in many developing countries, for instance, African countries, poses a challenge to the labour market and the overall socio-economic condition. The unemployment graduate is not only deprived of having income, but also deprived of the socialisation effect of work, eventually causing depression and frustration. Madoui (2015) ascertains that, in other developing countries (African countries), the unemployed graduate appears to experience disgrace, hardship and frustration as the resulting cause from unemployment. On its own, graduate unemployment results in a worthlessness, and an embarrassment when having less income value in society. Adawo *et al.*, (2012) stated that unemployment causes unhappiness to graduates who have to adapt in the world of material consideration where the unemployed are not socially and economically recognised because they are seen as liabilities in their societies. The pressure received from society make the unemployed graduates exhibit some negative social problems, for example, kidnapping and drug abuse. Sirat & Shuib (2012) is of the opinion that youth or graduates unemployment can be said to have contributed to the huge rise in social unrest and crime in the developing world. Aihie *et al.*, (2014), further ascertained that graduate unemployment has negative effects on youth; it results in circumstances like low self-esteem, frustration and depression, and anti-social behaviour such as prostitution in females and armed robbery or kidnapping in males.

## Is Student Entrepreneurship a Solution?

The high unemployment rate and rapid economic changes taking place within the South African workplace has caused most graduates to consider self-employment as a solution. The self-employed graduates can be seen as graduate entrepreneurs who study whilst running a small business for survival (Schreuder & Coetzee, 2006:41). Student entrepreneurship can be considered as a student who owns a business, requiring personal sacrifice, strategising, and risk-taking in order to create something valuable. Florin *et al.*, (2007:21) ascertain that the student entrepreneurial model implies that one is able to create employment and benefit by profiting from one's own working skills and connections, which may also create chances of employability for others. The dedication to self-employment requires innovation, commitment, a positive disposition, self-efficacy, and motivation. Bezuidenhout, (2011) adds that to achieve entrepreneurship, students who are in entrepreneurship while studying should have tolerance for ambiguity and be willing to take risks to pursue an entrepreneurial career more easily. Therefore, some students have to resort to entrepreneurship for them to be able to penetrate the market which is dominated by a high unemployment rate of students.

## University Education as a Seed for Student Entrepreneurship

Primordially, universities or institutions of higher learning came into existence as custodians of knowledge. Universities or institutions of higher education have been created to advance human capital in the form of knowledge production and dissemination. At the centre of these institutions is formal education of which Kgomoeswana (2020: 12) argues could be the key to facing challenges. Consolidating and increasing access to academic institutions by the democratic government has been the priority in post-apartheid South Africa (The Presidency, 2014). Universities in their different formation and focus represent knowledge, truth, discussions, inquiry, authenticity, care, understanding veracity, application, personal critique, development, and action (Clark, 1998, 2004). Socially and economically, the academic institutions are the epicenter of knowledge and education. The knowledge and education created by universities does not only mould educated people, but also has an impact on politics, administration, including industries, and commerce (Livingstone, 2016: 8). Viewed from the human capital theory, education plays a pivotal role in economic growth and can provide much needed skills for human development (Unterhalter, 2009: 2017). For Unterhalter (2009), education is instrumental in empowering a distributive force for social change and developing a critical mind.

Education is key in educating the nation, but also for broadening opportunities for economic growth and development in a knowledge society (Castells, 2017). Thus, demand for accessible and quality education is an investment towards advancing teaching and learning, research and community engagement; a higher institutions core business (Ramphele, 2008). Considering the socio-economic challenges faced by society, universities are custodians of knowledge production and dissemination for transformational and developmental purposes (Rothblatt, 2006). However, in the modern era, such institutions are challenged to embrace and play a developmental role as one of the critical stakeholders in addressing challenges faced by the modern world. An assumed developmental role saw nations particularly, the developed ones, investing huge sums of financial resources in institutions of higher learning with the targeted outcomes of having a skilled and competent workforce (Margison & Considine, 2011).

Knowledge produced by universities is often disseminated through theses and dissertations compiled by students for grading towards their degrees or qualifications. For students to play an active role in the knowledge economy, young people require better educational and economic opportunities to prosper in the labour market (NPC, 2011: 15). The establishment of these income projects is in line with the DHET and university policies with a particular focus on promoting student entrepreneurship. In order to deal with unemployment issues, Okechukwu (2019: 14) argues that qualifications are inadequate provided they are accompanied by entrepreneurial skills.

## University Support as the Driver for Student Entrepreneurship

For student entrepreneurship to succeed, human, financial and infrastructural support is needed. At national level, attempts to address graduate and youth unemployment, and the quest to encourage universities to establish the third-stream income, the promotion of student and graduate entrepreneurship was prioritised. The commitment to instil an entrepreneurial culture, saw the establishment of an Entrepreneurship Development in Higher Education (EDHE) in 2016 within the University Education Branch of the Department Higher Education and Training. The EDHE Programme has since been included in the University Capacity Development Programme (UCDP) of the Department Higher Education and Training (https://edhe.co.za/edhe-intervarsity).

The goals of the EDHE Programme are:

- **Student entrepreneurship:** Mobilising the national student and graduate resource to create successful enterprises that will ultimately lead to both wealth and job creation.
- **Entrepreneurship development in academia:** Support academics in instilling an entrepreneurial mindset in all students and graduates through the offering of relevant knowledge, transferral of practical skills and the application of business principles, not only to a specific discipline, but across disciplines.
- **Developing entrepreneurial universities:** Creating a conducive environment that will enable universities to adapt strategically and embark on projects whereby third-stream income can be generated through innovative business ideas (https://edhe.co.za/edhe-intervarsity).

In the main, the EDHE Programme was developed to boost the entrepreneurial capacity of students, academics and leaders. Due to challenges faced by students such as unemployed graduates, the programme intended to transform students into economically active citizens during and post their tertiary education. Through entrepreneurial activities, students can generate an additional income and fast-track the process of becoming economically active. Upon graduation, students would be able to consider entrepreneurship as a career, either as a first choice, or as an alternative, especially if they have difficulties in finding employment. In order to fulfil this mandate, students from all disciplines are encouraged to embrace an entrepreneurial mindset and culture based on entrepreneurship education and training (EDHE Lekgotla 2018).

Various universities have heeded the call to support students in their entrepreneurial journey. For example, Durban University of Technology (DUT) has also responded well to the DHET call on all South African higher education institutions to support student entrepreneurs who still want to grow their businesses (DUT, 2017). The Centre for Social Entrepreneurship (CSE) is the division in charge of ensuring student projects at DUT are supported with one of the highest pitching events with 300 applicants and where only 20 of them were chosen to present their business for funding in 2017 (Kunene, 2017). In the case of Mangosuthu University of Technology (MUT), on 12 April 2019, the Deputy Vice chancellor of MUT announced the launch of a Pilot project, Wadhwami Foundation (WF) Entrepreneurial Skills Training program to take MUT as one of the entrepreneurship development universities (MUT, 2019). Hence, student entrepreneurs were already visible on the MUT campus. In line with the national department of higher education, UKZN introduced a policy and Student Entrepreneurship Programme in 2018 to encourage entrepreneurship culture (UKZN InQubate, 2018). UKZN Inqubate also assists with technology transfer, which aims to assist student entrepreneurs with management of intellectual property, commercial contracts and licenses (UKZN Enspire, 2019). Innovatively, students from various disciplines across all five campuses were invited to enter competitions with awards and mentoring services.

## FUTURE REASERCH DIRECTIONS

Student entrepreneurship in South African higher educations is new and, as such, rigorous research is needed to instil a culture of student entrepreneurship. Opportunities and infrastructure available should be the point of departure to motivate graduates to start using knowledge acquired through their theses and dissertations for income-generating projects within and outside campus. With adequate human and financial support, graduates and youth in general could start to sustain their student entrepreneurial enterprises. From such research, role models for nurturing entrepreneurial students could have a stronger effect in both students and non-attending young people considering there is a lack of entrepreneurial culture among the university youth (Lafuente, Vaillant, & Rialp, 2007). Bergmann, Hundt & Sternberg (2016) argue that university programmes that support entrepreneurship among students are more effective when coordinated with respective strategies of the region where the university is located.

## CONCLUSION AND RECOMMENDATIONS

This chapter has deliberated on the scourge of graduates' unemployment in the context of the higher education sector. Slow economic growth, curriculum, mediocre quality and academic orientation of education systems were highlighted as contributory factors to rising graduate unemployment and underemployment in South Africa. Student entrepreneurship in South African higher educations is new and, as such, there is a need for research that focuses on the relevant support by various stakeholders. This entails the quantitative and qualitative impact of such support in growing sustainable student entrepreneurial enterprises. From such research, role models for nurturing entrepreneurial students could have a stronger effect in both students and non-attending young people considering there is a lack of entrepreneurial role models outside the university (Lafuente, Vaillant, & Rialp, 2007).

In response to challenges faced by students, universities have enacted entrepreneurial policies aimed at promoting entrepreneurship education among their students and staff. UKZN introduced a student entrepreneurship policy and student entrepreneurship programme in 2018 aimed at providing support for student entrepreneurs. Its focus was on postgraduate students who had acquired more skills at the university, but this opens up a debate on whether entrepreneurship is learned or a skill one is born with (Rengamani, 2015:38). Student livelihoods have improved and, as such, they have managed to minimise the financial challenges they faced within universities. Students have created employment for themselves and other students. Their entrepreneurial endeavours have opened up opportunities to beat hunger as well as other financial challenges although at a smaller scale.

This chapter recommends that through entrepreneurship, students can establish suitable income-generating projects. Support from institutions of higher learning could make a stark difference on the lives of the students. Universities are, therefore, urged to promote a culture and spirit of entrepreneurship at both undergraduate and post-graduate levels. Finally, in order to reduce the challenges of unemployment among youth and graduates alike, an entrepreneurial culture and education needs to be created as part of the university curriculum.

## REFERENCES

Adesina, O. S. (2013). Unemployment and security challenges in Nigeria. *International Journal of Humanities and Social Science, 03*(07).

Aihie, O. N. & Alika, H. I. (2014). Combating youth unemployment in Nigeria through effective school counselling. *Edo Journal of Counselling,* 201-218.

Arkes, J. (2010). Using unemployment rates as instruments to estimate returns to schooling. *Southern Economic Journal, 76*(3), 711–722. doi:10.4284ej.2010.76.3.711

Atkins, M. J. (1999). Oven-ready and self-basting: Taking stock of employability skills. *Teaching in Higher Education, 4*(2), 267–280. doi:10.1080/1356251990040208

Australian Council of Engineering Deans. (2018). *An update on the status and trends in Australia's higher education system for engineering*. Australian Council of Engineering Deans.

Balogun, K. (2016). *Unemployment in Africa.* Paper presented at African transformation forum organized by Africa Centre for Economic Transformation (ACET).

Barker, F. (2007). *The South African labour market* (5th ed.). Van Schaik publishers.

Bedard, K., & Herman, D. A. (2008). Who goes to graduate/professional school? The importance of economic fluctuations, undergraduate field, and ability. *Economics of Education Review, 27*(2), 197–210. doi:10.1016/j.econedurev.2006.09.007

Bezuidenhout, M. (2011). *The development and evaluation of a measure of graduate employability in the context of the new world of work* (Doctoral dissertation). University of Pretoria.

Brown, P., Hesketh, V., & Williams, S. (2002). *Employability in a knowledge economy*. Cardiff University.

CHEC (Cape Higher Education Consortium). (2013). *Pathways from university to work: a graduate destination survey of the 2010 cohort of graduates from the Western Cape Universities*. CHEC.

Crowley, L., Jones, K., Cominetti, N., & Gulliford, J. (2013). *International Lessons: Youth unemployment in the global context*. Lancaster University.

De Witte, H., Rothmann, S., & Jackson, L. T. (2012). The psychological consequences of unemployment in South Africa. *Suid-Afrikaanse Tydskrif vir Ekonomiese en Bestuurswetenskappe*, *15*(3), 235–252. doi:10.4102ajems.v15i3.153

Engineers Australia. (2017). *The engineering profession: A statistical overview* (13th ed.). Institution of Engineers Australia.

Farouq, A., & Adilovic, S. (2014). *Understanding Graduate Employability-Fit with the Company: The Employer Perspective*. Academic Press.

Florin, J., Karri, R., & Rossiter, N. (2007). Fostering entrepreneurial drive-in business education: An attitudinal approach. *Journal of Management Education*, *31*(1), 17–42. doi:10.1177/1052562905282023

GerardiK.HerkenhoffK.OhanianL. E.WillenP. (2013). Unemployment, negative equity, and strategic default. Available at SSRN 2293152.

Graham, L., & Mlatsheni, C. (2015). Youth Unemployment in South Africa: Understanding the challenge and working on solutions. *South African Child Gauge*, 51-59.

Herz, B., & van Rens, T. (2011). Structural unemployment. *Economics Working Papers*, 1276.

Honwana, A. (2013). *The Time of Youth; Works, social Change and Politics in Africa*. Kumarian Press.

Hwang, Y. (2017). What is the cause of graduates' unemployment? Focus on individual concerns and perspectives. *Journal of Educational Issues*, *3*(2), 1–10. doi:10.5296/jei.v3i2.11378

ILO (International Labour Organisation). (2014). *Global employment trends: risk of a jobless recovery? ILO.*

ILO (International Labour Organisation). (2015). *World employment and social outlook*. ILO.

International Monetary Fund (IMF). (2014). World Economic Outlook-Recovery Strengthens, Remains Uneven. International Monetary Fund.

Lafuente, E., Vaillant, Y., & Rialp, J. (2007). Regional differences in the influence of role models: Comparing the entrepreneurial process of rural Catalonia. *Regional Studies*, *41*(6), 779–796. doi:10.1080/00343400601120247

Lam, D. (2014). Youth bulges and youth unemployment. *IZA World of Labor: Evidence-Based Policy Making*. Advance online publication. doi:10.15185/izawol.26

Lesotho Bureau of Statistics. (2011). *2008 Lesotho integrated labour force survey*. www.bos.gov.ls

Lie, K. (2007). *Employer perception on graduate literacy in higher education in relation to the workplace*. http://www.esp-world.info/Articles_20/DOC/Koo_vp_employer_Journal18Oct09.pdf

Lingstone, R. (2016). *Some Thoughts on University Education*. Cambridge University Press.

Lovati, J. M. (1976). *The unemployment rate as an economic indicator*. Federal Reserve Bank of St. Louis.

Madoui, M. (2015). Unemployment among young graduates in Algeria, a sociological reading. *Open Journal of Social Sciences*, *3*(1), 35–41. doi:10.4236/jss.2015.311006

Marchand, J. M., & Hermens, A. H. (2014, December). Student entrepreneurship: a research agenda. *Australian and New Zealand Academy of Management Conference*.

Morley, L. (2001). Producing new workers: Quality, equality and employability in higher education. *Quality in Higher Education*, *7*(2), 131–138. doi:10.1080/13538320120060024

Morrissey, H. (2013). Your career is not predestined by degree choice. *Telegraph*. https://www.telegraph.co.uk/finance/comment/10264114/Your-career-is-notpredestined-by-degree-choice.html

Mseleku, Z. (2019). Graduate internship and employment opportunities: A case study of EThekwini Municipality, KwaZulu-Natal (PhD thesis). University of KwaZulu-Natal, Durban, South Africa.

NPC (National Planning Commission). (2011). *National development Plan. Our future: Make it work, Executive summary*. The Presidency.

OECD (Organisation for Economic Co-Operation and Development). (2014). Preventing unemployment and underemployment from becoming structural. OECD.

Oluwajodu, F., Greyling, L., Blaauw, D., & Kleynhans, E. P. (2015). Graduate unemployment in South Africa: Perspectives from the banking sector. *SA Journal of Human Resource Management*, *13*(1), 1–9. doi:10.4102ajhrm.v13i1.656

Omadjohwoefe, O. S. (2011). Education and the paradox of graduate unemployment: The dilemma of development in Nigeria. *An International Multi-Disciplinary Journal*, *5*(1), 253–265.

Onoyase, A. (2019). Causal factors and effects of unemployment on graduates of tertiary institutions in Ogun State South West Nigeria: Implications for counselling. *Journal of Educational and Social Research*, *9*(4), 119–127. doi:10.2478/jesr-2019-0061

Pauw, K., Oosthuizen, M., & Van Der Westhuizen, C. (2008). Graduate Unemployment In The Face Of Skills Shortages: A Labour Market Paradox1. *The South African Journal of Economics*, *76*(1), 45–57. doi:10.1111/j.1813-6982.2008.00152.x

Pauw, K., Oosthuizen, M., & Van Der Westhuizen, C. (2008). Graduate unemployment in the face of skills shortages: A labour market paradox. *The South African Journal of Economics*, *76*(1), 45–57. doi:10.1111/j.1813-6982.2008.00152.x

Rengamani, J., & Ramachandran, S. (2015). A Study on the entrepreneurial skills among students in Chennai. *International Journal of Advanced Research in Management*, *6*(3), 36–44.

ROA (Research Centre For Education and the Labour Market). (2012). *Maastricht University graduate surveys: 2012. ROA-F2012/3*. Maastricht University.

Ryan, C. (2012). *Field of Degree and Earnings by Selected Employment Characteristics: 2011. American Community Survey Briefs. ACSBR/11-10*. US Census Bureau.

Sankobe, Y. (2019). *The Narrative of an Unemployed Graduate in South Africa*. Samuel Centre for Social Connectedness. https://www.socialconnectedness.org/the-narrative-of-an-unemployed-graduate-in-south-africa/

Sara, S. S. (2008). *Evaluation of vocational training programmes among the in-mates of reformatory institutions in Jigawa State*. Unpublished seminar paper submitted to the Department of Education, University of Maiduguri.

Schreuder, A. M. G., & Coetzee, M. (2006). *Careers: an organisational perspective* (3rd ed.). Juta & Co.

Sehume, J. (2015). Solving poverty, unemployment and inequality. *Sunday Independent*, *24*(June), 15.

Sekatane, M. B. (2004). *The role of clothing manufacturing co-operatives in job creation and poverty alleviation in Sharpeville* (Doctoral dissertation). North-West University.

Singh, V. (2019). Student entrepreneurs on the rise in grim economy. *Sunday Tribune*, *6*(October), 20.

Sirat, M., & Shuib, M. (2012). *Employability in Malaysia*. Asian and Pacific Regional Bureau for Education UNESCO.

Sparber, C., & Fan, J. S. (2012). *Unemployment, Skills, and the Business Cycle Since 2000*. Academic Press.

Statistics South Africa. (2017). *Media Release: Quarterly Labour Force Survey – QLFS Q4: 2016*. www.statssa.gov.za/?p=9561

Statistics South Africa. (2018). National and Provincial Labour Market: Youth Statistical Release P0211.4.2. Pretoria, South Africa: Statistics South Africa. Retrieved from http://www.statssa.gov.za/publications/P02114.2/P02114.22015.pdf

Taudama, A. M. (2009). *Significance of self-employment among unemployed graduates in Kaduna State* (Unpublished PGDM Project report). Department of Social Management Sciences, Bayero University, Kano.

Tomlinson, M. (2008). The degree is not enough: Students' perceptions of the role of higher education credentials for graduate work and employability. *British Journal of Sociology of Education*, *29*(1), 49–61. doi:10.1080/01425690701737457

Tshishonga, N. (2020). Profiling Student Entrepreneurial Enterprises at Howard College Campus: Students' Livelihood Opportunities and Challenges. In A. O. Ayandibu (Ed.), *Reshaping Entrepreneurship Education with Strategy and Innovation* (pp. 197–216). IGI Global.

WEF. (2013). *Global agenda councils -youth unemployment visualization 2013*. WEF.

Wellman, N. (2010). The employability attributes required of new marketing graduates. *Marketing Intelligence & Planning*, *28*(7), 908–930. doi:10.1108/02634501011086490

Wilton, N. (2011). Do employability skills really matter in the UK graduate labour market? The case of business and management graduates. *Work, Employment and Society*, *25*(1), 85–100. doi:10.1177/0950017010389244

Winkelmann, R. (2009). Unemployment, social capital, and subjective well-being. *Journal of Happiness Studies*, *10*(4), 421–430. doi:10.100710902-008-9097-2

World Bank. (2013). *World development report: Jobs*. Author.

Worldwide, J. A. (2011). *Generation jobless: the challenge of global youth unemployment.* www.jaworldwide.org

## KEY TERMS AND DEFINITIONS

**Entrepreneurship:** Entrepreneurship is defined as an activity that involves the discovery, evaluation, and exploitation of opportunities to introduce new goods and services, which have not existed (Mbhele, 2012). Therefore, in entrepreneurship, entrepreneurs are exposed to new business that ascend in the face of risk and uncertainty.

**Student:** A young person or any other person who is registered in a university or institution of higher learning to obtain his or her degree or qualification.

**Student Entrepreneurs:** These are university or any higher education registered students who, within their capacity, decide to start their own enterprises to meet their basic needs.

**Student Entrepreneurship:** Student entrepreneurship is the practice where students start and run their own businesses enterprises in order to generate their own income.

**Unemployed Graduate:** Is the situation whereby students graduate but are still unable to secure employment in the job market.

# Chapter 9
# The Critical Importance of Enhancing Social Entrepreneurship Learning Pathways to Recover From the COVID-19 Economic Crisis

**Tim Pascoe**
*DICE Consortium, UK*

**Jeff Gow**
https://orcid.org/0000-0002-5726-298X
*DICE Consortium, UK*

**Andre Mostert**
*DICE Consortium, UK*

## EXECUTIVE SUMMARY

*Social enterprises (SE) have long been recognised as a significant part of society and as a yardstick for the wider concern of community stakeholders to the general wellbeing and quality of life of the population. Furthermore, in countries that have embraced the free market with limited government, particularly in post-financial-crisis enforced austerity fiscal budgets, the role of the SE is extremely important in contributing to community wellbeing. Now the COVID-19 pandemic of 2020 has dealt a crushing blow to many economic, social, and entrepreneurial activities with its associated lockdowns and government mandated restrictions on economic activities. It is imperative, given the devastating economic impact of the epidemic and subsequent lockdowns, that efforts to encourage SE and social entrepreneurship*

DOI: 10.4018/978-1-7998-7724-0.ch009

*be redoubled and receive government assisted training for these efforts. Creating robust and effective learning pathways informed by the need to support a building back better ethos is key to the future of social innovation and social enterprise-based economic activities.*

*Social entrepreneurship is emerging as an inventive approach for dealing with complex social needs. (Johnson, 2002)*

## OVERVIEW OF SOCIAL ENTREPRENEURSHIP

### Introduction and Problem Statement

The COVID-19 pandemic has caused an international emergency endangering people and economies across the world. At the start of the pandemic, most nations were not ready and reacting to new dangers needed new and evolving solutions. Social enterprises (SEs) or socially driven private enterprises have come to the fore to help – they have been particularly active as they are, by their nature, agile and flexible and have stepped up to provide relief. These enterprises will continue to be important as the pandemic develops and the world reacts as recovery is going to take time and vary across the globe. Indeed, we may have to learn to live with the virus!

In this context, the Global Partnership for Results-Based Approaches (GPRBA) has reviewed COVID-19. The GPRBA was established in 2003 and, since then, has been working to bring together public and private sector funders to maximise resources and design effective incentives for service providers to provide social solutions. The GPRBA has a history of working successfully with SEs and has produced a White Paper (Das et al 2020) providing guidance for stakeholders who engage in Result Based Financing (RBF) and who are dealing with the pandemic. Taking such an approach, it focuses on two overarching objectives, i.e., helping reduce the spread of COVID-19 cases and helping to minimise the socio-economic impact of the pandemic, especially on poor and excluded groups using SEs through an RBF model. Furthermore, it explores financial arrangements, tools and mechanisms that could be used to substantiate results working with SEs whilst taking into account the need to reduce face-to-face interactions in light of COVID-19.

SE have long been recognised as a significant part of society and as a yardstick for the wider concern of community stakeholders to the general wellbeing and quality of life of the population. Furthermore, in countries that have embraced the free market with limited government support particularly in postglobal financial crisis enforced austerity fiscal budgets, the role of the SE is extremely important in contributing to community wellbeing. Now the COVID-19 pandemic of 2020 has dealt a crushing blow to many economic, social and entrepreneurial activities with its associated lockdowns and government mandated restrictions on economic activities. It is imperative, given the devastating economic impact of the epidemic and subsequent lockdowns, that efforts to encourage SE and social entrepreneurship be redoubled and receive government assisted training for these efforts. This is particularly pertinent in that COVID has given many people the opportunity to reconsider their goals in life leading to the potential growth of new social entrepreneurs who, given support, can play a significant role in leading us out of the COVID crisis.

SE are businesses that engage in conventional trade and business activities in relevant markets to address social challenges and achieve social aims. SE endeavour to integrate people and communities to promote economic development and enhance social and community well-being. The official UK definition of social enterprise to which most social enterprise umbrella bodies subscribe is:

*A social enterprise is a business with primarily social objectives whose surpluses are principally reinvested for that purpose in the business or in the community, rather than being driven by the need to maximise profit for shareholders and owners. (DTI, 2002: 1).*

Villeneuve-Smith and Temple (2015:4) offer the following social enterprise aim at:

*Combining a sustainable business model with a clear social purpose, working and employing in the most challenging areas, and demonstrating that this can be done in an accountable, fair and inclusive way.*

The prevalent economic system in many countries has experienced a ‘growing critique of Western capitalism as far too focussed on financial transactions, putting shareholders above other stakeholders and short-term profits above longer-term value to society’ (Kanter 2011:52). Kanter identified a group of companies which she termed ‘supercorps’ for their ability to manoeuvre against the prevailing tide and combine innovation, profits, growth and social good. She also introduces the concept of the ‘supercoops’.

Employee-owned companies throughout the world have been shown to outperform their counterparts outside the sector (Arando et al 2011) and research indicates that employee-owned companies typically outperform their non-employee-owned counterparts.

The Mittelstand in Austria, Germany and Switzerland are attracting a lot of attention within the UK Coalition Government, who have singled out these companies for their consistent growth, contribution to society and long-term shareholder commitment. The prevailing manifestation of capitalism has evolved to the extent that it would appear we have been led up a one-way street that has turned out to be a dead end. As a result, that dead end has resulted in companies that are out of balance, heavily distorted in their operations as they seek to meet the demand of shareholders, banks or other sources of finance.

Finance in itself is no longer an enabler of business, analogous to the way that a combustion engine uses oil to run smoothly. We are effectively seeing finance as something that fuels the business and is the sole measure of success and, on many occasions, neglecting the need to sufficiently oil the machine – make the thing run more efficiently. The pressure to meet shareholders demands for returns has resulted in significant short-termism and a very volatile business environment.

Venture Capital backed companies are driven by financial short termism based on an exit strategy and are inefficient in terms of true wealth creation in the wider sense such that post-acquisition the contribution of the company to collective value is barely visible. At worst, acquisitions are inspired as part of a defensive strategy to quash a smaller competitor.

Presently, companies are finding it difficult to find financial support from the banks, which is to a large extent being blamed on the banks. However, it could be argued that banks are being more prudent in their lending activities and accurately assessing the probability of default. This would lead us to conclude that the contemporary business environment may not be sufficiently geared to meet the demands for fundamental people-focussed economic growth and to limit the impact of rent seeking activities.

SEs represent what is known as the 'social economy', which is a thriving and growing collection of organisations that fall in between the traditional private sector on the one hand, and the public sector on the other. The sector occupied by SEs is often referred to as the 'third sector', it includes voluntary and community organisations, foundations, and associations of many different types. SEs are differentiated from conventional businesses in that they use trading activities to achieve their social goals and aim for financial self-sufficiency, as opposed to seeking soft funding and other agency-based resources. They aim to combine entrepreneurial skills with a social mission characteristic of the social economy.

Most SEs often have a governance structure based on participation by the workforce and/or other stakeholder groups. This participation will vary according to the different models applied in diverse circumstances. SEs come in a variety of forms, which include:

- Employee-Owned Businesses creating jobs and rescuing jobs as part of economic development strategies.
- Credit Unions providing access to finance.

- Cooperatives and associations of persons united to meet common economic and social needs through jointly owned enterprises.
- Development Trusts who are key actors in community-based regeneration.
- Social Firms providing employment and training to people with disabilitics and other disadvantaged groups.
- Intermediate Labour Market Companies providing training and work experience for the long-term unemployed.
- Community Business Social Enterprises, which have a strong geographical definition and focus on local markets and local services.
- Charities' Trading Arms enabling them to meet their objectives in innovative ways, such as through Fair-Trade companies.

However, to be constrained by these criteria would not describe the phenomenon that is occurring in the UK and around the world. SEs are increasingly being started, driven and developed by Social Entrepreneurs. 'Social entrepreneurs are not content just to give a fish or teach how to fish. They will not rest until they have revolutionized the fishing industry.' (Drayton 2004). Skoll argues that 'Social entrepreneurship has emerged as a legitimate model for transformative social change' (Skoll 2009:3).

Despite this growth in the attention associated with social enterprise, 'the field of social entrepreneurship lacks rigour and is in its infancy compared to the wider field of entrepreneurship' (Abu-Saifan 2012:24). Notwithstanding this lack of rigour, the legitimacy of social enterprise is becoming widely accepted however, with the nurturing environment, support structures and other enablers being present which are often lacking in most economies.

The pandemic of 2020 has impacted all sectors of the economy not least that of the SE. The pandemic has shown that SEs are agile: according to a British Council study, two-thirds of SEs were able to pivot in the face of changing trading conditions, and are now effectively running different businesses. This pivoting was characterised by introduction of new products and services, adapted business models, with new targets, beneficiaries and stakeholders (British Council 2020). Inevitably, these activities have also been associated with adapting to increased focus in terms of operating online; with more than 50% moving provision or services online. The Council's report continues and highlights that many (1/3) SEs researched said that there were/are no suitable government support measures available to them, unsurprisingly limited government support has been most acutely lacking across South Asia and sub-Saharan Africa countries. The gap in provision for SE is not unique to these regions and was apparent in economies with higher levels of state support in response to the pandemic (British Council 2020).

Other studies have echoed the assessment of the British Council report, Social Enterprise UK concluded that most SEs' business models have undergone a shift;

and for many, this is likely to permanent. However, for some, more than half have reduced their services and/or ceased to operate. Whilst this study argues that less than 20% are operating as they did before the pandemic (Social Enterprise UK: 2020a).

In this chapter, we will firstly investigate the social entrepreneurship ecosystem, then examine the how, when and why of the social entrepreneur and the opportunities for training and learning in social entrepreneurship in the UK and EU. We will then give an overview of a suggested learning pathway programmes for driving SE training and SE development as a tool for building back better post pandemic.

## ACTORS IN THE SOCIAL ENTREPRENEURSHIP ECOSYSTEM

Internationally, there is growing interest in SE and the potential of it to address many social ills and intractable challenges that call for social entrepreneurial effectiveness.

*Figure 1.*
*Source: Wilkinson, C (2014) A Map of SE and Their Eco-systems in Europe. European Commission.*

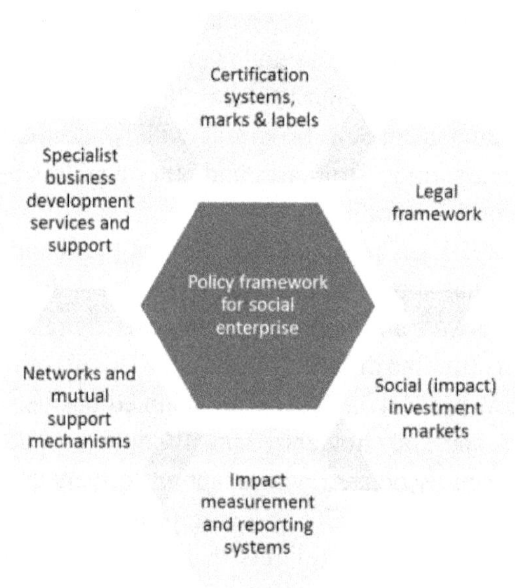


The UK has led the way in the mobilisation of social entrepreneurial solutions and the creation of nurturing eco-systems to support SE. 'The UK is viewed as a pioneer of social enterprise and the associated practices of social investment and social value. Government statistics identify around 70,000 SE in the UK, contributing

£24 billion to the economy and employing nearly a million people. Since 2005, over 11,000 Community Interest Companies have been founded, and the last five years have seen significant development of social investment to support the growth of this movement' (Villeneuve-Smith and Temple 2015: 4).

The Villeneuve-Smith and Temple report[1] offered the following findings:

- Close to half (49%) of all SEs are five years old or less. Thirty-five percent are three years old or less – more than three times the proportion of SME start-ups.
- The proportion of SEs that grew their turnover over the past 12 months is 52%. A greater proportion of SEs are growing than mainstream SMEs (40%).
- 50% of SEs reported a profit, with 26% breaking even. Almost all use the majority of those profits to further their social or environmental goals.
- 31% of SEs are working in the top 20% most deprived communities in the UK.
- The proportion of SEs that export or licence has grown to 14%. For over one-third of these, international trade accounts for between 11% and 50% of income.
- 73% of SEs earn more than 75% of their income from trade.
- 27% of SEs have the public sector as their main source of income, an increase on 2013 and 2011. Fifty-nine percent of SEs do some business with the public sector.
- The number of SEs introducing a new product or service in the last 12 months has increased to 59%. Among SMEs it has fallen to 38%.
- 40% of SEs are led by women; 31% have Black Asian Minority Ethnic directors; 40% have a director with a disability.
- 41% of SEs created jobs in the past 12 months compared to 22% of SMEs.
- 59% of SEs employ at least one person who is disadvantaged in the labour market. For 16% of social enterprises, this group forms at least half of all employees.
- The average pay ratio between social enterprise CEO pay and the lowest paid is just 3.6:1 – for FTSE 100 CEOs, this ratio stands at 150:1.
- 49% of SEs operating in public sector markets say they are yet to see support for SEs to arrive in tender documents – there is much to do before the Social Value Act works as intended.
- 44% of SEs sought funding or finance in the last 12 months and 39% believe its lack of availability is a barrier to their sustainability. Just 5% of SMEs think access to finance is a barrier.

These key findings were generated from the 'largest and most diverse' (ibid:8), the organisational structure from these samples showed (ibid:9) the results in Table 1.

*Table 1. Social enterprises organisational structure (%)*

| Organisational Structure | 2015 | 2013 | 2011 | 2009 |
|---|---|---|---|---|
| Company Limited by Guarantee (CLG) | 45% | 51% | 54% | 59% |
| Community Interest Company (CIC) | 20% | 17% | 10% | 17% |
| Company limited by Shares | 16% | 12% | 12% | 7% |
| Industrial and Provident Society (IPS) | 9% | 19% | 24% | 37% |
| Sole Proprietorship | 6% | 2% | | |
| Partnership | 3% | 2% | | |
| Limited Company | 1% | 1% | | |
| Limited Liability Partnership | 1% | | | |
| PLC | <0.5% | 1% | | |
| Other/Do not know/not provided | 16% | 11% | | |

Source: Villeneuve-Smith and Temple 2015: 9

A more recent study by Georgy and Mansfield (2019) showed the growth of the sector when assessed against the Villeneuve-Smith and Temple report:

- The start-up wave of social enterprises continues to surge, with 42% under 5 years old.
- 52% of social enterprises grew their turnover in the last 12 months.
- 77% of social enterprises earn more than 75% of their income from trading.
- 40% of social enterprises are led by women.
- 35% of social enterprises have BAME directors.
- 78% of social enterprises said they were a living wage employer.
- 88% of social enterprises actively aim to minimise environmental impacts.
- 65% of social enterprises expect to increase their focus on sustainability and environmental friendliness.
- 75% of social enterprises consider environmental impacts to be of equal or greater importance than cost.
- This movement is being driven by women and BAME-led start-ups, demonstrating the vibrancy and diversity of the sector.
- SEs create vital opportunities in uncertain times, employing those who are disadvantaged, and reinvesting over 75% of their profits into delivering their mission.

- SEs are proving commercially strong as well: with more than half growing their turnover in the last 12 months, and over three-quarters making a profit or breaking even.
- This is supported by the finding that they are more far innovativc than their mainstream counterparts, with 56% introducing a new product or service in 2019.
- In 2019, there were 100,000 SEs contributing £60bn to UK GDP.

KEY FINDINGS (GEORGY AND MANSFIELD, 2019)

- **Growing in Number:** Forty-two percent of social enterprises are less than 5 years old, which is three times the proportion of SMEs more widely (14%). Three in ten social enterprises are three years old or less, even higher than previously seen, showing that the start-up wave identified in previous research continues to surge.
- **Growing in Size:** Fifty-two percent of social enterprises grew their turnover in the last 12 months. This is higher than in 2017 and much higher than the 34% of SMEs who have seen an increase.
- **Independent Businesses:** SEs are businesses that earn their income through trading, competing in the marketplace – 77% of social enterprises earn more than 75% of their income from trading, up on our previous survey.
- **More Innovative:** The proportion of SEs introducing a new product or service was 56% in 2019, higher again than previous years and far outstripping SMEs, at 36%.
- **Commercially Successful:** Forty-eight percent of SEs made a profit in the past year, with 27% breaking even and a lower percentage losing money than in previous research. The longer an SE has been around, the more likely it is to make a profit. An SE eco-system is complex and not easily represented. However, Wilkinson offers the table shown in Table 2 as a representation of the UK situation.

The positive impacts that social enterprises can bring to the skills development and employability of the UK population is often assumed, but the evidence for this on a large-scale has been somewhat lacking. This review explores education; training and employment support delivered by social enterprises, in order to identify these gaps in our knowledge, and also to highlight the high efficacy of social enterprise interventions in disadvantaged areas, with socially excluded individuals, and in urban regeneration. Furthermore, the review shows how certain models of SE delivery focused on employee ownership could also benefit public service delivery and hence protect jobs and build community cohesion. The review frames this evidential

*Table 2. Social enterprise eco-system*

| | |
|---|---|
| **Policy makers** [2]- Governmental departments or institutions designing or implementing policy, support instruments and measures for SE and infrastructures | Department for Business, Innovation and Skills, Cabinet Office – Office for Civil Society, Department for Communities and Local, Government, Department for Work and Pensions Other Government Departments |
| **Customers** – authorities contracting social enterprises | Government Departments, Regional authorities, Local authorities / councils |
| Organisations promoting, certifying and awarding SE labels | Social Enterprise Mark company, Social Enterprise UK |
| Institutions, civil society initiatives or other SE promoting social entrepreneurship education and training, and presenting role models | School for Social Entrepreneurs, Striding Out, Inspire2Enterprise, Social enterprise support, networks/ representatives The Scottish Social Enterprise Academy |
| Organisations that have the capacity to act as an observatory and to monitor the development and to assess the needs and opportunities of social entrepreneurs/social enterprises | BIS, Social Enterprise UK, Social Firms UK, Co-Ops UK, The RBS SE100 Index, Locality |
| Providers of social enterprise start up and development support services and facilities (such as incubators) | UnLtd, Social enterprise support networks / representatives |
| Business support providers | UnLtd, The Plunkett Foundation, Social enterprise support networks / representatives |
| Facilitators of learning and exchange platforms for social enterprises | RBS 100SE Index, Inspire2Enterprise, Community Action Network (CAN) |
| Social enterprise (support) networks, associations | Social Enterprise UK, Social Enterprise NI, Social Enterprise Scotland, Wales Co-operative centre, CIC Association, Social Firms UK, Co-ops UK, NCVO, ACEVO, Locality, Community Action Network (CAN), ABCUL, UnLtd |
| Key providers of finance and intermediaries | Major banks (e.g., RBS), Big Lottery Fund, Big Society Capital, City of London Corporation, Social Finance UK, SIB Group, UnLtd, Clearlyso, Big Issue Invest, Key Fund, Bridges Futures, CAF Venturesome, Esmee Fairburn Foundation, CDFA on behalf of all CDFIs |
| Research institutions | Third Sector Research Centre (TSRC) at the University of Birmingham, Social Enterprise University Enterprise Network (Plymouth University), Market Stewardship Research Group, Social Investment Research Council |

Source: Wilkinson (2014:16-17)

exploration within a critique of the existing UK policy environment surrounding skills development and employment, to highlight how policy and funding could be used to grow the impact of SE in the above areas (Hazenberg 2021).

This SE eco-system carries a diverse cross section of training and support. However, due to limits of this report only a select cross section of providers will be identified. However, in research commissioned by the School of Social Entrepreneurs examining SE training in thc UK thc follow key findings emerged (McGlashan 2013):

- As a sector, SE under-invests in training.
- The biggest barrier to training is time.
- There is cross-sector interest in SE training.
- Social impact measures are the hot topic.
- Expert practitioners are key to a good training course.
- Training is beginning to move online.

Addressing these findings and developing a resource to nurture and enhance the SE eco-system across the EU is a key goal of the SETTLE project[3].

## SOCIAL ENTREPRENEUR

Throughout the world, there is growing recognition of the role and importance of entrepreneurship and enterprise (Abu-Saifan 2012: 22). The impact and effects of this focus has seen a growing focus on innovation, lower rates of unemployment and accelerated structural changes in economic activities (ibid). With this changing focus has come a growing recognition of the role and importance associated with SE. Abu-Saifan offers the following definition for a social entrepreneur:

*The social entrepreneur is a mission-driven individual who uses a set of entrepreneurial behaviours to deliver a social value to the less privileged, all through an entrepreneurially oriented entity that is financially independent, self-sufficient, or sustainable. (Abu-Saifan 2012: 25)*

Dees argues that social entrepreneurs have not received the same attention that conventional entrepreneurs enjoy and uses the term 'sub-species' which is perhaps a bit pejorative (Dees 1998). But despite this perspective, the obvious overlaps between commercial and social entrepreneurs have been long been recognised, (Catford, 1998; Dearlove, 2004; Dees, 1998a; Johnson, 2003; Nicholls, 2006b; Peredo & McLean, 2006; Roberts & Woods, 2005).

Table 3 shows comparison between profit-orientated and social entrepreneurs. This table opens much debate and some of the distinctions are questionable, i.e., are both not potentially high achievers, does profit not also represent social value, etc.? Indeed, profit is key to SE survival with the difference being that profit is

*Table 3. Profit-orientated vs. social entrepreneurs*

| Unique Characteristics of Profit-Orientated Entrepreneurs | Overlaps between the two | Unique Characteristics of Social Entrepreneurs |
|---|---|---|
| High Achiever | Innovator | Mission Leader |
| Risk bearer | Dedicated | Emotionally charged |
| Organiser | Initiative taker | Change agent |
| Strategic Thinker | Leader | Opinion Leader |
| Value creator | Opportunity alert | Social value creator |
| Holistic | Persistent | Social Alert |
| Arbitrageur | Committed | Manager/Visionary |

Source: Abu-Saifan (2012:25)

reinvested into the SE, not paid out as dividends. These issues aside, the table does offer a suitable base for engaging in a dialogue in what sets social entrepreneurs apart. However, at the core, all entrepreneurial activities are predicated on the need to create a sustainable business model that delivers value to the target audience. For the purpose of this report, the key distinction is the matter of how surplus funds generated are applied.

## OVERVIEW OF SELECTED SOCIAL ENTERPRISE LANDSCAPES

### Czech Republic

The SE sector in the Czech Republic is not well developed, but research shows there are a large number of active SEs. According to Dohnalova, Hrabetova, Slechtova, Legnerova, and Guri (2015) '[s]olidarity, mutual help, organisations, foundations and cooperatives exist in different forms for more than 100 years. Efforts to establish associations and cooperatives seem to be the 'roots' of Czech SE and can be found at the beginning of 19th century when a friendly environment for the development of civic organisations was created. A high number of associations between WW1 and WW2 followed the tradition started in the 18th and 19th century related to the Czech National Revival. Normalisation in the 1970s brought a more authoritarian socialism, where all public life was under the correction and no public organisations were allowed to operate. This remained in force till the end of communism in November 1989.' (Dohnalova et al 2915:5-6)

They continue that '[t]he 'Velvet' revolution brought civil liberty and a collapse of Communist Party. This regime changeover meant a renewal of many public associations. Wide range of new associations and cooperatives of social type were founded. The development of civic sector after 1989 brought nowadays basics of social enterprises.'

'The Czech concept of SE is broad with great emphasis on economic and social objectives (business and social missions) that should be in balance. Most of the existing SE in the CR are focused on the employment of disadvantaged people (the so-called integration social enterprises).' (Jetmar 2013:44).

According to the Euclid Network '[t]he sectors in the Czech Republic is moderately developed enjoying a generally positive relationship with the state. Civil Society Organisations are active and diverse.' The organization adds that '[d]espite the persisting impact of the previous communist regime on the civil society in the Czech Republic, legislations passed in the early 90s and increased foreign funding for civil society organisations have paved the way for the steady rise of the civil society. Thousands of new Civil Society Organizations (CSO) sprung up in the following years.'

Kaderabkova (2016) agrees that the SE sector is very young in the Czech Republic. 'The concept was first mentioned in the evaluation of innovativeness of the Operational Programme Human Resources and Employment (OPHRE) published in 2012. The guidelines for systemic support of social innovations, formulated by the researchers at the Centre for Innovation Studies in Prague, included 60 steps to be undertaken in coming years. One of the recommendations included organizing pilot calls for social innovation projects, which were indeed launched in 2013 and 2014.'

Kaderabkova (2016) further notes that '...17 projects were supported in OPHRE, the first in the country, which specifically targeted solutions of social problems through social innovations. The pilots were quite important as they offered a unique learning opportunity – how to develop the systemic support of social innovations, which would reflect the country and local specifics. Not only the novelty of the social innovation concept itself was important but also the implementation of self-evaluation of social impact as an instrument of learning and improvement. A comprehensive toolbox (together with an intense and individualized support) was created to guide the social innovators through the process starting with evaluation plan and finishing with final evaluation report. All the social innovation actors were learning continuously which practices work and which do not, what risks are imminent, what constrains are threatening'.

## Finland

The term 'social entrepreneur' or 'social enterprise' is not widely used in Finland, but the practice of contributing to a cooperative or a cooperative tradition is strong in Finland. In a report by the Nordic Council of Ministers (2015) it is pointed out that '…the term 'socialt entreprenörskap' is rarely used, but that enterprises designated 'sociala företag' or 'samhällsentreprenörskap' are similar to activities described as social entrepreneurship. 'As in other areas in Finland, SE are expected to improve the quality of public services, generate innovation, improve productivity and have a preventive effect on social and health problems.' (Nordic Council of Ministers, 2015).

Traditionally, Finland is a universal welfare state; whereby the state provides most public services including free education, housing and healthcare. In this context, SEs (as seen by the UK for instance) play a relatively minor role, but they have seen SE in the form of sheltered workshops and work centres since the 1950s (Marcel, 2015). Research by the Nordic Council of Ministers (2015) points out that '… Finland therefore has a long history in which 'citizenship organisations' played a role as producers of services. According to information from the Nordic working group, the development of SE has, however, been modest in Finland in recent years, and in decline compared with ordinary private enterprises.'

The early Finnish civil society mostly developed in civil movements. Later, the development of the welfare state influenced the development of civil society. In '…Finland, there are indications that SE and cooperatives acted as an important driving force for innovation in the development of industry, agriculture and local communities but that, for a time, the establishment and expansion of the welfare state led to a weakening of these phenomena because of the government taking over these tasks.' (Nordic Council of Ministers, 2015). The report added that they are 'seeing a new wave of interest in social entrepreneurship and SE in the 2000s. It was inspired by developments in Europe and the US, but also driven by a need to develop the Nordic welfare state through new forms of cooperation and partnership with civil society organisations. A press release by the Ministry of Economic Affairs and Employment (Valtioneuvosto, 2021) states that '[a]ccording to a survey completed in 2020, there are approximately 1,700 social enterprises in Finland, more than half of which are organisations providing health and social services to the public sector.' Wilkinson (2014) breaks it down to estimate that, '… around 2,500 to 3,200 SE in Finland that "comply" with the EU Operational Definition. National estimates of social enterprises, however, range from 5,000 to 10,000 organisations, depending on the definition used for measurement purposes.' This view, supported by a study in 2015 estimated 'that there are roughly 19,000 social enterprises in Finland' (Melkas, 2020).

There is a relatively broad non-profit sector (a number of formal associations per capita) in Finland and voluntary work comprises most of it. It is typical of Finnish civil society to have more CSO working in expressive fields such as culture and sports than in providing public services (Liuskari, n.d.), but according to Wilkinson (2014) '... SE are predominantly involved in the social services sector, they operate in a wide variety of sectors including health, education, construction, recycling, retail and leisure services.'

CSOs in Finland have a lower proportion of paid staff. In general, the Finnish state has mostly a very positive and open relationship with civil society. Civil society is institutionally recognised as an important part of society. Both political and financial support is provided. The autonomy of CSOs are respected and they are also seen as active associates. Nowadays, changes in the civil society field is observed and more NGOs are specialising and the local level is emphasised. This means that many associations and organisations are small and independent which lead to fewer connections to the state and municipalities (Liuskari, n.d.).

## Hungary

'The growth of the social enterprise economy in the past two decades is due to its success in addressing entrenched social and economic problems. The persistent problems of unemployment, poverty, social exclusion, poor social services, and environmental degradation – even in fast-growing emerging market economies – call for new, innovative solutions. Neither pure market-based nor pure public sector approaches have effectively confronted these problems.' (Etchart, 2015).

According to Jaksa and Eros (2016) '[s]ocial innovation has a rather brief history in Hungary. Primarily, social innovation is evoked in relation to market production (Schumpeter, 1912), focussing on the capacity of enterprises to employ a labour force, to diversify the skills of that labour force, and to increase mobility within the national economy.'

They continue '[t]he late 1980s unveiled a great need for social innovation, which had been supressed by the planned/centralized socialist economy; Hungary's entire system of social services had to be reinvented at once, following the transition in 1990. Social innovation was regarded as part of the answer to the 'arrested development' in social service provision, tackling social problems arising from marginalization and unemployment.'

Etchart, Horváth, Rosandić, and Spitálszky (2014) noted that 'SE in Hungary tend to be young. The SELUSI research found that their average age is 15.9 years, although according to the NESsT´s definition – enterprises that solve critical SE in a sustainable manner, SE are even younger, averaging about seven to eight years. Half of the SE are small (1–10 employees) and only 12% has above 1M €

revenues.' (p.1). They add however that the awareness about social entrepreneurship is growing '[d]espite the lack of a legal definition of social enterprise, and the fact that the non-profit and business sectors are still segregated in Hungary, non-profit organizations have recently started to show a growing interest in the self-financing and social entrepreneurship model.'

According to Edmiston (2015:1), citing Kengyel, '[d]espite limited institutional support or recognition of the concept, there is growing interest in social innovation in Hungary. A major factor impelling interest in its application and potential is the large inflow of European funds, much of which is tied to the promotion of social innovation'.

The social challenges Hungary faces are distinctive of Central European countries 'an ageing population, growing unemployment and a big Roma minority. According to the last census in 2001, there were approximately 190,000 members of the Roma minority living in Hungary…' (Hamburg, 2016). The report also adds other social problems including unemployment. Etchart et al (2014) lists the top five society challenges as:

1. Poverty and Social exclusion
2. Aging population
3. Labour market: Youth unemployment and too early exit of over 55-year-olds
4. Discrimination against Roma
5. Homelessness.

## Ireland

The concept of SE is rooted in local and community development, going right back to the early development of the cooperative movement up to the broad range of economic and social activities the sector is now engaged in today.' (Forfás, 2013, p3).

A report by Wilkinson (2014) adds that '[t]he term 'social enterprise' has only relatively recently entered policy discourse in Ireland. Research into what might be considered to be the social enterprise model has typically focussed on the wider social economy or not-for-profit community, which have a slightly longer tradition'.

A key finding of the Forfás (2013) report is 'that SE are in general not seeking additional state funding; rather, adjustments to some aspects of various policy areas including access to finance, procurement, capability building and ensuring supportive legislative frameworks. Such changes would help to reduce barriers to SE participating more fully in economic activity. The social enterprise sector in Ireland has the potential to develop enterprises that can be self-sustainable. Such sustainable, self-reliant business models are important to the survival and development of SE and it is in the shifting of the sector towards the commercially oriented model that job creation potential is foreseen.' (p3).

'Many SE in Ireland provide services that the government does not offer to citizens, either because the state has outsourced, or cannot provide these services to the same standard, or they do not provide them in the first place... In addition, SE provide services that may not be commercially viable for conventional enterprises, because while SE must be sustainable enterprises, they do not have the same requirements for financial rates of return as conventional enterprises and also can often draw on voluntary resources.' (Forfás, 2013:14).

In terms of public support and initiatives, the Irish government released a report in 2013 that seems to be guiding the development of the SE sector. This report contains 22 recommendations on developing the SE sector, covering the following areas:

- Policy development for the sector
- Capacity building in the sector
- Procurement
- Funding and finance
- Developing leaders and harnessing community support

## Poland

Poland has no formal or common definition of social enterprise, '...despite the gradual development of SE and their growing legal recognition in Poland, no unanimity or agreed understanding of this notion has yet been reached.' (Ciepielewska-Kowalik, Pieliński, Starnawska & Szymańska, 2015:4). They offer two reasons for the unclear status of the sector:

1. SE is a relatively new term in Poland. The term has been used by academics, government officials, professionals, and third sector organisations only in the years following Poland's integration into the European Union in 2004.
2. The link with the long history of SE in Poland. Long before the introduction of the term, there was a considerable number of organisations possessing features of SE in Poland, and there is no settled agreement as to which of those organisations should be called SEs.

In the country report on Poland, Wilkinson (2014: i) agrees '[t]here is no official definition of social enterprise in Poland. The term social enterprise is not much used in Poland. Instead, the concept of 'social economy' is more prevalent. SE are often perceived as a constituent of the 'social economy', a broader concept that itself does not have an official or commonly accepted definition in Poland. Official documents on the use of EU structural funds operationalise the term 'social economy entities' by listing legal and organisational forms.'

However, Wilkinson (2014) refers to the draft The National Programme of Social Economy Development (KPRES) released in 2013 for an attempt at a definition of an SE, which has demonstrated the following characteristics:

- Carrying out business activity with clear organisational boundaries and own financial reporting.
- The objective of business activity is either:
  - Social and employment integration of people at the risk of social exclusion (operationalised as employing a minimum of 50 per cent of staff from among those at risk of social exclusion or at least 30 per cent of disabled); or
  - Providing public benefit services whilst, at the same time, fulfilling pro-employment objectives.
- No distribution of profit or financial surplus among shareholders/partners; using profits or financial surplus to increase company capital, and in a certain share for:
  - Social and employment integration, in case of enterprises with pro-employment objectives; or
  - Providing public benefit services for the local community where an enterprise operates.
- Democratic governance or at least consultative role of employees and other stakeholders; and a salary cap for managers.

The National Programme (KPRES) envisages the adoption of an Act on Social Enterprise, which would introduce an SE status (organisations could register themselves as an SE provided, they fulfil certain conditions). The Government's rationale for creating a special legal status is as follows:

- To define and legitimise SEs;
- To enable clear identification of entities that are the subject of specific public policies;
- To help relevant entities identify their position in the socio-economic system of the country;
- To build public awareness on SEs, their role and their offer – both as providers of goods and services and as potential employers.

Poland has a long and complicated tradition of SE organisations reaching back to before the Second Word War (Ciepielewska-Kowalik et al, 2015). 'Since then, they have undergone very turbulent developments, wavering during the communist period, and experiencing a revival after 1989. This difficult history of social enterprise organisations has contributed strongly to the socio-economic potential, developmental opportunities, trends, challenges and—finally—obstacles for present-day models of social enterprise.' (p.5)

In their paper Ciepielewska-Kowalik and Pieliński (2015:1) refer to the 'third sector' economy '... has transformed itself very dramatically since the end of the communist rule in 1989. Today there are several tens of thousands third sector organizations, mainly non-profit organizations, which were set up in the last twenty-five years.' They describe how the third sector 'has changed on the structural level, the discussion on the third sector, and more widely on civil society, has also changed. There were high hopes for the civil society to thrive during the last years of the communist rule and in the beginning of the democratic era. Civil society was perceived as a better and more natural form of public life than state institutions.'

Another reason researchers are '... seeing an increasing interest in SE in Poland since 2004 is also attributable—beside the influence of integration in the EU—to the growing insufficiency of the public sector to fulfil social needs.' (Ciepielewska-Kowalik et al, 2015:8) they continue '...the role of SE as welfare service providers still remains underestimated in Poland. This is evident in the modest socio-economic and developmental potential of Polish SE when compared to the older EU members.'

'According to www.ngo.pl, there were about 17,000 foundations and 107,000 associations registered in Poland in 2014. These numbers include many inactive organizations that have not formally dissolved, estimated to account for roughly a quarter of all registered organizations. Around 800 organizations carry out the process of liquidation every year, but since it is not obligatory many organizations suspend or stop their activities without taking any formal steps to liquidate.' (USAID, 2014:170)

The report by Wilkinson (2014: ii) '...estimates that there are around 5,200 entities (2012) in Poland that could be classified as SE by applying the EU Operational, employing around 70,000 people. This represents around 0.3 per cent of all registered and active enterprises (including one-person enterprises) and around 0.4 per cent of the total employment in the economy.'

In operational terms, '[s]taff are largely project-based hires and not permanent employees. According to research published by Klon Jawor in October 2013, only 5 percent of organizations have more than five paid employees. Organizations do not seek volunteers. Those who want to volunteer are typically young people seeking work experience'. (USAID, 2014:171)

The report by USAID of 2014 found that local government is the main source of funding for CSOs. Wilkinson (2015:9) also found that 'Public funding is central to practically all support and infrastructure for SE (as well as the wider social economy sector) in Poland.'

'CSOs provide services in a wide range of fields including sports, tourism and leisure, culture and arts, training and education, social services and social aid, health care, local development, and to a lesser degree, environmental protection, human rights, science and research, employment, support to other organizations, and public safety.' (USAID, 2014:174) The report adds that in rural areas services are mostly limited to education and sport.

Ciepielewska-Kowalik et al (2015) identifies the main operational models of SE in Poland as, each following 'different institutional trajectories since their beginnings':

- Cooperatives:
  - Traditional cooperatives
  - Social cooperatives
- Entrepreneurial non-profit organisations.
- Work and social integration SEs.

## SOCIAL ENTERPRISE EDUCATION

Given the nature of enterprise development and its role in economic growth and development, the impact of the pandemic will have implications for how SE training will and should be delivered. As shown above, many SEs have reverted to an online model for business continuity. This will be driven by necessity and pragmatism, however, effective support for emerging social entrepreneurs may not be served through an only online approach[4]. Furthermore, as we come out of the pandemic, there will be a return to more traditional support and the result will be a combination of all approaches.

Prior to that discussion, we need to note what we mean by SE education because, as the sector developed, so has the terminology and the terms enterprise education and entrepreneurship education are often used interchangeably and differentiating between them can be difficult (Hytti, 2002; Hannon and Scott, 2006; Gibb, 1993; Jones and Iredale, 2010).

Over the last few years, whatever the title, SE education has and is being promoted at national level. This drive in the UK is reflected by the Dearing Report, which states: 'We recommend to higher education institutions that they consider the scope for encouraging entrepreneurship through innovative approaches to programme design and through specialist postgraduate programmes' (Dearing, 1997). The result of this support has been a growth of enterprise education programmes and research reviewing their content and impact. That work has looked at the programmes:

- Background, experience and motivation (Jones, 2010; Kuratko, 2005).
- Effectiveness, outcomes and outputs (Matlay, 2007; Hytti et al., 2010).
- Comparison and categorisation (Gibb, 1993; Hannon, 2005; Hytti, 2002; Hytti and O'Gorman, 2004).

A few papers (1010 ET 57,8/9) have taken a step further towards standardisation of programmes, for example, offering guidelines or even proposing standard content (for instance QAA, 2012).

It could be argued that the drive for SE is being 'fuelled' by public policy and public finance rather than open market demand. 'Educational, enterprise and entrepreneurship policy makers have allocated and spent public money on the premise that enterprise and entrepreneurship education can make a difference to life chances and business opportunities' (Jones and Iredale, 2010).

This is a worthy target but not one necessarily driving the programme deliverers. It has been suggested that, in many cases, the acceptance or adoption by higher education institutions (HEIs) of such enterprise objectives is reactionary to funding being made available rather than being proactive looking at what SE could deliver (Hannon, 2004). It has also been suggested that the motivation for many HEIs in engaging in enterprise education is that, in reality, they are simply following what other leading institutions do without reviewing their own need and context for delivering SE education programmes. Others are undertaking SE delivery as a tactical move to be seen to be in alignment with new and changing central and regional government policy agendas (sic) (Hannon, 2004) or being 'unwilling to depart from perceived "good practice"' (Matlay, 2006). Therefore, the consequences have meant programme content has been influenced by what other programmes appear to be doing (peer influence) or what the providers of the programme funding seem to want (financial influence). Therefore, they are reacting rather than leading on programme content and not delivering what the open market might demand. An example of this is the case of the Northern Ireland Centre for Entrepreneurship (NICENT) at Queen's University, Belfast and the University of Ulster where, due to its funding being provided though the local economic development agency, part of the funding conditions was that business and job creation targets would be set (Bridge et al., 2010), with the understanding that the programme would be developed to persuade and assist students to start businesses.

All '[u]niversities and other institutions may want to train and develop tomorrow's agents of change in order to bring about positive social change in disadvantaged communities (Prieto et al 2012: 1). The DICE Consortium along with partners is no exception.

As Johnson identified in his study of 2002, the goal of any training for social entrepreneurs, is its 'emphasis on problem-solving and social innovation, socially entrepreneurial activities blur the traditional boundaries between the public, private and non-profit sector, and emphasize hybrid models of for-profit and non-profit activities' (Cited in Prieto et al 2012: 1).

As we move potentially, to a post pandemic era, the need to apply critical paedagogic thinking to enterprise education and SE education more specifically becomes mission critical. In this vein, Foster's observation of Higher Education is apropos (Foster 2002:37):

*'Higher education... is directed to the continual recasting of knowledge and skills required to maintain the value of human capital in the technology-driven global economy. Higher education subserves the survival instinct of those societies (and within them, of those individuals) most ready to respond to change with cognitive and technological flexibility and self-reinvention'.*

The DICE team works with university partners and social innovators to drive solutions and support emerging social entrepreneurs. This chapter seeks to offer a learning pathway that can be adapted and applied in a post-pandemic context. As an analysis of critical paedagogic theory is beyond the scope of this chapter, the authors need to acknowledge that the framing of any post-pandemic intervention must be assessed within this paradigm.

## TRAINING AND LEARNING FOR SOCIAL ENTREPRENEURSHIP[5]

In the UK, there has been a proliferation of SE training programmes. This section aims to give a brief overview of some of these, to act as a tool for identifying the status quo and inform the design of any proposed programme.

A logical starting point would be the School for Social Entrepreneurs (SSE) (https://www.the-sse.org/our-courses/). According to their website, the SSE aims to '...empower people from all backgrounds to create positive social change. Our courses help individuals start, sustain, and scale social enterprises, charities and community projects. We'll help you build confidence and gain practical business skills in technical areas like marketing and finance'. SSE focusses on delivery of short courses ('generally last at least 6 days') and their programmes cover the following topics:

- Starting an SE
- Scaling an SE
- Replication and Social Franchising
- From Charity to SE – Transition to Trading
- Third-Sector Digital Leaders.

They also offer various shorter workshops, some examples are: Social Media Masterclass, Get Ahead in Sales, Sources of Funding for Charities and SE, Crowdfunding for Charities and SE, Action Learning Facilitator Training, Kickstart Your Social Media Strategy, Writing Successful Bids, Working with Corporates, Measuring Social Impact, Unlocking Social Investment and Developing a Fundraising Strategy. SSE also offers bespoke training to the sector.

The Department of Continuing Education at Oxford University offers an online distance learning course titled Social Entrepreneurship which carries 10 credits, (https://www.conted.ox.ac.uk/L100-9_.They are:

**Unit 1:** Introduction to social entrepreneurship: The journey ahead
**Unit 2:** Creating social change: The social value proposition and identifying a social business opportunity
**Unit 3:** Understanding poverty: The Millennium Development Goals
**Unit 4:** Human-Centred Design: Partnering with the targeted community to address social problems
**Unit 5:** Developing a theory of change: Starting with the social impact
**Unit 6:** Envisioning an innovative society: The role of social innovation
**Unit 7:** The business model: Creating a social business model
**Unit 8:** Funding social ventures: Strategies for success
**Unit 9:** The driving force behind social entrepreneurship: Measurement and scaling social impact
**Unit 10:** The future: Reflection and shared experiences

The course aims to:

- Expose students to the concept of social entrepreneurship and SE and how social entrepreneurs are transforming society to deliver social impact in their home communities and abroad.
- All students to understand the role of measuring impact and how to quantify the social impact for investors, donors, and beneficiaries to help ensure that scarce resources are utilised appropriately.
- Increase awareness of how they might apply social entrepreneurship skills in their future pursuits to address social problems.

Against this short course approach is Goldsmiths, University of London, which offers an MA in Social Entrepreneurship. This one-year full-time programme is built around five core modules:

- Theories of Creative, Cultural and Social Entrepreneurship
- Entrepreneurial Modelling
- Social Entrepreneurship: Policy and Frameworks
- Social Return on Investment: Principles and Practice
- Research or Project-Based Master's Dissertation

This programme has the following learning objectives:

- Develop a critical, sociologically informed understanding of this fast-evolving field.
- Develop tangible expertise in social return on investment and entrepreneurial modelling methodologies.
- Become part of London's social innovation community, a global centre of gravity in this field (with links to local social innovation communities virtually everywhere in the world).
- Access several future career paths in the growing social innovation sector.
- Develop a grasp of research methods, a significant body of written work and a public profile through assignments, debates and online/offline publication avenues, enabling some students to work as social innovation consultants/ knowledge leaders upon graduation.

Other organisations offer a diverse mix of training and support for social entrepreneurs, including UnLtd (https://unltd.org.uk/), Social Enterprise (http://www.socialenterprise.org.uk), Social Enterprise Solutions (http://www.socialenterprisesolutions.co.uk), Social Enterprise Works (http://www.socialenterpriseworks.org/). Some examples from this group:

- Changing the World: A Beginners Guide to Social Entrepreneurship
- From Ideas to Social Enterprise
- Ten Steps in Creating Your Own Social Enterprise
- Introduction to Social Enterprise for Public Sector
- What's Next for Your Social Enterprise?
- Eights Steps to a Public Sector Spin Out
- Business Planning for Social Enterprise
- Developing a Marketing Strategy that Translates into Sales
- Making Social Ventures Work

- Helping People Grow
- Social Enterprise Governance
- Making Your Venture Sustainable

This list is non-exhaustive but offers some insights into the diversity and spread of social enterprise training and support. The DICE Social Enterprise team[6], on the back of research and other support activities created a set of 'Train the Trainer' Level 7 units:

**Unit 1:** Strategic Enterprise Management
**Unit 2:** Research in Business
**Unit 3:** Social Enterprise Management
**Unit 4:** Strategic Management
**Unit 5:** Applied Financial Management
**Unit 6:** Applied Marketing
**Unit 7:** International Business Development
**Unit 8:** Funding and Finance for Social Enterprise

These units aimed to capture the essential areas for development of the social entrepreneur.

## EXISTING QUALIFICATIONS FOR SOCIAL ENTERPRISE IN UK

The current national qualification frameworks in England, Wales and Northern Ireland are the Regulated Qualification Framework (RQF) for qualifications regulated by Ofqual (general and vocational qualifications in England and vocational qualifications in Northern Ireland), the Credit and Qualifications Framework for Wales (CQFW) for qualifications in Wales, and the Framework for Higher Education Qualifications (FHEQ). The Scottish Credit and Qualifications Framework (SCQF) is the national credit transfer system for all levels of qualifications in Scotland.

The Register of Regulated Qualifications contains details of Regulated Qualifications in England (Ofqual), Wales (Welsh Government) and Northern Ireland (Ofqual for vocational qualifications and CCEA Accreditation for all other qualifications). https://register.ofqual.gov.uk/ The SCQF is found here https://scqf.org.uk/.

## FURTHER DEVELOPMENT PROPOSALS

The DICE Social Enterprise team, on the back of research and other support activities has developed some proposals for a common set of qualifications.

### Recommendations for a Social Enterprise Learning Pathway

EQF Level 4

**Candidate:** Someone with basic awareness but limited business administration or management experience.
**Delivery Context:** 5–8 sessions across 1–a 2 months with development of business plan as the key outcome.
At least 70% face-to-face interaction supported with on-line material
50–100 hours total learning.**Content**
**Unit 1:** Introduction to Entrepreneurship and Social Enterprise
**Unit 2:** Business idea and planning – services or products
**Unit 3:** Legal structures
**Unit 4:** Business administration – staffing, resources, location
**Unit 5:** Marketing & communications – selling/trading
**Unit 6:** Funding and Finance management – triple bottom line
**Unit 7:** Social impact or change.

EQF Level 5

**Candidate:** Someone who has launched an SE, interested in stabilising or maturing the SE.
**Delivery Context:** 12–16 sessions across 3–6 months.
Approximately 25% face-to-face interaction supported with extensive on-line material
150–250 hours total learning

**Content**

**Unit 1:** Introduction to Governance
**Unit 2:** Risk Management – Spreading the Risk
**Unit 3:** Procurement of Tenders and Evaluation/Reports on Social Impact
**Unit 4:** Refining or Relaunching Product/Service – Testing
**Unit 5:** Competition vs Collaboration/Co-operation (with Private/Public Sector) – IPR
**Unit 6:** Advanced Funding and Finance Management – Sustainability, Donations vs Grants/Projects, Membership Fees, Crowd Funding, Tax

**Unit 7:** Advanced HR management – Paid and Voluntary Staff
**Unit 8:** Advanced Marketing &Communications – Digital, Social Media, Networks, Stakeholders
**Unit 9:** Advanced Understanding of Regulatory Frameworks.

EQF Level 7

**Candidate:** Someone who has established one or more mature SEs, and is interested in innovation, growth or replication in additional locations.
Requires extremely specialist and nationally relevant content
Extremely time-poor due to leading the SEs
**Delivery Context:** 4–6 face-to-face sessions across 1–2 years.
On-line masters level material including 4–6 residential masterclass workshops
1200 hours total learning (2000 including dissertation)

Content

**Unit 1:** Strategic Enterprise Management – Transparent Governance and Change Management
**Unit 2:** Research and Innovations in Social Business and Enterprise
**Unit 3:** Social Enterprise leadership – Delegation and Oversight
**Unit 4:** Applied Resource Management – HR Recruitment and Retention of Specialist Personnel and Services
**Unit 5:** Applied Financial Management
**Unit 6:** Applied Marketing – Networking & Communications using Traditional and Digital Methods
**Unit 7:** Funding and Finance for Social Enterprise – Commissions, Consortia, Competition
**Unit 8:** International Business Development, Social Franchising and Replication
**Unit 9:** Political Dimension for Social Enterprise Community
**Unit 10:** Mentoring, Coaching and Training Social Enterprise.

## CONCLUSION

Developing a coherent and effective SE support and training platform demands that all relevant stakeholders are driven by the needs of the social entrepreneurs and their motivations and missions. The key to effective development is ensuring that the material, units, programmes etc. are flexible and meet the needs of diverse people, contexts, resources, access and training experience. Furthermore, it is important to consider how to enable and make more capable trainers using a 'Train the Trainer' approach. The project method outlined here will build an infrastructure to support the expansion of SE activities across the country and ensure that all social entrepreneurs and SEs can enhance the innate potential of social entrepreneurship to address many intractable social problems and assist in the economic recovery.

In the context of the COVID-19 pandemic and the devastating impact of lockdowns on economic activity in the UK over the past year, it now behoves the government to greatly expand access to social entrepreneurial training opportunities. In this chapter, we have outlined the social entrepreneurship ecosystem and offered a potential SE training framework to increase social capital through enhanced social entrepreneurship activities that have the potential, if adopted widely, to assist the UKand other economies to recover from the devastating impacts of the COVID-19 pandemic.

## REFERENCES


Abu-Saifan, S. (2012). Social Entrepreneurship: Definitions and Boundaries. *Technology Innovation Management Review*. https://timreview.ca/sites/default/files/article_PDF/Saifan_TIMReview_February2012_0.pdf

Arando, S., Gao, M., Jones, D. C., & Kato, T. (2011). *Efficiency in Employee-Owned Enterprises: An Econometric Case Study of Mondragon*. IZA Discussion Paper. https://cep.lse.ac.uk/conference_papers/26_05_2011/kato.pdf

Bacq, S., Hartog, C., Hoogendoorn, B., & Lepoutre, J. (2011). *Social and Commercial Entrepreneurship: Exploring Individual and Organizational Characteristics*. https://ondernemerschap.panteia.nl/pdf-ez/h201110.pdf

Bridge, S., Hegarty, C., & Porter, S. (2010). Rediscovering enterprise: Developing appropriate university entrepreneurship education. *Education + Training*, *52*(8/9), 722–734. doi:10.1108/00400911011089015

British Council, United Nations and Social Enterprise UK. (2020). *Innovation and resilience: A global snapshot of social enterprise responses to Covid-19*. British Council. https://www.britishcouncil.org/sites/default/files/socialenterprise_covidresponsesurvey_web_final_0.pdf?_ga=2.115436869.250335672.1622470098-1316689371.1622470098

Catford, J. (1998). Social Entrepreneurs are vital for health promotion - but they need supportive environments too. *Health Promotion International*, *13*(2), 95–98. doi:10.1093/heapro/13.2.95

Ciepielewska-Kowalik, A., & Pieliński, B. (2015). In search for a place for the third sector in the Polish welfare state: Toward a limited co-production. *EMES Conferences Selected Papers Series, ECSP-5EMES-13*. Retrieved from http://emes.net/content/uploads/publications/in-search for-a-placc-for-thc-third-sector-in-the-polish-welfare-state-toward-a-limited-co-production/ESCP-5EMES-13_Third_Sector_Polish_Welfare_State_Ciepielewska-Kowalik_Pielinski.pdf

Ciepielewska-Kowalik, A., Pieliński, B., Starnawska, M., & Szymańska, A. (2015). *Looking for Social Enterprise Models in Poland: Institutional and Historical Context*. ICSEM Working Papers, no. 11.

Das, M. B., Khan, I. A., & Tinsley, E. (2020). *Results-Based Financing Through Social Enterprises: A White Paper for the Global Partnership for Results-Based Approaches, in Response to the Covid-19 Pandemic*. World Bank. https://openknowledge.worldbank.org/handle/10986/34319

Dearing, R. (1997). *Higher Education in the Learning Society – Report of the National Committee of Inquiry into Higher Education*. HMSO.

Dearlove, D. (2004). Interview: Jeff Skoll. *Business Strategy Review*, *15*(2), 51–53.

Dees, J. G. (1998). Enterprising non-profits. *Harvard Business Review*, *76*(1), 54–67.

Dees, J. G. (1998a). *The Meaning of Social Entrepreneurship*. Stanford University: Draft Report for the Kauffman Center for Entrepreneurial Leadership. https://sehub.stanford.edu/sites/default/files/TheMeaningofsocialEntrepreneurship.pdf

Dohnalova, M., Legnerova, K., & Slechtova, V. (2015). *Social Enterprise in the Czech Republic*. ICSEM Working Papers No. 24. https://www.iap-socent.be/sites/default/files/Czech%20Republic%20-%20Dohnalova%20et%20al_0.pdf

Drayton, W. (2004). *How to Change the World: Social Entrepreneurs and the Power of New Ideas*. Oxford University Press.

Etchart, N., Horváth, A., Rosandić, A., & Spitálszky, A. (2014). *The state of social entrepreneurship in Hungary*. SEFORÏS Country Report. Retrieved from http://www.seforis.eu/upload/reports/Country_Report_Hungary.pdf

Forfás. (2013). *Social enterprise in Ireland: Sectoral opportunities and policy issues*. Retrieved from https://www.djei.ie/en/Publications/Social-Enterprise-in-Ireland-Sectoral-Opportunities-and-Policy-Issues.html

Foster, J. (2002). Sustainability, higher education and the learning society. *Environmental Education Research*, *8*(1), 35–41. doi:10.1080/13504620120109637

Gibb, A. A. (1993). The enterprise culture and education: understanding enterprise education and its links with small business, entrepreneurship and wider educational goals. International Small Business Journal, 11(3), 11-34. doi:10.1177/026624269301100301

Gibb, A. A. (2000). SME policy, academic research and the growth of ignorance, mythical concepts, myths, assumptions, rituals and confusions. *International Small Business Journal, 18*(3), 2–12. doi:10.1177/0266242600183001

Gregory, D., & Mansfield, C. (2019). *Capitalism in Crisis? Transforming our economy for people and planet.* Social Enterprise UK. https://www.socialenterprise.org.uk/wp-content/uploads/2019/11/Capitalism-in-Crisis.pdf

Hannon, D. (2004). *Philosophies of enterprise and entrepreneurship education and the challenges for higher education in the UK.* Paper presented at the 27th ISBA National Small Firms Conference, Newcastle, UK.

Hannon, D. (2005). *Graduate entrepreneurship in the UK: defining a research and enterprise policy framework.* Paper presented at the 28th ISBA National Small Firms Conference, Blackpool, UK.

Hannon, D., & Scott, J. (2006). *Mapping provision of enterprise education and support or entrepreneurship in England's HEIs.* Paper presented at the 29th ISBA National Small Firms Conference, Cardiff, UK.

Hazenberg, R. H. (2021). *The role of social enterprise in developing skills and creating employment opportunities in the UK.* https://www.enterpriseresearch.ac.uk/wp-content/uploads/2021/04/No50-The-role-of-social-enterprise-in-developing-skills-and-creating-employment-opportunities-in-the-UK-R.-Hazenberg.pdf

Hytti, U. (Ed.). (2002). State-of-Art of Enterprise Education in Europe – results from the Entredu project. Leonardo da Vinci -Programme of the European Commission.

Hytti, U., & O'Gorman, C. (2004). What is 'enterprise education'? An analysis of the objectives and methods of enterprise education programmes in four European countries. *Education + Training, 46*(1), 11–23. doi:10.1108/00400910410518188

Hytti, U., Stenholm, P., Heinonen, J., & Seikkula-Leino, J. (2010). Perceived learning outcomes in entrepreneurship education. *Education + Training, 52*(8/9), 587–606. doi:10.1108/00400911011088935

Jaksa, B., & Eros, B. (2016). *Social Innovations in Hungary.* https://www.siceurope.eu/sites/default/files/uploads/documents/social_innovations_in_hungary_2016.pdf

Jetmar, M. (2013). Social entrepreneurship: Challenge not only for developing countries but also for the EU. *CBU International Conference on Integration and Innovation in Science and Education*. www.cbuni.cz doi:10.12955/cbup.2013.13

Johnson, S. (2002). *Social entrepreneurship literature review*. Canadian Centre for Social Entrepreneurship. https://www.researchgate.net/profile/Leon-Prieto/publication/287854658_Social_entrepreneur_development_An_integration_of_critical_pedagogy_the_theory_of_planned_behavior_and_the_ACS_model/links/59ffab4d458515d0706e1ed9/Social-entrepreneur-development-An-integration-of-critical-pedagogy-the-theory-of-planned-behavior-and-the-ACS-model.pdf

Johnson, S. (2003). Young social entrepreneurs in Canada. *New Academy Review*, *2*(4).

Jones, B., & Iredale, N. (2010). Enterprise education as pedagogy. *Education + Training*, *52*(1), 7–19. doi:10.1108/00400911011017654

Kaderabkova, A. (2016). *Social Innovation in the Czech Republic*. CIS. Microsoft Word - Country Profile_ Czech Republic_2016.docx

Kanter, R. M. (2011). How Great Companies Think Differently. *Harvard Business Review*. http://gwmoon.knu.ac.kr/Lecture_Library_Upload/How_great_companies_think_differently.pdf

Kuratko, D. F. (2005). The emergence of entrepreneurship education: Development, trends and challenges. *Entrepreneurship Theory and Practice*, *29*(5), 577–597. doi:10.1111/j.1540-6520.2005.00099.x

LiuskariS. (n.d.). *Finland*. Retrieved from http://www.euclidnetwork.eu/programme-areas/geographical-areas-in-which-we-work/civil-society-in-europe-country-profiles/finland.html

Matlay, H. (2007). *The impact of entrepreneurship education on entrepreneurial outcomes*. Paper presented at the 30th ISBA National Small Firms Conference, Glasgow, UK.

McGlashan. (2013). Social Enterprise Training – The Facts. *The Guardian*. https://www.theguardian.com/social-enterprise-network/2013/sep/09/social-enterprise-training-research2

Melkas, H. (2020). Social enterprise: A study of its prevalence, role and characteristics in Swedish-Speaking regions of Finland. *Tijds. voor econ. en Soc. Geog.*, *111*(2), 101–116. doi:10.1111/tesg.12366

Nicholls, A. (Ed.). (2006). *Social Entrepreneurship: New Models of Sustainable Social Change*. Oxford University Press.

Nordic Council of Ministers, Nordic Council of Ministers Secretariat. (2015). *Social entrepreneurship and social innovation in the Nordic countries: Initiatives to promote social entrepreneurship and social innovation*. Retrieved from http://norden.diva-portal.org/smash/get/diva2:856045/FULLTEXT01.pdf doi:10.6027/TN2015-562

OECD Centre for Entrepreneurship, SMEs and Local Development. (2009). The Impact of the Global Crisis on SME and Entrepreneurship Financing and Policy Responses. Paris: OECD.

Opatrny-Yazell, C. M., Jensen, D. H., & McCord, M. H. (2021). The Dilemma of Social Entrepreneurship and Social Enterprise: An Exercise. *Entrepreneurship Education and Pedagogy*. https://journals.sagepub.com/doi/abs/10.1177/25151274211006896 doi:10.1177/25151274211006896

Peredo, A. M., & McLean, M. (2006). Social Entrepreneurship: A Critical Review of the Concept. *Journal of World Business*, *41*(1), 56–65. doi:10.1016/j.jwb.2005.10.007

Prieto, L. C., Phipps, S. T., & Friedrich, T. L. (2012). Social entrepreneur development: An integration of critical pedagogy, the theory of planned behavior and the ACS model. *Academy of Entrepreneurship Journal*, *18*(2), 2012.

Roberts, D., & Woods, C. (2005). Changing the world on a shoestring: The concept of social entrepreneurship. *University of Auckland Business Review*, *7*(1), 45–51.

Schumpeter, J. A. (1912). *Theorie der wirtschaftlichen Entwicklung*. Dunker und Humbolt.

Skoll, J. (2009). *In Innovations – Technology, Governance, Globalisation: Social Entrepreneurship: Shifting Power Dynamics. Skoll World Forum 2009*. MIT Press. http://www.pbs.org/now/shows/537/Shifting-Power-Dynamics.pdf

Social Enterprise UK. (2020a). *Social Enterprise Advisory Panel: June 2020 Highlights*. https://www.socialenterprise.org.uk/wp-content/uploads/2020/07/SEUK-SEAP-First-Survey-June-2020.pdf

Social Enterprise UK. (2020b). *2020 – a view from across the nations*. https://www.socialenterprise.org.uk/2020-a-view-from-across-the-nations/

The Economist. (2009). *After the Storm*. https://www.economist.com/node/14548881

United States Agency for International Development, Bureau for Europe and Eurasia, Office of Democracy, Governance and Social Transition (USAID). (2014). *2013 CSO Sustainability Index for Central and Eastern Europe and Eurasia*. USAID. Retrieved from https://www.usaid.gov/sites/default/files/documents/1863/EuropeEurasia_FY2014_CSOSI_Report.pdf

Valtioneuvosto. (2021). *Social enterprises to benefit from more advice and competence – A call for funding launched to establish a new centre of expertise*. Available at: https://valtioneuvosto.fi/en/-/1410877/social-enterprises-to-benefit-from-more-advice-and-competence-a-call-for-funding-launched-to-establish-a-new-centre-of-expertise

Villeneuve-Smith, F., & Temple, N. (2015). *Leading the World in Social Enterprise – State of Social Enterprise Survey 2015*. Social Enterprise UK. http://socialenterprise.org.uk/public/uploads/editor/SEUK_StateofSocialEnterprise_FINAL_WEB.pdf

Wilkinson, C. (2014). *A Map of SE and Their Eco-systems in Europe*. European Commission. https://www.wikipreneurship.eu/images/d/de/SE_mapping_results.pdf

Wilkinson, C. (2015). *A Map of SE and Their Eco-systems in Europe. Country Report*. European Commission. https://ec.europa.eu/social/BlobServlet?docId=13102&langId=

## ENDNOTES

1 15,198 SE in the target population with a total of 1.159 completed.

2 The report acknowledges that this is not a full representation of all the relevant actors but does give insight.

3 https://settle-project.eu/

4 DICE (Developing Innovative Community Solutions www.diceconsortium.com) is a specialist in the area and typifies this. The DICE SE team is presently engaged in an online only delivery pilot for emerging social entrepreneurs from six countries (Egypt, India, Mali, Pakistan, Tanzania, and South Africa) – please contact Dr Pascoe to learn more.

5 The analysis in this section is not exhaustive and aims to act as a resource to support discussions, design and development, etc.

6 www.diceconsortium.com

# Chapter 10
# Consulting for Sustainability and Social Impact in Social Enterprises and Not for Profits:
## How Does Consultancy Work?

**Onyekachi Wambu**
*AFFORD, UK*

**Amanda Rodrigues Amorim Adegboye**
*Coventry University, UK*

**Kumar Kotecha**
*University of Greenwich, UK*

**Natasha Bonsu**
*Emerald Castle, UK*

**Christine Locke**
*Diversity House, Sittingbourne, UK*

## EXECUTIVE SUMMARY

*A key remit of any consultant is to assist the client or organisation they work with to achieve their objectives by mapping out a strategy for developing and sustaining the work of the organisation. The aim of this chapter is to use an autoethnographic method and semi-structured questioning to reflect on our consultancy activity with social enterprises and not-for-profit organisations. As a part of their lived experience of engaging with clients, a group of diverse consultants reflect on their work of providing consultancy services to community groups, academics, and organisations.*

DOI: 10.4018/978-1-7998-7724-0.ch010

A key remit of any consultant is to assist their client or the organisation they work for to achieve their corporate and business objectives (see Chapter 1) and to develop a strategy for sustaining the work of the organisation. The aim of this chapter is to use an autoethnographic method of research woven with semi-structured questioning to reflect on our consultancy activity with social enterprises (SEs) and not-for-profit organisations. As a part of their lived experience, a group of consultants with diverse expertise and terms of reference reflect on their work of providing consultancy services to SEs, community groups, academics, and organisations. To find out more about the consultants background please check their biographies in the authors section. Their shared experiences, advice and learning cover the following key areas in building the capacity of the consultant and meeting client objectives:

- Professional entry points
- Mentoring
- Gaining formal qualifications and experiential training
- Developing TORs
- Models for evaluating NGOs/social enterprises
- Collaborative working
- Likes of the profession
- Measuring social impact and sustainability
- Learning from mistakes avoiding pitfalls
- Conducting internal evaluations on social enterprises
- Pricing models
- Consulting during Covid-19
- Use of ICT
- Social enterprises and development

Finally, in Figure 1, at the end of the chapter summarises some of the best practices and a series of do's and don'ts.

## CONSULTANT REFLECTIONS

Consultant Name: Onyekachi Wambu, AFFORD-UK, London

1. Tell us how you got involved in consultancy services?

AFFORD's mission is to enhance and expand the contributions Africans in the diaspora make to Africa's development. Those contributions are financial, intellectual, political, social, cultural and through volunteerism. It is a big agenda – so we have prioritised the creation of decent jobs in Africa via diaspora investment and entrepreneurial engagement in the small- and medium-sized enterprise sector. AFFORD is unique in that we undertake consultancy on behalf of different international organisations or institutions who are seeking to understand this diaspora economy, whilst at the same time, we employ consultants to support the businesses and SEs that we support. In the latter area, AFFORD provides Business Development Support (BDS) services that advise these diaspora SEs who are undertaking investments or expanding their businesses in Africa. We got into consultancy work through delivering on our mission, as we undertook a lot of research to fully understand the ways that diaspora support development in Africa. As one of the few organisations doing work in the migration and development nexus, we very quickly built-up expertise that has been very valuable to the development sector as it sought to understand the role that the diasporas play in development.

2. Did you have a mentor before you went into consultancy?

When AFFORD was first set up in 1994, the key figures who established the organisation were very experienced International Development consultants and experts. They provided the benchmark through which the organisation established its PMEAL (Planning, monitoring, evaluation, accountability, and learning) systems, which in turn shaped our external evaluation, project planning, and other consultancy processes. This cohort have continued over the years to be mentors for the organisation – supporting us in developing consultancies in different areas (including producing training toolkits), ensuring that those consultancies that we do undertake are delivered to the highest quality.

3. How did you go about developing the terms of reference?

Terms of Reference (TORs) are best developed in consultation with clients. In the case of our BDS services advising businesses, this is best done through a proper process of assessing the business with the business owner through completed pre-qualification questionnaires, business plans, budgets, or forecasts, as well as the long-term ambitions for the business and the social and other impacts they wish to make. Our checklists include:

- Templates for applications and business plans.
- Detailed budgets.
- Marketing strategy and action plans.
- Criteria for applicants, panel and partners, and a set of practical filters and procedures for due diligence at each phase.

- Operational Management Plan for all subcontractors, partners, and business advisors.
- Agreed metrics, assumptions, milestones, outcomes, outputs, tasks, deadlines, and responsibility.
- Regular review procedures to ensure that the business plans are SMART and responsive to the situation on the ground.
- Monitoring, evaluation, and review procedures.

4. What training did you undertake to be a consultant?

AFFORD built its expertise in consultancy work through its experiential process and with the support of its founders who were experienced consultants, cascading their own knowledge and skills. We have also harnessed the skills and experiences of BDS experts and consultants who have been brought in to support the organisation. One of these experts, for instance, has been one of the leading country experts on working with co-ops and SEs from Africa and Latin America focused on fair-trade agriculturally produced products. So, we have been able to harness our founders as mentors in shaping our offer and have brought in external experts when necessary to improve the offer. We have also participated in training programmes provided by trusted third-party organisations in specific areas in order to benchmark and deepen our skills – so they meet industry standards.

5. What do you like about the work you undertook?

Many of the businesses we work with are keen to grow their businesses in difficult trading conditions on the African continent. They are also keen to make a social impact particularly in creating jobs. Supporting them to successfully achieve their goals and have a social impact is always satisfying. Observing lives being transformed in Africa makes the work worthwhile. When we undertake research consultancies or training consultancies it is always satisfying to deliver new knowledge that will enable better policy making and also provide training that improves service delivery by government departments or international agencies.

6. What benefits did you gain from collaborating with your colleagues?

As an organisation delivering consultancy services, collaboration between colleagues is essential to any successful outcomes. Establishing roles and responsibilities as part of the project planning is also vital to successful delivery. Also assessing the strengths of different colleagues and apportioning them to an area that best draws out their expertise is equally important in enabling successful delivery. The role of the project coordinator is really to ensure that the team works effectively to ensure successful outcomes and happy clients.

7. How do you measure social impact and sustainability?

Quantitative and qualitative methods are used to collect data and measure impact. The businesses we support agree very specific objectives, indicators, outputs and outcomes, as well as the means for verification – these constitute the tools for data collection and measuring the impact of our work supporting job creation via diaspora SME interventions. For instance, quantitively these include the number of decent jobs directly created; those that are indirectly created; the quality of those jobs, whether they are protected by contracts or good working conditions; and qualitatively the psychological impact of having a job on individuals and how their lives are transformed as a result – i.e. children going to school or their ability to pay for healthcare, etc.

8. Have there been any mistakes you have made as a consultant and what pitfalls should others avoid?

Mistakes are usually always the result of not having been very clear in the TORs and managing expectations properly between the consultant and a client. Avoid assumptions. A great deal of work should be spent on precisely scoping out the consultancy and addressing the precise parameters of the project. Also, a clear idea of what success looks like at the end of this consultancy in terms of expected outcomes should also be factored in. Along the way, potential difficulties can also be mitigated by building in frequent reviews of progress to be able to identify any emerging problems and respond to them in a timely fashion. Despite the existence of some of these processes to manage particularly complex consultancies occasionally there will be difficulties and misunderstandings. These should then be dealt with through proper mediation protocols.

9. What models and theories do you use to evaluate an NGO/SE?

The businesses or SEs that we provide BDS consultancy support to usually engage with us because they agree with the Theory of Change that AFFORD works with. This would include the project cycle and the PMEAL tools that would be used.

10. What advice would you give to consultants taking on consultancy work?

Be clear about the terms of reference and the scope of the work, understand the broader context of the client's work including their constraints and challenges. Finally, understand what success looks like for them.

11. What advice would you give to social entrepreneurs conducting evaluations or reviews on their own organisations?

Pretend you are an investor and approach your business unemotionally and as an outsider so that you can understand the business. Ask yourself the questions the investor would. Separate the social impact (and the good you wish to bring about) from how well run and efficient the company is – the road to hell is frequently paved with good intentions. Always ask yourself the difficult questions. Also speak to and ask your staff, your suppliers and all those who exist in the ecosystem your business exists in does, the difficult questions. Sometimes it is impossible to be this neutral or expect staff members and others who are dependent on you to be equally neutral or frank. So, most of the time it is better to bring in an independent evaluator to provide such an honest appraisal of your company.

12. What pricing model do you use and what sharing formula do you use?

For our BDS work supporting businesses and SEs we work with their pricing model. The business development support that we provide is to look at that model critically and offer feedback as to whether the business is realistic or not, especially when considering competitors and other factors in the ecosystem. Our own pricing model when we undertake consultancies for others is to use competitive international day rates that international experts charge.

13. How did you consult during the Covid-9 pandemic period?

All activity during coverage was conducted online. Zoom or MS Teams were the central tools for focus group meetings and communication, as was WhatsApp. SurveyMonkey continued to be the tool for processing and analysing questionnaires. Later, some face-to-face meetings were possible after vaccine regimes were introduced.

14. How can Information Communication Technology (ICT) and Social Media improve the consulting process?

We have all learned how to do things better since Covid-19 via the role that ICT played. This is going to be very important moving forward in designing training, project implementation and other programmes that can be delivered online. Ironically it is actually much more cost effective and one might even say efficient, although without the warmth of human contact.

15. What advice would you give to SEs and NGO's working in the developing world?

In order to fulfil your social mission ensure that the enterprise is effective and efficient. Poor service delivery is frequently the bane of the poor and the excluded. Clearly define the social mission and social impact that you expect as a result of enacting that social mission. Take advice from local people who are in your ecosystem. Do not expect to micro-manage and run your social enterprise from the UK as a number of diaspora businesses sometimes do. Put in place a good management system on the ground to run the SEs and businesses. Always seek to add value or solve a problem in the social economy – do not distort the local economy or replicate or destroy what others are already doing. Find a gap where you can add value. Be agile and creative in responding to challenges – be prepared to pivot the SE with an eye always on solving problems in the social economy.

## Consultant Name: Amanda Amorim Adegboye

1. Tell us how you got involved in consultancy services?

Initially, I was invited by a senior academic colleague to join a consultancy team and contribute to the development of the quantitative data collection protocol and data analysis. My colleague received an invitation to submit a bid to a local authority in London, England to perform a service evaluation. After this experience, I have started looking for tenders on different government portals. However, most of my experience in consultancy or commercial research is based on invitations by colleagues or organisations.

2. Did you have a mentor before you went into consultancy?

I never had a formal mentor regarding consultancy. However, there was a time when I decided to reduce my working hours as a lecturer and apply for other research-related jobs outside academia (or high education institutions). I got an offer to conduct a service evaluation commissioned by a local Clinical Commissioning Group (CCG) in London. When I requested the faculty Dean to change my contract to part-time, she advised me on the impact that this would have on my pension and suggested whether I could take the job as a consultancy project. She explained the pros and cons of opening my own consultancy firm or doing consultancy under my current employer (University). Due to other personal commitments, I decided to do the consultancy work via the University. The main advantage was that the University was responsible for setting up the contract and liability. Being new to consultancy, having an established institution setting up the contract dctails was a great deal.

3. How did you go about developing the terms of reference?

Developing and agreeing on the TOR is a critical step as it defines all the features of how you (consultant) or the team will conduct the evaluation. Whenever possible, I follow the World Bank guidelines on how to write the TORs for an evaluation (Roberts et al 2011). The World Bank guidance document includes a modified checklist developed by the United Nations, which I find very useful for reviewing the quality of the TOR and ensuring that all necessary elements are included in the document. The process should start by understanding the scope, objectives, timeframe and resources required for the evaluation and consulting the commissioners about what is expected in terms of outputs and deliverables.

4. What training did you undertake to be a consultant?

I learned a lot on the job as each project is unique. However, I had acquired the top level of qualification in my field (PhD) when I first started conducting consultancy research and independent evaluations. I believe that to be a successful consultant, you need to be a self-learner. However, some courses on leadership, communication and presentation skills and project management are very useful. During my career, I have done several courses related to these areas, including presenting to the media and Agile methodology. I continue doing CPD courses to keep abreast with new developments in the area of monitoring & evaluation, leadership and project management.

5. What do you like about the work you undertook?

What I like the most about doing consultancy is the fact that my work has a direct or indirect impact on decisions. The best part of the evaluation report are the recommendations.

6. What benefits did you gain from collaborating with your colleagues?

Collaborative work allows for the sharing of skills, knowledge and experience and consequently leads to better outcomes for the beneficiaries of the project, for the consultancy team and the commissioner. An effective partnership enhances professional learning. Also, it is a great opportunity for expanding your professional network.

7. How do you measure social impact and sustainability?

Impact occurs when the programme, service or policy generates health, economic, cultural benefits (Greenhalgh et al, 2016). Measuring impact is very difficult particularly when you evaluate short-term projects and the impact of a particular programme will require time (for example, reduction in mortality rate or change in policy, improvement in quality of life and wellbeing). There is no recipe for measuring impact. It will depend on the nature of the evaluation. This should be guided by the logic model. The sustainability aspect goes hand-in-hand with the implementation process (Tumilowicz et al, 2018). It is assessed by asking the question – Is this intervention likely to be adopted or implemented by the organisation and Why? In order to perform a robust evaluation of the sustainability of a programme, service or interventions, other domains need to be assessed including governance, commitment, stakeholder engagement and financing.

8. Have there been any mistakes you have made as a consultant and what pitfalls should others avoid?

When tenders are competitive, consultants need to demonstrate value for money to win the contract. Frequently, the consultancy team tend to develop ambitious proposals and then find it difficult to deliver what has been agreed on the TOR. Having a realistic estimation of the time and resources needed to deliver the work is essential for a successful consultancy.

9. What models and theories do you use to evaluate an NGO/SE?

Evaluations should always be guided by the theory of change or logic models. 'A logic model is a graphic display or "map" of the relationship between a programme's resources, activities, and intended results, which also identifies the programme's underlying theory and assumptions' (W.K. Kellogg Foundation, 2004).

10. What advice would you give to consultants taking on consultancy work? Why and please expand and give some examples.

Consultants should invest time and effort in developing their unique skillset so they are differentiated in the market. Building a network is also critical as some opportunities for consultancy work may arise from the people you know. Registering successful stories and testimonials even for minor work or tasks delivered also help build credibility and enhance chances of getting new contracts.

11. What advice would you give to social entrepreneurs conducting evaluations or reviews on their own organisations?

Ensure that the team have adequate scientific, tech and analytical skills to conduct the work. Also, it is important to ensure that the team is not introducing bias when analysing and interpreting the results. Ideally, evaluation should be conducted by an independent team (not involved in the delivery of the project). Most funders allow institutions to include a dedicated budget for an independent evaluation, usually conducted by an external team.

12. What pricing model do you use and what sharing formula do you use?

As an academic, my consultancy experience is related to contract research and programme or research evaluation. I use the University pricing model for budget estimation. Depending on the client or funders I can charge VAT or overheads. In some instances, I can apply a full economic costing model where both direct and indirect costs (estates charges, central services) can be included. Please can you expand ion the University pricing model and any other model others are using.

13. How did you consult during the Covid -19 pandemic period?

I have used digital and teaching & learning tools to deliver e-consultancy. I have been recently involved in consultancy work (as part of the consultancy team) with the World Health Organisation (WHO) where inputs were received from a multitude of stakeholders, including educators, healthcare professionals, governmental and NGOs and the public sector. In fact, conducting the evaluation remotely proved to be cost-effective given the geographic spread of participants. Using a digital platform also facilitated simultaneous translation during the workshops and focus group discussion. We also made use of the simultaneous translation where attendees could select the audio channel in their preferred language.

14. How can Information Communication Technology (ICT) and Social Media improve the consulting process?

ICT and social media can help with the dissemination of your work, find new audiences and build your profile and credibility. You can expand your network via social media and connect with potential clients or users. It can facilitate creating a dialogue between your or your company and your stakeholders.

15. What advice would you give to social enterprises and NGO's working in the developing world?

Be committed to upskilling your workforce by promoting education and supporting autonomy. This will show your staff that you trust and value them. This will ultimately bring job satisfaction. Investing in capacity building and training, promoting autonomy and providing a clear path for career progression is important for the success of any organization, regardless of whether they are based in a low- or high-income country. Why? There are many free resources online that can be used for training.

## Consultant Name: Christine Locke

1. Tell us how you got involved in consultancy services?

When I fell into consulting, I had no idea what I was getting myself into. In 2005, the then-Medway Racial Equality Council asked me to undertake a community research project that looked into the perceptions and experiences of substance usage within Medway's South Asian communities. The research was financed by the Department of Health. Following the successful completion of my first consultation, the then Swale PCT invited me to conduct a needs assessment for the Black, Asian, and Minority Ethnic (BAME) populations in Swale. I enjoyed conducting both research and consulting so much that I began looking for work in corporate and non-profit organisations, which I have done for the past 15 years. However, invites from colleagues or organisations have resulted in the majority of my consulting (teaching and research) skills.

2. Did you have a mentor before you went into consultancy?

Some colleagues recommended my initial consulting contracts. Prior to receiving these recommendations and dabbling in consultancy, I had no mentoring or formal training as a consultant. However, in 2017, after conducting several years of soft-skills training, equity, diversity, and inclusion audits, and conducting project impact evaluations for organisations, I decided to enrol in the Consulting Institute to receive internationally accredited management consultant training and mentoring (CMC) qualifications. While studying at the Institute of Consulting, I met Tony Lavender, my mentor and role model.

3. How did you go about developing the terms of reference?

Developing and agreeing on the Terms of Reference (TOR) sets out the essential steps that a consultant and/or his/her team will follow in conducting the evaluation. Whenever possible, I follow the UNDP (2019) and the Management of Consultancy guidelines on how to write the TORs for an evaluation (Chartered Management Institute 2017). The UNDP and CMI guidance documents include templates or a checklist, which is useful for reviewing the quality of the TOR and ensuring that all necessary elements are included in the document. The process should start by understanding the scope, objectives, timeframe, and resources required for the evaluation and consulting the commissioners about what is expected in terms of outputs and deliverables.

4. What training did you undertake to be a consultant?

Initially, I learned a lot on the job as each project is unique. However, realising that a consultant needs some core skills, knowledge, and competency to operate effectively and efficiently (Nickols & Bergholz 2012), I registered with the Institute of Consulting for the CMI level qualification in professional consulting. I am currently a PhD candidate and working on my thesis as I believe that to be a successful consultant you need to be a continuous learner. According to the Institute of Consulting, an effective management consultant requires a balance of the following – behaviours, skills, and knowledge. Based on this argument, I have received training on several subjects including market capability and knowledge, consulting competence, professional behaviours, business/management competencies among others, to ensure that I operate ethically and at a high standard. I continue doing CPD courses to keep abreast with new developments in monitoring & evaluation, leadership, and project management.

5. What do you like about the work you undertook?

What I like the most about doing consultancy is the fact that my work has a direct or indirect impact on decisions. The best part of the evaluation report is the recommendations.

6. What benefits did you gain from collaborating with your colleagues?

I believe that there are three core reasons for collaborating with your colleagues as a consultant and these come under the acronym – ‘K’ (Know the past to understand the present), ‘G’ (Get to the truth), and ‘M’ (Maximise buy-in for change). The astronomer Carl Sagan famously said, 'you have to know the past to understand the present,' and his assertion is correct as an excellent way of knowing the up-to-date state of the organization, is to talk to those who were led by the people in your role in the past. Interacting and collaborating with your colleagues will ensure that you gain insiders' information on what was done right? What was done wrong? And what are the key challenges and the roadblocks preventing the organisation from overcoming them? Also, a consultant on taking a new contract may be confronted with challenges and blockades from employees of all levels at the organisation, therefore, there is no better way to address resistance to change than by communication and collaborating with these new colleagues.

7. How do you measure social impact and sustainability?

Social impact is the positive change that your organisation has created or effected over time (Future Learn. In the third sector where I do most of my consulting, understanding how they work to achieve better outcomes for their service users and stakeholders including sponsors. Social impact is critical to Social Impact Measurement is a process of understanding how much social change occurred and can be attributed to an organisation's activities. The Not-for-Profit sector uses a variety of approaches to gauge their social impact and some of these include MERL (Monitoring, Evaluation, Research and Learning), SROI (Social Return on Investment), QUAL (the quality-of-life scale), Social Accounting and Audit: a systematic analysis of the effects of an organisation on its communities of interest or stakeholders, with stakeholder input as part of the data analysed for the accounting statement, logic models or the logic approach to program (a framework that enables organisations to embed evaluation and performance assessment into the program design and life cycle process of their programs). There is a link between social impact and sustainability, as a good assessment of impact using the tools will enable an organisation to gauge and maintain at a certain rate or level the changes or impacts made by their programs.

8. Have there been any mistakes you have made as a consultant and what pitfalls should others avoid?

When tenders are competitive, consultants need to demonstrate value for money to win the contract. Frequently, the consultancy team tend to develop ambitious proposals and then find it difficult to deliver what has been agreed on the TOR. Having a realistic estimation of the time and resource needed to deliver the work is essential for a successful consultancy.

9. What models and theories do you use to evaluate an NGO/SE?

Change is a critical component in the work that NGOs do. The fast changes in government policies and meeting thc funding criteria of sponsors means that NGOs are faced with understanding and evaluating the changes and impacts that their programs make. Therefore, it is pertinent that appropriate theories and models are needed to effectively support the change process in shaping healthy work environments. Some of the theories and models include the Force Field Model and The Unfreezing-Change-Refreezing Mode (Kurt Lewin 1951), Planned Change (Lippitt, Watson, and Westley 1958), Innovation Diffusion Theory (Rogers 1995), the medicine change wheel, and the logic model (W.K. Kellogg Foundation, 2004).

10. What advice would you give to consultants taking on consultancy work?

There is much advice that can be given to a new consultant starting out in the consulting business, however, the most crucial advice is that he or she should be mindful of adhering to professional standards and ethical conducts such as: behaving in an open, honest, and trustworthy manner, disclosing any personal interest which may affect his or her decisions, to serve the client with integrity, cultivate confidence, trust, build rapport with colleagues at all levels, competence, independence, objectivity, and professionalism. Also, he or she should invest in workforce development. Allocate tasks according to the team's expertise and ambition to grow. When a consultant incorporates behaviours in the above highlighted manner, it ensures that his or her advice, findings and recommendations are adhered to. Also, this will guarantee that the consultant not only achieves then ultimate result in the current brief but also creates the opportunity for a recurring invitation for future jobs.

11. What advice would you give to social entrepreneurs conducting evaluations or reviews on their own organisations?

An internal consultant should be mindful of the three core competencies of consultancy, which are technical, business, and consulting (Nickols & Bergholz 2012). The consultant should confirm that his or her team have adequate scientific, technical and analytical skills to conduct the work. Also, it is important to ensure that the team is not introducing bias when analysing and interpreting the results. Ideally, evaluation should be conducted by an independent team (not involved in the delivery of the project). Most funders allow institutions to include a dedicated budget for an independent evaluation, usually conducted by an external team.

12. What pricing model do you use and what sharing formula do you use?

I use value-based pricing (Alan Weiss 2008) – The concept is that prior to suggesting a price, you have a detailed conversation with the prospect to understand and agree upon the value the engagement, if successful, would have on the business. Also, I use the price list from the NCVO.

13. How did you consult during the Covid-19 pandemic period?

During the global pandemic, I used the hybrid approach in my consultancy work whilst taking into consideration the social distancing directives. I used the digital platform to conduct Equality, Diversity, Inclusion, and Intersectionality audit for corporate organisations. During the period of the Covid-19, I carried out mental health training using platforms such as Skype for business, Zoom and WhatsApp. However, for the consultancy commission with the Office of the National Statistics to support the National Census 2021, I had to deliver this contract face-to-face at my Centre.

14. How can Information Communication Technology (ICT) and Social Media improve the consulting process?

Digital communication of all types will ensure that the consultant has an efficient form of communication both internally and externally. It allows different parties to express what they want to say and how they respond to each other.

15. What advice would you give to social enterprises and NGOs working in the developing world?

Be committed to upskilling your workforce by promoting and valuing education. Why? There are many free resources online that can be used for training.

## Consultant Name: Kumar KOTECHA, Charity Trustee and School Governor

1. Tell us how you got involved in consultancy services?

Essentially, I was asked by others based on perceived expertise, experience, knowledge etc. of mine. Noting my roles in charities, school governance and the third sector, such services have been provided *pro bono*.

2. Did you have a mentor before you went into consultancy?

I never had a formal mentor. However, most knowledge has been gained by way of acquired experience and detailed/qualitative research because of necessity.

3. How did you go about developing thc tcrms of reference?

Generic (e.g., The Independent Evaluation Blue Booklet re International Bank for Reconstruction & Development/World Bank) terms of reference(s) are used to describe/define various aspects, including requirements, expectations, objectives, scope, timeframe etc. re the task/evaluation. However, much is tailored in terms of the specific assignment, task, needs of the organisation etc. Indeed, developing TOR is a crucial step in terms of managing outputs re qualitative evaluation.

4. What training did you undertake to be a consultant?

None specifically, but all skills have been acquired by doing, including utilising experiences gained through high-profile local government employment etc. The skills are constantly refined by way of ongoing research and acquisition of knowledge etc.

5. What do you like about the work you undertook?

Getting to know the inner workings of organisations, its personnel, establishing long-term relationships etc. and noting the express and implied consequences for all concerned in terms of the evaluation undertaken.

6. What benefits did you gain from collaborating with your colleagues?

Establishment of ongoing professional relationships, networks, partnerships etc.

7. How do you measure social impact and sustainability?

Social impact and sustainability can be problematic to establish but key to assess change. Classic theory of change is necessary to use to establish how intervention works. Utilising aspects re interventions include common elements such as inputs, resources, implementation, outputs, outcomes, impact, context etc. Indeed, the use of a logic model is practical as it represents the theory of how an intervention produces its outcomes – essentially, facilitating how an intervention works.

8. Have there been any mistakes you have made as a consultant and what pitfalls should others avoid?

A key learning feature for me over the years has been about timescale and to always allow additional time for various eventualities.

9. What models and theories do you use to evaluate an NGO/SE?

Thc classic preferred model is the logic model as mentioned above and this has been used in the organisation where I discharge civic duties as a trustee, governor etc. The logic model is functional and somewhat straightforward to comprehend for all concerned.

10. What advice would you give to consultants taking on consultancy work?

As a lone operator, I always cross check all in terms of establishing Terms of Reference (TORs) and equally, cross reference as I make progress.

11. What advice would you give to social entrepreneurs conducting evaluations or reviews on their own organisations?

Follow a rigorous process, establish paraments/TORs, understanding any limitations, involve objective & skilled independent individuals to carry out the evaluation.

12. What pricing model do you use and what sharing formula do you use?

My work is not chargeable and always *pro bono.*

13. How did you consult during the Covid-19 pandemic period?

I have done no such work during the Covid-19 period.

14. How can Information Communication Technology (ICT) and social media improve the consulting process?

Facilitating remote meetings, gathering of data/information and certainly conducting any necessary research and much more as needed but being conscious of various safety/security measures, including general Data Protection Regulation (GDPR).

15. What advice would you give to social enterprises and NGOs working in the developing world?

Stay focused on the goals, be creative about acquiring and the use of available resources, learn from others and their successes & mistakes, be humble, embrace ideas and explore accordingly etc.

## Consultant Name: Natasha Bonsu, Emerald Castle Consultancy, London

1. Tell us how you got involved in consultancy services?

I have always enjoyed evaluating and developing strategies to improve my work and that of other people. I value self-reflection and assessing the strength and weakness of a project to justify my involvement. I attended an SE seminar and enjoyed hearing about the enhancements in peoples' lives because of these entrepreneurs. However, when I started talking to entrepreneurs it was obvious that many struggled to articulate their outcomes and impact. I knew from there I wanted to help, and I offered my services to consult.

2. Did you have a mentor before you went into consultancy?

Yes, I had a mentor before I decided to be a consultant, we discussed life after university and juggling family and career. When I decided to pursue a career in consultancy, I asked my mentor for support and he has guided me throughout. I have another mentor who specialises in SE and we discuss the industry at length to make sure I'm offering the right advice to my clients.

3. How did you go about developing the terms of reference?
4. What training did you undertake to be a consultant?

I did not complete any formal training to be consultant, however, I completed my Master's in economics which enhanced my analytical skills. I am a self-learner and continuously read about third-sector developments. I deepen my knowledge about good consultancy practice, time, and project management skills. Good consultants are good listeners and I make sure that I listen carefully to fully understand any problem before offering a solution. I attend numerous workshops and seminars about small business development, sales, and marketing.

5. What do you like about the work you undertook?

I enjoy seeing the difference my projects make to my client's organisation and highlighting how their SEs have a significant positive impact to their beneficiaries.

I enjoy analysing and interpreting outcomes to make informed evaluations and offering a sound strategy for the future. I enjoy my work even more when my reports are used to compliment a funding application and the award is granted to my client.

6. What benefits did you gain from collaborating with your colleagues?

I thoroughly enjoy collaboration and prefer to work with colleagues than alone. I like having colleagues to brainstorm and develop ideas with. I am a firm believer that it 'takes a village' to complete a project and each team member has a viable contribution according to their strengths and skills. My best work has been produced by working very closely with my client and their team to fully understand their needs. In addition, building a strong bond with colleagues to share sensitive data and the integrity to handle and interpret such information.

7. How do you measure social impact and sustainability?

My preferred method of measuring social impact and sustainability depends on the organisation and its size. Small grass roots SEs and voluntary groups require a firm understanding of their theory of change. In addition, realistic and measurable metrics to collect data and interpret. Once the organisation has been established for a few years and seen a sizeable growth; a combination of the theory of change and a logic model would be a viable method of measure.

8. Have there been any mistakes you have made as a consultant and what pitfalls should others avoid?

Mistakes and pitfalls will always occur in any type of work and it is being able to acknowledge the mistake, correct it and implement strategies for such mistakes not be repeated. I made the costly mistake of undertaking a project that I assumed required interpreting and evaluating alone. It was only when I delved deeper that I found that there was not enough data, and the quality of the data was very poor. This assumption meant that I needed to spend more time collecting data and within a limited time frame yet still produce a quality report. I have learnt from my mistake and I request to see all the data – good and bad – before accepting a project.

9. What models and theories do you use to evaluate an NGO/SE?
10. What advice would you give to consultants taking on consultancy work?

I would always advise consultants to be as neutral and unbiased as possible. We want to support and help our clients, but we can only be good consultants if we have integrity. Without integrity our report is flawed and is useless to our client. Secondly, seek a second opinion from a mentor or respected colleague to ensure that you have interpreted all data correctly and in an unbiased way.

11. What advice would you give to social entrepreneurs conducting evaluations or reviews on their own organisations?

Self-reflection is important as the entrepreneur lives and breathes their business. It is therefore important that they have built the skills and habits to constantly reflect their work and outcomes. However, self-reflection can be depressing when you realise that your work and organisation needs a major overhaul, and it is easier to stick our head in the sand than to deal with the issue. However, all leaders know the route to any destination is never straight but full of bendy roads in stormy weather and not just a on a summer's day. All these situations build resilience and encourage us to handle problems which will always arise, as an opportunity for growth and not failure.

12. How did you consult during the Covid-19 pandemic period?

As with everyone else, the power of online meetings using Zoom and MS Teams, emailing and telephone. Also, not just to talk about work, but to take a genuine interest in someone's life outside work and to develop a strong relationship.

13. How can Information Communication Technology (ICT) and Social Media improve the consulting process?

ICT will always be needed to aid a consultant to deliver their work. However, nothing beats meeting a client face-to-face and building rapport. Transferring large amounts of datasets using ICT will make our work quicker and improved statistical software to aid interpretation will also contribute significantly. Social media is still a very strong marketing tool and will always help create an awareness of the consultant and their work.

14. What advice would you give to social enterprises and NGOs working in the developing world?

Simplify the product and service as much as possible and have a clear customer in mind who will benefit from the business. Secondly, the organisation should be agile and adaptable to every changing economic climate. Finally, develop, train, and empower a core team to be proactive problem solvers thinking outside the box.

Figures 1-10 draw to a conclusion the reflections above in a tabularised summary of best practices and experiences of consultants for knowledge exchange consultancy work.

*Figure 1.*

Conclusion – the summary below from our consultants feedback is not exhaustive, but provides some useful tips to consider when undertaking projects with social enterprises/NGOs

| Area | Summary | Dos | Don'ts |
|---|---|---|---|
| Professional entry points | Diverse entry points are available, including experiential and qualification-based entries. Some consultants have built up a body of expertise which is then marketed through the consultancy for commercial or social benefit. Others have had their expertise in quantitative data collection and analysis recognized and been invited to join a team submitting an official tender. Each route is valuable, the key factor being the potential consultant's interest or passion for the profession and willingness to seize opportunities that present themselves. | Be proactive and consider enhancing your abilities in some of the generic skillsets that are critical for consultancy work – i.e., project planning and management, data collection and analysis, research and reporting writing, designing toolkits and sectoral professional packages, enhanced presentation, and communication techniques – as well as those that would be beneficial and tailored to supporting social enterprises and NGOs such as business development support (BDS) | Consultants build up expertise and share their knowledge and analysis of particular situations. Do not claim expertise that you don't have or pretend to know more than you know. Create a lifelong learning environment for yourself to acquire the expertise that you need to make yourself as indispensable as you can to future employers or clients. |
| Mentoring | Whether experiential or qualification based – seek out mentors and experienced professional consultants to support and advice you in order to build up and refine your expertise. | Do not be diffident in seeking mentoring or coaching from professionals operating in your key areas of focus – project management, BDS, etc. Offer to understudy or provide shadow support. Ask them for structured and constructive feedback. Also seek feedback from clients who | Do not ignore constructive feedback. View is as a part of your lifelong learning process and learn to integrate this kind of evaluation into your on-going activities. |

*Figure 2.*

| | | | |
|---|---|---|---|
| | | employ large numbers of consultants on what they specifically look for in well delivered projects. | |
| Gaining formal qualifications and experiential training | Professional qualifications to a post degree level in the specific sectors you are operating are important in reassuring clients. Years of on-the-job experience and the steady accumulation of knowledge are also considered invaluable. Both should be augmented by further courses provided by accredited services such as those provided Institute of Consulting or CPD in key business development areas such as project management, monitoring & evaluation, leadership, communications, consulting competence, business management, market capability, etc. | Seek out courses that enhance your abilities in some of the generic skillsets that are critical for consultancy work as well as those that would be beneficial and tailored to supporting social enterprises and NGOs such as business development support (BDS). Full, part time and distance learning options are all available to suit your own particular situation. | Create a lifelong learning environment for yourself to acquire the expertise that you need to make yourself as indispensable as you can to future employers or clients. |
| Developing TORs | Terms of Reference (TORs) are best developed in consultation with clients. It is key in defining the steps and scope of the project. In the case of the consultation before BDS advice to businesses, this is best done through a proper process of assessing the business with the business owner through completed pre-qualification questionnaires, business plans, budgets or forecasts, as well as the long-term ambitions for the business and the social and other impact they wish to make. Others work according to the World Bank guidelines on how to write the ToRs for an evaluation (Roberts et al 2011) which include the scope, objectives, timeframe, resources, and | Conduct a thorough consultation with the business owner ahead of drawing up a final TOR. A checklist would include some of the following items:<br>- Templates for applications and business plans<br>- Detailed budget<br>- Marketing strategy and action plans<br>- Criteria for applicants, panel and partners, and a set of practical | Be realistic about the business plan and timescales – and ensure that they demonstrate viability. Do not try to achieve an owner's 10-year vision in a 2 year business plan or cashflow. Achieving the vision needs realistic implementation. Ensure that the TOR reflects an accurate assessment of the business |

*Figure 3.*

| | | | |
|---|---|---|---|
| | deliverable outcomes. Yet still others work with the Chartered Management Institute 2017) and UNDP guidelines for evaluations. | filters and procedures for due diligence at each phase<br>- Operational Management Plan for all subcontractors, partners, and business advisors<br>- Agreed metrics, assumptions, milestones, outcomes, outputs, tasks, deadlines, and responsibility<br>- Regular review procedures to ensure that the business plans are SMART and responsive to the situation on the ground<br>- Monitoring, evaluation, and review procedures | |
| Evaluation models for NGO's/social enterprises | Evaluations should be guarded by the theories of change of the client and the expected outputs and outcomes of the action. Amanda Amorim Adegboye also describes it as a logic model – being "a graphic display or 'map' of the relationship between a programme's resources, activities, and intended results, which also identifies the programme's underlying theory and assumptions" (W.K. Kellogg Foundation, 2004). Meanwhile Christine Locke's models include Force Field Model and The Unfreezing-Change-Refreezing Model (Kurt Lewin 1951), Planned Change (Lippitt, Watson, and Westley 1958). | Do ensure that the theory of change or logic model is robust and makes sense. Ensure that the objectives, indicators, outputs, and outcomes of the actions clearly defined, and with a clear means of verification. This would enable a practical evaluation exercise. | Do not narrowly restrict the interpretation of data to indicators, outputs, and outcomes. Do also allow in the evaluation scope for measuring the things that didn't work, and unintended outcomes. |

*Figure 4.*


| | | | |
|---|---|---|---|
| | deliverable outcomes. Yet still others work with the Chartered Management Institute 2017) and UNDP guidelines for evaluations. | filters and procedures for due diligence at each phase<br>- Operational Management Plan for all subcontractors, partners, and business advisors<br>- Agreed metrics, assumptions, milestones, outcomes, outputs, tasks, deadlines, and responsibility<br>- Regular review procedures to ensure that the business plans are SMART and responsive to the situation on the ground<br>- Monitoring, evaluation, and review procedures | |
| Evaluation models for NGO's/social enterprises | Evaluations should be guarded by the theories of change of the client and the expected outputs and outcomes of the action. Amanda Amorim Adegboye also describes it as a logic model – being "a graphic display or 'map' of the relationship between a programme's resources, activities, and intended results, which also identifies the programme's underlying theory and assumptions" (W.K. Kellogg Foundation, 2004). Meanwhile Christine Locke's models include Force Field Model and The Unfreezing-Change-Refreezing Model (Kurt Lewin 1951), Planned Change (Lippitt, Watson, and Westley 1958). | Do ensure that the theory of change or logic model is robust and makes sense. Ensure that the objectives, indicators, outputs, and outcomes of the actions clearly defined, and with a clear means of verification. This would enable a practical evaluation exercise. | Do not narrowly restrict the interpretation of data to indicators, outputs, and outcomes. Do also allow in the evaluation scope for measuring the things that didn't work, and unintended outcomes. |

*Figure 5.*

| | | | |
|---|---|---|---|
| | Innovation Diffusion Theory (Rogers 1995), and the medicine change wheel. | | |
| | Quantitative and qualitative methods are used to collect data and measure impact linked to specific objectives, indicators, outputs, outcomes, as well as the means for verification. | | |
| Collaborative working | Delivering projects effectively requires collaborative working, and the utilization of diverse skills and expertise. Such collaborative working ensures cross learning across the team. Building and managing a team to successfuly deliver the project is a good indication of effective project management. The first step of collaborative working is working constructively and productively in partnership with the client and their team. Christine Lock dubs it the: K" (Know the past to understand the present), "G" (Get to the truth), and "M" (Maximise buy-in for change). Finally agree ethical framework for such collaboration. | Do assess the skills and competencies in the overall project team and best way to harness and deploy the expertise and knowledge others in the team are bring to the table. Create opportunities for team building which will enhance collaboration.<br>Regular meetings and report updates are important in keeping the project on track and discovering early whether team members are experiencing challenges that might result in project delays.<br>Do offer mechanisms for addressing differences or potential conflict. | Do not select an unbalanced team without the skills or expertise to collaborate effectively or deliver the project |
| Likes of the professions | Successful project delivery and ensuring clients meet their goals of social transformation. Also, personal development and learning which are also professionally satisfying. | Do focus on the positive aspects of the work that leads to transformational impact and sustainability | |

*Figure 6.*

| | | | |
|---|---|---|---|
| Measuring social impact and sustainability | Quantitative and qualitative methods are used to collect data and measure the impact of the social enterprise and the transformation changes that have been stimulated by the social enterprise.<br>Amanda Amorim Adegboye notes: Impact Measurement is a process of understanding how much social change occurred and can be attributed to an organisation's activities. The Not-for-Profit sector use a variety of approaches to gauge their social impact and some of these include MERL (Monitoring, Evaluation, Research and Learning), SROI (Social Return on Investment), QUAL (the quality-of-life scale), Social Accounting and Audit: a systematic analysis of the effects of an organisation on its communities of interest or stakeholders, with stakeholder input as part of the data that are analysed for the accounting statement, logic models or the logic approach to program and embedded into the programme design and project cycle, ensuring continuous performance review. | Clearly define what the social impact goals are as part of the theory of change, as well as the indicators, outputs, and means of verification.<br>Select your tools MERL, PMEAL, SROI etc and embed these in the project cycle. | Do not restrict your measure to just direct impact. Develop sophisticated tools to measure indirect impact which has resulted from the action – these may sometimes be psychological such as the effect on self-esteem. Ensure the tools are also flexible enough to assess unintended consequences, both positive and negative. |
| Learning from mistakes and avoiding pitfalls | Mistakes are usually always a function of poor planning, inadequate terms of reference, lack of due diligence, improper managing of expectations between the consultant and client, incompetence or other unforeseen circumstances that have not been factored into the planning. Mitigation | Do undertake a great deal of work on precisely scoping out the consultancy and addressing the precise parameters of the project. | Do not ignore issues around legal and other compliance<br>Don't underprepare the planning for the consultancy and avoid assumptions |

*Figure 7.*

| | | | |
|---|---|---|---|
| | processes can be put in place to minimise any potential damage. One of these involves frequent reviews and updates which can quickly identify any emerging issues. The approach to mitigate unforeseen issues involves the undertaking of a detailed risk assessment to scope out the potential risks, would be.<br><br>Despite the existence of some of these processes to manage particularly complex consultancies occasionally there will be difficulties and misunderstandings. These should then be dealt with through proper mediation protocols<br><br>Finally, another pitfall to avoid is to ensure that all professional insurance is up to date. A key is the professional indemnity insurance, to mitigate any downside from business recommendations you make. £5 million worth of insurance would provide reasonable coverage. Other key insurance include public liability or employer's liability, if you or others are hurt while visiting each other, or to legally cover employing others. | Do also have clear idea of what success looks like for the client at the end of the consultancy in terms of expected outcomes.<br><br>Do build in regular review period.<br><br>Ensure insurance and other legal requirements are up to date | Do not ignore project reviews or the issues that emerge from due diligence or risk assessments |
| Conducting internal evaluations on social enterprises | First ensure the team have the skillset to be able to conduct an internal evaluation. Establish protocols that will mitigate against bias and will be in favour of neutral analysis and appraisal of data. Since the evaluation is a tool of constructive learning, adopt | Do treat the evaluation as a constructive learning tool that will enable you to better understand your company and enhance performance | Do not bring in a sympathetic friend or cheat yourself by being less than honest with your own business |

*Figure 8.*

| | | | |
|---|---|---|---|
| | the attitude of an investor and ask the hard questions the investor would ask. Separate the social impact (and the good you wish to bring about) from how well run and efficient the company is – the road to hell is frequently paved with good intentions. Get frank and honest feedback from all stakeholders – customers/beneficiaries, staff, suppliers, etc. Sometimes it is impossible to be this neutral or expect staff members and others who are dependent on you to be equally neutral or frank. So, most of the time it is better to bring in an independent evaluator to provide such an honest appraisal of your company. Funders make provision for an independent evaluation in budgets, given that a good evaluation is an effective learning tool. | Do try and be as neutral as possible. If this is impossible do engage an external evaluator<br><br>Do ensure you speak to as many stakeholders as possible | |
| Pricing models | Several pricing models exist which can be used depending on your business. Some consultants have used the value base pricing (Alan Weiss 2008), others match competitive pricing by others in the same sector, or remain within broad bands provided by international organisations, depending on the level of expertise of the consultant. The important factors are understanding the needs and budget of the client, the precise added value your intervention is | At the very least do look at competitive pricing models in your sector<br><br>Do ensure that you have factored in your own costs and a margin.<br><br>Do ensure that you work within the budget of your client | Do not decide to operate a consultancy as a loss leader unless you are sure how it will be paid for, or you have properly calculated the short and medium term risk of operating below cost<br><br>Do not ignore these costs of yours. Given that you are operating in the social enterprise space with |

*Figure 9.*

| | | | |
|---|---|---|---|
| | expected to generate and, ensuring once you have considered these that you cover your own costs and additional margin. Close communication on the available budget is therefore crucial. However, this information is not always available in a tender situation – so assessing the competitive pricing environment and your own costs/margin should guide your pricing model. | | squeezed budgets delivering massive social goods, reflect the costs in the budget if necessary, as a one off discount you are offering or a pro bono element depending on the circumstances on client. |
| Consulting during Covid-19 | The Chinese ideograph for challenge is similar to that for opportunity. Or as businesses put it market failure is almost always a business opportunity. So Covid-19 created opportunities for certain sectors (tech firms such as Zoom, or home delivery such as Amazon, and increased fragility for other sectors such as hospitality and airlines. Others were able to creatively pivot away from existing businesses to seize opportunities in the new normal. For consultants activities increasingly moved online (Zoom, Ms Teams, WhatsApp, Survey Monkey) or hybrid techniques were deployed – while maintaining social distancing rules. The online techniques proved to be very cost effective – slashing travelling, hospitality and other costs. | Do follow social distancing and other Covi-19 prevention guidelines and mandates<br><br>Do pivot to online platforms and be creative getting the best results from them<br><br>Do build in a risk assessment that would integrate a risk strategy for major disasters or pandemics | Do not look at your model as frozen in ice – hold consultations with clients and stakeholders about alternative delivery methods. |

*Figure 10.*

| | | | |
|---|---|---|---|
| Use of ICT | Digital and teaching/learning tools have been deployed to deliver e-consultancies. Not only were they cost effective but enabled a wider international and geographic spread, involving multilingual working. | Do consider the latest e-learning and e-consultancy software<br><br>Do consider the bigger geographic and international market online activities have now opened up for you | Do not ignore on-line and ICT developments which going to grow in importance in delivering projects. Seek to enhance your skillset in this area. |
| Social enterprises and development | Both the enterprise and the social/development aspects of the social enterprise are important. It is important to ensure the enterprise aspect and the business viability (and sustainability) in order to be able to deliver the development agenda. Research the trends in your sector as much as you can, alongside consideration of the social and transformative impact you need to make. Understand the enterprise and social/development activities and clearly identify which sectors they would work most effectively in. Simplify the product and service as much as possible and have a clear customer in mind who will benefit from the business, and a beneficiary who will benefit from the social dimension – since they are often different demographics. The organization should be agile and adaptable to every changing economic climate. | Think about your added value as a social enterprise – what is your USP for your business – networks, markets, skills, worldly insights, etc?<br><br>Do not assume that because your business works elsewhere it will be the same process and issues in another country.<br><br>Operate within a clear ethical framework – this should be seen as part of the social developmental impact the business is contributing to the eco-system.<br><br>Develop yourself, your staff, encourage continuous learning. Enjoy your work and making a social impact. | While focusing on the enterprise dimension do not simply do business as usual in the country of operation on the basis that 'this is how everyone does it here.'<br><br>Do seek to operate or micro-manage a social enterprise long distance in a third country. Develop, train, and empower a core team to be proactive problem solvers thinking outside the box. |

## REFERENCES

Greenhalgh, T., Raftery, J., Hanney, S., & Glover, M. (2016). Research impact: A narrative review. *BMC Medicine, 14*(1), 78. doi:10.118612916-016-0620-8 PMID:27211576

Lewin, K. (1951). *Field theory in social sciences.* Harper & Row.

Lippitt, R., Watson, J., & Westley, B. (1958). *The dynamics of planned change.* Harcourt Brace.

Nickols, F., & Bergholz. (2012). *The Consultant's Competency Circle: A Tool for Gauging Your Success Potentials as an Independent Consultant.* Available at http://www.nickols.us/The _Consulting_Competency_Circle.pdf

Roberts, D., Khattri, N., & Wessel, A. (2011). *Writing terms of reference for an evaluation: A how-to guide. 2011 Independent Evaluation Group.* The World Bank. doi:10.22163/fteval.2011.134

Rogers, E. (1995). *Diffusion of innovations* (4th ed.). Free Press.

Template for confirmation of interest and Submission of Financial Proposal is available under the procurement section of UNDP Pacific Office in Fiji. (n.d.). www.pacific.undp.org

Tumilowicz, A., Ruel, M. T., Pelto, G., Pelletier, D., Monterrosa, E. C., Lapping, K., Kraemer, K., De Regil, L. M., Bergeron, G., Arabi, M., Neufeld, L., & Sturke, R. (2018). We need the full details and year implementation science in nutrition: Concepts and frameworks for an emerging field of science and practice. *Current Developments in Nutrition, 3*(3), nzy080. Advance online publication. doi:10.1093/cdn/nzy080 PMID:30864563

Weiss, A. (2004). *Logic Model Development Guide. Using Logic Models to Bring Together Planning, Evaluation, and Action.* https://www.aacu.org/sites/default/files/LogicModel.pdf

W.K. Kellogg Foundation. (2004). *Logic Model Development Guide. Using Logic Models to Bring Together Planning, Evaluation, and Action.* https://www.aacu.org/sites/default/files/LogicModel.pdf

## ADDITIONAL READING

Future Learn. (n.d.). *How and Why to Measure Social Impact*. Retrieved from https://www.futurelearn.com/info/courses/social-enterprise-growing-a-sustainable-business/0/steps/20920

# Compilation of References


Aaltonen, S., & Akola, E. (2014). *Lack of trust - The main obstacle for immigrant entrepreneurship?* University of Turku. Retrieved from: http://www.pyk2.aalto.fi/ncsb2012/aaltonen.pdf/

Aastrup, J., & Halldorsson, A. (2008). Epistemological Role of Case Studies in Logistics: A Critical Realist Perspective. *International Journal of Physical Distribution & Logistics Management, 38*(10), 746–763. doi:10.1108/09600030810926475

Abu-Saifan, S. (2012). Social Entrepreneurship: Definitions and Boundaries. *Technology Innovation Management Review*. https://timreview.ca/sites/default/files/article_PDF/Saifan_TIMReview_February2012_0.pdf

Abu-Saifan, S. (2012). Social entrepreneurship: Definition and boundaries. *Technology Innovation Management Review, 2*(2), 22–27. doi:10.22215/timreview/523

Adair, J. (1973). *Action-Centred Leadership*. McGraw Hill.

Adesina, O. S. (2013). Unemployment and security challenges in Nigeria. *International Journal of Humanities and Social Science, 03*(07).

Adida, C. L. (2015). *Immigrant Exclusion and Insecurity in Africa*. Cambridge University Press.

Adner, R., & Kapoor, R. (2010). Value creation in innovation ecosystems: How the structure of technological interdependence affects firm performance in new technology generations. *Strategic Management Journal, 31*(3), 306–333. doi:10.1002mj.821

Aihie, O. N. & Alika, H. I. (2014). Combating youth unemployment in Nigeria through effective school counselling. *Edo Journal of Counselling*, 201-218.

Ainsworth, S., & Cox, J. W. (2003). Families Divided: Culture and Control in Small Family Business. *Organization Studies, 24*(9), 1463–1485. doi:10.1177/0170840603249004

Alter, K. (2007). *Social Enterprise Typology*. http://www.virtueventures.com/setypology

Alter, K. (2007). *Social enterprise typology*. Virtue Ventures LLC.

Amtaika, A. (2017). Is Democratisation of Africa a Process or an Experiment" The Dissection of the Democratic Theory. In A. Amtaika (Ed.), *The Democratisation of Africa: Dynamics and Trends* (pp. 3–30). Pan African University Press.

Anderson, A. R., Drakopoulou Dodd, S., & Jack, S. L. (2012). Entrepreneurship as connecting: Some implications for theorising and practice. *Management Decision*, *50*(5), 958–971. doi:10.1108/00251741211227708

Anderson, A., Drakopoulou Dodd, S., & Jack, S. (2009). Aggressors; Winners; Victims and Outsiders, European Schools' Social Construction of the Entrepreneur. *International Small Business Journal*, *27*(1), 126–136. doi:10.1177/0266242608098349

Anderson, A., & Starnawska, M. (2008). Research practices in entrepreneurship. *Entrepreneurship and Innovation*, *9*(4), 221–230. doi:10.5367/000000008786208731

Anderson, A., & Warren, L. (2011). The Entrepreneur as a hero and jester: Enacting the entrepreneurial discourse. *International Small Business Journal*, *29*(6), 589–609. doi:10.1177/0266242611416417

Anderson, S. G. (2014). *New strategies for social innovation: Market-based approaches for assisting the poor*. Columbia University Press. doi:10.7312/ande15922

Antonakis, J. (2012). Transformational and charismatic leadership. *The Nature of Leadership*, *2*, 256-288.

Arando, S., Gao, M., Jones, D. C., & Kato, T. (2011). *Efficiency in Employee-Owned Enterprises: An Econometric Case Study of Mondragon*. IZA Discussion Paper. https://cep.lse.ac.uk/conference_papers/26_05_2011/kato.pdf

Arkes, J. (2010). Using unemployment rates as instruments to estimate returns to schooling. *Southern Economic Journal*, *76*(3), 711–722. doi:10.4284ej.2010.76.3.711

Ashoka. (2012). Social entrepreneurship: Definition and boundaries. *Technology Innovation Management Review*, (February), 24.

Atchison, C. J., Bowman, L., Vrinten, C., Redd, R., Pristera, P., Eaten, J., & Ward, H. (2020). Perceptions and Behavioural Responses of the General Public during the COVID-19 Pandemic: A Cross-sectional Survey of UK Adults. *BMJ (Clinical Research Ed.)*. Advance online publication. doi:10.1101/2020.04.01.20050039

Atkins, M. J. (1999). Oven-ready and self-basting: Taking stock of employability skills. *Teaching in Higher Education*, *4*(2), 267–280. doi:10.1080/1356251990040208

Aukes, L., Geertsma, J., Cohen-Schotanus, J., & Zweirsta, R. (2007). The Development of a Scale to Measure Personal Reflection in Medical Practice and Education. *Medical Teacher*, *29*(2-3), 177–182. Advance online publication. doi:10.1080/01421590701299272 PMID:17701630

Austin, J., Stevenson, H., & Wei-Skillern, J. (2006). Social and commercial entrepreneurship: Same, different, or both? *Entrepreneurship Theory and Practice*, *30*(1), 1–22. doi:10.1111/j.1540-6520.2006.00107.x

Australian Council of Engineering Deans. (2018). *An update on the status and trends in Australia's higher education system for engineering*. Australian Council of Engineering Deans.

Awaysheh, A., & Bonfiglio, D. (2017). Leveraging experiential learning to incorporate social entrepreneurship in MBA programs: A case study. *International Journal of Management Education*, *15*(2), 332–349. doi:10.1016/j.ijme.2017.04.001

Bacq, S., Hartog, C., Hoogendoorn, B., & Lepoutre, J. (2011). *Social and Commercial Entrepreneurship: Exploring Individual and Organizational Characteristics*. https://ondernemerschap.panteia.nl/pdf-ez/h201110.pdf

Bacq, S., & Janssen, F. (2011). The multiple faces of social entrepreneurship: A review of definitional issues based on geographical and thematic criteria. *Entrepreneurship and Regional Development*, *23*(5-6), 373–403. doi:10.1080/08985626.2011.577242

Baggot, R. (2013). *Partnership for Public Health and Well-being, policy, and practice*. Palgrave Macmillan.

Baker, C., Stokes, P., Lichy, J., Atherton, J., & Moss, D. (2011). *Values, beliefs and attitudes in the era of late-capitalism: A consideration of the re-emergence and re-positioning of faith and spirituality as spiritual capital in the workplace*. https://www.chester.ac.uk/sites/files/chester/Values,%20Beliefs%20and%20Attitudes%20in%20the%20Era%20of%20Late%20Capitalism.pdf

Ballatt, J., & Campling, P. (2011). *Intelligent Kindness: Reforming the Culture of healthcare*. RCPsych.

Balogun, K. (2016). *Unemployment in Africa*. Paper presented at African transformation forum organized by Africa Centre for Economic Transformation (ACET).

Barker, F. (2007). *The South African labour market* (5th ed.). Van Schaik publishers.

Bartram, D., Poros, M. V., & Monforte, P. (2012). *Key Concepts in Migration*. SAGE Publications.

Bedard, K., & Herman, D. A. (2008). Who goes to graduate/professional school? The importance of economic fluctuations, undergraduate field, and ability. *Economics of Education Review*, *27*(2), 197–210. doi:10.1016/j.econedurev.2006.09.007

Berti, M. (2017). *Elgar introduction to organizational discourse analysis*. Edward Elgar Publishing. doi:10.4337/9781784717056

Beugre, C. (2017). *Social Entrepreneurship Managing the Creation of Social Value*. Routledge.

Beugre, C. (2017). *Social entrepreneurship, managing the creation of social value*. Routhledge.

Bezuidenhout, M. (2011). *The development and evaluation of a measure of graduate employability in the context of the new world of work* (Doctoral dissertation). University of Pretoria.

Binks, M., & Vale, P. (1990). *Entrepreneurship and Economic Change*. McGraw-Hill.

Black, M. (1962). *Models and metaphors*. Cornell University Press. doi:10.7591/9781501741326

Bloemen-Bekx, M., Voordeckers, W., Remery, C., & Schippers, J. (2019). Following in parental footsteps? The influence of gender and learning experiences on entrepreneurial intentions. *International Small Business Journal, 37*(6), 642–663. doi:10.1177/0266242619838936

Blum, U., & Dudley, L. (2001). Religion and economic growth: Was Weber right? *Journal of Evolutionary Economics, 11*(2), 207–230. doi:10.1007/PL00003862

Bornstein, D. (2005). *How to change the world: social entrepreneurs and the power of new ideas*. Penguin Books.

Boschee, J. (2006) Social Entrepreneurship: The Promise New York.

Bourdieu, P. (1986). The forms of capital. In J. Richardson (Ed.), *Handbook of Theory and Research for the Sociology of Education*. Greenwood.

Bridge, S., Hegarty, C., & Porter, S. (2010). Rediscovering enterprise: Developing appropriate university entrepreneurship education. *Education + Training, 52*(8/9), 722–734. doi:10.1108/00400911011089015

British Council, Turkey. (2019). *The State of Social Enterprise in Turkey*. Available at: https://www.britishcouncil.org.tr/en/programmes/education/social-enterprise-research

British Council, United Nations and Social Enterprise UK. (2020). *Innovation and resilience: A global snapshot of social enterprise responses to Covid-19*. British Council. https://www.britishcouncil.org/sites/default/files/socialenterprise_covidresponsesurvey_web_final_0.pdf?_ga=2.115436869.250335672.1622470098-1316689371.1622470098

British Council. (2015) *Social Enterprise Landscape in Ghana*. British Council. https://www.britishcouncil.org/sites/default/files/social_enterprise_landscape_in_ghana_report_final.pdf

British Council. (2015) *Social Enterprise Landscape in Ghana*. British. https://www.britishcouncil.org/sites/britishcouncil.uk2/files/social_enterprise_landscape_in_ghana_report_final.pdf

British Council. (2019). *Report on Social Enterprises in Turkey*. https://www.britishcouncil.org.tr/programmes/education/social-enterprise-research

Brockhaus, R. H. (1982). The psychology of the entrepreneur. Encyclopedia of Entrepreneurship, 39 - 57.

Brown, G. (2017). *My Life, Our Times*. Penguin Random House.

Brown, P., Hesketh, V., & Williams, S. (2002). *Employability in a knowledge economy*. Cardiff University.

Burnes, B. (2004). Kurt Lewin and the Planned Approach to Change: A Re-appraisal. *Journal of Management Studies, 41*(6), 977–1002. doi:10.1111/j.1467-6486.2004.00463.x

Burns, P. (2011). *Entrepreneurship and small business start-up, growth and maturity*. Palgrave Macmillan.

Burns, P. (2011). *Entrepreneurship and small business, start up, growth and maturity*. Palgrave Macmillan. doi:10.1007/978-0-230-20848-3

Campbell, S. (1997). Social entrepreneurship: How to develop new social-purpose business ventures. *Health Care Strategic Management*, *16*(5), 17–18. PMID:10179045

Capaldi, N. (2005). Introduction. In N. Capaldi (Ed.), *Business and religion: A clash of civilizations?* M&M Scrivener Press.

Carswell, P., & Rolland, D. (2007). Religion and Entrepreneurship in New Zealand. *Journal of Enterprising Communities Peoples and Places in the Global Economy, 1*(2), 162-174.

Catford, J. (1998). Social Entrepreneurs are Vital for Health Promotion - but They Need Supportive Environments too. *Health Promotion International*, *13*(2), 95–98. doi:10.1093/heapro/13.2.95

Cavanagh, G. F. (1999). Spirituality for managers: Context and critique. *Journal of Organizational Change Management*, *12*(3), 186–199. doi:10.1108/09534819910273793

Cebekhulu, A. (2018). *Umhlaba Uyahlaba! The World is Thorny! Wandsbeck*. Reach Publishers.

Celik, S. (2019). Evaluation of the Migration Phenomenon as an Economics Dimension. In Immigration and Refugee Policy: Breakthroughs in Research and Practice (pp. 1-7). IGI Global.

Ceptureanu, S., Ceptureanu, E., Luchian, C., & Luchian, I. (2018). Community Based Programs Sustainability. A Multidimensional Analysis of Sustainability Factors. *Sustainability*, *870*(10), 1–15. doi:10.3390u10030870

Certo, S. T., & Miller, T. (2008). Social entrepreneurship: Key issues and concepts. *Business Horizons*, *51*(4), 267–271. doi:10.1016/j.bushor.2008.02.009

Chakravorty, I., Daga, S., Bhamrah, J.S., Menon, G., Dave. S., Chakravorty, S., Bhala, N. & Mehta, R. (2020). Self-reported Occupational Risk for COVID-19 in Hospital Doctors from Black Asian and Minority Ethnic Communities in UK. *The Physician, 6*(1). doi:10.38192/1.6.1.9

Chandra, Y. (2017). Social entrepreneurship as emancipatory work. *Journal of Business Venturing*, *32*(6), 657–673. doi:10.1016/j.jbusvent.2017.08.004

Chandra, Y. (2018). New narratives of development work? Making sense of social entrepreneurs' development narratives across time and economies. *World Development*, *107*, 306–326. doi:10.1016/j.worlddev.2018.02.033

Chanphirun, S., & Peter, V. (2014). Understanding the concept of the entrepreneurial university from the perspective of higher education models. *Higher Education*, *68*(6), 891–908. doi:10.100710734-014-9750-0

Chan-Serafin, S., Brief, A., & George, J. (2013). How Does Religion Matter and Why? *Religion and Organisational Sciences*, *24*(5), 1585–1600. doi:10.1287/orsc.1120.0797

Charity, E. C. T. (2021) *A Brief History of Ealing Community Transport*. https://ectcharity.co.uk/files_uploads/A_Brief_History_of_ECT_Charity_(April_2016).pdf

CHEC (Cape Higher Education Consortium). (2013). *Pathways from university to work: a graduate destination survey of the 2010 cohort of graduates from the Western Cape Universities*. CHEC.

Chimphondah, A. (2019). The Past, present & future of affordable housing in Africa. *Affordable Housing Investment Summit Africa*.

Chisala, C. (2020). Immigrant Entrepreneurship in Africa: A Zambian Perspective. In Impact of Immigration and Xenophobia on Development in Africa (pp. 224- 245). IGI Global.

Chlosta, S., Patzelt, H., Klein, S. B., & Christian, D. (2012). Parental role models and the decision to become self-employed: The moderating effect of personality. *Small Business Economics*, *38*(1), 121–138. doi:10.100711187-010-9270-y

Choi, S., & Schnurr, S. (2014). Exploring distributed leadership: Solving disagreements and negotiating consensus in a "leaderless" team. *Discourse Studies*, *16*(1), 3–24. doi:10.1177/1461445613508891

Ciepielewska-Kowalik, A., & Pieliński, B. (2015). In search for a place for the third sector in the Polish welfare state: Toward a limited co-production. *EMES Conferences Selected Papers Series, ECSP-5EMES-13*. Retrieved from http://emes.net/content/uploads/publications/in-search-for-a-place-for-the-third-sector-in-the-polish-welfare-state-toward-a-limited-co-production/ESCP-5EMES-13_Third_Sector_Polish_Welfare_State_Ciepielewska-Kowalik_Pielinski.pdf

Ciepielewska-Kowalik, A., Pieliński, B., Starnawska, M., & Szymańska, A. (2015). *Looking for Social Enterprise Models in Poland: Institutional and Historical Context*. ICSEM Working Papers, no. 11.

Coetzee, M. (2016). *Introduction to social enterprises in South Africa*. Presented at the Graduate School of Business, University of Cape Town.

Colquitt, J. A., & George, G. (2011). Publishing in AMJ—Part 1: Topic choice. *Academy of Management Journal*, *54*(3), 432–435. doi:10.5465/amj.2011.61965960

Community Housing Aotearoa. (2015). *Details matter: Taking stock of the community housing sector in Aotearoa*. Community Housing Aotearoa.

Cornelissen, J. P. (2006a). Making sense of theory construction: Metaphor and disciplined imagination. *Organization Studies*, *27*(11), 1579–1597. doi:10.1177/0170840606068333

Cornelissen, J. P. (2006b). Metaphor and the dynamics of knowledge in organization theory: A case study of the organizational identity metaphor. *Journal of Management Studies*, *43*(4), 683–709. doi:10.1111/j.1467-6486.2006.00607.x

Costa, P. T. Jr, McCrae, R. R., & Kay, G. G. (1995). Persons, Places, and Personality: Career Assessment Using the Revised NEO Personality Inventory. *Journal of Career Assessment*, *3*(2), 123–139. doi:10.1177/106907279500300202

Coulter, A. (2004). When I'm 64: Health Choices. *Health Expectations*, *7*(2), 95–97. doi:10.1111/j.1369-7625.2004.00269.x PMID:15117383

Crowley, L., Jones, K., Cominetti, N., & Gulliford, J. (2013). *International Lessons: Youth unemployment in the global context*. Lancaster University.

Crush, J., & Ramachandran, S. (2015). Doing business with Xenophobia. In Mean Streets: Migration, Xenophobia and Informality in South Africa (pp. 25-59). Southern African Migration Programme, the African Centre for Cities and the International Development Research Centre. doi:10.2307/j.ctvh8r45r.6

Crush, J., Cikanda, A., & Skinner, C. (2015). Migrant Entrepreneuship and Infomality in South African Cities. In Mean Streets: Migration, Xenophobia and Informality in South Africa (pp. 25-59). Southern African Migration Programme, the African Centre for Cities and the International Development Research Centre.

Dalhammar, T. (2004). *Voices of entrepreneurship and small business- Immigrant enterprises in Kista* [Unpublished PhD Thesis]. Royal Institute of Technology.

Das, M. B., Khan, I. A., & Tinsley, E. (2020). *Results-Based Financing Through Social Enterprises: A White Paper for the Global Partnership for Results-Based Approaches, in Response to the Covid-19 Pandemic*. World Bank. https://openknowledge.worldbank.org/handle/10986/34319

Davidson, P., & Wiklund, J. (1996). Values, belief and regional variations in new firm formation rates. *Journal of Economic Psychology*, *18*(2-3), 179–199. doi:10.1016/S0167-4870(97)00004-4

De Witte, H., Rothmann, S., & Jackson, L. T. (2012). The psychological consequences of unemployment in South Africa. *Suid-Afrikaanse Tydskrif vir Ekonomiese en Bestuurswetenskappe*, *15*(3), 235–252. doi:10.4102ajems.v15i3.153

Dearing, R. (1997). *Higher Education in the Learning Society – Report of the National Committee of Inquiry into Higher Education*. HMSO.

Dearlove, D. (2004). Interview: Jeff Skoll. *Business Strategy Review*, *15*(2), 51–53.

Dees, J. G. (1998a). *The Meaning of Social Entrepreneurship*. Stanford University: Draft Report for the Kauffman Center for Entrepreneurial Leadership. https://sehub.stanford.edu/sites/default/files/TheMeaningofsocialEntrepreneurship.pdf

Dees, J. (2007). *Taking Social Entrepreneurship Seriously Transaction Social Science and Modern Society*. Academic Press.

Dees, J. G. (1998). Enterprising non-profits. *Harvard Business Review*, *76*, 54–67. PMID:10176919

Dees, J. G. (1998, January/February). Enterprising Nonprofits: What Do You Do When Traditional Sources of Funding Fall Short? *Harvard Business Review*, 55–67.

Dees, J. G. (2007). Taking Social Entrepreneurship Seriously. *Transaction Social Science and Modern Society*, *44*(3), 24–31.

Defourny, J., & Nyssens, M. (2001). Belgium: Social enterprises in community services. Academic Press.

Defourny, J., & Nyssens, M. (2010). Social Enterprise. In K. Hart, J.-L. Laville, & D. Cattani (Eds.), *The Human Economy: A Citizen's Guide* (pp. 284–292). Polity Press.

Deloitte. (2021). *Is It Worth It.* https://www2.deloitte.com/content/dam/Deloitte/global/Documents/gx-is-it-worth-it.pdf

Denzin, N., & Lincoln, Y. (2003). *Collecting and interpreting qualitative materials.* Sage publications.

Department of Trade and Industry (DTI). (2004). www.dti.gov.uk/socialenterprise/

Department of Trade and Industry. (2002). *Social Enterprise: A Strategy for Success.* DTI.

Devine Chocolate. (2021). *The Beginnings and Structure of Kuapa Kokoo | Blog - Divine Chocolate.* http://www.Devinechocolate.com/devineworld

Dey, K., & Grant, S. (2014). Maori communities as social enterprise. In H. Douglas & S. Grant (Eds.), *Social entrepreneurship and enterprise. Concepts in context* (pp. 194–216). Tilde University Press.

Di Domenico, M., Haugh, H., & Tracey, P. (2010). Social bricolage: Theorizing social value creation in social enterprises. *Entrepreneurship Theory and Practice, 34*(4), 681–703. doi:10.1111/j.1540-6520.2010.00370.x

Dinham, A. (2007). *Faiths and Frontiers on the Starship: boldly going as faith-based entrepreneurs?* Faith-Based Regeneration Network. http://www.fbrn.org.uk/files/STARSHIP.pdf

Dinham, A. (2007). *Faiths and Frontiers on the Starship: boldly going as faith-based entrepreneurs?* Faith Based Regeneration Network UK.

Dixon, S. E. A., & Clifford, A. (2007). Ecopreneurship—A new approach to managing the triple bottom line. *Journal of Organizational Change Management, 20*(3), 326–345. doi:10.1108/09534810710740164

Doering-Whitea, J., Sanchez, J., & Creasey, H. (2021). Entrepreneurship as a community practice strategy: Lessons from Detroit. *Journal of Community Practice, 29*(1), 46–61. doi:10.1080/10705422.2021.1881935

Doherty, B., Huagh, H., & Lyon, F. (2014). Social Enterprises as Hybrid Organisations: A Review and Research Agenda. *International Journal of Management Review, 16*, 417-436.

Dohnalova, M., Legnerova, K., & Slechtova, V. (2015). *Social Enterprise in the Czech Republic.* ICSEM Working Papers No. 24. https://www.iap-socent.be/sites/default/files/Czech%20Republic%20-%20Dohnalova%20et%20al_0.pdf

Dooms, T., & Pillay, P. (2020). Black entrepreneurship journeys. In A. Cawe & K. Mabasa (Eds.), *Beyond Tenderpreneurship: Rethinking Black Business and Economic Empowerment* (pp. 336–358). Mapungubew Institute for Strategic Reflection.

Dorado, S. (2006). Social entrepreneurial ventures: Different values so different process of creation, no? *Journal of Developmental Entrepreneurship*, *11*(4), 319–343. doi:10.1142/S1084946706000453

Down, S. (2010). *Enterprise Entrepreneurship and Small Business*. Sage.

Drayton, W. (2004). *How to Change the World: Social Entrepreneurs and the Power of New Ideas*. Oxford University Press.

Dubos, R. (2017). *Social capital: Theory and research*. Routledge.

Edler, J., & Fagerber, J. (2017). Innovation policy: What, why, and how. *Oxford Review of Economic Policy*, *33*(1), 2–23. doi:10.1093/oxrep/grx001

Edwards-Schachter, M., & Wallace, M. (2017). 'Shaken but not Stirred': Sixty years of defining social innovation. *Technological Forecasting and Social Change*, *119*, 64–79. doi:10.1016/j.techfore.2017.03.012

Eisenmann, T. R. (2013). Entrepreneurship: A Working Definition. *Harvard Business Review*, *10*, 1–4.

Eloff, T. (2017). *Turning Point: South Africa at the Crossroards*. Tafelberg.

Emerson, J. (2003). The Blended Value Proposition: Integrating Social and Financial Returns. *California Review Management*, *45*(4), 35–51. doi:10.2307/41166187

Emoh, F. I., Ajator, U. O., & Ugonabo, C. U. (2016). Urban infrastructure financing and management in Nigeria. *Global Journal of Advanced Research*, *3*(6), 492–504.

Engineers Australia. (2017). *The engineering profession: A statistical overview* (13th ed.). Institution of Engineers Australia.

English, B., & Bennett, P. (2015). *Social housing reform programme: Overview (Paper one)*. New Zealand Government.

English, B., & Coleman, J. (2015). *Budget 2015: Social bond to focus on mental health*. New Zealand Government.

Etchart, N., Horváth, A., Rosandić, A., & Spitálszky, A. (2014). *The state of social entrepreneurship in Hungary*. SEFORÏS Country Report. Retrieved from http://www.seforis.eu/upload/reports/Country_Report_Hungary.pdf

Farouq, A., & Adilovic, S. (2014). *Understanding Graduate Employability-Fit with the Company: The Employer Perspective*. Academic Press.

Fauconnier, G., & Turner, M. (1998). Conceptual integration networks. *Cognitive Science*, *22*(2), 133–187. doi:10.120715516709cog2202_1

First Fruit Group. (2021). *About us*. https://www.firstfruit.org.uk/aboutus.htm

Florin, J., Karri, R., & Rossiter, N. (2007). Fostering entrepreneurial drive-in business education: An attitudinal approach. *Journal of Management Education*, *31*(1), 17–42. doi:10.1177/1052562905282023

Forbes. (2021). *Change the World Rankings*. https://fortune.com/change-the-world/2020/search/

Forfás. (2013). *Social enterprise in Ireland: Sectoral opportunities and policy issues*. Retrieved from https://www.djei.ie/en/Publications/Social-Enterprise-in-Ireland-Sectoral-Opportunities-and-Policy-Issues.html

Forouharfar, A., Rowshan, S. A., & Salarzehi, H. (2019). Social entrepreneurship strategic grid: Visualizing classification, orientation and dimensionality in the strategic paradigms of governmental-scale social entrepreneurship (A literature-based approach). *Cogent Business and Management*, *6*(1), 1644714. doi:10.1080/23311975.2019.1644714

Foster, D. (2006). Exploring Cultural Mode Amidst Others in the Church of England. In A. Nicholls (Ed.), *Social Entrepreneurship New Models of Social Change*. Oxford University Press.

Foster, J. (2002). Sustainability, higher education and the learning society. *Environmental Education Research*, *8*(1), 35–41. doi:10.1080/13504620120109637

Fowler, A. (2000). NGDOs as a moment in history: Beyond aid to social entrepreneurship or civic innovation? *Third World Quarterly*, *21*(4), 637–654. doi:10.1080/713701063

Francis, R. (2013). *Report of the Mid Staffordshire NHS Foundation Trust Public Inquiry: Executive Summary*. The Stationary Office.

Fukuyama, F. (2004). *Social Capital and the Global Economy Foreign Affairs*. http://public.gettysburg.edu/~dborock/courses/Spring/p344/ps344read/fukuyama-social%20capital%20and%20globalization.pdf

Fukuyama, F. (2005). Building Democracy After Conflict: "Stateness" First. *Journal of Democracy*, *16*(1), 84–88. doi:10.1353/jod.2005.0006

Geldres-Weiss, V. V., Gambetta, N., Massa, N. P., & Geldres-Weiss, S. L. (2021). Materiality Matrix Use in Aligning and Determining a Firm's Sustainable Business Model Archetype and Triple Bottom Line Impact on Stakeholders. *Sustainability*, *13*(3), 1065. doi:10.3390u13031065

Genesis Housing Association. (2014). *Annual accounts*. https://www.genesisha.org.uk/PDF/Finance_Statements_2014.pdf

George, G., Mcgahan, A. M., & Prabhu, J. (2012). Innovation for Inclusive Growth: Towards a Theoretical Framework and Research Agenda. *Journal of Management Studies*, *49*(4), 661–683. doi:10.1111/j.1467-6486.2012.01048.x

GerardiK.HerkenhoffK.OhanianL. E.WillenP. (2013). Unemployment, negative equity, and strategic default. Available at SSRN 2293152.

Germak, A. J., & Robinson, J. A. (2014). Exploring the motivation of nascent social entrepreneurs. *Journal of Social Entrepreneurship*, *5*(1), 5–21. doi:10.1080/19420676.2013.820781

Gibb, A. A. (1993). The enterprise culture and education: understanding enterprise education and its links with small business, entrepreneurship and wider educational goals. International Small Business Journal, 11(3), 11-34. doi:10.1177/026624269301100301

Gibb, A. A. (2000). SME policy, academic research and the growth of ignorance, mythical concepts, myths, assumptions, rituals and confusions. *International Small Business Journal*, *18*(3), 2–12. doi:10.1177/0266242600183001

Gibbs, G. (1988). *Learning by Doing: A Guide to Teaching and Learning Methods*. Further Education Trust.

Gibbs, P., & Ilkan, M. (2008). The ethics of marketing in Islamic and Christian communities Insights for global marketing. *Cross Cultural Management*, *15*(2), 162–175. doi:10.1108/13527600810870606

Giddens, A., & Sutton, P. W. (2013). *Sociology* (7th ed.). Polity Press.

Gileya. (2017). *The typology of a personality in social philosophical dimension. Peculiarities of a marginal personality in the modern world*. Academic Press.

Goleman, D. (1995). *Emotional intelligence*. Bantam Books.

Goleman, D. (2000). Leadership that Gets Results. *Harvard Business Review*, *78*(2), 78–90.

Good Finance. (2021). *Measuring Social Impact*. https://www.goodfinance.org.uk/measuring-social-impact

Gordon, S. L. (2010). Migrants in a 'state of exception' xenophobia and the role of the post-apartheid state. In Contemporary Social Issues in Africa: Cases in Gaborone, Kampala and Durban (pp. 45-64). Africa Institute of Africa (AISA).

Gotsis, G., & Kortezi, Z. (2009). The impact of Greek Orthodoxy on entrepreneurship: A theoretical framework. *Journal of Enterprising Communities People and Places in the Global Economy*, *3*(2), 152–175. doi:10.1108/17506200910960851

Graafland, J., Kaptein, M., & Mazereeuw-van Der Duijn Schouten, C. (2007). Conceptions of God, Normative Convictions, and Socially Responsible Business Conduct. *Business & Society*, *46*(3), 331–368. doi:10.1177/0007650306296085

Graham, L., & Mlatsheni, C. (2015). Youth Unemployment in South Africa: Understanding the challenge and working on solutions. *South African Child Gauge*, 51-59.

Grant, R., & Jordan, J. (2013). *Foundations of Strategy*. Willey.

Grant, S. (2015). *Social Housing in New Zealand: Does social enterprise fit into this mix?* University of Waikato.

Greenhalgh, T., Raftery, J., Hanney, S., & Glover, M. (2016). Research impact: A narrative review. *BMC Medicine*, *14*(1), 78. doi:10.118612916-016-0620-8 PMID:27211576

Gregory, D., & Mansfield, C. (2019). *Capitalism in Crisis? Transforming our economy for people and planet*. Social Enterprise UK. https://www.socialenterprise.org.uk/wp-content/uploads/2019/11/Capitalism-in-Crisis.pdf

Gupta, A. K. (2013). Tapping the Entrepreneurial Potential of Grassroots Innovation. *Stanford Social Innovation Review*, *11*(3), 18–20.

Hailey, J. (2014). *The sustainable NGO: Why resourcing matters*. INTRAC Online. Accessible via https://www.intrac.org/sustainable-ngo-resourcing-matters/

Hannon, D. (2004). *Philosophies of enterprise and entrepreneurship education and the challenges for higher education in the UK*. Paper presented at the 27th ISBA National Small Firms Conference, Newcastle, UK.

Hannon, D. (2005). *Graduate entrepreneurship in the UK: defining a research and enterprise policy framework*. Paper presented at the 28th ISBA National Small Firms Conference, Blackpool, UK.

Hannon, D., & Scott, J. (2006). *Mapping provision of enterprise education and support or entrepreneurship in England's HEIs*. Paper presented at the 29th ISBA National Small Firms Conference, Cardiff, UK.

Harding, R. (2007). Understanding social entrepreneurship. *Industry and Higher Education*, *21*(1), 73–84. doi:10.5367/000000007780222723

Hare, P., Jones, D., & Blackledge, G. (2007). Understanding social enterprise: A case study of the childcare sector in Scotland. Social Enterprise Journal, 3(1).

Hartley, J., & Benington, J. (2010). *Leadership for healthcare*. The Policy Press.

Haugh, H. M., & Mckee, L. (2003). 'It's Just like a Family' – shared Values in the Family Firm. *Community Work & Family*, *6*(2), 141–158. doi:10.1080/13668800302541

Hay Group. (2015). *Iceberg Model*. Mary Seacole Workshop 1 Slides.

Hayday, M. (2016). Managing Trends in Finance and Social Finance for Social Enterprise. In C. Oham & D. Macdonald (Eds.), Leading and Managing a Social. Academic Press.

Hazenberg, R. H. (2021). *The role of social enterprise in developing skills and creating employment opportunities in the UK*. https://www.enterpriseresearch.ac.uk/wp-content/uploads/2021/04/No50-The-role-of-social-enterprise-in-developing-skills-and-creating-employment-opportunities-in-the-UK-R.-Hazenberg.pdf

Heifetz, R. (2006). Mobilizing for adaptive work. In Making Policy Happen. Routledge.

Heifetz, R. (1994). *Leadership Without Easy Answers*. The Belknap Press of Havard University Press.

Herz, B., & van Rens, T. (2011). Structural unemployment. *Economics Working Papers*, 1276.

Heywood, A. (2013). *Politics* (4th ed.). Palgrave MacMillan. doi:10.1007/978-1-137-27244-7

Hiller, H., & DiLuzio, L. (2004). The Interviewee and the Research Interview: Analysing a Neglected Dimension in Research. *Canadian Review of Sociology and Anthroplogy*, *41*(1), 1–26. doi:10.1111/j.1755-618X.2004.tb02167.x

Holt, C. L., Schulz, E., Williams, B., Clark, E. M., Wang, M. Q., & Southward, P. L. (2012). Assessment of Religious and Spiritual Capital in African American Communities. *Journal of Religion and Health*, *51*(4), 1061–1074. doi:10.100710943-012-9635-4 PMID:22810197

Honwana, A. (2013). *The Time of Youth; Works, social Change and Politics in Africa*. Kumarian Press.

Hoogendoorn, B., Pennings, E., & Thurik, R. (2012). Conceptual Overview of What We Know about Social Entrepreneurship. In J. Defilippis & S. Saegert (Eds.), *The Community Development Reader* (pp. 117–124). Routledge.

Hwang, Y. (2017). What Is the Cause of Graduates' Unemployment? Focus on Individual Concerns and Perspectives. *Journal of Educational Issues*, *3*(2), 1–10. doi:10.5296/jei.v3i2.11378

Hytti, U. (Ed.). (2002). State-of-Art of Enterprise Education in Europe – results from the Entredu project. Leonardo da Vinci -Programme of the European Commission.

Hytti, U., & O'Gorman, C. (2004). What is 'enterprise education'? An analysis of the objectives and methods of enterprise education programmes in four European countries. *Education + Training*, *46*(1), 11–23. doi:10.1108/00400910410518188

Hytti, U., Stenholm, P., Heinonen, J., & Seikkula-Leino, J. (2010). Perceived learning outcomes in entrepreneurship education. *Education + Training*, *52*(8/9), 587–606. doi:10.1108/00400911011088935

Ibimilua, A. F., & Ibitoye, O. A. (2015). Housing policy in Nigeria: An overview. *American International Journal of Contemporary Research*, *5*(2).

Ibrahim, N. A., & Angelidis, J. P. (2005). The Long Term Performance of Small Businesses: Are there Differences Between "Christian Based Companies and Their Secular Counterparts"? *Journal of Business Ethics*, *58*(1-3), 187–193. doi:10.100710551-005-1413-8

ILO (International Labour Organisation). (2014). *Global employment trends: risk of a jobless recovery? ILO.*

ILO (International Labour Organisation). (2015). *World employment and social outlook*. ILO.

International Labour Organisation. (2016). *Private and public procurement and the social economy project: best practice case studies from South Africa*. ILO.

International Monetary Fund (IMF). (2014). World Economic Outlook-Recovery Strengthens, Remains Uneven. International Monetary Fund.

Investopedia What Factors Go in Calculating Social Return on Investment. (n.d.). https://www.investopedia.com/ask/answers/070314/what-factors-go-calculating-social-return-investment-sroi.asp

Iyortsuun, A. S. (2015). A conceptual overview of social entrepreneurship and its relevance to the Nigeria's third sector. *International Journal of Small Business and Entrepreneurship Research*, *3*(4), 32-51. www.eajournals.org

Jack, S. L., & Anderson, A. R. (1999). Entrepreneurship education within the enterprise culture: Producing reflective practitioners. *International Journal of Entrepreneurial Behaviour & Research*, *5*(3), 110–125. doi:10.1108/13552559910284074

Jager, U. (2010). *Managing Social Business: Mission Governance Strategy and Accountability*. Palgrave Macmillan. doi:10.1057/9780230292420

Jaksa, B., & Eros, B. (2016). *Social Innovations in Hungary*. https://www.siceurope.eu/sites/default/files/uploads/documents/social_innovations_in_hungary_2016.pdf

Jetmar, M. (2013). Social entrepreneurship: Challenge not only for developing countries but also for the EU. *CBU International Conference on Integration and Innovation in Science and Education*. www.cbuni.cz doi:10.12955/cbup.2013.13

Jiang, D., Hayward, S. D., & Morris, M. L. (2017). Raising entrepreneurs: Can parenting style amplify entrepreneurial intentions and behaviours? *International Journal of Management and Enterprise Development*, *16*(1/2), 13–33. doi:10.1504/IJMED.2017.082544

Johnson, G., Sholes, K., & Whittington, R. (2009). *Fundamentals of Strategy Pearson Education*. Academic Press.

Johnson, S. (2002). *Social entrepreneurship literature review*. Canadian Centre for Social Entrepreneurship. https://www.researchgate.net/profile/Leon-Prieto/publication/287854658_Social_entrepreneur_development_An_integration_of_critical_pedagogy_the_theory_of_planned_behavior_and_the_ACS_model/links/59ffab4d458515d0706e1ed9/Social-entrepreneur-development-An-integration-of-critical-pedagogy-the-theory-of-planned-behavior-and-the-ACS-model.pdf

Johnson, S. (2003). Young social entrepreneurs in Canada. *New Academy Review, 2*(4).

Johnson, G., & Scholes, K. (1999). *Exploring Corporate Strategy* (5th ed.). Prentice Hall Europe.

Johnson, L. (2017). The Lives and Identities of UK Black and South Asian Head Teachers. *Educational Management Administration & Leadership*, *45*(5), 842–862. doi:10.1177/1741143217717279

Jokela, M. (2008). Personality predicts migration within and between U.S. states. *Journal of Research in Personality*.

Jones, B., & Iredale, N. (2010). Enterprise education as pedagogy. *Education + Training*, *52*(1), 7–19. doi:10.1108/00400911011017654

Justyna Łukaszewska-Bezulska, J. (2020). The Role of Social Capital in Labour-Related Migrations: The Polish Example. *Journal of International Migration and Integration*, *3*, 1–8. Retrieved May 9, 2021, from. doi:10.100712134-020-00776-z

Kaderabkova, A. (2016). *Social Innovation in the Czech Republic*. CIS. Microsoft Word - Country Profile_ Czech Republic_2016.docx

Kandler, C., & Bleidorn, W. (2015). The Genetic and Environmental Contributions to Personality Differences and Development. The International Encyclopedia of Social and Behavioral Sciences (2nd ed., pp. 884-890). doi:10.1016/B978-0-08-097086-8.25011-3

Kanter, R. M. (2011). How Great Companies Think Differently. *Harvard Business Review*. http://gwmoon.knu.ac.kr/Lecture_Library_Upload/How_great_companies_think_differently.pdf

Katzenbach, J.R., & Smith, D. (1993). The discipline of teams. *Harvard Business Review, 83*(7-8), 162–71.

Kauanui, S. K., Thomas, K. D., Sherman, C. L., Waters, G. R., & Gilea, M. (2008). Exploring Entrepreneurship Through the Lens of Spirituality. *Journal of Management, Spirituality & Religion*, *5*(2), 160–189. doi:10.1080/14766080809518698

Keller, J. G., & Helfenbein, R. (2008). Spirituality, Economics, and Education: A Dialogic Critique of “Spiritual Capital.” *Spirituality. Economics and Education*, *5*(4), 109–128.

Kerlin, J. A. (2010b). *Historical institutionalism and social enterprise development: Towards a conceptual framework for comparative social enterprise*. Working Paper. www.istr.org/resource/resmgr/Istanbul_abstracts/ISTR2010_0580.pdf

Kerlin, J. A. (2006). *Social enterprise in the United States and Europe: Understanding and learning from the differences*. International Society for Third-Sector Research and The Johns Hopkins University.

Kerlin, J. A. (2010a). A comparative analysis of the global emergence of social enterprise. *Voluntas*, *21*(2), 162–179.

Kolade, O., Egbetokun, A., Rae, D., & Hussain, J. (2020). Entrepreneurial resilience in turbulent environments: the role of spiritual capital. In P. Sinha, J. Gibb, M. Akorie, & J. M. Scott (Eds.), *Research Handbook in Business and Management series*. Elgar Online. doi:10.4337/9781788973717.00028

Kolb, D. A. (1984). *Experiential learning: Experience as the Source of Learning and Development*. Prentice-Hall Inc.

Krueger, A. (1974). The political economy of the rent seeking society. *The American Economic Review*, *64*, 291–303.

Kuratko, D. F. (2005). The emergence of entrepreneurship education: Development, trends and challenges. *Entrepreneurship Theory and Practice*, *29*(5), 577–597. doi:10.1111/j.1540-6520.2005.00099.x

Lafuente, E., Vaillant, Y., & Rialp, J. (2007). Regional Differences in the Influence of Role Models: Comparing the Entrepreneurial Process of Rural Catalonia. *Regional Studies*, *41*(6), 779–796. doi:10.1080/00343400601120247

Lam, D. (2014). Youth bulges and youth unemployment. *IZA World of Labor: Evidence-Based Policy Making*. Advance online publication. doi:10.15185/izawol.26

Landua, L. B., & Segatti, A. (2013). Urbanisation and migration: The governance of mobility and spatial inequalities. In U. Pillay, G. Hagg, & F. Nyamnjoh (Eds.), *State of the Nation South Africa 2012-2013*. HSRC Press.

Langley, G. L., Nolan, K. M., Nolan, T. W., Norman, C. L., & Provost, L. P. (2009). *The Improvement Guide: a practical approach to enhancing organizational performance* (2nd ed.). Jossey-Bass Publishers.

Laspita, S., Breugst, N., Heblich, S., & Patzelt, H. (2012). Intergenerational Transmission of Entrepreneurial Intentions. *Journal of Business Venturing*, *27*(4), 414–435. doi:10.1016/j.jbusvent.2011.11.006

Lawrence, P. (2018). Challenging th Hegemony of Neoliberal Economics: Is Another Way Possible? In Building Blocks Towards an African Century: Essays in Honour of Thabo Mbeki, Former President of the Republic of South, Africa (pp. 136-165). Johannesburg: Real African Publishers.

Lee, K., McCann, P., & Ching, M. (2003). Christ and Business Culture: A study of Christian Executive in Hong Kong. *Journal of Business Ethics*, *43*(1/2), 103–110. doi:10.1023/A:1022967300183

Lesotho Bureau of Statistics. (2011). *2008 Lesotho integrated labourforce survey*. www.bos.gov.ls

Lewin, K. (1951). *Field theory in social sciences*. Harper & Row.

Lewis, C. (2019). *Sovereign entrepreneurs: Cherokee small-business owners and the making of economic sovereignty*. University of North Carolina Press. doi:10.5149/northcarolina/9781469648590.001.0001

Liao, J., & Welsch, H. (2003). Social capital and entrepreneurial growth aspiration: A comparison of technology- and non-technology-based nascent entrepreneurs. *The Journal of High Technology Management Research*, *14*(1), 149–170. doi:10.1016/S1047-8310(03)00009-9

Lie, K. (2007). *Employer perception on graduate literacy in higher education in relation to the workplace*. http://www.esp-world.info/Articles_20/DOC/Koo_vp_employer_Journal18Oct09.pdf

Lindquist, M., Sol, J., & Praag, M. (2015). Why Do Entrepreneurial Parents Have Entrepreneurial Children? *Journal of Labor Economics*, *33*(2), 269–296. doi:10.1086/678493

Lingstone, R. (2016). *Some Thoughts on University Education*. Cambridge University Press.

Lippitt, R., Watson, J., & Westley, B. (1958). *The dynamics of planned change*. Harcourt Brace.

LiuskariS. (n.d.). *Finland*. Retrieved from http://www.euclidnetwork.eu/programme-areas/geographical-areas-in-which-we-work/civil-society-in-europe-country-profiles/finland.html

Lovati, J. M. (1976). *The unemployment rate as an economic indicator.* Federal Reserve Bank of St. Louis.

Lucey, T. A. (2019). Examining a measure of spiritual capital: Perceptions of business and education majors. *Citizenship, Social and Economics Education, 18*(1), 3-15.

Łukaszewska-Bezulska, J. (2014). Social capital and migrations: an analysis of interactions in light of particular theoretical concepts - Problemy Polityki Społecznej - Numer nr 4 (2014) - BazEkon - Yadda, Problemy Polityki Społecznej. *Studia i Dyskusje, 27*(4), 23–40. Available at: http://www. problemypolitykispolecznej.pl/images/czasopisma/27/PPS-27-23-40.pdf

Lumpkin, G., Moss, T., Gras, D., Kato, S., & Amezcua, A. (2013). Entrepreneurial Processes in Social Contexts: How Are They Different, If at All? *Small Business Economics, 40*(3), 1–23. doi:10.100711187-011-9399-3

Lundmark, E., Krzeminska, A., & Shepherd, D. A. (2019). Images of Entrepreneurship: Exploring Root Metaphors and Expanding Upon Them. *Entrepreneurship Theory and Practice, 43*(1), 138–170. doi:10.1177/1042258717734369

Lutomia, A. N., Bravo, J. B., & Seck, F. (2019). Becoming an African Hair Salon Entrepreneur in the United States of America. In Immigration and Refugee Policy: Breakthroughs in Research and Practice (pp. 31-51) IGI Global.

Maathai, W. (2009). *The Challenge for Africa: A New Vision.* William Heinemann.

Madoui, M. (2015). Unemployment among young graduates in Algeria, a sociological reading. *Open Journal of Social Sciences, 3*(1), 35–41. doi:10.4236/jss.2015.311006

Mahlobo, T. (2016). *The New Economy: Ancient Hope for Modern Economies.* Johannesburg: LCBN Ltd. and LEAD2020.

Malach-Pines, A., Sadeh, A., Dvir, D., & Yofe-Yanai, O. (2002). Entrepreneurs and managers: Similar yet different. *The International Journal of Organizational Analysis, 10*(2), 172–190. doi:10.1108/eb028949

Malloch, T. R. (2005). Spirituality and entrepreneurship. In N. Capaldi (Ed.), *Business and Religion A Clash of Civilizations?* M&M Scrivener Press.

Malloch, T. R. (2005). Spirituality and Entrepreneurship. In N. Capaldi (Ed.), *Business and Religion A Clash of Civilizations?* M&M Scrivener Press.

Malloch, T. R. (2008). *Doing virtuous business: The remarkable success of spiritual enterprise.* Thomas Nelson.

Malloch, T. R. (2008). *Doing Virtuous Business: The Remarkable Success of Spiritual Enterprise.* Thomas Nelson.

Marchand, J. M., & Hermens, A. H. (2014, December). Student entrepreneurship: a research agenda. *Australian and New Zealand Academy of Management Conference.*

Markides, C. (2006). Disruptive innovation: In need of better theory. *Journal of Product Innovation Management*, *23*(1), 19–25. doi:10.1111/j.1540-5885.2005.00177.x

Martin, R. L. & Osberg, S. (2007). Social Entrepreneurship: The Case for Definition. *Stanford Innovation Review*, 28-39.

Martin, J., & Novicevic, M. (2010). Social Entrepreneurship among Kenyan farmers: A case example of acculturation challenges and program successes. *International Journal of Intercultural Relations*, *34*(5), 482–492. doi:10.1016/j.ijintrel.2010.05.007

Marx, K. (1959). *Das Kapital, a critique of political economy*. H. Regnery.

Mary Seacole Programme. (2015). *Participant Learning Journal: Leadership Workshop One*. NHS Leadership Academy.

Mas-Machuca, M., & Marimon, F. (2019). Holistic spiritual capital: Definition and its measurement. *International Journal of Organization Theory and Behavior*, *22*(1), 96–110. doi:10.1108/IJOTB-05-2018-0057

Matlay, H. (2007). *The impact of entrepreneurship education on entrepreneurial outcomes*. Paper presented at the 30th ISBA National Small Firms Conference, Glasgow, UK.

Mazereeuw-van der Duijn Schouten, C., Graafland, J., & Kaptein, M. (2014). Religiosity, CSR Attitudes, and CSR Behavior: An Empirical Study of Executives' Religiosity and CSR. *Journal of Business Ethics*, *123*(3), 437–459. doi:10.100710551-013-1847-3

McGlashan. (2013). Social Enterprise Training – The Facts. *The Guardian*. https://www.theguardian.com/social-enterprise-network/2013/sep/09/social-enterprise-training-research2

Melkas, H. (2020). Social Enterprise: A Study of Its Prevalence, Role and Characteristics in Swedish-Speaking Regions of Finland. *Tijds. voor econ. en Soc. Geog.*, *111*(2), 101–116. doi:10.1111/tesg.12366

Meyer, J. (2000). Qualitative research in health care: Using qualitative methods in health related action research. *BMJ (Clinical Research Ed.)*, *320*(7228), 178–181. doi:10.1136/bmj.320.7228.178 PMID:10634744

Millman, J., Ferguson, J., Tricket, D., & Condemi, B. (1999). Spirit and community at South West Airlines: An investigation of a spiritual values-based model. *Journal of Organizational Change*, *12*(3), 221–223. doi:10.1108/09534819910273928

Mills, G., & Herbst, J. (2012). *Africa's Third Liberation*. Penguin Books.

Mlambo, D. N. (2019). A South African perspective on immigrants and Xenophobia in post-1994 South Africa. *African Renaissance*, *16*(4), 53–67. doi:10.31920/2516-5305/2019/16n4a3

Mohammed, A. A. (2018). *Entrepreneurship Lecture Notes*. https://www.researchgate.net/publication/326190494_Entrepreneurship_lecture_note

Molecke, G., & Pinkse, J. (2017). Accountability for Social impact: A bricolage perspective on impact measurement in social enterprises. *Journal of Business Venturing*, *32*(5), 550–568. doi:10.1016/j.jbusvent.2017.05.003

Mondragon Corporation. (2020). *Annual Report 2019*. https://www.mondragon-corporation.com/2019urtekotxostena/assets/downloads/eng/annual-report-2019.pdf

Moore, J. F. (1993). Predators and prey: A new ecology of competition. *Harvard Business Review*, *71*, 75–86. PMID:10126156

Morgan, G. (2006). Images of organization (updated ed.). Sage.

Morgan, G. (1980). Paradigms, metaphors, and puzzle solving in organization theory. *Administrative Science Quarterly*, *25*(4), 605–622. doi:10.2307/2392283

Morgan, G. (2016). Commentary: Beyond Morgan's eight metaphors. *Human Relations*, *69*(4), 1029–1042. doi:10.1177/0018726715624497

Morgan, G., Gliner, J., & Harmon, R. (1999). Definition, Purposes, and Dimensions of Research. *Journal of the American Academy of Child and Adolescent Psychiatry*, *38*(2), 217–219. Retrieved March 10, 2020, from https://www.jaacap.org/article/S0890-8567(09)62901-4/pdf

Morley, L. (2001). Producing new workers: Quality, equality and employability in higher education. *Quality in Higher Education*, *7*(2), 131–138. doi:10.1080/13538320120060024

Morris, M., & Schindehutte, M. (2005). Entrepreneurial values and the ethnic enterprise: An examination of six sub Cultures. *Journal of Small Business Management*, *43*(4), 453–479. doi:10.1111/j.1540-627X.2005.00147.x

Morrison, A. (2000). Entrepreneurship: What triggers it? *International Journal of Entrepreneurial Behaviour & Research*, *6*(2), 59–71. doi:10.1108/13552550010335976

Morrissey, H. (2013). Your career is not predestined by degree choice. *Telegraph*. https://www.telegraph.co.uk/finance/comment/10264114/Your-career-is-notpredestined-by-degree-choice.html

Mosselson, A. (2010). There is no Difference between Citizen and Non-Citizen Anymore: Violent Xenophobia, Citizenship and the Political of Belonging in Post-Apartheid South Africa. *Journal of Southern African Studies*, *36*(3), 641–655. doi:10.1080/03057070.2010.507570

Mseleku, Z. (2019). Graduate internship and employment opportunities: A case study of EThekwini Municipality, KwaZulu-Natal (PhD thesis). University of KwaZulu-Natal, Durban, South Africa.

Municipality, İ. (2017). *Report on stray animals*. https://www.trthaber.com/haber/yasam/istanbuldaki-sahipsiz-kedi-kopek-sayisi-aciklandi-311559.html

Murphy, K. M., Shleifer, A., & Vishny, R. W. (1991). The allocation of talent: Implication for Growth. *The Quarterly Journal of Economics*, (May), 503–530.

Murphy, P. J., & Coombes, S. M. (2009). A model of social entrepreneurial discovery. *Journal of Business Ethics*, *87*(3), 325–336. doi:10.100710551-008-9921-y

Naidoo, N. (2011). What is research? A conceptual understanding. *African Journal of Emergency Medicine*, *2011*(1), 47–48. Retrieved March 10, 2020, from https://www.researchgate.net/profile/Navindhra_Naidoo/publication/265704878_What_is_research_A_conceptual_understanding/links/54197fc60cf2218008bf83cf/What-is-research-A-conceptual-understanding.pdf?origin=publication_detail

Neal, J. A., Benyamin, M., Lichtenstein, B., & Banner, D. (1999). Spiritual Perspectives on Individual, Organisational and Societal Transformation. *Journal of Organizational Change Management*, *12*(3), 175–186. doi:10.1108/09534819910273757

Neubert, M. J., Bradley, S. W., Ardianti, R., & Simiyu, E. M. (2017). The Role of Spiritual Capital in Innovation and Performance: Evidence from Developing Economies. *Entrepreneurship Theory and Practice*, *41*(4), 621–640. doi:10.1111/etp.12172

Neuman, S. (1986). Religious observance within a human capital framework: Theory and application. *Applied Economics*, *18*(11), 1193–1202. doi:10.1080/00036848600000072

Ng'ambi, H. C. (2018). Advancing the Developmental Goals of Africa through Rare and Total Leadership: The case of Thabo Mbeki. In Building Blocks Towards an African Century: Essays in Honour of Thabo Mbeki, Former President of the Republic of South, Africa (pp. 70-100). Johannesburg: Real African Publishers.

Nicholls, A. (Ed.). (2006). *Social Entrepreneurship: New Models of Sustainable Social Change*. Oxford University Press.

Nicholls, A., & Cho, A. (2007). Social Entrepreneurship: The Structuration Field. In A. Nichols (Ed.), *Social Entrepreneurship New Models of Sustainable Social Change*. Oxford University Press.

Nicholls, A., & Young, P. (2006). Preface to Paperback Edition. In A. Nicholls (Ed.), *Social Entrepreneurship New Models for Sustainable Social Change*. Oxford University Press.

Nickols, F., & Bergholz. (2012). *The Consultant's Competency Circle: A Tool for Gauging Your Success Potentials as an Independent Consultant.* Available at http://www.nickols.us/The_Consulting_Competency_Circle.pdf

Nicole, B. (2003). *The Base of the Pyramid (BOP): Reperceiving Business from the Bottom Up.* Global Business Network (GBN) Working Paper.

Nliam, A. (2021). *N200bn social housing facility ready for disbursement.* https://von.gov.ng/amp/2021/05/31/n200bn-social-housing-facility-ready-for-disbursement

Nordic Council of Ministers, Nordic Council of Ministers Secretariat. (2015). *Social entrepreneurship and social innovation in the Nordic countries: Initiatives to promote social entrepreneurship and social innovation*. Retrieved from http://norden.diva-portal.org/smash/get/diva2:856045/FULLTEXT01.pdf doi:10.6027/TN2015-562

Northouse, P. G. (2018). Leadership: Theory and practice. *Sage (Atlanta, Ga.).*

NPC (National Planning Commission). (2011). *National development Plan. Our future: Make it work, Executive summary*. The Presidency.

O'Leary, Z. (2014). *The Essential Guide to Doing Your Research Project*. Sage.

Odumeru, J. A., & Ifeanyi, G. O. (2013). Transformational vs. Transactional Leadership Theories: Evidence in Literature. *International Review of Management and Business Research*, *2*(2), 355–361.

OECD (Organisation for Economic Co-Operation and Development). (2014). Preventing unemployment and underemployment from becoming structural. OECD.

OECD Centre for Entrepreneurship, SMEs and Local Development. (2009). The Impact of the Global Crisis on SME and Entrepreneurship Financing and Policy Responses. Paris: OECD.

OECD. (2003). *The non-profit sector in a changing economy*. OECD.

OECD/ILO. (2018). *How Immigrants Contribute to South Africa's Economy*. OECD Publishing. doi:10.1787/9789264085398-en

Oham & McDonald. (2016). *Leading and Managing a Social Enterprise in Health and Social Care*. Community Training Partners.

Oham, C., & Durkin, C. (2016). Social Innovation Management and Capital Literacy. In C. Oham & D. MacDonald (Eds.), Leading and Managing a Social Enterprise in Health and Social Care. Academic Press.

Oham, C. (2013). Could there be treasures in our faith? The recognition and utilisation of spiritual capital values. In D. Singleton (Ed.), *Faith With Its Sleeves Rolled Up*. Faith Action.

Oham, C. (2016). Why Social Enterprise? In C. Oham & D. Macdonald (Eds.), *Leading and Managing a Social Enterprise in Health and Social Care*. Community Training Partners.

Oham, C., & Macdonald, D. (2016). *Leading and managing a social enterprise in health and social Care*. Community Training Partners.

Oham, C., Stewart, J., & Cornish, Y. (2009). Social Capital Social Enterprise and Community Development. In J. Stewart & Y. Cornish (Eds.), *Professional Practice in Public Health* (pp. 191–206). Devon Reflect Press Devon.

Oham, C., Stewart, J., & Cornish, Y. (2009). Social capital, social enterprise and community development. In J. Stewart & Y. Cornish (Eds.), *Professional Practice in Public Health*. Reflect Press.

Okhomina, D. A. (2010). Entrepreneurial postures and psychological traits: The sociological influences of education and environment. *Research in Higher Education*, 2–20.

Oluwajodu, F., Greyling, L., Blaauw, D., & Kleynhans, E. P. (2015). Graduate unemployment in South Africa: Perspectives from the banking sector. *SA Journal of Human Resource Management*, *13*(1), 1–9. doi:10.4102ajhrm.v13i1.656

Omadjohwoefe, O. S. (2011). Education and the Paradox of Graduate Unemployment: The Dilemma of Development in Nigeria. *An International Multi-Disciplinary Journal*, *5*(1), 253–265.

Onoyase, A. (2019). Causal Factors and Effects of Unemployment on Graduates of Tertiary Institutions in Ogun State South West Nigeria: Implications for Counselling. *Journal of Educational and Social Research*, *9*(4), 119–127. doi:10.2478/jesr-2019-0061

Opatrny-Yazell, C. M., Jensen, D. H., & McCord, M. H. (2021). The Dilemma of Social Entrepreneurship and Social Enterprise: An Exercise. *Entrepreneurship Education and Pedagogy*. https://journals.sagepub.com/doi/abs/10.1177/25151274211006896 doi:10.1177/25151274211006896

Orloff, A. (2020). *Remaking modernity: Politics, history, and sociology*. Duke University Press.

Pacor, I. (2015). Shiza Shahid's 3 Lessons for Being a Change-Maker (Capes and Masks Not Included). *Educational Tours*. Retrieved from https://blog.eftours.com/ef/events/shiza-shahids-3-lessons-for-being-a-change-maker

Parkinson, C., & Howorth, C. (2008). The language of social entrepreneurs. *Entrepreneurship and Regional Development*, *20*(3), 285–309. doi:10.1080/08985620701800507

Pauw, K., Oosthuizen, M., & Van Der Westhuizen, C. (2008). Graduate Unemployment In The Face Of Skills Shortages: A Labour Market Paradox1. *The South African Journal of Economics*, *76*(1), 45–57. doi:10.1111/j.1813-6982.2008.00152.x

Pawson, R., & Tilley, N. (2004). *Realist Evaluation*. University College London.

Payne, A., Frow, P., & Eggert, A. (2017). The customer value proposition: Evolution, development and application in marketing. *Journal of the Academy of Marketing Science*, *45*(4), 467–489. doi:10.100711747-017-0523-z

Pearce, J. A. II, Fritz, D. A., & Davis, P. S. (2010). Entrepreneurial Orientation and the Performance of Religious Congregations as Predicted by Rational Choice Theory. *Entrepreneurship Theory and Practice*, *34*(1), 219–248. doi:10.1111/j.1540-6520.2009.00315.x

Peattie, K., & Morley, A. (2008). *Diversity and Dynamics Contexts and Contributions*. Social Enterprise Coalition and Centre for Business Relationships, Accountability, Sustainability and Society Cardiff University. Available at http://orca.cf.ac.uk/30775/1/SE%20Monograph%20 Published.pdf

Peredo, A. M., & McLean, M. (2006). Social entrepreneurship: A critical review of the concept. *Journal of World Business*, *41*(1), 56–65. doi:10.1016/j.jwb.2005.10.007

Pietersen, E. (2021). Entrepreneurship leadership. In E. van Zyl (Ed.), *Leadership in the African Context* (2nd ed.). Juta and Company Ltd.

Porter, M. E. (1985). *Competitive Advantage*. The Free Press.

Porter, M. E., & Kramer, M. R. (2011). Creating shared value. *Harvard Business Review*, *89*(1/2), 62–77.

Prabhu, J., & Jain, S. (2015). Innovation and entrepreneurship in India: Understanding jugaad. *Asia Pacific Journal of Qualitative. Management*, *32*(4), 843–868.

Prahalad, C. K. (2006). *The fortune at the bottom of the pyramid*. Pearson Prentice Hall.

Prieto, L. C., Phipps, S. T., & Friedrich, T. L. (2012). Social Entrepreneur Development: An Integration of Critical Pedagogy, The Theory of Planned Behavior and the ACS Model. *Academy of Entrepreneurship Journal*, *18*(2), 2012.

Putnam, R. (2000). *Bowling Alone: The Collapse and Revival of American Community*. Simon and Schuster.

Radjou, N., & Prabhu, J. (2016). Frugal innovation. How to do better with less. *The Economist*.

Ramsey, C. M. (2012). Developing Productive Inquiry, Section 4, (B839), Making a difference: the management initiative. The Open University.

Ramus, T., Cara, B.L., Vaccaro, A., & Brusoni, S. (2019). Social or Commercial? Innovation Strategies in Social Enterprise at Times of Turbulence. *Business Ethics Quarterly*, *28*(4), 463-492.

Rengamani, J., & Ramachandran, S. (2015). A Study on the Entrepreneurial Skills among Students in Chennai. *International Journal of Advanced Research in Management*, *6*(3), 36–44.

Rima, S. D., & Lessens, R. (2005). *Spiritual Capital Research Project, Letter of Intent*. Metanexus Institute.

ROA (Research Centre For Education and the Labour Market). (2012). *Maastricht University graduate surveys: 2012. ROA-F2012/3*. Maastricht University.

Roberts, D., Khattri, N., & Wessel, A. (2011). *Writing terms of reference for an evaluation: A how-to guide. 2011 Independent Evaluation Group*. The World Bank. doi:10.22163/fteval.2011.134

Roberts, D., & Woods, C. (2005). Changing the World on a Shoestring: The Concept of Social Entrepreneurship. *University of Auckland Business Review*, *7*(1), 45–51.

Rogers, E. (1995). *Diffusion of innovations* (4th ed.). Free Press.

Royce, M. (2007). Using human resource management tools to support social enterprise: Emerging themes from the sector. *Social Enterprise Journal*, *3*(1), 10–19. doi:10.1108/17508610780000718

Royce, M. (2009). *Management for Social Enterprise*. Sage.

Roy, M. J., Donaldson, C., Baker, R., & Kerr, S. (2014). The potential of social enterprise to enhance health and well-being: A model and systematic review. *Social Science & Medicine*, *123*, 182–193. doi:10.1016/j.socscimed.2014.07.031 PMID:25037852

Rudigi, R. J. (2010). 'The journey from death to life: I was told that life is out there' - a case study of Congolese immigrants in Durban, South Africa. In Contemporary Social Issues in Africa: Cases in Gaborone, Kampala and Durban (pp. 65-78). Africa Institute of Africa (AISA).

Ryan, C. (2012). *Field of Degree and Earnings by Selected Employment Characteristics: 2011. American Community Survey Briefs. ACSBR/11-10.* US Census Bureau.

Sabella, A., & Niveen, L. (2016). A strategic perspective of social enterprise. *Journal of General Management*, *41*(4), 71–89. doi:10.1177/030630701604100405

Sahin, M, Nijkamp, P., & Baycan-Levent, T. (2006). *Migrant Entrepreneurship from the Perspective of Cultural Diversity.* file:///C:/Users/TSHISH~1/AppData/Local/Temp/Migrant_Entrepreneurship_from_the_Perspective_of_C.pdf

Sankobe, Y. (2019). *The Narrative of an Unemployed Graduate in South Africa.* Samuel Centre for Social Connectedness. https://www.socialconnectedness.org/the-narrative-of-an-unemployed-graduate-in-south-africa/

Sara, S. S. (2008). *Evaluation of vocational training programmes among the in-mates of reformatory institutions in Jigawa State.* Unpublished seminar paper submitted to the Department of Education, University of Maiduguri.

Sarason, Y., Dean, T., & Dillard, J. (2006). Entrepreneurship as the nexus of individual and opportunity: A structuration view. *Journal of Business Venturing*, *21*(3), 285–305. doi:10.1016/j.jbusvent.2005.02.007

Sarason, Y., Dean, T., & Dillard, J. (2010). How can we know the dancer from the dance? *Journal of Business Venturing*, *25*(2), 238–243. doi:10.1016/j.jbusvent.2008.06.003

Savitz, A., & Weber, K. (2006). *The triple bottom line: How today's best-run companies are achieving economic, social, and environmental success - and how you can too.* Jossey-Bass.

Schafer, D. S. (1990). Level of entrepreneurship and scanning source usage in very small businesses. *Entrepreneurship Theory and Practice*, *15*(2), 19–21. doi:10.1177/104225879101500204

Schein, E. H. (2004). The levels of culture. In Organizational Collaboration: Themes and Issues. Routledge.

Schreuder, A. M. G., & Coetzee, M. (2006). *Careers: an organisational perspective* (3rd ed.). Juta & Co.

Schumpeter, J. A. (1912). *Theorie der wirtschaftlichen Entwicklung.* Dunker und Humbolt.

Schwandt, T. A. (1993). Theory for the moral sciences: Crises of identity and purpose. In G. Mills & D. J. Flinders (Eds.), *Theory and concepts in qualitative research* (pp. 5–13). Teachers College Press.

Sehume, J. (2015). Solving poverty, unemployment and inequality. *Sunday Independent*, *24*(June), 15.

Seibert, S. E., Crant, J. M., & Kraimer, M. L. (1999). Proactive personality and career success. *The Journal of Applied Psychology, 84*(3), 416–427. doi:10.1037/0021-9010.84.3.416 PMID:10380421

Sekatane, M. B. (2004). *The role of clothing manufacturing co-operatives in job creation and poverty alleviation in Sharpeville* (Doctoral dissertation). North-West University.

Senior, B., & Fleming, J. (2006). The Leadership of Change. In *Organizational change* (3rd ed.). Prentice Hall.

Servon, L. J. (2011). *Bootstrap capital: Microenterprises and the American poor*. Brookings Institution Press.

Shaw, E., & Carter, S. (2007). Social entrepreneurship: Theoretical antecedents and empirical analysis of entrepreneurial processes and outcomes. *Journal of Small Business and Enterprise Development, 14*(3), 418–434. doi:10.1108/14626000710773529

Short, J. C., Todd, W. M., & Lumpkin, G. T. (2009). Research in social entrepreneurship: Past contributions and future opportunities. *Strategic Entrepreneurship Journal, 3*(2), 161–194. doi:10.1002ej.69

Singh, V. (2019). Student entrepreneurs on the rise in grim economy. *Sunday Tribune, 6*(October), 20.

Sirat, M., & Shuib, M. (2012). *Employability in Malaysia*. Asian and Pacific Regional Bureau for Education UNESCO.

Skoll, J. (2009). *In Innovations – Technology, Governance, Globalisation: Social Entrepreneurship: Shifting Power Dynamics. Skoll World Forum 2009*. MIT Press. http://www.pbs.org/now/shows/537/Shifting-Power-Dynamics.pdf

Social Enterprise Alliance. (2004). www.se-alliance.org

Social Enterprise Alliance. (2018). *Trends in giving report*. https://socialenterprise.us/article/trends-in-giving-report-2018/

Social Enterprise UK. (2020a). *Social Enterprise Advisory Panel: June 2020 Highlights*. https://www.socialenterprise.org.uk/wp-content/uploads/2020/07/SEUK-SEAP-First-Survey-June-2020.pdf

Social Enterprise UK. (2020b). *2020 – a view from across the nations*. https://www.socialenterprise.org.uk/2020-a-view-from-across-the-nations/

Social Enterprise UK. (2021). *The London Early Years Foundation*. Social Enterprise UK.

South Africa Social Housing Act No.16 of 2008.

Sparber, C., & Fan, J. S. (2012). *Unemployment, Skills, and the Business Cycle Since 2000*. Academic Press.

Sparrow, S., & Robinson, J. (1994). Action Research: an appropriate design for research in nursing? *Educational Action Research, 2*(3). doi:10.1080/0965079940020304

Staniewski, M. W., & Awruk, K. (2021). Parental Attitudes and Entrepreneurial Success. *Journal of Business Research, 123*, 538–546. doi:10.1016/j.jbusres.2020.10.039

Statistics South Africa. (2017). *Media Release: Quarterly Labour Force Survey – QLFS Q4: 2016*. www.statssa.gov.za/?p=9561

Statistics South Africa. (2018). National and Provincial Labour Market: Youth Statistical Release P0211.4.2. Pretoria, South Africa: Statistics South Africa. Retrieved from http://www.statssa.gov.za/publications/P02114.2/P02114.22015.pdf

Steiner, A., & Teasdale, S. (2017). Unlocking the potential of rural social enterprise. *Journal of Rural Studies, 70*, 144–154. doi:10.1016/j.jrurstud.2017.12.021 PMID:31787801

Storey, J., & Holti, R. (2013). *Towards a New Model of Leadership for the NHS*. National Leaderrship Academy.

Sullivan, M. (2003). Social entrepreneurship: Towards conceptualisation. *International Journal of Nonprofit and Voluntary Sector Marketing, 8*(1), 76–88. doi:10.1002/nvsm.202

Swann, S. L., & Morgan, M. (Eds.). (2002). Social capital: Insights from qualitative research. Academic Press.

Tang, J. (2008). Environmental munificence for entrepreneurs: Entrepreneurial alertness and commitment. *International Journal of Entrepreneurial Behaviour & Research, 14*(3), 128–151. doi:10.1108/13552550810874664

Taudama, A. M. (2009). *Significance of self-employment among unemployed graduates in Kaduna State* (Unpublished PGDM Project report). Department of Social Management Sciences, Bayero University, Kano.

Teece, D. J. (2010). Business models, business strategy and innovation. *Long Range Planning, 43*(2-3), 172–194. doi:10.1016/j.lrp.2009.07.003

Template for confirmation of interest and Submission of Financial Proposal is available under the procurement section of UNDP Pacific Office in Fiji. (n.d.). www.pacific.undp.org

Terreblanche, S. (2012). *Lost in Transformation: South Africa's search for a New Future Since 1986*. KMM Review Publishing Company.

The Economist. (2009). *After the Storm*. https://www.economist.com/node/14548881

The Holy Bible, Literal Standard Version (LSV). (2020). *Covenant Press, Covenant Christian Coalition*. Retrieved from http://self.gutenberg.org/

The Nigerian National Housing Policy (2012).

The Open University. (2014). *'Unit 6: Your initiative: developing options for action', B718: Mary Seacole Programme*. The Open University.

The Open University. (2015). *'Methods of inquiry: other sources of information', B718: Mary Seacole Programme*. The Open University.

The Open University. (n.d.). *Evaluating the quality of information: The PROMPT criteria*. Available at http://learn.open.ac.uk/mod/oucontent/view.php?id=451704

Thompson, J., Alvy, G., & Lees, A. (2000). Social Entrepreneurship: A New Look at the People and the Potential. *Management Decision, 38*(5).

Thompson, J. L. G., Alvy, G., & Lees, A. (2000). Social entrepreneurship – A new look at the people and the potential. *Management Decision, 38*(5), 328–338. doi:10.1108/00251740010340517

Thompson, J. L., & Doherty, B. (2006). The diverse world of social enterprise. *International Journal of Social Economics, 33*(5/6), 361–375. doi:10.1108/03068290610660643

Tomlinson, M. (2008). The degree is not enough: Students' perceptions of the role of higher education credentials for graduate work and employability. *British Journal of Sociology of Education, 29*(1), 49–61. doi:10.1080/01425690701737457

Torrington, D., & Hall, L. (1998). *Human Resource Management*. Prentice Hall Europe.

Tortella, G., Quiroga, G., & Moral-Arce, I. (2011). *Nature or Nurture? Factors of Entrepreneurship: A Comparative Approach*. Institute of Latin American Studies Columbia University.

Tshishonga, N. (2021). Economic Survival: Towards balancing the Financial and Intellectual Act? In Higher Education, Community Engagement and Entrepreneurship in Southern Africa (pp. 68-95). Cambridge Scholars Publishing.

Tshishonga, N. (2020). Profiling Student Entrepreneurial Enterprises at Howard College Campus: Students' Livelihood Opportunities and Challenges. In A. O. Ayandibu (Ed.), *Reshaping Entrepreneurship Education with Strategy and Innovation* (pp. 197–216). IGI Global.

Tuckman, B., & Jensen, M. (1977). Stages of small-group development revisited. *Group & Organization Studies, 2*, 419–427.

Tumilowicz, A., Ruel, M. T., Pelto, G., Pelletier, D., Monterrosa, E. C., Lapping, K., Kraemer, K., De Regil, L. M., Bergeron, G., Arabi, M., Neufeld, L., & Sturke, R. (2018). we need the full details and year Implementation Science in Nutrition: Concepts and Frameworks for an Emerging Field of Science and Practice. *Current Developments in Nutrition, 3*(3), nzy080. Advance online publication. doi:10.1093/cdn/nzy080 PMID:30864563

Tusting, L. S., Bisanzio, D., Alabaster, G., Cameron, E., Cibulskis, R., Davies, M., Flaxman, S., Gibson, H. S., Jakob Knudsen, J., Mbogo, C., Okumu, F. O., von Seidlein, L., Weiss, D. J., Lindsay, S. W., Gething, P. W., & Bhatt, S. (2019). Mapping changes in housing in sub-Saharan Africa from 2000 to 2015. *Nature Research Letter*. doi:10.1038/s41586-019-1050-5

Tusting, L. S., Gething, P. W., Gibson, H. S., Greenwood, B., Knudsen, J., Lindsay, S. W., & Bhatt, S. (2020). Housing and child health in Sub-Saharan Africa: A cross-sectional analysis. *PLoS Medicine, 17*(3). https://doi.org/10.1371/journal.pmed.1003055

United Nations. (n.d.). *The 17 Goals. Department of Economic and Social Affairs*. Retrieved from: https://sdgs.un.org/goals

United States Agency for International Development, Bureau for Europe and Eurasia, Office of Democracy, Governance and Social Transition (USAID). (2014). *2013 CSO Sustainability Index for Central and Eastern Europe and Eurasia*. USAID. Retrieved from https://www.usaid.gov/sites/default/files/documents/1863/EuropeEurasia_FY2014_CSOSI_Report.pdf

Valtioneuvosto. (2021). *Social enterprises to benefit from more advice and competence – A call for funding launched to establish a new centre of expertise*. Available at: https://valtioneuvosto.fi/en/-/1410877/social-enterprises-to-benefit-from-more-advice-and-competence-a-call-for-funding-launched-to-establish-a-new-centre-of-expertise

van Aaken, D., & Buchner, F. (2020). Religion and CSR: A systematic literature review. *Journal of Business Economics*, *90*(5-6), 917–945. doi:10.100711573-020-00977-z

Van De Van, A. H., Sapienza, H. J., & Villanueva, J. (2007). Entrepreneurial pursuits of self and collective interests. *Strategic Entrepreneurship Journal*, *1*(3-4), 353–370. doi:10.1002ej.34

Van Iwaarden, J., Van Der Wiele, T., Williams, R., & Moxham, C. (2009). Charities: How important is performance to donors? *International Journal of Quality & Reliability Management*, *10*(2), 2–22. doi:10.1108/02656710910924143

Vanguard. (2016). *FG plans #1trn social housing scheme*. www.vanguard.com/2016/10/fgplans-n1trn-social housing-scheme/

Vasconcelos, A. F. (2020). Individual spiritual capital: Meaning, a conceptual framework. *Journal of Work-Applied Management*, *13*(1), 117–141. doi:10.1108/JWAM-08-2020-0038

Verheul, I., & Van Mil, L. (2011). What determines the growth ambition of Dutch early-stage entrepreneurs? *International Journal of Entrepreneurial Venturing*, *3*(2), 183–207. doi:10.1504/IJEV.2011.039340

Verstraete, T. (2002). Essay on the singularity of entrepreneurship as a research domain. *Éditions de l'ADREG*.

Villeneuve-Smith, F., & Temple, N. (2015). *Leading the World in Social Enterprise – State of Social Enterprise Survey 2015*. Social Enterprise UK. http://socialenterprise.org.uk/public/uploads/editor/SEUK_StateofSocialEnterprise_FINAL_WEB.pdf

Vincent Ponroy, J., Lê, P., & Pradies, C. (2019). In a Family Way? A model of family firm identity maintenance by non-family members. *Organization Studies*, *40*(6), 859–886. doi:10.1177/0170840619836707

Vivar, C. G., Canga Armayor, A., & Canga Armayor, N. (2011). *Qualitative Research Proposal: A Model to Help Novice Researchers*. Available at: https://www.researchgate.net/profile/Ana_Armayor/publication/282700875_Qualitative_research_proposal_A_model_to_help_novice_researchers/links/56447b0608ae451880a7d221/Qualitative-research-proposal-A-model-to-help-novice-researchers.pdf?

W.K. Kellogg Foundation. (2004). *Logic Model Development Guide. Using Logic Models to Bring Together Planning, Evaluation, and Action.* https://www.aacu.org/sites/default/files/LogicModel.pdf

Waddock, S. A., & Post, J. E. (1991). Social entrepreneurs and catalytic change. *Public Administration Review, 51*(5), 393–401. doi:10.2307/976408

Weber, M. (1905). The Protestant Ethic and the Spirit of Capitalism. In *Die protestantische Ethik und der Geist des Kapitalismus.* Academic Press.

Weber, M. (1965). *The Sociology of Religion.* Methuen.

Weber, M. (2011). The Protestant Ethic and Spirit of Capitalism. In S. Kalberg (Ed.), *The Protestant Ethic and The Spirit of Capitalism.* Oxford University Press.

Weerawardena, J., & Mort, S. G. (2006). Investigating social entrepreneurship: A multidimensional model. *Journal of World Business, 41*(1), 21–35. doi:10.1016/j.jwb.2005.09.001

WEF. (2013). *Global agenda councils -youth unemployment visualization 2013.* WEF.

Weiss, A. (2004). *Logic Model Development Guide. Using Logic Models to Bring Together Planning, Evaluation, and Action.* https://www.aacu.org/sites/default/files/LogicModel.pdf

Wellman, N. (2010). The employability attributes required of new marketing graduates. *Marketing Intelligence & Planning, 28*(7), 908–930. doi:10.1108/02634501011086490

West, M. (2012). *Effective Teamwork: Practical Lessons from Organizational Research.* BPS Blackwell. (Original publication 1994)

Wheatley, M., & Frieze, D. (2011). *Walk Out Walk On: A Learning Journey Into Communities Daring to Live the Future Now.* Berrett-Koehler Publishers.

Whitehead, C., & Scanlon, K. J. (Eds.). (2007). *Social housing in Europe.* London School of Economics and Political Science.

Whittington, R. (1993). What is Strategy and does it matter? Thomson Business Press.

Wijaya, N. H. S., & Rinaldi, E. (2018). Parenting Style, Risk Propensity, and Entrepreneurial Interest. *Proceedings of the 7th International Conference on Entrepreneurship and Business Management, 1*, 296-301. 10.5220/0008492102960301

Wilkinson, C. (2014). *A Map of SE and Their Eco-systems in Europe.* European Commission. https://www.wikipreneurship.eu/images/d/de/SE_mapping_results.pdf

Wilkinson, C. (2015). *A Map of SE and Their Eco-systems in Europe. Country Report.* European Commission. https://ec.europa.eu/social/BlobServlet?docId=13102&langId=

Wilton, N. (2011). Do employability skills really matter in the UK graduate labour market? The case of business and management graduates. *Work, Employment and Society, 25*(1), 85–100. doi:10.1177/0950017010389244

Winkelmann, R. (2009). Unemployment, social capital, and subjective well-being. *Journal of Happiness Studies, 10*(4), 421–430. doi:10.100710902-008-9097-2

Wongtschowski, A. (2015) social enterprise capabilities and human development *DPU Working Paper* No.174, Special Issue on Capability Approach in Development Planning and Urban Design

World Bank Group. (2018). *An Incomplete Transition: Overcoming the Legacy of Exclusion in South Africa*. UCT Press.

World Bank. (2013). *World development report: Jobs*. Author.

Worldwide, J. A. (2011). *Generation jobless: the challenge of global youth unemployment*. www.jaworldwide.org

Yin, R. (2003). Applied Social Research Methods Series: Vol. 34. *Applications of case study research* (2nd ed.). Sage.

Yukl, G. (2013). *Leadership in Organizations* (Global edition). Pearson.

Zahra, S. A., Rawhouser, H. N., Bhawe, N., Neubaum, D. O., & Hayton, J. C. (2008). Globalization of social entrepreneurship opportunities. *Strategic Entrepreneurship Journal*, *2*(2), 117–131. doi:10.1002ej.43

# Related References

To continue our tradition of advancing information science and technology research, we have compiled a list of recommended IGI Global readings. These references will provide additional information and guidance to further enrich your knowledge and assist you with your own research and future publications.

Abtahi, M. S., Behboudi, L., & Hasanabad, H. M. (2017). Factors Affecting Internet Advertising Adoption in Ad Agencies. *International Journal of Innovation in the Digital Economy*, *8*(4), 18–29. doi:10.4018/IJIDE.2017100102

Agrawal, S. (2017). The Impact of Emerging Technologies and Social Media on Different Business(es): Marketing and Management. In O. Rishi & A. Sharma (Eds.), *Maximizing Business Performance and Efficiency Through Intelligent Systems* (pp. 37–49). Hershey, PA: IGI Global. doi:10.4018/978-1-5225-2234-8.ch002

Alnoukari, M., Razouk, R., & Hanano, A. (2016). BSC-SI: A Framework for Integrating Strategic Intelligence in Corporate Strategic Management. *International Journal of Social and Organizational Dynamics in IT*, *5*(2), 1–14. doi:10.4018/IJSODIT.2016070101

Alnoukari, M., Razouk, R., & Hanano, A. (2016). BSC-SI, A Framework for Integrating Strategic Intelligence in Corporate Strategic Management. *International Journal of Strategic Information Technology and Applications*, *7*(1), 32–44. doi:10.4018/IJSITA.2016010103

Altındağ, E. (2016). Current Approaches in Change Management. In A. Goksoy (Ed.), *Organizational Change Management Strategies in Modern Business* (pp. 24–51). Hershey, PA: IGI Global. doi:10.4018/978-1-4666-9533-7.ch002

Alvarez-Dionisi, L. E., Turner, R., & Mittra, M. (2016). Global Project Management Trends. *International Journal of Information Technology Project Management*, *7*(3), 54–73. doi:10.4018/IJITPM.2016070104

Anantharaman, R. N., Rajeswari, K. S., Angusamy, A., & Kuppusamy, J. (2017). Role of Self-Efficacy and Collective Efficacy as Moderators of Occupational Stress Among Software Development Professionals. *International Journal of Human Capital and Information Technology Professionals*, *8*(2), 45–58. doi:10.4018/IJHCITP.2017040103

Aninze, F., El-Gohary, H., & Hussain, J. (2018). The Role of Microfinance to Empower Women: The Case of Developing Countries. *International Journal of Customer Relationship Marketing and Management*, *9*(1), 54–78. doi:10.4018/IJCRMM.2018010104

Arsenijević, O. M., Orčić, D., & Kastratović, E. (2017). Development of an Optimization Tool for Intangibles in SMEs: A Case Study from Serbia with a Pilot Research in the Prestige by Milka Company. In M. Vemić (Ed.), *Optimal Management Strategies in Small and Medium Enterprises* (pp. 320–347). Hershey, PA: IGI Global. doi:10.4018/978-1-5225-1949-2.ch015

Aryanto, V. D., Wismantoro, Y., & Widyatmoko, K. (2018). Implementing Eco-Innovation by Utilizing the Internet to Enhance Firm's Marketing Performance: Study of Green Batik Small and Medium Enterprises in Indonesia. *International Journal of E-Business Research*, *14*(1), 21–36. doi:10.4018/IJEBR.2018010102

Atiku, S. O., & Fields, Z. (2017). Multicultural Orientations for 21st Century Global Leadership. In N. Baporikar (Ed.), *Management Education for Global Leadership* (pp. 28–51). Hershey, PA: IGI Global. doi:10.4018/978-1-5225-1013-0.ch002

Atiku, S. O., & Fields, Z. (2018). Organisational Learning Dimensions and Talent Retention Strategies for the Service Industries. In N. Baporikar (Ed.), *Global Practices in Knowledge Management for Societal and Organizational Development* (pp. 358–381). Hershey, PA: IGI Global. doi:10.4018/978-1-5225-3009-1.ch017

Ávila, L., & Teixeira, L. (2018). The Main Concepts Behind the Dematerialization of Business Processes. In M. Khosrow-Pour, D.B.A. (Ed.), Encyclopedia of Information Science and Technology, Fourth Edition (pp. 888-898). Hershey, PA: IGI Global. doi:10.4018/978-1-5225-2255-3.ch076

Bartens, Y., Chunpir, H. I., Schulte, F., & Voß, S. (2017). Business/IT Alignment in Two-Sided Markets: A COBIT 5 Analysis for Media Streaming Business Models. In S. De Haes & W. Van Grembergen (Eds.), *Strategic IT Governance and Alignment in Business Settings* (pp. 82–111). Hershey, PA: IGI Global. doi:10.4018/978-1-5225-0861-8.ch004

Bashayreh, A. M. (2018). Organizational Culture and Organizational Performance. In W. Lee & F. Sabetzadeh (Eds.), *Contemporary Knowledge and Systems Science* (pp. 50–69). Hershey, PA: IGI Global. doi:10.4018/978-1-5225-5655-8.ch003

Bedford, D. A. (2018). Sustainable Knowledge Management Strategies: Aligning Business Capabilities and Knowledge Management Goals. In N. Baporikar (Ed.), *Global Practices in Knowledge Management for Societal and Organizational Development* (pp. 46–73). Hershey, PA: IGI Global. doi:10.4018/978-1-5225-3009-1.ch003

Benmoussa, F., Nakara, W. A., & Jaouen, A. (2016). The Use of Social Media by SMEs in the Tourism Industry. In I. Lee (Ed.), *Encyclopedia of E-Commerce Development, Implementation, and Management* (pp. 2159–2170). Hershey, PA: IGI Global. doi:10.4018/978-1-4666-9787-4.ch155

Berger, R. (2016). Indigenous Management and Bottom of Pyramid Countries: The Role of National Institutions. In U. Aung & P. Ordoñez de Pablos (Eds.), *Managerial Strategies and Practice in the Asian Business Sector* (pp. 107–123). Hershey, PA: IGI Global. doi:10.4018/978-1-4666-9758-4.ch007

Bharwani, S., & Musunuri, D. (2018). Reflection as a Process From Theory to Practice. In M. Khosrow-Pour, D.B.A. (Ed.), Encyclopedia of Information Science and Technology, Fourth Edition (pp. 1529-1539). Hershey, PA: IGI Global. doi:10.4018/978-1-5225-2255-3.ch132

Bhatt, G. D., Wang, Z., & Rodger, J. A. (2017). Information Systems Capabilities and Their Effects on Competitive Advantages: A Study of Chinese Companies. *Information Resources Management Journal, 30*(3), 41–57. doi:10.4018/IRMJ.2017070103

Bhushan, M., & Yadav, A. (2017). Concept of Cloud Computing in ESB. In R. Bhadoria, N. Chaudhari, G. Tomar, & S. Singh (Eds.), *Exploring Enterprise Service Bus in the Service-Oriented Architecture Paradigm* (pp. 116–127). Hershey, PA: IGI Global. doi:10.4018/978-1-5225-2157-0.ch008

Bhushan, S. (2017). System Dynamics Base-Model of Humanitarian Supply Chain (HSCM) in Disaster Prone Eco-Communities of India: A Discussion on Simulation and Scenario Results. *International Journal of System Dynamics Applications, 6*(3), 20–37. doi:10.4018/IJSDA.2017070102

Biswas, A., & De, A. K. (2017). On Development of a Fuzzy Stochastic Programming Model with Its Application to Business Management. In S. Trivedi, S. Dey, A. Kumar, & T. Panda (Eds.), *Handbook of Research on Advanced Data Mining Techniques and Applications for Business Intelligence* (pp. 353–378). Hershey, PA: IGI Global. doi:10.4018/978-1-5225-2031-3.ch021

Bücker, J., & Ernste, K. (2018). Use of Brand Heroes in Strategic Reputation Management: The Case of Bacardi, Adidas, and Daimler. In A. Erdemir (Ed.), *Reputation Management Techniques in Public Relations* (pp. 126–150). Hershey, PA: IGI Global. doi:10.4018/978-1-5225-3619-2.ch007

Bureš, V. (2018). Industry 4.0 From the Systems Engineering Perspective: Alternative Holistic Framework Development. In R. Brunct-Thornton & F. Martinez (Eds.), *Analyzing the Impacts of Industry 4.0 in Modern Business Environments* (pp. 199–223). Hershey, PA: IGI Global. doi:10.4018/978-1-5225-3468-6.ch011

Buzady, Z. (2017). Resolving the Magic Cube of Effective Case Teaching: Benchmarking Case Teaching Practices in Emerging Markets – Insights from the Central European University Business School, Hungary. In D. Latusek (Ed.), *Case Studies as a Teaching Tool in Management Education* (pp. 79–103). Hershey, PA: IGI Global. doi:10.4018/978-1-5225-0770-3.ch005

Campatelli, G., Richter, A., & Stocker, A. (2016). Participative Knowledge Management to Empower Manufacturing Workers. *International Journal of Knowledge Management, 12*(4), 37–50. doi:10.4018/IJKM.2016100103

Căpusneanu, S., & Topor, D. I. (2018). Business Ethics and Cost Management in SMEs: Theories of Business Ethics and Cost Management Ethos. In I. Oncioiu (Ed.), *Ethics and Decision-Making for Sustainable Business Practices* (pp. 109–127). Hershey, PA: IGI Global. doi:10.4018/978-1-5225-3773-1.ch007

Carneiro, A. (2016). Maturity in Health Organization Information Systems: Metrics and Privacy Perspectives. *International Journal of Privacy and Health Information Management, 4*(2), 1–18. doi:10.4018/IJPHIM.2016070101

Chan, R. L., Mo, P. L., & Moon, K. K. (2018). Strategic and Tactical Measures in Managing Enterprise Risks: A Study of the Textile and Apparel Industry. In K. Strang, M. Korstanje, & N. Vajjhala (Eds.), *Research, Practices, and Innovations in Global Risk and Contingency Management* (pp. 1–19). Hershey, PA: IGI Global. doi:10.4018/978-1-5225-4754-9.ch001

Chandan, H. C. (2016). Motivations and Challenges of Female Entrepreneurship in Developed and Developing Economies. In N. Baporikar (Ed.), *Handbook of Research on Entrepreneurship in the Contemporary Knowledge-Based Global Economy* (pp. 260–286). Hershey, PA: IGI Global. doi:10.4018/978-1-4666-8798-1.ch012

Charlier, S. D., Burke-Smalley, L. A., & Fisher, S. L. (2018). Undergraduate Programs in the U.S: A Contextual and Content-Based Analysis. In J. Mendy (Ed.), *Teaching Human Resources and Organizational Behavior at the College Level* (pp. 26–57). Hershey, PA: IGI Global. doi:10.4018/978-1-5225-2820-3.ch002

Chaudhuri, S. (2016). Application of Web-Based Geographical Information System (GIS) in E-Business. In U. Panwar, R. Kumar, & N. Ray (Eds.), *Handbook of Research on Promotional Strategies and Consumer Influence in the Service Sector* (pp. 389–405). Hershey, PA: IGI Global. doi:10.4018/978-1-5225-0143-5.ch023

Choudhuri, P. S. (2016). An Empirical Study on the Quality of Services Offered by the Private Life Insurers in Burdwan. In U. Panwar, R. Kumar, & N. Ray (Eds.), *Handbook of Research on Promotional Strategies and Consumer Influence in the Service Sector* (pp. 31–55). Hershey, PA: IGI Global. doi:10.4018/978-1-5225-0143-5.ch002

Dahlberg, T., Kivijärvi, H., & Saarinen, T. (2017). IT Investment Consistency and Other Factors Influencing the Success of IT Performance. In S. De Haes & W. Van Grembergen (Eds.), *Strategic IT Governance and Alignment in Business Settings* (pp. 176–208). Hershey, PA: IGI Global. doi:10.4018/978-1-5225-0861-8.ch007

Damnjanović, A. M. (2017). Knowledge Management Optimization through IT and E-Business Utilization: A Qualitative Study on Serbian SMEs. In M. Vemić (Ed.), *Optimal Management Strategies in Small and Medium Enterprises* (pp. 249–267). Hershey, PA: IGI Global. doi:10.4018/978-1-5225-1949-2.ch012

Daneshpour, H. (2017). Integrating Sustainable Development into Project Portfolio Management through Application of Open Innovation. In M. Vemić (Ed.), *Optimal Management Strategies in Small and Medium Enterprises* (pp. 370–387). Hershey, PA: IGI Global. doi:10.4018/978-1-5225-1949-2.ch017

Daniel, A. D., & Reis de Castro, V. (2018). Entrepreneurship Education: How to Measure the Impact on Nascent Entrepreneurs. In A. Carrizo Moreira, J. Guilherme Leitão Dantas, & F. Manuel Valente (Eds.), *Nascent Entrepreneurship and Successful New Venture Creation* (pp. 85–110). Hershey, PA: IGI Global. doi:10.4018/978-1-5225-2936-1.ch004

David, F., van der Sijde, P., & van den Besselaar, P. (2016). Enterpreneurial Incentives, Obstacles, and Management in University-Business Co-Operation: The Case of Indonesia. In J. Saiz-Álvarez (Ed.), *Handbook of Research on Social Entrepreneurship and Solidarity Economics* (pp. 499–518). Hershey, PA: IGI Global. doi:10.4018/978-1-5225-0097-1.ch024

David, R., Swami, B. N., & Tangirala, S. (2018). Ethics Impact on Knowledge Management in Organizational Development: A Case Study. In N. Baporikar (Ed.), *Global Practices in Knowledge Management for Societal and Organizational Development* (pp. 19–45). Hershey, PA: IGI Global. doi:10.4018/978-1-5225-3009-1.ch002

Delias, P., & Lakiotaki, K. (2018). Discovering Process Horizontal Boundaries to Facilitate Process Comprehension. *International Journal of Operations Research and Information Systems*, *9*(2), 1–31. doi:10.4018/IJORIS.2018040101

Denholm, J., & Lee-Davies, L. (2018). Success Factors for Games in Business and Project Management. In *Enhancing Education and Training Initiatives Through Serious Games* (pp. 34–68). Hershey, PA: IGI Global. doi:10.4018/978-1-5225-3689-5.ch002

Deshpande, M. (2017). Best Practices in Management Institutions for Global Leadership: Policy Aspects. In N. Baporikar (Ed.), *Management Education for Global Leadership* (pp. 1–27). Hershey, PA: IGI Global. doi:10.4018/978-1-5225-1013-0.ch001

Deshpande, M. (2018). Policy Perspectives for SMEs Knowledge Management. In N. Baporikar (Ed.), *Knowledge Integration Strategies for Entrepreneurship and Sustainability* (pp. 23–46). Hershey, PA: IGI Global. doi:10.4018/978-1-5225-5115-7.ch002

Dezdar, S. (2017). ERP Implementation Projects in Asian Countries: A Comparative Study on Iran and China. *International Journal of Information Technology Project Management*, *8*(3), 52–68. doi:10.4018/IJITPM.2017070104

Domingos, D., Martinho, R., & Varajão, J. (2016). Controlled Flexibility in Healthcare Processes: A BPMN-Extension Approach. In M. Cruz-Cunha, I. Miranda, R. Martinho, & R. Rijo (Eds.), *Encyclopedia of E-Health and Telemedicine* (pp. 521–535). Hershey, PA: IGI Global. doi:10.4018/978-1-4666-9978-6.ch040

Domingos, D., Respício, A., & Martinho, R. (2017). Reliability of IoT-Aware BPMN Healthcare Processes. In C. Reis & M. Maximiano (Eds.), *Internet of Things and Advanced Application in Healthcare* (pp. 214–248). Hershey, PA: IGI Global. doi:10.4018/978-1-5225-1820-4.ch008

Dosumu, O., Hussain, J., & El-Gohary, H. (2017). An Exploratory Study of the Impact of Government Policies on the Development of Small and Medium Enterprises in Developing Countries: The Case of Nigeria. *International Journal of Customer Relationship Marketing and Management*, *8*(4), 51–62. doi:10.4018/IJCRMM.2017100104

Durst, S., Bruns, G., & Edvardsson, I. R. (2017). Retaining Knowledge in Smaller Building and Construction Firms. *International Journal of Knowledge and Systems Science*, *8*(3), 1–12. doi:10.4018/IJKSS.2017070101

Edvardsson, I. R., & Durst, S. (2017). Outsourcing, Knowledge, and Learning: A Critical Review. *International Journal of Knowledge-Based Organizations*, *7*(2), 13–26. doi:10.4018/IJKBO.2017040102

Edwards, J. S. (2018). Integrating Knowledge Management and Business Processes. In M. Khosrow-Pour, D.B.A. (Ed.), Encyclopedia of Information Science and Technology, Fourth Edition (pp. 5046-5055). Hershey, PA: IGI Global. doi:10.4018/978-1-5225-2255-3.ch437

Ejiogu, A. O. (2018). Economics of Farm Management. In *Agricultural Finance and Opportunities for Investment and Expansion* (pp. 56–72). Hershey, PA: IGI Global. doi:10.4018/978-1-5225-3059-6.ch003

Ekanem, I., & Abiade, G. E. (2018). Factors Influencing the Use of E-Commerce by Small Enterprises in Nigeria. *International Journal of ICT Research in Africa and the Middle East*, *7*(1), 37–53. doi:10.4018/IJICTRAME.2018010103

Ekanem, I., & Alrossais, L. A. (2017). Succession Challenges Facing Family Businesses in Saudi Arabia. In P. Zgheib (Ed.), *Entrepreneurship and Business Innovation in the Middle East* (pp. 122–146). Hershey, PA: IGI Global. doi:10.4018/978-1-5225-2066-5.ch007

El Faquih, L., & Fredj, M. (2017). Ontology-Based Framework for Quality in Configurable Process Models. *Journal of Electronic Commerce in Organizations*, *15*(2), 48–60. doi:10.4018/JECO.2017040104

El-Gohary, H., & El-Gohary, Z. (2016). An Attempt to Explore Electronic Marketing Adoption and Implementation Aspects in Developing Countries: The Case of Egypt. *International Journal of Customer Relationship Marketing and Management*, *7*(4), 1–26. doi:10.4018/IJCRMM.2016100101

Entico, G. J. (2016). Knowledge Management and the Medical Health Librarians: A Perception Study. In J. Yap, M. Perez, M. Ayson, & G. Entico (Eds.), *Special Library Administration, Standardization and Technological Integration* (pp. 52–77). Hershey, PA: IGI Global. doi:10.4018/978-1-4666-9542-9.ch003

Faisal, M. N., & Talib, F. (2017). Building Ambidextrous Supply Chains in SMEs: How to Tackle the Barriers? *International Journal of Information Systems and Supply Chain Management*, *10*(4), 80–100. doi:10.4018/IJISSCM.2017100105

Fernandes, T. M., Gomes, J., & Romão, M. (2017). Investments in E-Government: A Benefit Management Case Study. *International Journal of Electronic Government Research*, *13*(3), 1–17. doi:10.4018/IJEGR.2017070101

Fouda, F. A. (2016). A Suggested Curriculum in Career Education to Develop Business Secondary Schools Students' Career Knowledge Management Domains and Professional Thinking. *International Journal of Technology Diffusion*, *7*(2), 42–62. doi:10.4018/IJTD.2016040103

Gallardo-Vázquez, D., & Pajuelo-Moreno, M. L. (2016). How Spanish Universities are Promoting Entrepreneurship through Your Own Lines of Teaching and Research? In L. Carvalho (Ed.), *Handbook of Research on Entrepreneurial Success and its Impact on Regional Development* (pp. 431–454). Hershey, PA: IGI Global. doi:10.4018/978-1-4666-9567-2.ch019

Gao, S. S., Oreal, S., & Zhang, J. (2018). Contemporary Financial Risk Management Perceptions and Practices of Small-Sized Chinese Businesses. In I. Management Association (Ed.), Global Business Expansion: Concepts, Methodologies, Tools, and Applications (pp. 917-931). Hershey, PA: IGI Global. doi:10.4018/978-1-5225-5481-3.ch041

Garg, R., & Berning, S. C. (2017). Indigenous Chinese Management Philosophies: Key Concepts and Relevance for Modern Chinese Firms. In B. Christiansen & G. Koc (Eds.), *Transcontinental Strategies for Industrial Development and Economic Growth* (pp. 43–57). Hershey, PA: IGI Global. doi:10.4018/978-1-5225-2160-0.ch003

Gencer, Y. G. (2017). Supply Chain Management in Retailing Business. In U. Akkucuk (Ed.), *Ethics and Sustainability in Global Supply Chain Management* (pp. 197–210). Hershey, PA: IGI Global. doi:10.4018/978-1-5225-2036-8.ch011

Giacosa, E. (2016). Innovation in Luxury Fashion Businesses as a Means for the Regional Development. In L. Carvalho (Ed.), *Handbook of Research on Entrepreneurial Success and its Impact on Regional Development* (pp. 206–222). Hershey, PA: IGI Global. doi:10.4018/978-1-4666-9567-2.ch010

Giacosa, E. (2018). The Increasing of the Regional Development Thanks to the Luxury Business Innovation. In L. Carvalho (Ed.), *Handbook of Research on Entrepreneurial Ecosystems and Social Dynamics in a Globalized World* (pp. 260–273). Hershey, PA: IGI Global. doi:10.4018/978-1-5225-3525-6.ch011

Gianni, M., & Gotzamani, K. (2016). Integrated Management Systems and Information Management Systems: Common Threads. In P. Papajorgji, F. Pinet, A. Guimarães, & J. Papathanasiou (Eds.), *Automated Enterprise Systems for Maximizing Business Performance* (pp. 195–214). Hershey, PA: IGI Global. doi:10.4018/978-1-4666-8841-4.ch011

Gianni, M., Gotzamani, K., & Linden, I. (2016). How a BI-wise Responsible Integrated Management System May Support Food Traceability. *International Journal of Decision Support System Technology*, *8*(2), 1–17. doi:10.4018/IJDSST.2016040101

Glykas, M., & George, J. (2017). Quality and Process Management Systems in the UAE Maritime Industry. *International Journal of Productivity Management and Assessment Technologies*, *5*(1), 20–39. doi:10.4018/IJPMAT.2017010102

Glykas, M., Valiris, G., Kokkinaki, A., & Koutsoukou, Z. (2018). Banking Business Process Management Implementation. *International Journal of Productivity Management and Assessment Technologies*, *6*(1), 50–69. doi:10.4018/IJPMAT.2018010104

Gomes, J., & Romão, M. (2017). The Balanced Scorecard: Keeping Updated and Aligned with Today's Business Trends. *International Journal of Productivity Management and Assessment Technologies*, *5*(2), 1–15. doi:10.4018/IJPMAT.2017070101

Gomes, J., & Romão, M. (2017). Aligning Information Systems and Technology with Benefit Management and Balanced Scorecard. In S. De Haes & W. Van Grembergen (Eds.), *Strategic IT Governance and Alignment in Business Settings* (pp. 112–131). Hershey, PA: IGI Global. doi:10.4018/978-1-5225-0861-8.ch005

Grefen, P., & Turetken, O. (2017). Advanced Business Process Management in Networked E-Business Scenarios. *International Journal of E-Business Research*, *13*(4), 70–104. doi:10.4018/IJEBR.2017100105

Haider, A., & Saetang, S. (2017). Strategic IT Alignment in Service Sector. In S. Rozenes & Y. Cohen (Eds.), *Handbook of Research on Strategic Alliances and Value Co-Creation in the Service Industry* (pp. 231–258). Hershey, PA: IGI Global. doi:10.4018/978-1-5225-2084-9.ch012

Haider, A., & Tang, S. S. (2016). Maximising Value Through IT and Business Alignment: A Case of IT Governance Institutionalisation at a Thai Bank. *International Journal of Technology Diffusion*, *7*(3), 33–58. doi:10.4018/IJTD.2016070104

Hajilari, A. B., Ghadaksaz, M., & Fasghandis, G. S. (2017). Assessing Organizational Readiness for Implementing ERP System Using Fuzzy Expert System Approach. *International Journal of Enterprise Information Systems*, *13*(1), 67–85. doi:10.4018/IJEIS.2017010105

Haldorai, A., Ramu, A., & Murugan, S. (2018). Social Aware Cognitive Radio Networks: Effectiveness of Social Networks as a Strategic Tool for Organizational Business Management. In H. Bansal, G. Shrivastava, G. Nguyen, & L. Stanciu (Eds.), *Social Network Analytics for Contemporary Business Organizations* (pp. 188–202). Hershey, PA: IGI Global. doi:10.4018/978-1-5225-5097-6.ch010

Hall, O. P. Jr. (2017). Social Media Driven Management Education. *International Journal of Knowledge-Based Organizations*, *7*(2), 43–59. doi:10.4018/IJKBO.2017040104

Hanifah, H., Halim, H. A., Ahmad, N. H., & Vafaei-Zadeh, A. (2017). Innovation Culture as a Mediator Between Specific Human Capital and Innovation Performance Among Bumiputera SMEs in Malaysia. In N. Ahmad, T. Ramayah, H. Halim, & S. Rahman (Eds.), *Handbook of Research on Small and Medium Enterprises in Developing Countries* (pp. 261–279). Hershey, PA: IGI Global. doi:10.4018/978-1-5225-2165-5.ch012

Hartlieb, S., & Silvius, G. (2017). Handling Uncertainty in Project Management and Business Development: Similarities and Differences. In Y. Raydugin (Ed.), *Handbook of Research on Leveraging Risk and Uncertainties for Effective Project Management* (pp. 337–362). Hershey, PA: IGI Global. doi:10.4018/978-1-5225-1790-0.ch016

Hass, K. B. (2017). Living on the Edge: Managing Project Complexity. In Y. Raydugin (Ed.), *Handbook of Research on Leveraging Risk and Uncertainties for Effective Project Management* (pp. 177–201). Hershey, PA: IGI Global. doi:10.4018/978-1-5225-1790-0.ch009

Hassan, A., & Privitera, D. S. (2016). Google AdSense as a Mobile Technology in Education. In J. Holland (Ed.), *Wearable Technology and Mobile Innovations for Next-Generation Education* (pp. 200–223). Hershey, PA: IGI Global. doi:10.4018/978-1-5225-0069-8.ch011

Hassan, A., & Rahimi, R. (2016). Consuming "Innovation" in Tourism: Augmented Reality as an Innovation Tool in Digital Tourism Marketing. In N. Pappas & I. Bregoli (Eds.), *Global Dynamics in Travel, Tourism, and Hospitality* (pp. 130–147). Hershey, PA: IGI Global. doi:10.4018/978-1-5225-0201-2.ch008

Hawking, P., & Carmine Sellitto, C. (2017). Developing an Effective Strategy for Organizational Business Intelligence. In M. Tavana (Ed.), *Enterprise Information Systems and the Digitalization of Business Functions* (pp. 222–237). Hershey, PA: IGI Global. doi:10.4018/978-1-5225-2382-6.ch010

Hawking, P., & Sellitto, C. (2017). A Fast-Moving Consumer Goods Company and Business Intelligence Strategy Development. *International Journal of Enterprise Information Systems, 13*(2), 22–33. doi:10.4018/IJEIS.2017040102

Hawking, P., & Sellitto, C. (2017). Business Intelligence Strategy: Two Case Studies. *International Journal of Business Intelligence Research, 8*(2), 17–30. doi:10.4018/IJBIR.2017070102

Haynes, J. D., Arockiasamy, S., Al Rashdi, M., & Al Rashdi, S. (2016). Business and E Business Strategies for Coopetition and Thematic Management as a Sustained Basis for Ethics and Social Responsibility in Emerging Markets. In M. Al-Shammari & H. Masri (Eds.), *Ethical and Social Perspectives on Global Business Interaction in Emerging Markets* (pp. 25–39). Hershey, PA: IGI Global. doi:10.4018/978-1-4666-9864-2.ch002

Hee, W. J., Jalleh, G., Lai, H., & Lin, C. (2017). E-Commerce and IT Projects: Evaluation and Management Issues in Australian and Taiwanese Hospitals. *International Journal of Public Health Management and Ethics, 2*(1), 69–90. doi:10.4018/IJPHME.2017010104

Hernandez, A. A. (2018). Exploring the Factors to Green IT Adoption of SMEs in the Philippines. *Journal of Cases on Information Technology, 20*(2), 49–66. doi:10.4018/JCIT.2018040104

Hernandez, A. A., & Ona, S. E. (2016). Green IT Adoption: Lessons from the Philippines Business Process Outsourcing Industry. *International Journal of Social Ecology and Sustainable Development, 7*(1), 1–34. doi:10.4018/IJSESD.2016010101

Hollman, A., Bickford, S., & Hollman, T. (2017). Cyber InSecurity: A Post-Mortem Attempt to Assess Cyber Problems from IT and Business Management Perspectives. *Journal of Cases on Information Technology, 19*(3), 42–70. doi:10.4018/JCIT.2017070104

Igbinakhase, I. (2017). Responsible and Sustainable Management Practices in Developing and Developed Business Environments. In Z. Fields (Ed.), *Collective Creativity for Responsible and Sustainable Business Practice* (pp. 180–207). Hershey, PA: IGI Global. doi:10.4018/978-1-5225-1823-5.ch010

Ilahi, L., Ghannouchi, S. A., & Martinho, R. (2016). A Business Process Management Approach to Home Healthcare Processes: On the Gap between Intention and Reality. In M. Cruz-Cunha, I. Miranda, R. Martinho, & R. Rijo (Eds.), *Encyclopedia of E-Health and Telemedicine* (pp. 439–457). Hershey, PA: IGI Global. doi:10.4018/978-1-4666-9978-6.ch035

Iwata, J. J., & Hoskins, R. G. (2017). Managing Indigenous Knowledge in Tanzania: A Business Perspective. In P. Jain & N. Mnjama (Eds.), *Managing Knowledge Resources and Records in Modern Organizations* (pp. 198–214). Hershey, PA: IGI Global. doi:10.4018/978-1-5225-1965-2.ch012

Jabeen, F., Ahmad, S. Z., & Alkaabi, S. (2016). The Internationalization Decision-Making of United Arab Emirates Family Businesses. In N. Zakaria, A. Abdul-Talib, & N. Osman (Eds.), *Handbook of Research on Impacts of International Business and Political Affairs on the Global Economy* (pp. 1–22). Hershey, PA: IGI Global. doi:10.4018/978-1-4666-9806-2.ch001

Jain, P. (2017). Ethical and Legal Issues in Knowledge Management Life-Cycle in Business. In P. Jain & N. Mnjama (Eds.), *Managing Knowledge Resources and Records in Modern Organizations* (pp. 82–101). Hershey, PA: IGI Global. doi:10.4018/978-1-5225-1965-2.ch006

Jamali, D., Abdallah, H., & Matar, F. (2016). Opportunities and Challenges for CSR Mainstreaming in Business Schools. *International Journal of Technology and Educational Marketing*, *6*(2), 1–29. doi:10.4018/IJTEM.2016070101

James, S., & Hauli, E. (2017). Holistic Management Education at Tanzanian Rural Development Planning Institute. In N. Baporikar (Ed.), *Management Education for Global Leadership* (pp. 112–136). Hershey, PA: IGI Global. doi:10.4018/978-1-5225-1013-0.ch006

Janošková, M., Csikósová, A., & Čulková, K. (2018). Measurement of Company Performance as Part of Its Strategic Management. In R. Leon (Ed.), *Managerial Strategies for Business Sustainability During Turbulent Times* (pp. 309–335). Hershey, PA: IGI Global. doi:10.4018/978-1-5225-2716-9.ch017

Jean-Vasile, A., & Alecu, A. (2017). Theoretical and Practical Approaches in Understanding the Influences of Cost-Productivity-Profit Trinomial in Contemporary Enterprises. In A. Jean Vasile & D. Nicolò (Eds.), *Sustainable Entrepreneurship and Investments in the Green Economy* (pp. 28–62). Hershey, PA: IGI Global. doi:10.4018/978-1-5225-2075-7.ch002

Jha, D. G. (2016). Preparing for Information Technology Driven Changes. In S. Tiwari & L. Nafees (Eds.), *Innovative Management Education Pedagogies for Preparing Next-Generation Leaders* (pp. 258–274). Hershey, PA: IGI Global. doi:10.4018/978-1-4666-9691-4.ch015

Joia, L. A., & Correia, J. C. (2018). CIO Competencies From the IT Professional Perspective: Insights From Brazil. *Journal of Global Information Management*, *26*(2), 74–103. doi:10.4018/JGIM.2018040104

Juma, A., & Mzera, N. (2017). Knowledge Management and Records Management and Competitive Advantage in Business. In P. Jain & N. Mnjama (Eds.), *Managing Knowledge Resources and Records in Modern Organizations* (pp. 15–28). Hershey, PA: IGI Global. doi:10.4018/978-1-5225-1965-2.ch002

K., I., & A, V. (2018). Monitoring and Auditing in the Cloud. In K. Munir (Ed.), *Cloud Computing Technologies for Green Enterprises* (pp. 318-350). Hershey, PA: IGI Global. doi:10.4018/978-1-5225-3038-1.ch013

Kabra, G., Ghosh, V., & Ramesh, A. (2018). Enterprise Integrated Business Process Management and Business Intelligence Framework for Business Process Sustainability. In A. Paul, D. Bhattacharyya, & S. Anand (Eds.), *Green Initiatives for Business Sustainability and Value Creation* (pp. 228–238). Hershey, PA: IGI Global. doi:10.4018/978-1-5225-2662-9.ch010

Kaoud, M. (2017). Investigation of Customer Knowledge Management: A Case Study Research. *International Journal of Service Science, Management, Engineering, and Technology*, *8*(2), 12–22. doi:10.4018/IJSSMET.2017040102

Kara, M. E., & Fırat, S. Ü. (2016). Sustainability, Risk, and Business Intelligence in Supply Chains. In M. Erdoğdu, T. Arun, & I. Ahmad (Eds.), *Handbook of Research on Green Economic Development Initiatives and Strategies* (pp. 501–538). Hershey, PA: IGI Global. doi:10.4018/978-1-5225-0440-5.ch022

Katuu, S. (2018). A Comparative Assessment of Enterprise Content Management Maturity Models. In N. Gwangwava & M. Mutingi (Eds.), *E-Manufacturing and E-Service Strategies in Contemporary Organizations* (pp. 93–118). Hershey, PA: IGI Global. doi:10.4018/978-1-5225-3628-4.ch005

Khan, M. A. (2016). MNEs Management Strategies in Developing Countries: Establishing the Context. In M. Khan (Ed.), *Multinational Enterprise Management Strategies in Developing Countries* (pp. 1–33). Hershey, PA: IGI Global. doi:10.4018/978-1-5225-0276-0.ch001

Khan, M. A. (2016). Operational Approaches in Organizational Structure: A Case for MNEs in Developing Countries. In M. Khan (Ed.), *Multinational Enterprise Management Strategies in Developing Countries* (pp. 129–151). Hershey, PA: IGI Global. doi:10.4018/978-1-5225-0276-0.ch007

Kinnunen, S., Ylä-Kujala, A., Marttonen-Arola, S., Kärri, T., & Baglee, D. (2018). Internet of Things in Asset Management: Insights from Industrial Professionals and Academia. *International Journal of Service Science, Management, Engineering, and Technology*, *9*(2), 104–119. doi:10.4018/IJSSMET.2018040105

Klein, A. Z., Sabino de Freitas, A., Machado, L., Freitas, J. C. Jr, Graziola, P. G. Jr, & Schlemmer, E. (2017). Virtual Worlds Applications for Management Education. In L. Tomei (Ed.), *Exploring the New Era of Technology-Infused Education* (pp. 279–299). Hershey, PA: IGI Global. doi:10.4018/978-1-5225-1709-2.ch017

Kożuch, B., & Jabłoński, A. (2017). Adopting the Concept of Business Models in Public Management. In M. Lewandowski & B. Kożuch (Eds.), *Public Sector Entrepreneurship and the Integration of Innovative Business Models* (pp. 10–46). Hershey, PA: IGI Global. doi:10.4018/978-1-5225-2215-7.ch002

Kumar, J., Adhikary, A., & Jha, A. (2017). Small Active Investors' Perceptions and Preferences Towards Tax Saving Mutual Fund Schemes in Eastern India: An Empirical Note. *International Journal of Asian Business and Information Management, 8*(2), 35–45. doi:10.4018/IJABIM.2017040103

Lassoued, Y., Bouzguenda, L., & Mahmoud, T. (2016). Context-Aware Business Process Versions Management. *International Journal of e-Collaboration, 12*(3), 7–33. doi:10.4018/IJeC.2016070102

Lavassani, K. M., & Movahedi, B. (2017). Applications Driven Information Systems: Beyond Networks toward Business Ecosystems. *International Journal of Innovation in the Digital Economy, 8*(1), 61–75. doi:10.4018/IJIDE.2017010104

Lazzareschi, V. H., & Brito, M. S. (2017). Strategic Information Management: Proposal of Business Project Model. In G. Jamil, A. Soares, & C. Pessoa (Eds.), *Handbook of Research on Information Management for Effective Logistics and Supply Chains* (pp. 59–88). Hershey, PA: IGI Global. doi:10.4018/978-1-5225-0973-8.ch004

Lederer, M., Kurz, M., & Lazarov, P. (2017). Usage and Suitability of Methods for Strategic Business Process Initiatives: A Multi Case Study Research. *International Journal of Productivity Management and Assessment Technologies, 5*(1), 40–51. doi:10.4018/IJPMAT.2017010103

Lee, I. (2017). A Social Enterprise Business Model and a Case Study of Pacific Community Ventures (PCV). In V. Potocan, M. Üngan, & Z. Nedelko (Eds.), *Handbook of Research on Managerial Solutions in Non-Profit Organizations* (pp. 182–204). Hershey, PA: IGI Global. doi:10.4018/978-1-5225-0731-4.ch009

Lee, L. J., & Leu, J. (2016). Exploring the Effectiveness of IT Application and Value Method in the Innovation Performance of Enterprise. *International Journal of Enterprise Information Systems, 12*(2), 47–65. doi:10.4018/IJEIS.2016040104

Lee, Y. (2016). Alignment Effect of Entrepreneurial Orientation and Marketing Orientation on Firm Performance. *International Journal of Customer Relationship Marketing and Management*, *7*(4), 58–69. doi:10.4018/IJCRMM.2016100104

Leon, L. A., Seal, K. C., Przasnyski, Z. H., & Wiedenman, I. (2017). Skills and Competencies Required for Jobs in Business Analytics: A Content Analysis of Job Advertisements Using Text Mining. *International Journal of Business Intelligence Research*, *8*(1), 1–25. doi:10.4018/IJBIR.2017010101

Leu, J., Lee, L. J., & Krischke, A. (2016). Value Engineering-Based Method for Implementing the ISO14001 System in the Green Supply Chains. *International Journal of Strategic Decision Sciences*, *7*(4), 1–20. doi:10.4018/IJSDS.2016100101

Levy, C. L., & Elias, N. I. (2017). SOHO Users' Perceptions of Reliability and Continuity of Cloud-Based Services. In M. Moore (Ed.), *Cybersecurity Breaches and Issues Surrounding Online Threat Protection* (pp. 248–287). Hershey, PA: IGI Global. doi:10.4018/978-1-5225-1941-6.ch011

Levy, M. (2018). Change Management Serving Knowledge Management and Organizational Development: Reflections and Review. In N. Baporikar (Ed.), *Global Practices in Knowledge Management for Societal and Organizational Development* (pp. 256–270). Hershey, PA: IGI Global. doi:10.4018/978-1-5225-3009-1.ch012

Lewandowski, M. (2017). Public Organizations and Business Model Innovation: The Role of Public Service Design. In M. Lewandowski & B. Kożuch (Eds.), *Public Sector Entrepreneurship and the Integration of Innovative Business Models* (pp. 47–72). Hershey, PA: IGI Global. doi:10.4018/978-1-5225-2215-7.ch003

Lhannaoui, H., Kabbaj, M. I., & Bakkoury, Z. (2017). A Survey of Risk-Aware Business Process Modelling. *International Journal of Risk and Contingency Management*, *6*(3), 14–26. doi:10.4018/IJRCM.2017070102

Li, J., Sun, W., Jiang, W., Yang, H., & Zhang, L. (2017). How the Nature of Exogenous Shocks and Crises Impact Company Performance?: The Effects of Industry Characteristics. *International Journal of Risk and Contingency Management*, *6*(4), 40–55. doi:10.4018/IJRCM.2017100103

Lu, C., & Liu, S. (2016). Cultural Tourism O2O Business Model Innovation-A Case Study of CTrip. *Journal of Electronic Commerce in Organizations*, *14*(2), 16–31. doi:10.4018/JECO.2016040102

Machen, B., Hosseini, M. R., Wood, A., & Bakhshi, J. (2016). An Investigation into using SAP-PS as a Multidimensional Project Control System (MPCS). *International Journal of Enterprise Information Systems*, *12*(2), 66–81. doi:10.4018/IJEIS.2016040105

Malega, P. (2017). Small and Medium Enterprises in the Slovak Republic: Status and Competitiveness of SMEs in the Global Markets and Possibilities of Optimization. In M. Vemić (Ed.), *Optimal Management Strategies in Small and Medium Enterprises* (pp. 102–124). Hershey, PA: IGI Global. doi:10.4018/978-1-5225-1949-2.ch006

Malewska, K. M. (2017). Intuition in Decision-Making on the Example of a Non-Profit Organization. In V. Potocan, M. Üngan, & Z. Nedelko (Eds.), *Handbook of Research on Managerial Solutions in Non-Profit Organizations* (pp. 378–399). Hershey, PA: IGI Global. doi:10.4018/978-1-5225-0731-4.ch018

Maroofi, F. (2017). Entrepreneurial Orientation and Organizational Learning Ability Analysis for Innovation and Firm Performance. In N. Baporikar (Ed.), *Innovation and Shifting Perspectives in Management Education* (pp. 144–165). Hershey, PA: IGI Global. doi:10.4018/978-1-5225-1019-2.ch007

Martins, P. V., & Zacarias, M. (2017). A Web-based Tool for Business Process Improvement. *International Journal of Web Portals*, *9*(2), 68–84. doi:10.4018/IJWP.2017070104

Matthies, B., & Coners, A. (2017). Exploring the Conceptual Nature of e-Business Projects. *Journal of Electronic Commerce in Organizations*, *15*(3), 33–63. doi:10.4018/JECO.2017070103

McKee, J. (2018). Architecture as a Tool to Solve Business Planning Problems. In M. Khosrow-Pour, D.B.A. (Ed.), Encyclopedia of Information Science and Technology, Fourth Edition (pp. 573-586). Hershey, PA: IGI Global. doi:10.4018/978-1-5225-2255-3.ch050

McMurray, A. J., Cross, J., & Caponecchia, C. (2018). The Risk Management Profession in Australia: Business Continuity Plan Practices. In N. Bajgoric (Ed.), *Always-On Enterprise Information Systems for Modern Organizations* (pp. 112–129). Hershey, PA: IGI Global. doi:10.4018/978-1-5225-3704-5.ch006

Meddah, I. H., & Belkadi, K. (2018). Mining Patterns Using Business Process Management. In R. Hamou (Ed.), *Handbook of Research on Biomimicry in Information Retrieval and Knowledge Management* (pp. 78–89). Hershey, PA: IGI Global. doi:10.4018/978-1-5225-3004-6.ch005

Mendes, L. (2017). TQM and Knowledge Management: An Integrated Approach Towards Tacit Knowledge Management. In D. Jaziri-Bouagina & G. Jamil (Eds.), *Handbook of Research on Tacit Knowledge Management for Organizational Success* (pp. 236–263). Hershey, PA: IGI Global. doi:10.4018/978-1-5225-2394-9.ch009

Mnjama, N. M. (2017). Preservation of Recorded Information in Public and Private Sector Organizations. In P. Jain & N. Mnjama (Eds.), *Managing Knowledge Resources and Records in Modern Organizations* (pp. 149–167). Hershey, PA: IGI Global. doi:10.4018/978-1-5225-1965-2.ch009

Mokoqama, M., & Fields, Z. (2017). Principles of Responsible Management Education (PRME): Call for Responsible Management Education. In Z. Fields (Ed.), *Collective Creativity for Responsible and Sustainable Business Practice* (pp. 229–241). Hershey, PA: IGI Global. doi:10.4018/978-1-5225-1823-5.ch012

Muniapan, B. (2017). Philosophy and Management: The Relevance of Vedanta in Management. In P. Ordóñez de Pablos (Ed.), *Managerial Strategies and Solutions for Business Success in Asia* (pp. 124–139). Hershey, PA: IGI Global. doi:10.4018/978-1-5225-1886-0.ch007

Muniapan, B., Gregory, M. L., & Ling, L. A. (2016). Marketing Education in Sarawak: Looking at It from the Employers' Viewpoint. In B. Smith & A. Porath (Eds.), *Global Perspectives on Contemporary Marketing Education* (pp. 112–130). Hershey, PA: IGI Global. doi:10.4018/978-1-4666-9784-3.ch008

Murad, S. E., & Dowaji, S. (2017). Using Value-Based Approach for Managing Cloud-Based Services. In A. Turuk, B. Sahoo, & S. Addya (Eds.), *Resource Management and Efficiency in Cloud Computing Environments* (pp. 33–60). Hershey, PA: IGI Global. doi:10.4018/978-1-5225-1721-4.ch002

Mutahar, A. M., Daud, N. M., Thurasamy, R., Isaac, O., & Abdulsalam, R. (2018). The Mediating of Perceived Usefulness and Perceived Ease of Use: The Case of Mobile Banking in Yemen. *International Journal of Technology Diffusion*, *9*(2), 21–40. doi:10.4018/IJTD.2018040102

Naidoo, V. (2017). E-Learning and Management Education at African Universities. In N. Baporikar (Ed.), *Management Education for Global Leadership* (pp. 181–201). Hershey, PA: IGI Global. doi:10.4018/978-1-5225-1013-0.ch009

Naidoo, V., & Igbinakhase, I. (2018). Opportunities and Challenges of Knowledge Retention in SMEs. In N. Baporikar (Ed.), *Knowledge Integration Strategies for Entrepreneurship and Sustainability* (pp. 70–94). Hershey, PA: IGI Global. doi:10.4018/978-1-5225-5115-7.ch004

Nayak, S., & Prabhu, N. (2017). Paradigm Shift in Management Education: Need for a Cross Functional Perspective. In N. Baporikar (Ed.), *Management Education for Global Leadership* (pp. 241–255). Hershey, PA: IGI Global. doi:10.4018/978-1-5225-1013-0.ch012

Ndede-Amadi, A. A. (2016). Student Interest in the IS Specialization as Predictor of the Success Potential of New Information Systems Programmes within the Schools of Business in Kenyan Public Universities. *International Journal of Information Systems and Social Change*, *7*(2), 63–79. doi:10.4018/IJISSC.2016040104

Nedelko, Z., & Potocan, V. (2016). Management Practices for Processes Optimization: Case of Slovenia. In G. Alor-Hernández, C. Sánchez-Ramírez, & J. García-Alcaraz (Eds.), *Handbook of Research on Managerial Strategies for Achieving Optimal Performance in Industrial Processes* (pp. 545–561). Hershey, PA: IGI Global. doi:10.4018/978-1-5225-0130-5.ch025

Nedelko, Z., & Potocan, V. (2017). Management Solutions in Non-Profit Organizations: Case of Slovenia. In V. Potocan, M. Üngan, & Z. Nedelko (Eds.), *Handbook of Research on Managerial Solutions in Non-Profit Organizations* (pp. 1–22). Hershey, PA: IGI Global. doi:10.4018/978-1-5225-0731-4.ch001

Nedelko, Z., & Potocan, V. (2017). Priority of Management Tools Utilization among Managers: International Comparison. In V. Wang (Ed.), *Encyclopedia of Strategic Leadership and Management* (pp. 1083–1094). Hershey, PA: IGI Global. doi:10.4018/978-1-5225-1049-9.ch075

Nedelko, Z., Raudeliūnienė, J., & Črešnar, R. (2018). Knowledge Dynamics in Supply Chain Management. In N. Baporikar (Ed.), *Knowledge Integration Strategies for Entrepreneurship and Sustainability* (pp. 150–166). Hershey, PA: IGI Global. doi:10.4018/978-1-5225-5115-7.ch008

Nguyen, H. T., & Hipsher, S. A. (2018). Innovation and Creativity Used by Private Sector Firms in a Resources-Constrained Environment. In S. Hipsher (Ed.), *Examining the Private Sector's Role in Wealth Creation and Poverty Reduction* (pp. 219–238). Hershey, PA: IGI Global. doi:10.4018/978-1-5225-3117-3.ch010

Nycz, M., & Pólkowski, Z. (2016). Business Intelligence as a Modern IT Supporting Management of Local Government Units in Poland. *International Journal of Knowledge and Systems Science*, *7*(4), 1–18. doi:10.4018/IJKSS.2016100101

Obaji, N. O., Senin, A. A., & Olugu, M. U. (2016). Supportive Government Policy as a Mechanism for Business Incubation Performance in Nigeria. *International Journal of Information Systems and Social Change*, *7*(4), 52–66. doi:10.4018/IJISSC.2016100103

Obicci, P. A. (2017). Risk Sharing in a Partnership. In *Risk Management Strategies in Public-Private Partnerships* (pp. 115–152). Hershey, PA: IGI Global. doi:10.4018/978-1-5225-2503-5.ch004

Obidallah, W. J., & Raahemi, B. (2017). Managing Changes in Service Oriented Virtual Organizations: A Structural and Procedural Framework to Facilitate the Process of Change. *Journal of Electronic Commerce in Organizations, 15*(1), 59–83. doi:10.4018/JECO.2017010104

Ojasalo, J., & Ojasalo, K. (2016). Service Logic Business Model Canvas for Lean Development of SMEs and Start-Ups. In N. Baporikar (Ed.), *Handbook of Research on Entrepreneurship in the Contemporary Knowledge-Based Global Economy* (pp. 217–243). Hershey, PA: IGI Global. doi:10.4018/978-1-4666-8798-1.ch010

Ojo, O. (2017). Impact of Innovation on the Entrepreneurial Success in Selected Business Enterprises in South-West Nigeria. *International Journal of Innovation in the Digital Economy, 8*(2), 29–38. doi:10.4018/IJIDE.2017040103

Okdinawati, L., Simatupang, T. M., & Sunitiyoso, Y. (2017). Multi-Agent Reinforcement Learning for Value Co-Creation of Collaborative Transportation Management (CTM). *International Journal of Information Systems and Supply Chain Management, 10*(3), 84–95. doi:10.4018/IJISSCM.2017070105

Ortner, E., Mevius, M., Wiedmann, P., & Kurz, F. (2016). Design of Interactional Decision Support Applications for E-Participation in Smart Cities. *International Journal of Electronic Government Research, 12*(2), 18–38. doi:10.4018/IJEGR.2016040102

Pal, K. (2018). Building High Quality Big Data-Based Applications in Supply Chains. In A. Kumar & S. Saurav (Eds.), *Supply Chain Management Strategies and Risk Assessment in Retail Environments* (pp. 1–24). Hershey, PA: IGI Global. doi:10.4018/978-1-5225-3056-5.ch001

Palos-Sanchez, P. R., & Correia, M. B. (2018). Perspectives of the Adoption of Cloud Computing in the Tourism Sector. In J. Rodrigues, C. Ramos, P. Cardoso, & C. Henriques (Eds.), *Handbook of Research on Technological Developments for Cultural Heritage and eTourism Applications* (pp. 377–400). Hershey, PA: IGI Global. doi:10.4018/978-1-5225-2927-9.ch018

Parry, V. K., & Lind, M. L. (2016). Alignment of Business Strategy and Information Technology Considering Information Technology Governance, Project Portfolio Control, and Risk Management. *International Journal of Information Technology Project Management, 7*(4), 21–37. doi:10.4018/IJITPM.2016100102

Pashkova, N., Trujillo-Barrera, A., Apostolakis, G., Van Dijk, G., Drakos, P. D., & Baourakis, G. (2016). Business Management Models of Microfinance Institutions (MFIs) in Africa: A Study into Their Enabling Environments. *International Journal of Food and Beverage Manufacturing and Business Models, 1*(2), 63–82. doi:10.4018/IJFBMBM.2016070105

Patiño, B. E. (2017). New Generation Management by Convergence and Individual Identity: A Systemic and Human-Oriented Approach. In N. Baporikar (Ed.), *Innovation and Shifting Perspectives in Management Education* (pp. 119–143). Hershey, PA: IGI Global. doi:10.4018/978-1-5225-1019-2.ch006

Pawliczek, A., & Rössler, M. (2017). Knowledge of Management Tools and Systems in SMEs: Knowledge Transfer in Management. In A. Bencsik (Ed.), *Knowledge Management Initiatives and Strategies in Small and Medium Enterprises* (pp. 180–203). Hershey, PA: IGI Global. doi:10.4018/978-1-5225-1642-2.ch009

Pejic-Bach, M., Omazic, M. A., Aleksic, A., & Zoroja, J. (2018). Knowledge-Based Decision Making: A Multi-Case Analysis. In R. Leon (Ed.), *Managerial Strategies for Business Sustainability During Turbulent Times* (pp. 160–184). Hershey, PA: IGI Global. doi:10.4018/978-1-5225-2716-9.ch009

Perano, M., Hysa, X., & Calabrese, M. (2018). Strategic Planning, Cultural Context, and Business Continuity Management: Business Cases in the City of Shkoder. In A. Presenza & L. Sheehan (Eds.), *Geopolitics and Strategic Management in the Global Economy* (pp. 57–77). Hershey, PA: IGI Global. doi:10.4018/978-1-5225-2673-5.ch004

Pereira, R., Mira da Silva, M., & Lapão, L. V. (2017). IT Governance Maturity Patterns in Portuguese Healthcare. In S. De Haes & W. Van Grembergen (Eds.), *Strategic IT Governance and Alignment in Business Settings* (pp. 24–52). Hershey, PA: IGI Global. doi:10.4018/978-1-5225-0861-8.ch002

Perez-Uribe, R., & Ocampo-Guzman, D. (2016). Conflict within Colombian Family Owned SMEs: An Explosive Blend between Feelings and Business. In J. Saiz-Álvarez (Ed.), *Handbook of Research on Social Entrepreneurship and Solidarity Economics* (pp. 329–354). Hershey, PA: IGI Global. doi:10.4018/978-1-5225-0097-1.ch017

Pérez-Uribe, R. I., Torres, D. A., Jurado, S. P., & Prada, D. M. (2018). Cloud Tools for the Development of Project Management in SMEs. In R. Perez-Uribe, C. Salcedo-Perez, & D. Ocampo-Guzman (Eds.), *Handbook of Research on Intrapreneurship and Organizational Sustainability in SMEs* (pp. 95–120). Hershey, PA: IGI Global. doi:10.4018/978-1-5225-3543-0.ch005

Petrisor, I., & Cozmiuc, D. (2017). Global Supply Chain Management Organization at Siemens in the Advent of Industry 4.0. In L. Saglietto & C. Cezanne (Eds.), *Global Intermediation and Logistics Service Providers* (pp. 123–142). Hershey, PA: IGI Global. doi:10.4018/978-1-5225-2133-4.ch007

Pierce, J. M., Velliaris, D. M., & Edwards, J. (2017). A Living Case Study: A Journey Not a Destination. In N. Silton (Ed.), *Exploring the Benefits of Creativity in Education, Media, and the Arts* (pp. 158–178). Hershey, PA: IGI Global. doi:10.4018/978-1-5225-0504-4.ch008

Radosavljevic, M., & Andjelkovic, A. (2017). Multi-Criteria Decision Making Approach for Choosing Business Process for the Improvement: Upgrading of the Six Sigma Methodology. In J. Stanković, P. Delias, S. Marinković, & S. Rochhia (Eds.), *Tools and Techniques for Economic Decision Analysis* (pp. 225–247). Hershey, PA: IGI Global. doi:10.4018/978-1-5225-0959-2.ch011

Radovic, V. M. (2017). Corporate Sustainability and Responsibility and Disaster Risk Reduction: A Serbian Overview. In M. Camilleri (Ed.), *CSR 2.0 and the New Era of Corporate Citizenship* (pp. 147–164). Hershey, PA: IGI Global. doi:10.4018/978-1-5225-1842-6.ch008

Raghunath, K. M., Devi, S. L., & Patro, C. S. (2018). Impact of Risk Assessment Models on Risk Factors: A Holistic Outlook. In K. Strang, M. Korstanje, & N. Vajjhala (Eds.), *Research, Practices, and Innovations in Global Risk and Contingency Management* (pp. 134–153). Hershey, PA: IGI Global. doi:10.4018/978-1-5225-4754-9.ch008

Raman, A., & Goyal, D. P. (2017). Extending IMPLEMENT Framework for Enterprise Information Systems Implementation to Information System Innovation. In M. Tavana (Ed.), *Enterprise Information Systems and the Digitalization of Business Functions* (pp. 137–177). Hershey, PA: IGI Global. doi:10.4018/978-1-5225-2382-6.ch007

Rao, Y., & Zhang, Y. (2017). The Construction and Development of Academic Library Digital Special Subject Databases. In L. Ruan, Q. Zhu, & Y. Ye (Eds.), *Academic Library Development and Administration in China* (pp. 163–183). Hershey, PA: IGI Global. doi:10.4018/978-1-5225-0550-1.ch010

Ravasan, A. Z., Mohammadi, M. M., & Hamidi, H. (2018). An Investigation Into the Critical Success Factors of Implementing Information Technology Service Management Frameworks. In K. Jakobs (Ed.), *Corporate and Global Standardization Initiatives in Contemporary Society* (pp. 200–218). Hershey, PA: IGI Global. doi:10.4018/978-1-5225-5320-5.ch009

Renna, P., Izzo, C., & Romaniello, T. (2016). The Business Process Management Systems to Support Continuous Improvements. In W. Nuninger & J. Châtelet (Eds.), *Handbook of Research on Quality Assurance and Value Management in Higher Education* (pp. 237–256). Hershey, PA: IGI Global. doi:10.4018/978-1-5225-0024-7.ch009

Rezaie, S., Mirabedini, S. J., & Abtahi, A. (2018). Designing a Model for Implementation of Business Intelligence in the Banking Industry. *International Journal of Enterprise Information Systems, 14*(1), 77–103. doi:10.4018/IJEIS.2018010105

Riccò, R. (2016). Diversity Management: Bringing Equality, Equity, and Inclusion in the Workplace. In J. Prescott (Ed.), *Handbook of Research on Race, Gender, and the Fight for Equality* (pp. 335–359). Hershey, PA: IGI Global. doi:10.4018/978-1-5225-0047-6.ch015

Romano, L., Grimaldi, R., & Colasuonno, F. S. (2017). Demand Management as a Success Factor in Project Portfolio Management. In L. Romano (Ed.), *Project Portfolio Management Strategies for Effective Organizational Operations* (pp. 202–219). Hershey, PA: IGI Global. doi:10.4018/978-1-5225-2151-8.ch008

Rostek, K. B. (2016). Risk Management: Role and Importance in Business Organization. In D. Jakóbczak (Ed.), *Analyzing Risk through Probabilistic Modeling in Operations Research* (pp. 149–178). Hershey, PA: IGI Global. doi:10.4018/978-1-4666-9458-3.ch007

Rouhani, S., & Savoji, S. R. (2016). A Success Assessment Model for BI Tools Implementation: An Empirical Study of Banking Industry. *International Journal of Business Intelligence Research, 7*(1), 25–44. doi:10.4018/IJBIR.2016010103

Ruan, Z. (2016). A Corpus-Based Functional Analysis of Complex Nominal Groups in Written Business Discourse: The Case of “Business”. *International Journal of Computer-Assisted Language Learning and Teaching, 6*(2), 74–90. doi:10.4018/IJCALLT.2016040105

Ruhi, U. (2018). Towards an Interdisciplinary Socio-Technical Definition of Virtual Communities. In M. Khosrow-Pour, D.B.A. (Ed.), Encyclopedia of Information Science and Technology, Fourth Edition (pp. 4278-4295). Hershey, PA: IGI Global. doi:10.4018/978-1-5225-2255-3.ch371

Ryan, J., Doster, B., Daily, S., & Lewis, C. (2016). A Case Study Perspective for Balanced Perioperative Workflow Achievement through Data-Driven Process Improvement. *International Journal of Healthcare Information Systems and Informatics, 11*(3), 19–41. doi:10.4018/IJHISI.2016070102

Safari, M. R., & Jiang, Q. (2018). The Theory and Practice of IT Governance Maturity and Strategies Alignment: Evidence From Banking Industry. *Journal of Global Information Management, 26*(2), 127–146. doi:10.4018/JGIM.2018040106

Sahoo, J., Pati, B., & Mohanty, B. (2017). Knowledge Management as an Academic Discipline: An Assessment. In B. Gunjal (Ed.), *Managing Knowledge and Scholarly Assets in Academic Libraries* (pp. 99–126). Hershey, PA: IGI Global. doi:10.4018/978-1-5225-1741-2.ch005

Saini, D. (2017). Relevance of Teaching Values and Ethics in Management Education. In N. Baporikar (Ed.), *Management Education for Global Leadership* (pp. 90–111). Hershey, PA: IGI Global. doi:10.4018/978-1-5225-1013-0.ch005

Sambhanthan, A. (2017). Assessing and Benchmarking Sustainability in Organisations: An Integrated Conceptual Model. *International Journal of Systems and Service-Oriented Engineering, 7*(4), 22–43. doi:10.4018/IJSSOE.2017100102

Sambhanthan, A., & Potdar, V. (2017). A Study of the Parameters Impacting Sustainability in Information Technology Organizations. *International Journal of Knowledge-Based Organizations, 7*(3), 27–39. doi:10.4018/IJKBO.2017070103

Sánchez-Fernández, M. D., & Manríquez, M. R. (2018). The Entrepreneurial Spirit Based on Social Values: The Digital Generation. In P. Isaias & L. Carvalho (Eds.), *User Innovation and the Entrepreneurship Phenomenon in the Digital Economy* (pp. 173–193). Hershey, PA: IGI Global. doi:10.4018/978-1-5225-2826-5.ch009

Sanchez-Ruiz, L., & Blanco, B. (2017). Process Management for SMEs: Barriers, Enablers, and Benefits. In M. Vemić (Ed.), *Optimal Management Strategies in Small and Medium Enterprises* (pp. 293–319). Hershey, PA: IGI Global. doi:10.4018/978-1-5225-1949-2.ch014

Sanz, L. F., Gómez-Pérez, J., & Castillo-Martinez, A. (2018). Analysis of the European ICT Competence Frameworks. In V. Ahuja & S. Rathore (Eds.), *Multidisciplinary Perspectives on Human Capital and Information Technology Professionals* (pp. 225–245). Hershey, PA: IGI Global. doi:10.4018/978-1-5225-5297-0.ch012

Sarvepalli, A., & Godin, J. (2017). Business Process Management in the Classroom. *Journal of Cases on Information Technology, 19*(2), 17–28. doi:10.4018/JCIT.2017040102

Satpathy, B., & Muniapan, B. (2016). Ancient Wisdom for Transformational Leadership and Its Insights from the Bhagavad-Gita. In U. Aung & P. Ordoñez de Pablos (Eds.), *Managerial Strategies and Practice in the Asian Business Sector* (pp. 1–10). Hershey, PA: IGI Global. doi:10.4018/978-1-4666-9758-4.ch001

Saygili, E. E., Ozturkoglu, Y., & Kocakulah, M. C. (2017). End Users' Perceptions of Critical Success Factors in ERP Applications. *International Journal of Enterprise Information Systems*, *13*(4), 58–75. doi:10.4018/IJEIS.2017100104

Saygili, E. E., & Saygili, A. T. (2017). Contemporary Issues in Enterprise Information Systems: A Critical Review of CSFs in ERP Implementations. In M. Tavana (Ed.), *Enterprise Information Systems and the Digitalization of Business Functions* (pp. 120–136). Hershey, PA: IGI Global. doi:10.4018/978-1-5225-2382-6.ch006

Seidenstricker, S., & Antonino, A. (2018). Business Model Innovation-Oriented Technology Management for Emergent Technologies. In M. Khosrow-Pour, D.B.A. (Ed.), Encyclopedia of Information Science and Technology, Fourth Edition (pp. 4560-4569). Hershey, PA: IGI Global. doi:10.4018/978-1-5225-2255-3.ch396

Senaratne, S., & Gunarathne, A. D. (2017). Excellence Perspective for Management Education from a Global Accountants' Hub in Asia. In N. Baporikar (Ed.), *Management Education for Global Leadership* (pp. 158–180). Hershey, PA: IGI Global. doi:10.4018/978-1-5225-1013-0.ch008

Sensuse, D. I., & Cahyaningsih, E. (2018). Knowledge Management Models: A Summative Review. *International Journal of Information Systems in the Service Sector*, *10*(1), 71–100. doi:10.4018/IJISSS.2018010105

Sensuse, D. I., Wibowo, W. C., & Cahyaningsih, E. (2016). Indonesian Government Knowledge Management Model: A Theoretical Model. *Information Resources Management Journal*, *29*(1), 91–108. doi:10.4018/irmj.2016010106

Seth, M., Goyal, D., & Kiran, R. (2017). Diminution of Impediments in Implementation of Supply Chain Management Information System for Enhancing its Effectiveness in Indian Automobile Industry. *Journal of Global Information Management*, *25*(3), 1–20. doi:10.4018/JGIM.2017070101

Seyal, A. H., & Rahman, M. N. (2017). Investigating Impact of Inter-Organizational Factors in Measuring ERP Systems Success: Bruneian Perspectives. In M. Tavana (Ed.), *Enterprise Information Systems and the Digitalization of Business Functions* (pp. 178–204). Hershey, PA: IGI Global. doi:10.4018/978-1-5225-2382-6.ch008

Shaikh, A. A., & Karjaluoto, H. (2016). On Some Misconceptions Concerning Digital Banking and Alternative Delivery Channels. *International Journal of E-Business Research*, *12*(3), 1–16. doi:10.4018/IJEBR.2016070101

Shams, S. M. (2016). Stakeholder Relationship Management in Online Business and Competitive Value Propositions: Evidence from the Sports Industry. *International Journal of Online Marketing*, *6*(2), 1–17. doi:10.4018/IJOM.2016040101

Shamsuzzoha, A. (2016). Management of Risk and Resilience within Collaborative Business Network. In R. Addo-Tenkorang, J. Kantola, P. Helo, & A. Shamsuzzoha (Eds.), *Supply Chain Strategies and the Engineer-to-Order Approach* (pp. 143–159). Hershey, PA: IGI Global. doi:10.4018/978-1-5225-0021-6.ch008

Shaqrah, A. A. (2018). Analyzing Business Intelligence Systems Based on 7s Model of McKinsey. *International Journal of Business Intelligence Research, 9*(1), 53–63. doi:10.4018/IJBIR.2018010104

Sharma, A. J. (2017). Enhancing Sustainability through Experiential Learning in Management Education. In N. Baporikar (Ed.), *Management Education for Global Leadership* (pp. 256–274). Hershey, PA: IGI Global. doi:10.4018/978-1-5225-1013-0.ch013

Shetty, K. P. (2017). Responsible Global Leadership: Ethical Challenges in Management Education. In N. Baporikar (Ed.), *Innovation and Shifting Perspectives in Management Education* (pp. 194–223). Hershey, PA: IGI Global. doi:10.4018/978-1-5225-1019-2.ch009

Sinthupundaja, J., & Kohda, Y. (2017). Effects of Corporate Social Responsibility and Creating Shared Value on Sustainability. *International Journal of Sustainable Entrepreneurship and Corporate Social Responsibility, 2*(1), 27–38. doi:10.4018/IJSECSR.2017010103

Škarica, I., & Hrgović, A. V. (2018). Implementation of Total Quality Management Principles in Public Health Institutes in the Republic of Croatia. *International Journal of Productivity Management and Assessment Technologies, 6*(1), 1–16. doi:10.4018/IJPMAT.2018010101

Smuts, H., Kotzé, P., Van der Merwe, A., & Loock, M. (2017). Framework for Managing Shared Knowledge in an Information Systems Outsourcing Context. *International Journal of Knowledge Management, 13*(4), 1–30. doi:10.4018/IJKM.2017100101

Soares, E. R., & Zaidan, F. H. (2016). Information Architecture and Business Modeling in Modern Organizations of Information Technology: Professional Career Plan in Organizations IT. In G. Jamil, J. Poças Rascão, F. Ribeiro, & A. Malheiro da Silva (Eds.), *Handbook of Research on Information Architecture and Management in Modern Organizations* (pp. 439–457). Hershey, PA: IGI Global. doi:10.4018/978-1-4666-8637-3.ch020

Sousa, M. J., Cruz, R., Dias, I., & Caracol, C. (2017). Information Management Systems in the Supply Chain. In G. Jamil, A. Soares, & C. Pessoa (Eds.), *Handbook of Research on Information Management for Effective Logistics and Supply Chains* (pp. 469–485). Hershey, PA: IGI Global. doi:10.4018/978-1-5225-0973-8.ch025

Spremic, M., Turulja, L., & Bajgoric, N. (2018). Two Approaches in Assessing Business Continuity Management Attitudes in the Organizational Context. In N. Bajgoric (Ed.), *Always-On Enterprise Information Systems for Modern Organizations* (pp. 159–183). Hershey, PA: IGI Global. doi:10.4018/978-1-5225-3704-5.ch008

Steenkamp, A. L. (2018). Some Insights in Computer Science and Information Technology. In *Examining the Changing Role of Supervision in Doctoral Research Projects: Emerging Research and Opportunities* (pp. 113–133). Hershey, PA: IGI Global. doi:10.4018/978-1-5225-2610-0.ch005

Studdard, N., Dawson, M., Burton, S. L., Jackson, N., Leonard, B., Quisenberry, W., & Rahim, E. (2016). Nurturing Social Entrepreneurship and Building Social Entrepreneurial Self-Efficacy: Focusing on Primary and Secondary Schooling to Develop Future Social Entrepreneurs. In Z. Fields (Ed.), *Incorporating Business Models and Strategies into Social Entrepreneurship* (pp. 154–175). Hershey, PA: IGI Global. doi:10.4018/978-1-4666-8748-6.ch010

Sun, Z. (2016). A Framework for Developing Management Intelligent Systems. *International Journal of Systems and Service-Oriented Engineering*, *6*(1), 37–53. doi:10.4018/IJSSOE.2016010103

Swami, B., & Mphele, G. T. (2016). Problems Preventing Growth of Small Entrepreneurs: A Case Study of a Few Small Entrepreneurs in Botswana Sub-Urban Areas. In N. Baporikar (Ed.), *Handbook of Research on Entrepreneurship in the Contemporary Knowledge-Based Global Economy* (pp. 479–508). Hershey, PA: IGI Global. doi:10.4018/978-1-4666-8798-1.ch020

Tabach, A., & Croteau, A. (2017). Configurations of Information Technology Governance Practices and Business Unit Performance. *International Journal of IT/Business Alignment and Governance*, *8*(2), 1–27. doi:10.4018/IJITBAG.2017070101

Talaue, G. M., & Iqbal, T. (2017). Assessment of e-Business Mode of Selected Private Universities in the Philippines and Pakistan. *International Journal of Online Marketing*, *7*(4), 63–77. doi:10.4018/IJOM.2017100105

Tam, G. C. (2017). Project Manager Sustainability Competence. In *Managerial Strategies and Green Solutions for Project Sustainability* (pp. 178–207). Hershey, PA: IGI Global. doi:10.4018/978-1-5225-2371-0.ch008

Tambo, T. (2018). Fashion Retail Innovation: About Context, Antecedents, and Outcome in Technological Change Projects. In I. Management Association (Ed.), Fashion and Textiles: Breakthroughs in Research and Practice (pp. 233-260). Hershey, PA: IGI Global. doi:10.4018/978-1-5225-3432-7.ch010

Tambo, T., & Mikkelsen, O. E. (2016). Fashion Supply Chain Optimization: Linking Make-to-Order Purchasing and B2B E-Commerce. In S. Joshi & R. Joshi (Eds.), *Designing and Implementing Global Supply Chain Management* (pp. 1–21). Hershey, PA: IGI Global. doi:10.4018/978-1-4666-9720-1.ch001

Tandon, K. (2016). Innovative Andragogy: The Paradigm Shift to Heutagogy. In S. Tiwari & L. Nafees (Eds.), *Innovative Management Education Pedagogies for Preparing Next-Generation Leaders* (pp. 238–257). Hershey, PA: IGI Global. doi:10.4018/978-1-4666-9691-4.ch014

Tantau, A. D., & Frăţilă, L. C. (2018). Information and Management System for Renewable Energy Business. In *Entrepreneurship and Business Development in the Renewable Energy Sector* (pp. 200–244). Hershey, PA: IGI Global. doi:10.4018/978-1-5225-3625-3.ch006

Teixeira, N., Pardal, P. N., & Rafael, B. G. (2018). Internationalization, Financial Performance, and Organizational Challenges: A Success Case in Portugal. In L. Carvalho (Ed.), *Handbook of Research on Entrepreneurial Ecosystems and Social Dynamics in a Globalized World* (pp. 379–423). Hershey, PA: IGI Global. doi:10.4018/978-1-5225-3525-6.ch017

Trad, A., & Kalpić, D. (2016). The E-Business Transformation Framework for E-Commerce Architecture-Modeling Projects. In I. Lee (Ed.), *Encyclopedia of E-Commerce Development, Implementation, and Management* (pp. 733–753). Hershey, PA: IGI Global. doi:10.4018/978-1-4666-9787-4.ch052

Trad, A., & Kalpić, D. (2016). The E-Business Transformation Framework for E-Commerce Control and Monitoring Pattern. In I. Lee (Ed.), *Encyclopedia of E-Commerce Development, Implementation, and Management* (pp. 754–777). Hershey, PA: IGI Global. doi:10.4018/978-1-4666-9787-4.ch053

Trad, A., & Kalpić, D. (2018). The Business Transformation Framework, Agile Project and Change Management. In M. Khosrow-Pour, D.B.A. (Ed.), Encyclopedia of Information Science and Technology, Fourth Edition (pp. 620-635). Hershey, PA: IGI Global. doi:10.4018/978-1-5225-2255-3.ch054

Trad, A., & Kalpić, D. (2018). The Business Transformation and Enterprise Architecture Framework: The Financial Engineering E-Risk Management and E-Law Integration. In B. Sergi, F. Fidanoski, M. Ziolo, & V. Naumovski (Eds.), *Regaining Global Stability After the Financial Crisis* (pp. 46–65). Hershey, PA: IGI Global. doi:10.4018/978-1-5225-4026-7.ch003

Turulja, L., & Bajgoric, N. (2018). Business Continuity and Information Systems: A Systematic Literature Review. In N. Bajgoric (Ed.), *Always-On Enterprise Information Systems for Modern Organizations* (pp. 60–87). Hershey, PA: IGI Global. doi:10.4018/978-1-5225-3704-5.ch004

van Wessel, R. M., de Vries, H. J., & Ribbers, P. M. (2016). Business Benefits through Company IT Standardization. In K. Jakobs (Ed.), *Effective Standardization Management in Corporate Settings* (pp. 34–53). Hershey, PA: IGI Global. doi:10.4018/978-1-4666-9737-9.ch003

Vargas-Hernández, J. G. (2017). Professional Integrity in Business Management Education. In N. Baporikar (Ed.), *Management Education for Global Leadership* (pp. 70–89). Hershey, PA: IGI Global. doi:10.4018/978-1-5225-1013-0.ch004

Vasista, T. G., & AlAbdullatif, A. M. (2017). Role of Electronic Customer Relationship Management in Demand Chain Management: A Predictive Analytic Approach. *International Journal of Information Systems and Supply Chain Management, 10*(1), 53–67. doi:10.4018/IJISSCM.2017010104

Vergidis, K. (2016). Rediscovering Business Processes: Definitions, Patterns, and Modelling Approaches. In P. Papajorgji, F. Pinet, A. Guimarães, & J. Papathanasiou (Eds.), *Automated Enterprise Systems for Maximizing Business Performance* (pp. 97–122). Hershey, PA: IGI Global. doi:10.4018/978-1-4666-8841-4.ch007

Vieru, D., & Bourdeau, S. (2017). Survival in the Digital Era: A Digital Competence-Based Multi-Case Study in the Canadian SME Clothing Industry. *International Journal of Social and Organizational Dynamics in IT, 6*(1), 17–34. doi:10.4018/IJSODIT.2017010102

Vijayan, G., & Kamarulzaman, N. H. (2017). An Introduction to Sustainable Supply Chain Management and Business Implications. In M. Khan, M. Hussain, & M. Ajmal (Eds.), *Green Supply Chain Management for Sustainable Business Practice* (pp. 27–50). Hershey, PA: IGI Global. doi:10.4018/978-1-5225-0635-5.ch002

Vlachvei, A., & Notta, O. (2017). Firm Competitiveness: Theories, Evidence, and Measurement. In A. Vlachvei, O. Notta, K. Karantininis, & N. Tsounis (Eds.), *Factors Affecting Firm Competitiveness and Performance in the Modern Business World* (pp. 1–42). Hershey, PA: IGI Global. doi:10.4018/978-1-5225-0843-4.ch001 von Rosing, M., Fullington, N., & Walker, J. (2016). Using the Business Ontology and Enterprise Standards to Transform Three Leading Organizations. *International Journal of Conceptual Structures and Smart Applications*, *4*(1), 71–99. doi:10.4018/IJCSSA.2016010104

von Rosing, M., & von Scheel, H. (2016). Using the Business Ontology to Develop Enterprise Standards. *International Journal of Conceptual Structures and Smart Applications*, *4*(1), 48–70. doi:10.4018/IJCSSA.2016010103

Walczak, S. (2016). Artificial Neural Networks and other AI Applications for Business Management Decision Support. *International Journal of Sociotechnology and Knowledge Development*, *8*(4), 1–20. doi:10.4018/IJSKD.2016100101

Wamba, S. F., Akter, S., Kang, H., Bhattacharya, M., & Upal, M. (2016). The Primer of Social Media Analytics. *Journal of Organizational and End User Computing*, *28*(2), 1–12. doi:10.4018/JOEUC.2016040101

Wang, C., Schofield, M., Li, X., & Ou, X. (2017). Do Chinese Students in Public and Private Higher Education Institutes Perform at Different Level in One of the Leadership Skills: Critical Thinking?: An Exploratory Comparison. In V. Wang (Ed.), *Encyclopedia of Strategic Leadership and Management* (pp. 160–181). Hershey, PA: IGI Global. doi:10.4018/978-1-5225-1049-9.ch013

Wang, F., Raisinghani, M. S., Mora, M., & Wang, X. (2016). Strategic E-Business Management through a Balanced Scored Card Approach. In I. Lee (Ed.), *Encyclopedia of E-Commerce Development, Implementation, and Management* (pp. 361–386). Hershey, PA: IGI Global. doi:10.4018/978-1-4666-9787-4.ch027

Wang, J. (2017). Multi-Agent based Production Management Decision System Modelling for the Textile Enterprise. *Journal of Global Information Management*, *25*(4), 1–15. doi:10.4018/JGIM.2017100101

Wiedemann, A., & Gewald, H. (2017). Examining Cross-Domain Alignment: The Correlation of Business Strategy, IT Management, and IT Business Value. *International Journal of IT/Business Alignment and Governance*, *8*(1), 17–31. doi:10.4018/IJITBAG.2017010102

Wolf, R., & Thiel, M. (2018). Advancing Global Business Ethics in China: Reducing Poverty Through Human and Social Welfare. In S. Hipsher (Ed.), *Examining the Private Sector's Role in Wealth Creation and Poverty Reduction* (pp. 67–84). Hershey, PA: IGI Global. doi:10.4018/978-1-5225-3117-3.ch004

Wu, J., Ding, F., Xu, M., Mo, Z., & Jin, A. (2016). Investigating the Determinants of Decision-Making on Adoption of Public Cloud Computing in E-government. *Journal of Global Information Management*, *24*(3), 71–89. doi:10.4018/JGIM.2016070104

Xu, L., & de Vrieze, P. (2016). Building Situational Applications for Virtual Enterprises. In I. Lee (Ed.), *Encyclopedia of E-Commerce Development, Implementation, and Management* (pp. 715–724). Hershey, PA: IGI Global. doi:10.4018/978-1-4666-9787-4.ch050

Yablonsky, S. (2018). Innovation Platforms: Data and Analytics Platforms. In *Multi-Sided Platforms (MSPs) and Sharing Strategies in the Digital Economy: Emerging Research and Opportunities* (pp. 72–95). Hershey, PA: IGI Global. doi:10.4018/978-1-5225-5457-8.ch003

Yusoff, A., Ahmad, N. H., & Halim, H. A. (2017). Agropreneurship among Gen Y in Malaysia: The Role of Academic Institutions. In N. Ahmad, T. Ramayah, H. Halim, & S. Rahman (Eds.), *Handbook of Research on Small and Medium Enterprises in Developing Countries* (pp. 23–47). Hershey, PA: IGI Global. doi:10.4018/978-1-5225-2165-5.ch002

Zanin, F., Comuzzi, E., & Costantini, A. (2018). The Effect of Business Strategy and Stock Market Listing on the Use of Risk Assessment Tools. In *Management Control Systems in Complex Settings: Emerging Research and Opportunities* (pp. 145–168). Hershey, PA: IGI Global. doi:10.4018/978-1-5225-3987-2.ch007

Zgheib, P. W. (2017). Corporate Innovation and Intrapreneurship in the Middle East. In P. Zgheib (Ed.), *Entrepreneurship and Business Innovation in the Middle East* (pp. 37–56). Hershey, PA: IGI Global. doi:10.4018/978-1-5225-2066-5.ch003

# About the Contributors

**Charles Oham** is a Senior Lecturer in Social Enterprise at the University of Greenwich, London, United Kingdom. He also serves as the Social and Commercial Lead for the School of Human Sciences and has led on his university's collaboration with Aspect Consortium UK, a £5.6 million Research England Connecting Communities Fund project. Previously he has held positions in lecturing and innovation at the Open University and the University of East London. His research interest and work are in the fields of social entrepreneurship, spiritual capital, community development, and entrepreneurship. Charles's career in the public and third sector has included remits in regeneration and community development, social entrepreneurship, volunteering, enterprise, innovation, and international development. He sits on the board of two social enterprises in East London. Charles has over 20 publications on social enterprise and spiritual capital and is a reviewer for journal publications and books in the field of social entrepreneurship.

***

**Amanda Rodrigues Amorim Adegboye** is currently Associate Head of School for Research at the School of Nursing, Midwifery and Health, Coventry University (CU), UK. She is also a member of the Centre for Healthcare Research, CU and the Centre for Care Excellence which is a joint venture between CU and the University Hospitals Coventry and Warwickshire, NHS Trust. Amanda is a PhD holder in Epidemiology with over 15 years' experience in the field of Public Health and Nutrition. She has a strong background in intervention design, service evaluation, and evidence synthesis. She is an Associate Membert of the Faculty of Public Health of the Royal Colleges of Physicians and a Fellow of the Higher Education Academy (FHEA). She completed her first degree in Human Nutrition at Rio de Janeiro State University in Brazil. In 2001, she did postgraduate training in Nutrition & Infectious Diseases at the Evandro Chagas Hospital/ Research Centre in Brazil. In 2006, she completed an exchange PhD programme in Sweden (Obesity Unit at Karolinska Institute). She obtained her PgCert in Higher Education from the University of Westminster in

2016. Having previously worked at a number of higher education institutions both nationally and internationally, she maintains a wide network of collaborations in Brazil, Denmark, the USA, UK and West Africa. She has a healthy of experience in contract research, consultancy and conducting independent impact and process evaluation of research projects and programmes.

**Natasha Bonsu** is the Co-Founder of Emerald Castle, they measure, motivate and inspire organisations to demonstrate their value and social impact as a business strategy for growth. Natasha encourages organisations to work ON their business rather than IN their business. We help organisations identify risks and problems before they occur, highlight services that are BOTH impactful and profitable. Once a business strategy is identified, articulating the new ethos throughout the organisation and external stakeholders. Natasha's has experience in economic development in developing countries and social enterprise businesses focused on job creation. She is a mentor to social entrepreneurs within the School of Social Entrepreneurs and provides guidance on start-up and growth strategies. Former work experience includes operational and project analyst within global asset management companies. Natasha has long been interested in the power of small and medium businesses to create positive social and environmental change. She is passionate about business being mindful about their intentions and purpose.

**Jeff Gow** is a leading expert in the application of Data Envelope Analysis (DEA) in a public health context and has advised Governments and NGOs, including UNAIDS, the World Health Organisation, UNICEF, Deutsche Gesellschaft für Technische Zusammenarbeit (German Government Development Corporation) (GTZ, now GIZ), the Departments of Health and Education in the KwaZulu-Natal Provincial Government, the Departments of Social Welfare and Correctional Services in the South African Government and the Ford Foundation. His work for South African Government Departments has resulted in changed policies. For example, his UNICEF cost effectiveness study on different models of orphan care provided strong evidence that caring for children in the extended family was the best outcome for the children and the government budget, using an DEA framework. His work resulted in the introduction two years later of the first child welfare payment to be implemented in Africa. This benefited 3.5 million children in South Africa orphaned by their death of their parents. Prof Gow has worked with DICE consortium and a number of other partners to develop suitable frameworks for social impact analysis, he was a key member of the UKEIRI team who developed the Social Enterprise Programme for India and the EU.

**Kumar Kotecha** has been a proactive academic at Greenwich University for over 3 decades (10 years as a part-time secondee), initially and substantially focusing on Youth & Community Studies. Furthermore, he has been a social entrepreneur in various guises from his late teens, focused on serving young people and communities at large. He continues to maintain his outright passion for engaging with and facilitating young people's learning, and at Greenwich university he is focused on education to include Education Studies, Childhood & Youth Studies, Teacher Training etc., including at MA level. Outside Greenwich, Kumar engages at different levels with communities, public & community service providers etc., including the private sector, enabling them in different ways to function not only in a mutually and socially cohesive manner, but thrive and not simply survive within multiple and challenging conditions. Many years back, Greenwich University had set precedent in the country by establishing the first BA in Youth & Community Studies undergraduate degree programme (JNC and validated by the National Youth Agency), following years of providing the Certificate and Post Graduate Diploma version of the same. Kumar was implicit in developing and delivering the BA Youth & Community Studies programme as a core team member, leading a specific module on finance/management/enterprise/entrepreneurship in the community context, enabling students and graduates to acquire, develop and discharge entrepreneurial skills within their work or begin new endeavours and ventures. In this respect, Kumar provided hands on mentoring to numerous students in their field work placement or at their workplace, including providing non-managerial supervision. During this time, one of the follow-on and the most innovative developments Kumar initiated, developed, and discharged was delivering the Greenwich University BA Youth & Community Studies at a local level and specifically at the Professional Development Centre of an Inner London Borough and its youth service provision, equally serving neighbouring boroughs. The additional inventive element was that Kumar secured various sponsors to provide £5,000 bursary per year to each student. Numerous impacts of this initiative continue to be evident to this day, serving not only young people but the communities at large in creative and cohesive manner, and this despite sever pressures on public funding since the abolition of the Inner London Education Authority in April 1990. In the 90s Kumar led a group of Greenwich University students to Belgium, participating on a two-week multilateral (9 additional universities) Intensive Programme (EU Leonardo de Vinci Programme), focusing on various aspects of Youth and Community work across Europe. The students and Kumar from Greenwich focused on sharing best practise and creative forms of youth & community work to include social enterprise and entrepreneurship. Kumar continues to engage and participate annually on teaching visits to Scandinavia, focusing on social enterprise and entrepreneurship, including sharing best practise and learning from the Scandinavians. He also leads on Erasmus with his School of Education at university, facilitating student and teacher exchange visits. More recently Kumar was an integral team member in embedding Social Enterprise and Entrepreneurship into the curriculum of two (Education Studies and Childhood & Youth Studies) undergraduate degree programmes, delivering the two with one other colleague. The core modules also included creating a social enterprise in groups, developing and producing an actual business model, key policies to include governance, financial planning, budgeting. Cores experiences gained from undertaking a field placement in a social enterprise setting and entering the annual Greenwich University Enterprise challenge. Equally Kumar mentoring several winners of the Challenge across the years, noting that one highly developed social enterprise initiative was to provide on-site childcare provision for students and in conjunction and partnership with the university. Other graduates from the university have gone on to set up their own enterprises, serving young people and or communities. Indeed, Kumar continues to be a grassroots operator/academic/practitioner, enabling and informing his work at Greenwich University and beyond.

**Gladius Kulothungan** teaches, researches, and facilitates business and social innovation and entrepreneurship in the UK, Europe and Asia. He has been a Senior Lecturer at the University of East London and a visiting lecturer at Roskilde University, Denmark. He currently lectures in VIA University College in Denmark.as a Visiting Professor; and is now a Programme Director at the University of Wales Trinity Saint David in, London, UK, leading their MBA Programme and supervising Doctoral candidates. Dr Gladius has published extensively in international journals on social innovation and social entrepreneurship.

**Christine Locke** is the founder and CEO of Diversity House, a charitable organisation she initiated over thirteen years ago to address social inequalities. The charity provides prisons, schools, and community-based services to promote individuals and families health and well-being. Also, Christine is the Senior Partner at COGOL Concerns, a consultancy firm that supports businesses in training, equality, diversity and inclusion audit, research and development. Christine is a Doctoral Candidate at Canterbury Church University, Kent. She holds a B. A (Hons) in Modern European Languages (French/English), a National Higher Diploma in French Education, a post-graduate certificate in Community Research, a post-graduate diploma in French Translation, a post-graduate diploma in Addictive Behaviour, an MA in Community Cohesion Management and an MSc. in Health Promotion and Public Health, among others. Christine is a qualified teacher, administrator, bilingual secretary, and chartered banker. She is a keen social activist and an intersectional feminist. Her passion for equality, inclusion, and justice led to her becoming a signatory to the United Nations Global Compact to support the Millennium Development Goals (MDGs), which has now evolved to Sustainable Development Goals (SDGs). Christine enjoys giving talks and motivational speeches. Her passion for social transformation has led her to present at: United Nations Assembly, New York; United Nations Conference Centre, Bonn, Germany; Young Women's Trust, Nottingham; Greenwich University, London; Her Royal Majesty's Prisons, Isle of Sheppey; Royal Overseas League, London. Christine is married with two daughters.

**Nathaniel Massa** is resident senior faculty at the University of Malta's Department of Management, where he is also Council representative and founding member on the Centre for Entrepreneurship and Business Incubation board. Holding a PhD in Business and Management and an MBA, his research interests include international business strategy, internationalisation and entrepreneurship; and organisational behaviour and family business studies. Associated with the Community for Internationalisation and Enterprise Research at the Adam Smith Business School, University of Glasgow; he has held membership at the Academy of International Business (AIB), USA, and the British Academy of Management (BAM), UK.

**Andre Mostert** is an academic practitioner working for and with several social enterprises with extensive experience in teacher education, materials development, qualification development, teaching and learning across all levels of education, etc. Andre has led on numerous projects for the TDA, BECTA, QIA, Erasmus+, British Council, ASIA Invest, and Foundation for Human Rights, etc. His research interests are focused around enterprise and enterprise development, creating enterprise development Eco-systems (student enterprise, new start-ups, etc.), teacher education, etc. this work is complemented by work in technological determinism, employability and social enterprise. Andre is working with the Karditsa local government in Greece to develop the business start-up and social enterprise development in the region through creation of a Social Enterprise Development Hub. As an academic practitioner his work delivers a mix of practical solutions development, that straddle different sectors, agriculture, youth development, local government capacity building, etc. and some philosophical work in fields of language and language development. Current research is addressing the impact of technology on language and thought, and through several international consortia, areas of sustainable agricultural, social enterprise development, social enterprise qualifications, supporting SMEs and social technology. Andre has trained businesses, design solutions for SMEs, trained researchers in financial development and research commercialization, etc.

**John-Paul Okeke** is a Senior Lecturer in Business Studies and Programme Manager for the Doctoral Research programme at the University of Wales Trinity Saint David London Campus. He has received a PhD in Business Studies from the

University of East London. He obtained an MA in Management from the London Metropolitan University UK and graduated in Business Management at Imo State University Nigeria. Dr John-Paul Okeke is an experienced professional, successful Business School lecturer with an outstanding career record in institutional leadership, team building, professional leadership, and programme development. John-Paul has led significant initiatives in knowledge transfer and knowledge development partnership involvement. He is an experienced mentor and advisor to younger faculty and consulting colleagues in Entrepreneurship. Dr Okeke has initiated management development and capacity building projects using his role. John-Paul has demonstrated an innovative spirit and a strategically oriented mind, with a proven capacity to lead change and manage people and teams, excellent relationship management and negotiation skills and the ability to influence high-level decisions. John-Paul is passionate about entrepreneurs and uses his practical experiences in entrepreneurship to support entrepreneurs, students in academia and family businesses using insights from his human resource background, knowledge management, strategic management as well as scholarship in the field of Entrepreneur.

**Alessia Pisoni** is Associate Professor at the Department of Economics - University of Insubria, where she teaches Innovation Management. She holds a Ph.D. in Economics of Production and Development, and coordinates the research unit of the Research Centre for Innovation and Life Sciences Management (CRESIT). Since 2010, she has also been collaborating with Mind the Bridge Foundation's research activities on European ICT startup ecosystems. Nowadays, her research interests are in the area of innovation, internationalization and entrepreneurship. She is author of an extensive list of articles and books in the fields of innovation, entrepreneurship, corporate governance, and international business.

**Nicoletta Sciutti**, MD GEEM Graduate - University of Insubria in Varese (Global Entrepreneurship, Economics and Management - GEEM - with a specialization in "International Business and Entrepreneurship"), is Erasmus student at Liverpool John Moores University in Liverpool - UK (MSc Entrepreneurship). Trainee at the General Consulate of Italy in Edinburgh - UK (Internship offered by Ministero degli Affari Esteri e della Cooperazione Internazionale). Management Consulting Analyst at Accenture.

**Ela Burcu Uçel** is a graduate of Hacettepe University, Business Administration. She had the opportunity to experience corporate life for 12 years. Then, she earned a scholarship from Izmir University of Economics and completed her PhD in organizational behavior. She has been teaching management, strategy and HRM at Izmir University of Economics since 2011. She also is an experienced trainer: she actively takes part in adult training programs in mediation, negotiation, and culture. She loves teaching, writing, learning, and volunteering. Her areas of interest are gender studies, education management, human resources, and climate change. She is actively learning and teaching these topics and taking part in related research.

**Onyekachi Wambu** is the Executive Director at the African Foundation for Development (AFFORD), a charity that seeks to enhance the contributions that Africans in the diaspora make to Africa's development. AFFORD is a pioneer and innovator in the field of policy and practice of 'diaspora-development'. Founded in 1994, it responded to the disjuncture between mainstream international development and actual diaspora action. There was a lack of understanding, acknowledgement, recognition and acceptance of the reality and potential of diaspora input in the development of countries of origin or heritage. Onyekachi Wambu was educated at the University of Essex and completed his M.Phil in International Relations at Selwyn College, Cambridge. Before AFFORD, he worked extensively as a journalist and television documentary maker. His publications include Under the Tree of Talking: Leadership for Change in Africa (ed) and Empire Windrush: 50 years of writing about black Britain (ed).

# Index

## L



## M



## N



## P



## Q



## R



## S

## T



## U



## X

www.ingramcontent.com/pod-product-compliance
Lightning Source LLC
LaVergne TN
LVHW081339300926
849161LV00008B/2023